Indian America

Indian America

A TRAVELER'S COMPANION

Fourth Edition

EAGLE/WALKING TURTLE

John Muir Publications
Santa Fe, New Mexico

John Muir Publications, P.O. Box 613, Santa Fe, NM 87504

Copyright © 1995, 1993, 1991, 1989 by Gary McLain
Cover © 1995 by John Muir Publications
All rights reserved.
Printed in the United States of America

Fourth edition. Second printing August 1997

Eagle Walking Turtle.
    Indian America : a traveler's companion / Eagle/Walking Turtle.—4th ed.
    p.   cm.
    Includes bibliographical references and index.
    ISBN 1-56261-238-7 : $18.95
    1. Indians of North America. 2. United States—Guidebooks.
I. Title
E77.E117 1995   95-3589
917.304'929—dc20   CIP

Editorial: Elizabeth Wolf, Dianna Delling, Karen Moye
Production: Kathryn Lloyd-Strongin, Janine Lehmann
Designer: Joanna V. Hill
Typeface: New Baskerville
Typesetter: Go West Graphics
Printer: Publishers Press

Distributed to the book trade by
Publishers Group West
Emeryville, California

Cover painting "Sundance II" by Eagle/Walking Turtle

Indian America is dedicated to Grandpa Iron and the
whole of all living things

Contents

Preface

Indian America is your guide to the world of the native people of America. Because many tribes may not be located on major highways, it is suggested that you consult a road atlas in addition to the information provided here.

It is important to realize that some tribes have a very small population and do not practice ceremonies; some do not welcome visitors. For this reason, you may find limited information for some tribes within these pages. But it is also important to know that most tribes welcome the public and cordially invite you to attend pow-wows and ceremonies and visit their reservations.

The brief histories accompanying the listings will most often end at the turn of the century. This is when Native Americans experienced dislocation from their lands and the intrusion of foreigners and, for all intents and purposes, ceased the practice of their own cultures free of non-Indian influence.

Welcome to Indian country. Enjoy your journey.

Acknowledgments

The Elk Dreamer Society's song included these words: "Whoever considers themselves more beautiful than me has no heart." So, when we consider that the whole creation is truly more beautiful than we are, how can we take credit for, or acknowledge the individual's participation in, the production of one small addition to the hope for love in the whole of all living things?

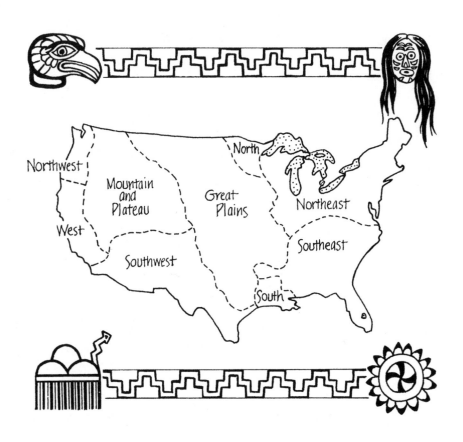

Native American Cultural Areas

Introduction

More than 50,000 years ago, our people arrived on this continent. There were seven original people—three men and four women. They came from Man Carrier (our name for the Big Dipper). From these seven people, our people developed.

In the early days men were strong, living without fire, hunting small animals and birds, using sharp shells, stones, or bones to butcher their kills. Later, one of the people, named Moves Walking, had a vision from the sun and learned how to make fire. From then on, our people cooked their meat by boiling it in water heated by hot stones.

All of our people lived together on the shores of a great sea in the south, known now as the Gulf of Mexico. They had chiefs to lead them, and warrior societies developed to maintain order. When our people became too numerous, a medicine person called Slow Buffalo had a vision that everyone should disperse throughout the land. The main council of chiefs divided our people into seven bands, appointed a chief for each band, and divided the common fire among them to establish a permanent relationship.

Oral history recalls only three of the band chiefs appointed at the council. High Hollow Horn led his people east to little Turtle Island (Atlantis). Slow Buffalo led his people west; they found the sacred arrows, and eventually they found the horse. These people became the Cheyenne, Kiowa, and other tribes. Moves Walking (probably a direct descendant of Moves Walking who was one of the original people) led his people north; they domesticated the dog and were given the Sacred Pipe Bundle. These people became the Sioux and the Arapahoe.

Slow Buffalo named the directions and created kinship relations that became the standards for living in peace and harmony.

As our people dispersed, names were created for everything, and languages became different. Customs grew from the differences found in the environment. Because of our living together like relatives, we were doing just fine. We roamed the country wild and free; there was plenty, and we were never in want. The Great Spirit gave us our spirituality, based on the four directions and on the four-legged animals. Through them we sent our voices and prayers to Him that created us all and intended us all to be relatives.

So, our story is cosmic and reflects our relationship with the universe and with the whole of all living things.

Long before the coming of Europeans to this continent, a man named Wooden Cup foresaw in visions the coming of white men, the disappearance of all animals back into the earth, and the destruction of our lifeways. Prophecies such as this taught our people that certain events were inevitable and that the outward defeat of our culture was a part of a cosmic plan, not the result of individual failings. This lifted the burden of responsibility from us all, our people and foreigners alike.

But, unfortunately, the foreigners did not comprehend the relationship that our people had with all living things. The foreigners had been native people, and they had had such a relationship centuries before, but with the coming of their industrial revolution everything had been lost. They did not know that the four-leggeds and the wings of the air and our Grandmother Earth were supposed to be relatives.

Then the foreigners came on us like floods of water. They covered every bit of land we had. We looked for islands where we were free to save our people, but we could not do it. We were always leaving our lands as the flood of foreigners devoured the people and the four-leggeds even as we tried to flee. Eventually we came to these small islands where we are today, and the flood and its influences are all around us.

Even the four-leggeds have been forced to live on islands created by the foreigners. The four-leggeds will vanish because the greed of foreigners will eliminate their environment. The flood closes in on us continually. The spirituality that our people had was left behind as they fled.

Now we are nothing but prisoners of war on our small islands. We are surrounded by the people we had befriended when they first arrived on our lands.

The first thing our people learn as children is to love each other and to be relatives to the four-leggeds. The next thing is to stand by your word. The Great Spirit made men all alike, and we should treat all our fellowmen alike. We tried to love the foreign people as we did ourselves. On account of this, many of our people are now in misery. The foreign people were men like us in all but their color, and we wanted to live in harmony with them. But now we see that the foreign people have done harm to our people.

As you read *Indian America*, you will find that our people live today on reservations. Even these small islands have been broken up by private and other government land within the reservation. In many places, our people live in communities without any reservation left at all. Our housing is often built with the help of HUD, and the policies of the federal government combined with the policies of our own sovereign governments have created a system that provides houses, mainly for relatives of those on the tribal council. Greed has spread to our own people; it may be one of the worst traits that the foreigners brought with them.

The houses are often in project tracts in rows. Some are Easter egg houses in pink, turquoise, and blue; stucco houses to imitate adobe in the Southwest; and urban development solar-heated styles similar to the one that you may live in. Shacks and log houses are here. Beer cans and dogs and wrecked cars may be in the yards of our people. The dome-shaped structure behind the house is a sweat lodge. The tipis are usually for Peyote meetings of the Native American Church. What you see will depend on what part of our country you are in. Reservations and our people's lifestyles vary greatly in America. Watch for the bumper stickers on our cars: America Is Indian Country; Fry Bread Power; Custer Wore Arrow Shirts; Custer Died For Your Sins; Indians Should Have Had Better Immigration Laws; and more. Indian humor is tongue-in-cheek, but we know why we are laughing.

And our sense of humor is reviving along with our spirituality. The spirit and philosophy of our ceremonies is becoming strong again in the Offerings Lodge (the Sun Dance), the Native American Church, the Sweat Lodge, the Stomp Dance, and the Kiva. We are aware of the sun, the moon, the planets, the stars, and all living things within the whole of all living things that form the spokes of our Medicine Wheel. Each breath and act of our lives is reflected in our ceremonies and is tied to the spirit of the whole of all living things.

Our people on the small island reservations carry the spirit of the past in their hearts. Adjusting from the culture we left behind to the culture of the foreigners has not been easy. As you visit our small islands, you will be reminded of the atrocities committed against us by racial prejudice, greed, and government policies. You may be appalled by some of our living conditions. But if you attend one of our ceremonies or one of our powwows, the spirit of the goodness of the past will remind you of the time when your ancestors lived in tribes and felt a relationship with all living things. The great hoop of the Medicine Wheel is so big that everything is within it. It is the great hoop of all living things in the universe. We all are within it and have available the goodness only it can teach us.

Do not be afraid to follow the path of the Medicine Wheel with our people. Be extremely respectful at our ceremonies. Wear clothing that reflects that respect; maintain a quiet and respectful attitude; and follow the manners of the native people who are there. You will learn that the Medicine Wheel and the sacred places and the sacred relationship you desire are always beneath your feet. Look up to pray with the whole of all living things; look down to pray with our Grandmother Earth. All places are sacred, and the great hoop of the Medicine Wheel is always with us. It is with us everywhere, not just in a church building but in the mountains, in the hills, in the woods and streams, in the plains and valleys, and in the cities of our Grandmother. Within the great hoop there is a center. The heart of all living things resides there. It is where the Tree of Life will grow, leaf, bloom, and fill with singing birds from the wisdom of the elders—if we follow their direction. It is our responsibility to heed their words and warnings and to follow their teachings. The safety and everlasting life of our spirit is found beneath the Tree of Life. Do not be afraid to ask the elders and medicine people about our relationship with the whole of all living things. They will communicate to you the beauty of the great hoop, the Medicine Wheel.

Four quarters define the four directions around the great hoop. Each quarter has its own sacred colors and sacred objects that represent the four directions, the whole of all living things, Grandmother Earth, and our own individual self.

The spiritual relationship with the Medicine Wheel and the whole of all living things can and must be reestablished and maintained. The survival of the human race and all other living things depends on it.

We are earnestly pursuing the building of a bridge between our cultures that will bring the best of both into a new culture that portrays the goodness that the world holds for us with a place for all living things to live in happiness.

With one word, defined and acted on and placed into reality, we can accomplish peace, harmony, happiness, and love throughout the whole of all living things. This one word is *respect*.

Aho.

THE GREAT PLAINS

MONTANA:
Blackfeet /
Flathead /
Chippewa Cree /
Gros-Ventre /
Assiniboine / Sioux /
Crow / N. Cheyenne

MONTANA

WYOMING:
Northern Arapahoe / Shoshone

KANSAS: Iowa / Kickapoo / Potawatomi /
Sac and Fox

OKLAHOMA: Absentee-Shawnee /
Apache / Otoe-Missouria / Caddo /
Pawnee / Cheyenne-Arapahoe /
Potawatomi / Ponca / Comanche /
Delaware / Iowa / Kaw / Sac and Fox /
Kickapoo / Kiowa / Tonkawa /
Wichita / Cherokee / Chickasaw /
Choctaw / Creek / Eastern Shawnee /
Miami / Modoc / Osage / Ottawa /
Peoria / Quapaw / Seminole / Seneca-Cayuga /
Wyandotte

NORTH DAKOTA: Turtle Mountain
Chippewa / Devils Lake Sioux /
Arikara-Hidatsa-Mandan /
Standing Rock Sioux

SOUTH DAKOTA:
Cheyenne River
Sioux / Crow Creek
Sioux / Santee Sioux /
Brule Sioux / Oglala
Sioux / Rosebud
Sioux / Sisseton-
Wahpeton
Sioux / Yankton
Sioux

IOWA: Mesquakie

NEBRASKA: Santee
Sioux / Winnebago /
Omaha

MISSOURI:
Eastern Shawnee

NORTH DAKOTA
SOUTH DAKOTA
WYOMING
NEBRASKA
IOWA
KANSAS
MISSOURI
OKLAHOMA
TEXAS
Alabama-Coushatta

The Great Plains of North America stretch from the Mississippi River in the east to the Rocky Mountains in the west and from Texas in the south to the Canadian Provinces in the north. It is an area of about a million square miles, and the terrain consists of bluffs and crags, of flat-topped mesas several hundred feet high, of richly wooded valleys and glistening streams. It contains rugged terrain in terraces, cliffs, and chasms with colors ranging from spectacular to the very drab; but mostly the Great Plains are grasslands.

This is the land of our people. Nomadic in nature, they followed the migrations of the buffalo and wandered the plains with spiritual respect for their environment and for all living things. The land was unbroken before the Europeans brought the plow; the grasses were as high as a horse's flanks and the buffalo herds stretched as wide as day; and the earth stayed young. When the winds of winter blew from the north down our plains, our people stayed in river bottoms in the trees out of the hard winds and close to water. In the summers of growth and warmth from the south, when the winds blew up clouds full of rains and the sun brought life, our people hunted the buffalo and followed the happiness of freedom, always in respect for life and thankful for the blessings from Grandfather, the Creator.

There was time then. Time to develop one of the greatest cultures ever to exist on our Grandmother Earth. Our people developed into a culture rich in beautiful art forms. Spiritually moving ceremonies in praise for our Grandfather the Creator, definite ways of living, rich in their grasp of human values and morality—the people of the plains were exceptional indeed.

The buffalo gave the people time. Food and everything needed for life, including shelter, came from the buffalo. The meat was used for food. The hide provided clothing and covers for tipis and bedding. The bones were used for cooking utensils and weapons. Sinew was formed into thread for sewing, and even the fat of the animal was used for light. When the buffalo was plentiful and easy to hunt, the people had time to do beautiful artwork with quills and willow and buckskins. And dances and songs and chants developed for social entertainment and spiritual appreciation of the creation of all living things.

Medicines for the body and spirit evolved with time also. Sage, cedar, and sweetgrass were used in the sacred ceremonies of our people. The Creator provided the knowledge of how to use these sacred medicines through the Medicine People found in every tribe.

The people cared for each other, and the old were cared for in the home. Young people were praised for their caring and for their aid to the elders of the tribe. The elders taught the young the ways passed down to them from their elders in years gone by; the circle was never broken. The sacred hoop of the people was whole and round. And it was good. It was very, very good.

The men formed societies for the protection and well-being of the whole of all the people. The women formed societies dedicated to caring and embracing the welfare of all the people. And they bore the babies and raised the children. And it was good. It was very, very good.

The heartbeat of our Grandmother Earth was heard and felt with the drum, and the flute from Father Sky played the prayers of the people. It is true that life could still be difficult and often was, but it was difficult in an honorable and clean way. The people never forgot to maintain their respect for the whole of all living things; they never forgot to play the drum to keep the heartbeat of Grandmother Earth alive; they never forgot to pray the flute to romance the heartbeat of all living things.

With the coming of the intruders to the Plains the circle was broken. The buffalo was exterminated by a society of people who were not in tune with the goodness of all living things. Without the buffalo, the culture of our people broke apart and suffered permanent wounds that will never heal without leaving scars.

The tribes in these pages are descendants of our people, and you can find among them remnants of this great culture. You can still hear the drum play out the heartbeat of our Grandmother Earth in ceremony and powwow across the Plains. And you will hear the flute pray in the homes and in the open spaces of the wind. The Medicine People use sage, cedar, and sweetgrass, and the sweet smell carries the healing forward from the past into the future in the Sweat Lodge, Offerings Lodge, Native American Church, and sacred dances of our people across the land.

Join with them to honor their ancestors and to honor our Creator, our Grandmother Earth, our Moon, our Sun, and the whole of all living things in the whole of all Creation. You will find that it is good. It is very, very good.

Aho . . .

They made us many promises, more than I can remember, but they never kept but one; they promised to take our land, and they took it.
—Unidentified Old Lakota

The Great Spirit raised both the white man and the Indian. I think he raised the Indian first. He raised me in this land. It belongs to me. The white man was raised over the great waters, and his land is over there. Since they crossed the sea, I have given them room. There are now white people all about me. I have but a small spot of land left. The Great Spirit told me to keep it.
—Red Cloud (Lakota)

This war did not spring up here in our land; this war was brought upon us by the children of the Great Father who came to take our land from us without price, and who, in our land, do a great many evil things. The Great Father and his children are to blame for this trouble. . . . It has been our wish to live here in our country peaceably, and do such things as may be for the welfare and good of our people, but the Great Father has filled it with soldiers who think only of our death.
— Spotted Tail (Lakota)

If a man loses anything and goes back and looks carefully for it he will find it, and that is what the Indians are doing now when they ask you to give them the things that were promised them in the past; and I do not consider that they should be treated like beasts, and that is the reason I have grown up with the feelings I have.
—Sitting Bull (Lakota)

There was not hope on earth, and God seemed to have forgotten us. Some said they saw the Son of God; others did not see Him. If He had come, He would do some great things as He had done before. We doubted it because we had seen neither Him nor His works.

The people did not know; they did not care. They snatched at the hope. They screamed like crazy men to Him for mercy. They caught at the promise they heard He had made.

The white men were frightened and called for soldiers. We had begged for life, and the white men thought we wanted theirs. We heard that soldiers were coming. We did not fear. We hoped that we could tell them our troubles and get help. A white man said the soldiers meant to kill us. We did not believe it.

— Red Cloud (Lakota),
after Wounded Knee

. . . today, by reason for the immense augmentation of the American population, and the extension of their settlements throughout the entire West, covering both slopes of the Rocky Mountains, the Indian races are more seriously threatened with a speedy extermination than ever before in the history of the country.

—Ely Parker, the first
Indian Commissioner
of Indian Affairs

No white person or persons shall be permitted to settle upon or occupy any portion of the territory, or without the consent of the Indians to pass through the same.

—Treaty of 1868

One does not sell the earth upon which the people walk.
— Crazy Horse (Lakota)

If we make peace, you will not hold it.
— Gall (Lakota)

We, too, have children, and we wish to bring them up well.
— Red Cloud (Lakota)

My heart is very strong.
— Satanta (Kiowa)

May the white man and the Indian speak truth to each other today.
— Blackfoot (Crow)

The whites think we don't know about the mines, but we do.
— Blackfoot (Crow)

This country south of the Arkansas is our country.
— Kicking Bird (Kiowa)

Osages have talked like blackbirds in spring; nothing has come from their hearts.
— Governor Joe (Osage)

The Tonkawa killed him—it make my heart hot.
— Quanah Parker
(Comanche)

I want my people follow after white way.
—Quanah Parker
(Comanche)

Some white people do that, too.
— Quanah Parker
(Comanche)

We want the privilege of crossing the Arkansas to kill buffalo.
— Black Kettle
(Cheyenne)

It is our great desire and wish to make a good, permanent peace.
— Little Raven
(Arapahoe)

I am the man that makes it rain.
— Lone Wolf (Kiowa)

You sent for us; we came here.
—Tall Bull (Cheyenne)

Do not ask us to give up the buffalo for sheep.
— Ten Bears (Comanche)

Teach us the road to travel, and we will not depart from it forever.
— Satank (Kiowa)

I love the land and the buffalo and will not part with it.
— Satanta (Kiowa)

We preferred our own way of living.
— Crazy Horse (Lakota)

I see that my friends before me are men of age and dignity.
— Spotted Tail (Lakota)

I feel that my country has gotten a bad name.
— Sitting Bull (Lakota)

You are living in a new path.
— Sitting Bull (Lakota)

I bring you word from your fathers the ghosts.
— Kicking Bear (Lakota)

We love the Great Spirit.
— Petalesharo (Pawnee)

By peace our condition has been improved in the pursuit of civilized life.
— John Ross (Cherokee)

They have not got forked tongues.
— Washakie (Shoshone)

The only good Indian is a dead Indian.
— General Sheridan

IOWA

Sac and Fox
3137 F Ave.
Tama, IA 52339
(515) 484-4678 or (515) 484-5358
Fax (515) 484-5424

Mesquakie, "foxes" (Muskwakiwuk, "red earth people")

Location: To find Tama, look in your atlas between Marshalltown and Cedar Rapids on U.S. Highway 30.

Public Ceremony or Powwow Dates: During the second weekend in August, beginning on Thursday and running through Sunday, you will find the Mesquakie celebration powwow.

Art Forms: Arts and crafts are offered for sale during the powwow. The Mesquakie are known for their intricate beadwork, which features Eastern Woodlands floral designs.

Visitor Information: The village that is built for the powwow is likely to show wigwams and Plains-style tipis.

Early French explorers found the Sac near Saginaw Bay, Michigan. They settled in Wisconsin in the middle of the seventeenth century. Later, the Sac united with the Fox (Mesquakie). They were tricked into signing a treaty in 1804 which deprived them of all their lands east of the Mississippi River. The Black Hawk War of 1832 was in protest against this treaty. The Sac are found today in Iowa, Kansas, and Oklahoma. They are in the Algonquian language division.

The Fox are also of the Algonquian tradition. They lived close to the Fox River and Lake Winnebago, Wisconsin. French traders who had allied with the Chippewa, Potawatomi, and Menominee drove them south about 1746. In 1780, the Fox were nearly wiped out by the Chippewa, and the survivors joined with the Sac for protection. The Fox are found today in Iowa, Kansas, and Oklahoma.

For more information, see Oklahoma, Sac and Fox; Kansas, Sac and Fox.

KANSAS

Iowa of Kansas
Route 1, Box 58A
White Cloud, KS 66094
(913) 595-3258
Fax (913) 595-6610

Iowa ("sleepy ones")

Visitor Information: The Iowa live today on two reservations, here and in Oklahoma.

By their own oral history, the Iowa moved to the Plains from the Great Lakes area. During the 1700s, they lived in the Iowa, Minnesota, and Missouri region. During this time, they raised corn, hunted buffalo, and traded hides and furs with St. Louis traders. In 1836, the Iowa were moved to a reservation in northeastern Kansas. In 1883, some Iowa moved to a reservation in Oklahoma. The Iowa live today in Kansas, Nebraska, and Oklahoma. They are of the Sioux language division.

For more information, see Oklahoma, Iowa.

Kickapoo of Kansas
P.O. Box 271
Horton, KS 66349
(913) 486-2131
Fax (913) 486-2801

Kiwigapawa ("he stands about")

Location: The reservation is seven miles west of Horton.

Public Ceremony or Powwow Dates: The Kickapoo hold an annual powwow about the third weekend in July from Friday through Sunday at their powwow grounds. You will see traditional dancing as well as powwow dancing. The traditional Kickapoo Green Corn Dance is also done. This is one of my favorite powwows. I love the Eastern Woodlands songs.

Art Forms: Arts and crafts are sold at the powwow. You will find leatherwork, beadwork, wood carvings, and jewelry. Local Kickapoo artists as well as artists from other tribes in the area are there. For buying at other times, check with the senior citizens center in the housing area for information about craftspeople and artists who live nearby.

Joe Vetter, Iowa Indian, December 18, 1903
Photo by Thomas W. Smillie; Courtesy Museum of New Mexico, Neg. No. 87000

Visitor Information: The community has a bingo enterprise for visitors who like to play games of chance.

In 1670, the Kickapoo lived where Wisconsin is today. In 1765, they moved to the present site of central Illinois. They aided the British in the War of 1812, and some Kickapoo joined with Black Hawk against the United States in 1832. They ceded their lands in 1809 and 1819 and moved to Missouri, then to Kansas where some Kickapoo live on a reservation.

In 1852, a large group of the Kickapoo moved to Texas and then to Mexico. Some remain in Texas today. Others moved to a reservation in Oklahoma in 1873. The Kickapoo are of the Algonquian language division and are closely related to the Sac and Fox.

For more information, see Oklahoma, Kickapoo; Texas, Kickapoo.

Prairie Band Potawatomi
14880 K Road
Mayetta, KS 66509
(913) 966-2255
Fax (913) 966-2144

Potawatomi (Potawatamink or Potawaganink, "people of the place of the fire")

Location: This band of the Potawatomi is located west of Mayetta. Look for the bingo signs along Highway 75 at Mayetta.

Public Ceremony or Powwow Dates: The tribe holds their annual powwow during the summer. Call for dates and times.

Art Forms: Call the tribal office for details on art and craft work available from tribal members.

Visitor Information: The tribe has a herd of buffalo that stays behind the tribal complex. The beauty and size of these great animals is awe-inspiring. Be sure to look at the old photographs on the walls of the hall at the tribal office.

The Potawatomi, the "people of the place of the fire," are often called the Fire Nation. They lived where lower Michigan, northern Indiana, and northern Illinois are today. The Potawatomi were allies with the French during the colonial wars and aided the English during the War of 1812. They ceded most of their lands between 1836 and 1841. Many of the Potawatomi moved to Kansas and to Oklahoma. Some of the people stayed in Michigan and Wisconsin. The

Potawatomi are of the Algonquian language division and are closely related to the Chippewa and Ottawa.

For more information, see Oklahoma, Citizen Band; Wisconsin, Forest County.

Sac and Fox of Missouri in Kansas and Nebraska
Rural Route 1, Box 60
Reserve, KS 66434-9723
(913) 742-7471
Fax (913) 742-3785

Sauk (Osa Kiwug, "people of the yellow earth")
Foxes (Muskwakiwuk, "red earth people")

Location: The tribal offices and store are located in Reserve. Follow the signs from Highway 73.

Visitor Information: The tribe operates a small arts and crafts shop next to the tribal office building. An addition includes a small convenience store with a "smoke shop."

For more information, see Iowa, Sac and Fox; Oklahoma, Sac and Fox.

MISSOURI

Eastern Shawnee of Oklahoma
P.O. Box 350
Seneca, MO 64865
(918) 666-2435
Fax (918) 666-3325

Shawnee (Shawun, "south")

Visitor Information: This tribe usually participates in events around Miami, Oklahoma. Read more about them under the Miami of Oklahoma.

Keo-kuk, Jr. (Watchful Fox), Head Chief of the Fox, 1868
Photo by A. Zeno Shindler; Courtesy Museum of New Mexico, Neg. No. 56181

The Shawnee first met Europeans about 1670 near the Savannah River in what is now the state of South Carolina. Another group was located in the Cumberland Valley. Some trouble with the Cherokee and Catawba caused the first group to move to where New York and Pennsylvania are today. They finally settled in the Ohio Valley during the late 1700s to escape from non-Indians and from the Iroquois. The Shawnee joined with the British during the Revolutionary War and continued to fight against the invading foreigners after the war. Tecumseh was badly beaten at the battle of Tippecanoe in 1811 before he could organize our people against the invasion. Many Shawnee moved to the west, but some helped the British in the War of 1812. Eventually, the main body of the Shawnee settled in Oklahoma near the Cherokee Nation. They are of the Algonquian language division.

For more information, see Oklahoma, Absentee-Shawnee.

MONTANA

Blackfeet
P.O. Box 850
Browning, MT 59417
(406) 338-7276
Fax (406) 338-7530

Siksika (Blackfoot People)
Pikuni

Location: The town of Browning is the hub of the Blackfeet reservation, where you will find the Blackfeet Tribal Business Council, the Bureau of Indian Affairs, the Blackfeet Public Health Service hospital, the Manpower office, the Blackfeet Native American Programs office, the Blackfeet Housing Authority, the Browning public schools, and the Blackfeet Community College.

Public Ceremony or Powwow Dates: The North American Indian Days celebration is held in Browning the second week in July. It is an intriguing way to see authentic Indian tradition. Tipis are pitched on the powwow grounds for four days of Indian dancing, games, sports events, and socializing. The celebration is located at the Blackfeet Tribal Fairgrounds, adjacent to the Museum of the Plains Indian. Comprising one of the largest gatherings of U.S. and Canadian tribes, the celebration is an unforgettable experience. Once you hear and feel the mystery of the drum, the traditional and fancy dancing, the many proud native people, you will begin to understand their endurance in times of hardship which enabled them to keep at least some of their lands.

Art Forms: You will find traditional forms among these Plains Indians, including quill work, beadwork, leather work, feather work, and moccasins. Call the tribal office for more information.

Visitor Information: The Blackfeet Indian Reservation, one of the outstanding recreation areas in North America, is on 1.5 million acres of panoramic beauty. The location is ideal for vacationers since it is next to Glacier National Park and within easy driving distance of Yellowstone National Park. The eight major lakes and 175 miles of rivers and streams offer prime fishing. The reservation offers a summer and winter playground of hiking, camping, fishing, hunting, boating, picnicking, swimming, horseback riding, rodeos, water skiing, snow skiing, and snowmobiling. A nine-hole golf course is located in East Glacier. The Blackfeet were among the most powerful Indian tribes of the Northwest Plains. At one time, their territory extended west of the Rocky Mountains from the North Saskatchewan River to the headwaters of the Missouri River (now called Yellowstone National Park).

The Blackfeet Indian Reservation is located in the mountains of northern Montana. On the north, it borders the Canadian province of Alberta and to the south includes Glacier County. The western boundary is at the base of the magnificent Rocky Mountains, which make up Glacier National Park. The majority of the land consists of high rolling plains, historically the hunting grounds for the Blackfeet people. Elevation varies from 3,400 feet to the east to over 9,000 feet at Chief Mountain to the west.

Browning has been the headquarters for the Blackfeet Indian Reservation since 1895. The town was named after the Indian Affairs Commissioner of that time, Daniel Browning. You will find motels, cafes, gift shops, and automobile services. Relax, enjoy, and let a part of history come alive in nature's wilderness on the Blackfeet Reservation.

The modern Blackfeet Nation descended from three of the most powerful Indian tribes in the Northwestern Plains: the Northern Piegan (Pikuni), the Blackfeet (Sisaka) or Southern Piegan, and the Blood (Kainai) Indians. All speak a common language. The Blood ranged primarily in Canada, while the Northern Piegans

Manny Shot, Blackfoot
Photo by H. Pollard; Courtesy Museum of New Mexico, Neg. No. 111167

inhabited the high plains along the eastern slopes of the Rockies on both sides of the United States-Canada border. The Blackfeet dwelled almost exclusively in Montana, a territory also occupied by the Gros Ventre and Assiniboine, a distant relative of the Dakota or Sioux Indians. Observers on the early frontier spoke erroneously of these two latter tribes as members of the Blackfeet. However, these two tribes, along with the Shoshone to the south, were inveterate enemies of the Blackfeet. When the early missionaries and treaty-makers first attempted to contact these tribes, they were often caught in tribal wars being fought between the Blackfeet and their enemies.

The non-Indian population, which had migrated from Europe in their quest for freedom, began their westward move from the eastern part of the United States in search of furs, land, and riches. The 1700s saw the entrance of the fur trade in Blackfeet Territory, with the buffalo robe becoming an important item of trade. The westward expansion of white society demanded more land for settlers, fur companies, railroads, and the businesses and military establishments necessary for protection of the railroads and settlers. Thus, the Blackfeet people's land was needed and the Treaty-making Era began.

In exchange for land, the U.S. government ratified treaties with the Blackfeet people promising peace, protection, agricultural goods, services, education, money, health care, and inviolate land—promises that usually were not kept.

At the end of the treaty-making period (1871), the United States had other methods of securing more land. Through presidential orders and congressional acts, the Blackfeet land base dwindled to its current size. From an original territory that extended from the Yellowstone River to the Saskatchewan River in Canada and from the Continental Divide to the confluence of the Missouri and Yellowstone rivers, Blackfeet land was reduced to a small 1.5-million-acre tract in northwestern Montana.

In early times, the buffalo contributed a great deal to Blackfeet existence: meat for the staple diet, hides for the lodges and clothing, robes for the lodges, and bones for some of the tools. The Blackfeet at that time required very little else to maintain their way of life.

Although the Blackfeet had only a minor interest in trapping, they were skillful hunters. Therefore, as the fur trade entered the Blackfeet Territory in the mid-1700s, the buffalo became a vital part of the trade. In 1874, the northwestern buffalo herd was estimated at four million; by 1879, five years later, there were only a few buffalo left on the Plains; by 1883-84, the buffalo were virtually exterminated. Some had been killed to feed the railroad crews, but most had been massacred for their hides. Their naked carcasses spotted the prairies, where they rotted and became fair game for bone pickers.

With their natural economy gone, the Blackfeet became dependent on the government for food and supplies. The government was ill-prepared for such a crisis, and winter rations were greatly underestimated. This caused a catastrophe during the winter of 1883-84 as the annuities for the Indians did not arrive. Some 600 Piegan starved or froze to death that winter. Bones and bodies were scattered about until public health officers hauled them away for burial on a small ridge to the east. This burial grounds became known as "Ghost Ridge."

The arrival of missionaries among the Blackfeet in the early 1800s is another part of the history of the tribe. In 1859, the first mission school was opened for the Blackfeet near Choteau, Montana, which was reservation land at that time. Three log cabins were erected and called the St. Peters Mission. In 1883, a small one-room mission school was opened at Robare. The Catholics, or "Black Robes," were the first religious group to have an impact on the Blackfeet, although other religious groups were present.

The government and public schools began providing educational services in the late 1800s and early 1900s. Willow Creek School was established by the government in 1892. In 1904, the Cut Bank boarding school was opened for 125 students. The first government day school opened at Heart Butte, Old Agency, and Starr School in 1915. The first public school opened at Four Persons Agency in Choteau in 1872 and closed in 1876 because of poor attendance. Altyn opened a school for white children only in 1898 in the Babb valley. The first public school in Browning opened in 1905 with an enrollment of 20 students. Government boarding schools off the reservation, such as Carlisle Indian School, were the primary source of education for many years, with many of the Indian children taken from their homes forcibly to attend these schools.

A particularly interesting event in the history of the reservation took place in 1903-04. A fence was built around the entire reservation with exits only at Whiskey Gap on the Canadian line, Robare on Birch Creek, and Cut Bank. Whether or not an Indian was allowed to leave the reservation was the decision of the "agent" or superintendent of the Bureau of Indian Affairs. It was also necessary for whites to obtain a pass to enter. Regular line riders patrolled the fences to ensure they remained intact and that those within stayed in and those without stayed out. According to records, the real reason for the fence was to ensure that the Indian cattle did not mingle with those of the whites; but, whatever the reasons, the fence was gone by 1909.

Discovery of oil in the Swift Current Valley between Babb and Many Glacier made history. Three wells were drilled. At Boulder Creek, oil was found. Although none of these wells proved to have commercial value, they did lead to later exploration and oil industry expansion on the reservation. The next major event that affected the Blackfeet was the Allotment Act of 1907. All of the 2,450 Blackfeet people on the tribal rolls were allotted land (320 acres). Some acreage was reserved for the town sites of Browning and Babb, with all remaining lands sold under the Homestead Act.

The Great Northern Railroad's promotional campaign brought more people to this area to seek their fortune. This, in turn, led to the need for more organized communities. The "Old West" with its lawless, untamed frontiers was gone. The farmer migrated west, bringing an end to the open range. Towns with local governments, churches, and law and order were established. It was during this time that the right to patent land was granted to Indians by the U.S. government. Those who obtained trust patents could now trade their land to another Indian or sell it to anyone if he had obtained a fee patent. In 1919, the government realized that the acreage allotted to the Indians was not enough to sustain them, so an additional 80 acres was given to each Indian. Many of the new allotments were in choice locations, and as a result, some Indians had patents forced on them so they would have to sell their land. In any case, most of them did not understand what the patent process was, and they sold their property for unbelievably low prices. It was not unusual for a man to trade his acreage for one horse. Also, many Indian people lost their lands to local merchants for grocery and supply bills.

In February 1919, Glacier County was established. On December 1, 1919, Browning became incorporated; the battle for the county seat between Browning and Cut Bank was on. Browning had the advantage of being near the center of the county and was the site of the Blackfeet Agency. A vote was held, and a few Blackfeet who had their land patents at the time cast their vote for Browning, even though the majority of Indians could not vote. If they could have, Browning would almost certainly be the county seat for Glacier County. (Indians were not granted full status as citizens with the right to vote until 1924, although they did fight in World War I for the United States prior to 1924.)

The Indian Reorganization Act (IRA) passed by Congress in 1934 allowed for tribes to organize a tribal government and made provisions for education (Johnson O'Malley funds) and a credit program, among others. With the reestablishment of tribal powers in 1935, the Blackfeet formed the Blackfeet Tribal Business Council with a constitution outlining powers and authority. Since 1934, the Blackfeet have made slow but steady progress toward becoming the proud and industrious people they were prior to the arrival of the white man approximately 200 years before. In the 50 years since the IRA, the Blackfeet tribe has made progress in all areas—economic development, education, social services, increasing the tribal land base, population, improved health standards, physical systems, housing, and management skills. The population has increased from a low of 2,000 members in 1920 (a result of a small-pox epidemic along with the massacre of many Blackfeet women and children) to 13,200 enrolled tribal members as of January 1988 (an increase of approximately 630% in 68 years).

Other congressional acts resulted from various studies, such as the Merriam Report and the Kennedy Subcommittee on Indian Education, that pointed out the needs of Indian people. These included the Civil Rights Act of 1968, the Indian Self-Determination Act and Education Assistance Act of 1975, the Elementary and Secondary Education Act, and others that led to increased self-government and decision making by tribes. These acts provided for expanded opportunities for improved education, improved housing, improved social services, health care, economic development activities, and other services that tribes took advantage of.

Although the quality of life and the standard of living for the Blackfeet people have improved dramatically in the last fifty years, a great deal remains to be done. A tribal plan identifies the needs and priorities for continued progress for the Blackfeet Reservation and tribe.

Chippewa Cree
Rocky Boy Rt., P.O. Box 544
Box Elder, MT 59521
(406) 395-4282
Fax (406) 395-4497

Chippewa (Ojibwa, "to roast till puckered up," referring to the puckered seam on their moccasins)
Cree (contraction from Kristinaux, French form of Kenistenoag, given as one of their own names)

Location: The reservation is located 15 miles south of U.S. Highway 2 on State Highway 234 near Havre.

Public Ceremony or Powwow Dates: Rocky Boy Indian Days is usually the first weekend in August. Call the tribal office for dates and times.

Art Forms: Call the tribal office for the names of individuals who do traditional forms of arts and crafts.

Visitor Information: The tribe sells permits for fishing and camping. Tipis can be rented for camping, and there are trailer hookups. The Bear Paw Ski Bowl offers good skiing during the winter.

The Cree lived between the Red River and the Saskatchewan River and traveled the area that is now Manitoba, Saskatchewan, North Dakota, and Montana. They are closely related to the Ojibwa and usually were allies with the Assiniboin against the Sioux and Siksika. The Cree are in the Algonquian language division.

For more information, see Minnesota, Ojibwa.

Confederated Salish and Kootenai
Box 278
Pablo, MT 59855-0278
(406) 675-2700
Fax (406) 675-2806

Salish (Okinagan: salst, "people")
Kuronaqa (one of their names for themselves)

Location: Look in your atlas in northwest Montana for the Flathead Indian Reservation.

Public Ceremony or Powwow Dates: The Fourth of July Powwow is held in Arlee, Montana.

Art Forms: Arts and crafts are sold at the powwow.

Visitor Information: At the powwow, the people celebrate with a rodeo, carnival, rock music, traditional Indian music, and hand games. Tipis are set up on the grounds.

Cree Woman with Fur Robe, 1926
Photo by Edward S. Curtis; Courtesy Museum of New Mexico, Neg. No. 122943

The Salish are a large and powerful division of the Salishan family, to which they gave their name, living in much of western Montana and centering around Flathead Lake and Valley. A more popular designation for this tribe is Flathead, given to them by the surrounding people, not because they artificially deformed their heads but because, in contrast to most tribes farther west, they left them in their natural condition, flat on top.

The Salish lived primarily by hunting. With the related Pend d'Oreille and Kootenai, they ceded to the United States their lands in Montana and Idaho, by the treaty of Hell Gate, Montana, July 16, 1855. They also joined in the peace treaty signed at the mouth of Judith River, Montana, on October 17, 1855. Lewis and Clark estimated their population in 1806 to be 600. Their probable number in 1853 was 325, a decrease said to be due to wars with the Siksika (Blackfeet). The number of Flatheads under the Flathead Agency in Montana (1909) was 598.

The Kootenai are a distinct language group who inhabit parts of southeast British Columbia and northern Montana and Idaho, from the lakes near the source of the Columbia River to Pend d'Oreille Lake. Their legends and traditions indicate that they were driven westward by the Siksika, their hereditary enemies. Before the buffalo disappeared from the plains from overhunting and destruction by non-Indians, they often had joint hunting expeditions. Memory of the treatment of the Kootenai by the Siksika remains, however, in the name they give the latter, Sahantla (Bad People). They also held a bad opinion of the Assiniboine (Tlutlamaeka, "Cutthroats") and the Cree (Gutskiawe, "Liars"). In 1890, the number of Kootenai in Idaho and Montana was 400 to 500; in 1905, the Flathead Agency, Montana, reported 554.

For more information, see Idaho, Kootenai and Coeur d'Alene.

Crow
P.O. Box 159
Crow Agency, MT 59022
(406) 638-2601
Fax (406) 638-7283

Crow (translation from French *gens des corbeaux*, for their own name, Absaroke, "crow," "sparrowhawk," or "bird people")

Unidentified woman, Flathead (Salish)
Photo by Edward S. Curtis; Courtesy Museum of New Mexico, Neg. No. 103019

Location: Crow Agency is located on Interstate 90 south of Hardin, Montana.

Public Ceremony or Powwow Dates: The Crow Fair is generally held in August. This is one of the biggest powwows in the lower 48 states and is considered one of the best. The Crow love tipis, and the area will be filled with them. Call the tribal office for dates and times.

Art Forms: The Crow are known for their fabulous beadwork, usually in floral designs. Look for the beautiful beaded horse gear during the Crow Fair parade. The visitors center at the Little Big Horn Battlefield also has arts and crafts.

Visitor Information: There is traditional dancing, powwow dancing, Indian food, arts and crafts sales, and more during the fair. The Crow flatten their roach headdresses and are distinctive during the dancing.

Custer Battlefield National Monument is located two miles southeast of Crow Agency on Interstate 90, exit 510.

The Crow are a Siouan tribe forming part of the Hidatsa tribe. According to tradition, they separated from the Hidatsa about 1776. One story says that this separation was the result of a factional dispute between two chiefs who were desperate men with a nearly equal number of followers. They were then residing on the Missouri River. One of the two bands, which afterward became the Crow, withdrew and moved to the vicinity of the Rocky Mountains, where they continued to roam until forced onto the reservation. Since their separation from the Hidatsa, their traditional lifestyle has been similar to that of most tribes of the plains. Their chief enemies were the Siksika and the Dakota. At the time of Lewis and Clark (1804), they lived on the Bighorn River; in 1817, they were located on the Yellowstone and the east side of the Rocky Mountains; in 1834, they lived on the south branch of the Yellowstone.

The tipis of the Crow were similar to those of the Sioux. On the poles there were small pieces of colored cloth, chiefly red, that floated like streamers in the wind. According to one observer, their camp swarmed with wolflike dogs. The Crow were wandering hunters, only occasionally planting a few small patches of tobacco. They lived at that time in some 400 tipis and possessed between 9,000 and 10,000 horses. In stature and dress, they were similar to the Hidatsa and were proud of their long hair. The women were skillful in many kinds of artwork. Their shirts and dresses made of bighorn leather as well as their buffalo robes embroidered and orna-

Perits-har-sts and wife, Crow Indians, Washington, D.C., 1873
Photo by Ulke; Courtesy Museum of New Mexico, Neg. No. 58639

Curley, Crow Indian scout for Gen. G. Custer at Battle of Little Big Horn in 1876
Photo by Finn; Courtesy Museum of New Mexico, Neg. No. 2511

mented with dyed porcupine quills are particularly beautiful. The men were skilled in making weapons, especially their large bows, which were covered with horn from elk or bighorn and often with rattlesnake skin. The Crow were skillful horsemen and could throw themselves from side to side during battle. Their dead were usually placed on scaffolds elevated on poles in the prairie.

The population was estimated by Lewis and Clark (1804) at 350 lodges and 3,500 individuals. In 1829 and 1834, the population was 4,500; in 1843, there were 400 tipis. Their number in 1890 was 2,287; and in 1904, 1,826. The Crow have been officially classified as the Mountain Crow and the River Crow, the former so-called because of their custom of hunting and roaming near the mountains away from the Missouri River, the latter, because they left the mountain region about 1859 and occupied the country along the river. There was no difference between them.

Fort Belknap
P.O. Box 249
Harlem, MT 59526
(406) 353-2205
Fax (406) 353-2797

Gros Ventre (Big Bellies)
Assiniboine-Sioux (u sin, "stone"; u pwawa, "he cooks by roasting"; one who cooks with a stone)

Location: This reservation is located in north-central Montana directly north of Billings.

Public Ceremony or Powwow Dates: Call the tribal office for dates and times.

Some writers have confused the Gros Ventre with the Hidatsa and the Atsina. They are very distinct tribes and are not related to each other. The two tribes have also been distinguished as Gros Ventre of the Missouri (Hidatsa) and Gros Ventre of the Prairie (Atsina). The name as applied to the Atsina originates from the Indian sign by which they are designated in sign language—a sweeping pass with both hands in front of the abdomen, intended to convey the idea of "hungry." A clue to its application to the Hidatsa is that the Hidatsa formerly tattooed parallel stripes across the chest and were thus sometimes distinguished in picture writings. The gesture sign to indicate this style of tattooing would be sufficiently similar to that used to designate the Atsina to lead the careless observer to interpret both

Chief Red Whip, Gros Ventre, 1913
Photo by Joseph A. Dixon; Courtesy Museum of New Mexico, Neg. No. 68011

Tipi, Gros Ventre
Photo by V. C. Traphagen; Courtesy Museum of New Mexico, Neg. No. 77735

as "Gros Ventre." The ordinary sign now used by the Southern Plains tribes to indicate the Hidatsa is interpreted to mean "spreading tipis," or "row of lodges."

The Assiniboin lived along the Saskatchewan and Assiniboine rivers in Canada and north of the Milk and Missouri rivers where Montana is today. They were allies with the Cree against Sioux tribes. They were a large tribe until 1836, when smallpox brought by non-Indians killed 4,000, leaving only about 6,000 survivors. Today, the Assiniboin live on reservations at Fort Belknap and at Fort Peck in Montana. There are some reserves in Canada where others live. They are of the Sioux language division and are closely related to the Yanktonai.

Fort Peck Assiniboine-Sioux
P.O. Box 1027
Poplar, MT 59255
(406) 768-5155
Fax (406) 768-5478

Assiniboine-Sioux

The Assiniboin lived along the Saskatchewan and Assiniboine rivers in Canada and north of the Milk and Missouri rivers where Montana is today. They were allies with the Cree against Sioux tribes. They were a large tribe until 1836, when smallpox brought by foreigners killed 4,000, leaving only about 6,000 survivors. Today, the Assiniboin live on reservations at Fort Belknap and at Fort Peck in Montana. There are some reserves in Canada where others live. They are of the Sioux language division and are closely related to the Yanktonai.

Northern Cheyenne
P.O. Box 128
Lame Deer, MT 59043
(406) 477-8284
Fax (406) 477-6210

Sha-Hi'yena, Shai-ena (from Sioux)
Shai-ela (from Teton)

Cheyenne

Location: This reservation is in south-central Montana bordering the Wyoming state line.

Public Ceremony or Powwow Dates: The Northern Cheyenne hold a powwow, usually in July. They often hold stick-games and other interesting events.

Art Forms: The Northern Cheyenne do traditional forms of artwork. Individual artisans can be contacted through the tribal office.

Visitor Information: The Northern Cheyenne Tribal Museum, Lame Deer, presents the history and culture of the Cheyenne Indian people.

The Cheyenne are of the greater Algonquian language division. They call themselves Dzi tsi stas, "people alike," that is, "Our People"; with a slight change of accent, it might also mean "gashed ones," from *ehistai,* "he is gashed," or possibly "tall people."

The popular name has no connection with the French *chien,* "dog," as has sometimes been erroneously supposed. In sign language, they are indicated by a gesture that has often been interpreted to mean "cut arms" or "cut fingers," being made by drawing the right index finger several times rapidly across the left, but which appears really to indicate "striped arrows," by which name they are known to the Hidatsa, Shoshone, Comanche, Caddo, and probably other tribes, an allusion to their old-time preference for turkey feathers for winging arrows.

The earliest home of the Cheyenne, before the year 1700, seems to have been that part of Minnesota bounded roughly by theMississippi, Minnesota, and upper Red rivers. The Sioux, then living closer to the Mississippi, to the east and southeast, came in contact with the French as early as 1667, but the Cheyenne are first mentioned in 1680, under the name of Chaa, when a party of that tribe, described as living on the head of the great river, the Mississippi, visited La Salle's Fort on the Illinois River to invite the French to come to their country, which they said had great numbers of beaver and other fur-bearing animals. The veteran Sioux missionary, Williamson, says that according to Sioux tradition, the Cheyenne occupied the upper Mississippi region prior to the Sioux and were found by them already established on the Minnesota. At a later period, they moved over to the Cheyenne branch of Red River, North Dakota, which thus acquired its name, being known to the Sioux as "the place where the Cheyenne plant," showing that the latter were still an agricultural people. This westward movement was due to pressure from the Sioux, who were retreating from the Chippewa, then already in possession of guns from the east.

Honii-Watoma (Wolf Robe), Cheyenne, 1909
Photo by DeLancey Gill; Courtesy Museum of New Mexico, Neg. No. 86994

Driven out by the Sioux, the Cheyenne moved west toward the Missouri River, where their further progress was opposed by the Sutaio, a people who had preceded them to the west and who were then living between the river and the Black Hills. After a period of hostility, the two tribes became friendly, some time after which the Cheyenne crossed the Missouri below the entrance of the Cannonball River and later took refuge in the Black Hills around the head of the Cheyenne River of South Dakota. Lewis and Clark found them there in 1804, since which time they moved west and south until they were confined to reservations. Up to the time of Lewis and Clark, they conducted war with the Mandan and Hidatsa, who probably helped to drive them from the Missouri River. They seem, however, to have kept on good terms with the Arikara.

According to their own history, the Cheyenne, while living in Minnesota and on the Missouri River, occupied fixed villages, practiced agriculture, and made pottery but lost these arts on being driven out into the plains to become roving buffalo hunters. On the Missouri, and perhaps also farther east, they occupied earth-covered log houses. Some Cheyenne had cultivated fields on the Little Missouri River as late as 1850. This was probably a recent settlement, as they are not mentioned in that area by Lewis and Clark. At least one man among them still understood the art of making beads and figurines from pounded glass, as formerly practiced by the Mandan. In a sacred tradition recited only by the priestly keeper, they still tell how they "lost the corn" after leaving the eastern country.

Although the friendship between the Sutaio and the Cheyenne dates from the crossing of the Missouri River by the latter, the actual incorporation of the Sutaio into the Cheyenne tribe probably occurred within the last two hundred years. The Cheyenne say also that they obtained the Sun Dance and the buffalo head medicine from the Sutaio but claim the Medicine Arrow Ceremony as their own from the beginning. Up to 1835, and probably until reduced by the cholera epidemic of 1849, the Sutaio kept their distinctive dialect, dress, and ceremonies and camped apart from the Cheyenne. In 1851, they were still to some extent a distinct people. Now they exist only as one of the component divisions of the Southern Cheyenne tribe. Under the name Staitan, they are mentioned by Lewis and Clark in 1804 as a small and savage tribe roving west of the Black Hills.

There is some doubt as to when or where the Cheyenne first met the Arapahoe, with whom they have long been friends; neither do they appear to have any clear idea as to the date of the friendship between the two tribes, which has continued. Their connection with the Arapahoe is of friendship, without assimilation, while the Sutaio have been incorporated into the tribe.

Their written history may be said to begin with the expedition of Lewis and Clark in 1804. Constantly pressed farther onto the plains by the Sioux, they found homes for themselves on the upper branches of the Platte, driving the Kiowa, in turn, farther to the south. They made their first treaty with the U.S. government in 1825 at the mouth of the Teton River, on the Missouri, at the present site of Pierre, South Dakota. After the building of Bent's Fort on the upper Arkansas in Colorado in 1832, a large part of the tribe decided to make permanent homes on the Arkansas, while the rest continued to live around the headwaters of the North Platte and Yellowstone rivers. This separation was made permanent by the treaty of Fort Laramie in 1851, the two sections being now known, respectively, as Southern and Northern Cheyenne. The distinction is purely geographic, although it has changed their former compact tribal organization.

The Southern Cheyenne are known in the tribe as Sowonia, "Southerners," while the Northern Cheyenne are commonly designated as O Mi Sis eaters, from the division most numerously represented among them. Their arrival on the Arkansas brought them into constant collision with the Kiowa, who, with the Comanche, claimed the territory to the south. The old men of both tribes told of numerous encounters during the next few years, the main one being a battle on an upper branch of Red River in 1837, in which the Kiowa killed an entire party of 48 Cheyenne warriors of the Bowstring society, and a battle in summer 1838, in which the Cheyenne and Arapaho attacked the Kiowa and Comanche on Wolf Creek, northwest Oklahoma, with considerable losses on both sides. About 1840, the Cheyenne made peace with the Kiowa in the south, having already made peace with the Sioux in the north. Since this time all these tribes, together with the Arapaho, Kiowa, Kiowa Apache, and Comanche, usually acted as allies in the wars with other tribes and with non-Indians. For a long time the Cheyenne were friends with the western Sioux, after whom they patterned many details of their dress and ceremony. They did not suffer badly from the smallpox epidemic of 1837-1839, having been warned in time to escape to the mountains. But like other prairie tribes, they suffered terribly from cholera in 1849, when several of their bands were nearly wiped out. They lost about 200 lodges, esti-

Sun Dance Pledgers, Cheyenne 1911
Photo by Edward S. Curtis; Courtesy Museum of New Mexico, Neg. No. 65118

mated at 2,000 people, or about two-thirds of their whole number before the epidemic.

Their peace with the Kiowa enabled them to extend their hunting expeditions farther to the south, and in 1853, they made their first raid into Mexico but with disastrous results, losing all but three men in a fight with Mexican lancers. From 1860 to 1878, they were involved in border warfare, acting with the Sioux in the north and with the Kiowa and Comanche in the south. And they probably lost more in conflict with non-Indians than any other tribe of the plains, in proportion to their number. In 1864, the southern band suffered a severe blow in the notorious Chivington massacre in Colorado and again in 1868 at the hands of Custer in the massacre at the Washita. They took a leading part in the general outbreak of the southern tribes in 1874-75.

The Northern Cheyenne joined with the Sioux in the battles against the intruders in 1876 and were active participants in the victory over Custer. Later in the year they received a severe blow from General Mackenzie and were forced to surrender. In the winter of 1878-79, a band of Northern Cheyenne under Dull Knife, Wild Hog, and Little Wolf, who had been taken as prisoners to Fort Reno to be colonized with the southern portion of the tribe in what is now Oklahoma, made a desperate attempt to escape. Of an estimated 89 men and 146 women and children who broke away on the night of September 9, about 75, including Dull Knife and most of the warriors, were killed in the pursuit that continued to the Dakota border, in the course of which about 50 non-Indians lost their lives. Thirty-two of the Cheyenne slain were killed in a second break for liberty from Fort Robinson, Nebraska, where the captured people had been confined. Little Wolf, with about 60 followers, escaped to safety in the north. At a later period, the Northern Cheyenne were assigned to the present reservation in Montana. The Southern Cheyenne were assigned to a reservation in western Oklahoma by treaty of 1867 but refused to remain there until after the surrender of 1875, when a number of the most prominent warriors were deported to Florida for a term of three years. In 1901-02, the lands of the Southern Cheyenne were allotted in severalty and the Indian people were offered American citizenship. Those in the north seemed to hold their own in population, while those of the south steadily decreased. In 1904, the Northern Cheyenne numbered 1,409; the Southern Cheyenne, 1,903.

Although originally an agricultural people of the timber country, the Cheyenne for generations were a typical prairie tribe, living in buffalo hide tipis, following the buffalo over great areas, traveling and fighting on horseback. They commonly buried their dead in trees or on scaffolds but occasionally in caves or in the ground. Polygamy was practiced, as was usual among the prairie tribes. Under their old system, before the division of the tribe, they had a council of 44 elective chiefs, four of whom constituted a higher body, with power to elect one of their own number as head chief of the tribe. In all councils that concerned the relations of the Cheyenne with other tribes, one member of the council was appointed to argue as the proxy or "devil's advocate" for the absent people. This council of 44 is still symbolized by a bundle of 44 invitation sticks, kept with the sacred medicine arrows and formerly sent around when the assembly was to be convened.

The set of four medicine arrows, each of a different color, constitutes the tribal palladium that they have had from the beginning of the world and is exposed with appropriate rites once a year if previously "pledged" and on those rare occasions when a Cheyenne has been killed by one of his own tribe, the purpose of the ceremony being to wipe away from the murderer the stain of a brother's blood. The rite did not die with the final separation of the two sections of the tribe in 1851. The bundle is still religiously preserved by the Southern Cheyenne. Besides the public ceremony there is also a rite spoken of as "fixing" the arrows, held at shorter intervals, which concerns the arrow priests alone. The public ceremony is always attended by delegates from the Northern Cheyenne. No woman or non-Indian has ever been allowed to come near the sacred arrows.

Their great tribal ceremony for generations has been the Sun Dance (Offerings Lodge), which they themselves say came to them from the Sutaio, after they moved to the open plains. So far as is known, this ceremony belongs exclusively to the tribes of the plains or to those in close contact with them. The Buffalo Head Ceremony, which was formerly connected with the Sun Dance but has been obsolete for many years, also came from the Sutaio. The Ghost Dance was enthusiastically taken up by the tribe at its first appearance, about 1890, and the Peyote Ceremony is now popular. They also had until the early 1900s a Fire Dance, something like that credited to the Navajo, in which the initiated performers danced over a fire of blazing coals until they extinguished it with their bare feet. In priestly dignity the keepers of the Medicine Arrow (Cheyenne) and Sun Dance (Sutaio) ceremonies stood first and equal.

At the Sun Dance, and on other occasions where the whole tribe was assembled, they formed their camp circle in eleven sections. Within the memory of old men still living in 1905, the ancient number did not exceed seven. Although it is quite probable that the Cheyenne may have had the clan system in ancient times while still a sedentary people, it is almost as certain to have disappeared so long ago as to be no longer even a memory.

The Northern Cheyenne were known as the most aggressive of all warrior tribes until they were defeated, with the loss of their chief, Tall Bull, by General Carr's forces in 1869.

For more information, see Oklahoma, Cheyenne.

NEBRASKA

Omaha of Nebraska
Omaha Tribal Council
P.O. Box 368
Macy, NE 68039
(402) 837-5391
Fax (402) 837-5308

U'mon'ha

Location: The Omaha Reservation is located in northeast Nebraska bordering the Winnebago Reservation.

Public Ceremony or Powwow Dates: The Omaha tribe, the originator of the modern-day "powwow," called their annual dance and celebration the "Whe'wahchee" or "Dance of Thanksgiving." It is the oldest powwow in the United States. In 1993, the Omaha celebrate their 190th annual dance. The first full moon during the month of August determines the time for the celebration. According to ancient traditions, a full moon almost always guarantees no rain. So, leave your umbrella at home and join the Omaha in their celebration.

The Omaha are in the Sioux language division. Earliest contact with the Europeans places them on the Ohio and Wabash rivers. Lewis and Clark mention the Omaha Dance of Thanksgiving in their journal. Their contact with the Omaha was in 1803 and took place in present-day northeastern Nebraska.

Ponca
Ponca Tribe of Nebraska
P.O. Box 288
Niebra, NE 66760
(402) 857-3391
Fax (402) 857-3736

For more information, see Oklahoma, Ponca.

Santee Sioux
Route 2
Niobrara, NE 68760
(402) 857-3302
Fax (402) 857-2307

Sioux (Isanyati)

Location: The reservation is located in northeastern Nebraska directly west of Sioux City, Iowa.

The Santee Sioux are an eastern division of the Dakota. The Mdewakanton and Wahpekute, sometimes also the Sisseton and Wahpeton, comprise part of this division.
For more information, see South Dakota, Sioux.

Winnebago
Winnebago, NE 68071
(402) 878-2272
Fax (402) 878-2963

Winnebago (Winipig)

Location: The reservation is located in northeast Nebraska on the Missouri River.

Public Ceremony or Powwow Dates: The annual powwow is usually held in late July, but you must call the tribal office for exact dates and times.

French explorers found the Winnebago living south of Green Bay and inland as far as Lake Winnebago. They later moved to the Fox, Wisconsin, and Rock rivers. The Winnebago fought for the British in the War of 1812. A reservation in Iowa was their home imposed by treaties in 1825 and 1832. Later, they were moved by the government to Minnesota and then again to the Omaha reservation. Many Winnebago still live in Wisconsin. They are in the Sioux language division.
For more information, see Wisconsin, Wisconsin Winnebago.

NORTH DAKOTA

Arikara, Hidatsa, and Mandan
Fort Berthold
P.O. Box 220
New Town, ND 58763
(701) 627-4782
Fax (701) 627-3805

Arikara, Hidatsa, and Mandan

Location: The Arikara, Hidatsa, and Mandan occupy west central North Dakota within six counties: McLean, McKenzie, Mountrail, Dunn, Mercer, and Ward. Look on your map of North Dakota, northwest of Bismarck and southeast of Williston on the Missouri River.

Public Ceremony or Powwow Dates: The powwows held on the Fort Berthold Reservation are colorful annual events, and visitors are welcome. There is no admission charge for the powwows, and many concession stands are available. The organizers do not allow any alcohol or drugs on the grounds during the events. Law enforcement personnel will strictly enforce these regulations.

The Arikara Celebration is held annually at White Shield, North Dakota, the second weekend of July. The Mandaree Celebration is held annually at Mandaree, North Dakota, the third weekend of July. The Little Shell Celebration is held at New Town, North Dakota, the second weekend of August, and the Twin Buttes Celebration is held at Twin Buttes, North Dakota, the third weekend of August.

Art Forms: You will find beadwork and star quilts handmade by local artisans. Call the tribe at the main office telephone number for more information. •

Visitor Information: The nearby cities of New Town and Parshall, North Dakota, have all services needed by the traveler. The Three Affiliated Tribes Museum is located in New Town.

The Fort Berthold Reservation is the home of the Mandan, Hidatsa, and Arikara tribes, who joined together as the Three Affiliated Tribes under the Indian Reorganization Act of June 18, 1934, with a Federal Corporation Charter ratified April 23, 1937, with a subsequent amendment November 27, 1961. They operate under a constitution and by-laws approved on June 28, 1936, with subsequent amendments.

All three tribes lived in permanent earth-lodge villages for many centuries before the arrival of the white man. Despite a basic similarity of economic and social life, these village peoples differed markedly in language and customs. The Mandan and Hidatsa speak a Siouan dialect, while the Arikara are members of the Caddoan linguistic group, being related closest to the Pawnee.

When first visited by traders and explorers in the middle eighteenth century, the Mandan and Hidatsa lived very near their present location. The Hidatsa had three earth-lodge villages at the mouth of the Knife River, north of the present town of Stanton, North Dakota, and the Mandan had a half-dozen or more villages near the mouth of the Heart River at Mandan, North Dakota. The Arikara were located in central South Dakota, with some of their villages ranging as high as the Grand River area.

The village people seem to have been moving slowly upstream in a long-term migration that began well back in prehistoric times. In the latter third of the eighteenth century, this migration was sharply accelerated because of the ravages resulting from the smallpox epidemic. This affected the Mandan to a greater degree than the other tribes, so that at the beginning of the nineteenth century they had moved to a location a few miles south of the Hidatsa. The Hidatsa controlled the hunting to the north, and the Arikara controlled the hunting to the south.

The Mandan and Hidatsa were the "farmers, merchants, and bankers" of the Northern Plains. Evidence has been found which indicates that these people were dealing with the native peoples of the deep Southwest. The Arikara, however, insisted on acting as brokers between the agricultural Hidatsa and Mandan in their bartering with the Mexican and deep Southwest people in trading for corn during the recurrent droughts that often plagued the Southwest.

The year 1837 marks the last of the violent smallpox epidemics that hit the general area. This epidemic resulted in the decimation of the Mandan tribe to a point where it could no longer exist as an independent unit. The Hidatsa were also hard hit. But inasmuch as members of this tribe were out on the prairies for their annual summer buffalo hunts, the Hidatsa were affected to a lesser degree by the ravages of smallpox.

The Arikara, who had been increasingly harassed by the Sioux from both the south and the east, chose this time to abandon their villages. When the Arikara found the Mandan villages empty, they moved into the hastily abandoned houses. In the meantime, the

Bear's Teeth, Arikara, 1908
Photo by Edward S. Curtis; Courtesy Museum of New Mexico, Neg. No. 103168

Mandan and Hidatsa, over a period of years, continued to move slowly upstream where they finally constructed a new village in a beautiful bend on the Missouri River. This location was the famous "Like a Fishhook Village."

Recorded history relating to the Fort Berthold Reservation area dates back to the 1790s when early explorers traversed the area and slightly later when the Lewis and Clark expedition traveled on their Missouri River voyage through the Louisiana Territory. However, definitive history of the reservation begins with the Treaty of Fort Laramie of 1851, which defined the boundary of the Gros Ventre (a misnomer for the Hidatsa), Mandan, and Arikara Indian nations, now called the Three Affiliated Tribes. The Fort Laramie Treaty established a vast area of land vaguely described as the entire right bank of the Missouri River from the mouth of the Yellowstone River and from the mouth of the Powder River to the headwaters of the Heart River. This territory, which included parts of Montana, Wyoming, North Dakota, and South Dakota, was named Fort Berthold in honor of an American Fur Company founder, Bartholomay Berthold.

Between 1851, when the Fort Laramie Treaty was signed, and 1891, a succession of executive orders and congressional acts changed the size of the reservation from a maximum of roughly 13,500,000 acres to a gross area (including white-owned land) of approximately 930,000 acres. During 1954, the reservation lost an additional 152,300 acres of land to the U.S. Army Corps of Engineers for the filling of the Garrison Reservoir (Lake Sakakawea). The waters of Lake Sakakawea inundated most of the well-built-up bottom and access roads and divided the reservation into five isolated segments that are not contiguous with each other. The flooding of the bottom lands destroyed the long-established Indian population centers, with the Tribal Agency itself being moved to the city of New Town. Since 1954, several small communities have sprung up, the principal ones being White Shield, Mandaree, and Twin Buttes.

The immense loss of natural resources occasioned by the flooding of Lake Sakakawea was cause for only a part of the adjustments that have had to be made by the Indian people. No attempt was made to reestablish duplicates of the small Indian villages that existed; thus, Indian families were forced to relocate on isolated holdings scattered throughout the reservation. Consequently, social and clan lines were crossed and recrossed, with former neighbors becoming widely separated. This extreme stress on the Indian people has been partly responsible for movement off the reservation.

Devils Lake Sioux
Sioux Community Center
Fort Totten, ND 58335
(701) 766-4221
Fax (701) 766-4126

Sioux

Location: The Fort Totten Reservation is located in northeast-central North Dakota close to Devils Lake on Federal Highway 2.

In 1908, the tribes placed on this reservation were the Assiniboine, Cuthead (Pabaksa), Santee, Sisseton, Yankton, and Wahpeton Sioux.
For more information, see South Dakota, Sioux.

Standing Rock Sioux
Fort Yates, ND 58538
(701) 854-7201
Fax (701) 854-7299

Sioux

Location: This reservation is located in south-central North Dakota and north-central South Dakota. Look straight south of Bismarck, North Dakota, on your map.

Public Ceremony or Powwow Dates: Call the tribal office for dates and times of their powwow at Little Eagle, South Dakota. It is usually held in July.

In 1908, the tribes placed on this reservation were the Blackfoot (Sihasapa), Hunkpapa, and Lower and Upper Yanktonai Sioux.
For more information, see South Dakota, Sioux.

Turtle Mountain Ojibwa
Belcourt, ND 58316
(701) 477-6451
Fax (701) 477-6836

Ojibwa (Chippewa)

Location: The reservation is located in north-central North Dakota just south of Manitoba, Canada.

The range of the Chippewa was along both shores of Lake Huron and Lake Superior extending across Minnesota to Turtle Mountain, North Dakota. This band is the Pembina.
For more information, see Minnesota, Ojibwa.

OKLAHOMA

Absentee-Shawnee
2025 S. Gordon Cooper Drive
Shawnee, OK 74801-9381
(405) 275-4030
Fax (405) 275-5637

Shawnee (*Shawun*, "south")

Visitor Information: All three branches of the Shawnee tribe are located in Oklahoma today. Shawnee stomp dance leaders and shell shakers dance traditional forms during stomp dance competitions at powwows. Look for them at the Quapaw powwow.

For more information, see Missouri, Eastern Shawnee.

Apache of Fort Sill
Route 2, Box 121
Apache, OK 73006
(405) 588-2298
Fax (405) 588-3133

Apache (probably from *apachu*, "enemy," the Zuñi name for the Navajo, who were designated "Apaches de Nabaju" by the early Spaniards in New Mexico)

Visitor Information: After the Apache wars with the blue coats in the Southwest were over in 1886, Chiricahua Apache Chief Geronimo was imprisoned at Fort Sill north of Lawton, Oklahoma. The guardhouse and cell where Geronimo and his warriors were imprisoned is still here. Many of Geronimo's people still live in the area today.

For more information, see Arizona, White Mountain Apache.

Apache
P.O. Box 1220
Anadarko, OK 73005
(405) 247-9493
Fax (405) 247-3153

Apache (probably from *apachu* "enemy," the Zuñi name for Navajo)

Visitor Information: This Indian community has several tribes living in it or nearby. They are the Apache, Arapaho, Caddo, Cheyenne,

Tennyson Berry (Sekûñtekûñ or War Bonnet), Kiowa-Apache, 1913
Photo by DeLancey Gill; Courtesy Museum of New Mexico, Neg. No. 59438

Nai-chi-ti (Nachez) and wife, Chiricahua Apache, ca. 1882
Photo by Ben Wittick; Courtesy School of American Research Collections in the
Museum of New Mexico, Neg. No. 15903

Comanche, Delaware, Kiowa-Apache, Kiowa, and Wichita. There are also other tribes represented by marriage, employment, and choice. The Apache call themselves N de, Dine, Tinde, or Inde, "People." For more information, see Arizona, White Mountain Apache.

Caddo
P.O. Box 487
Binger, OK 73009
(405) 656-2344
Fax (405) 247-2005

Caddo (Hasinai)

Visitor Information: The Caddo people live out their traditions in song, music, and dance. Labor Day is their biggest single celebration with three days of dancing, but the whole season of June through September is busy with dances. Call the tribal office for dates and times and arrangements.

The Caddo are the leading tribe of the Caddo Confederacy, which included the Arikara and Pawnee of the Plains and related tribes in the south. The explorer, LaSalle, found some Caddo villages along the Red River in 1687. The Caddo became involved in the wars between the French and the Spanish and as a result, moved westward into Texas. In 1859, a reservation was established in Oklahoma. Traditional Caddoans had conical-shaped thatched houses. They were farmers and buffalo hunters and wove cloth. The Caddo Confederacy included eight to twelve tribes, among them the Anadarko, Nacogdoches, and Natchitoches.

Cherokee of Oklahoma
P.O. Box 948
Tahlequah, OK 74465
(918) 456-0671
Fax (918) 456-6485

United Keetoowah Band of Cherokee
P.O. Box 746
Tahlequah, OK 74464-0746
(918) 456-9462
Fax (918) 456-3648

Buffalo Goad, June 1871
Photo by Jeremiah Gurney and Son; Courtesy Museum of New Mexico, Neg. No. 4853

The tribal name is a corruption of Tsalagi or Tsaragi, the name by which they commonly called themselves. It may be derived from the Choctaw *chiluk ki*, "cave people," in allusion to the numerous caves in their mountain country. They sometimes also call themselves Ani-Yun-wiya, "real people," or Ani-Kitu hwagi, "people of Kituhwa," one of their most important ancient settlements. Their northern kinsmen, the Iroquois, called them Oyata ge ronon, "inhabitants of the cave country," and the Delaware and connected tribes called them Kittuwa, from the settlement above.

Location: The Cherokee Heritage Center, Tsa-la-gi, is three miles south of Tahlequah on Highway 62, then one mile east. Tsa-la-gi Lodge is one mile more down Highway 62, four miles south of Tahlequah.

Public Ceremony or Powwow Dates: The Cherokee National Holiday is celebrated in early September. The Fall Festival is usually held in Jay, Oklahoma, around October. The Red Bird Smith ceremonial grounds near Vian, Oklahoma, host stomp dances each August 17 honoring Red Bird Smith. Call the tribal office for dates, times, and arrangements to attend ceremonials.

Art Forms: Traditional arts and crafts are sold at the Heritage Center.

The Cherokee are probably the same people as the Rickohockans, who invaded central Virginia in 1658, and the ancient Talligewi, of Delaware tradition. Oral history says that the Cherokee were driven southward from the upper Ohio River region by the combined forces of the Iroquois and Delaware.

Traditional, linguistic, and archaeological evidence shows that the Cherokee originated in the north, but they were found living in the south Allegheny region when first encountered by de Soto in 1540. Their relations with the Carolina colonies began 150 years later. In 1736, the Jesuit Priber started the first mission among them and attempted to organize their government on a "civilized" basis. In 1759, under the leadership of Oconostota, they began war with the English of Carolina. In the American Revolution, they aided the Americans and continued the struggle almost continuously until 1794. During this period, parties of the Cherokee pushed down the Tennessee River and formed new settlements at Chickamauga and other points around the Tennessee-Alabama line. Shortly after 1800, they became subject to missionary and educational work, and in 1820, they adopted a regular form of government modeled on that of the Iroquois Confederacy. In the meantime, large numbers of the more conservative Cherokee, wearied by the encroachments of non-Indians, had crossed the Mississippi and made new homes in the wilderness in what is now Arkansas. A year or two later, Sequoya, a celebrated Cherokee chief, invented their alphabet.

At the height of their prosperity, gold was discovered near the present Dahlonega, Georgia, within the limits of the Cherokee Nation, and at once powerful agitation was begun by non-Indians for the removal of the Indians. After years of hopeless struggle under the leadership of their great chief, John Ross, they were compelled to submit to the inevitable, and by the treaty of New Echota, December 29, 1835, the Cherokee sold their entire remaining territory and agreed to move beyond the Mississippi to a country there to be set apart for them—the Cherokee Nation in Indian Territory. Their removal, known as the Trail of Tears, was accomplished in the winter of 1838-39. It caused terrible hardship and the loss of nearly one fourth of their number: the unwilling Indians were driven out by military force and made the long journey on foot. On reaching their destination, they reorganized their national government, established their capital at Tahlequah, and admitted to equal privileges the earlier emigrants, known as "old settlers."

A part of the Arkansas Cherokee had previously moved to Texas, where they had obtained a grant of land in the eastern part of the state from the Mexican government. The later Texan revolutionists refused to recognize their rights, and in spite of the efforts of General Sam Houston, who defended the Indian claim, a conflict broke out, resulting in 1839 in the killing of the Cherokee chief, Bowl, with a large number of his men, by the Texan troops and the expulsion of the Cherokee from Texas.

When the main body of the tribe was removed to the West, several hundred fugitives escaped to the Stone Mountains, where they lived as refugees, until 1842, when through the efforts of William H. Thomas, an influential trader, they received permission to remain on lands set apart for their use in western North Carolina. They constitute the present eastern band of Cherokee, residing chiefly on the Qualla Reservation in Swain and Jackson counties, with several outlying settlements.

The Cherokee in the Cherokee Nation were for years divided into two hostile factions, those who had favored and those who had opposed the treaty of removal. Just when these differences were settled, the War Between the States was declared. Being slave owners and surrounded by southern influences, a large part of each of the

Five Civilized Tribes of the territory (Cherokee, Chickasaw, Choctaw, Creek, Seminole) enlisted in the service of the Confederacy, while others sided with the northern government. The territory of the Cherokee was overrun by both armies in turn. By the close of the war, they were devastated. By treaty in 1866, they were readmitted to the protection of the United States but were obliged to liberate their black slaves and admit them to equal citizenship. In 1867 and 1870, the Delaware and Shawnee, respectively, numbering together about 1,750, were admitted from Kansas and incorporated with the Nation. In 1889, the Cherokee Commission was created for the purpose of abolishing the tribal governments and opening the territories to non-Indian settlement, with the result that after 15 years of negotiation, an agreement was made by which the government of the Cherokee Nation came to an end on March 3, 1906. The Indian lands were divided, and the Cherokee people, native and adopted, became citizens of the United States without a reservation.

The Cherokee have seven clans: Wolf, Deer, Bird, Paint, Ani Saha ni, Ani Ga tagewi, Ani Gi la hi. In ancient times, there were fourteen. The wolf clan is the largest.

For more information, see North Carolina, Cherokee.

Cheyenne-Arapaho of Oklahoma

P.O. Box 38
Concho, OK 73022
(405) 262-0345
Fax (405) 262-0745

Cheyenne (Shai-ela)
Arapaho (Inunaina)

Location: The Southern Cheyenne and Southern Arapaho share their tribal office in Concho.

Public Ceremony or Powwow Dates: The Southern Arapaho usually have a powwow over Labor Day weekend. The Southern Cheyenne participate in the American Indian Exposition each year at Anadarko. Call the tribal office for dates and times. The Southern Arapaho attend the Sun Dance (Offerings Lodge) with the Northern Arapahoe in Wyoming each year. The Southern Cheyenne hold a Sun Dance (Offerings Lodge) in Oklahoma each year.

Art Forms: Please call the tribal office to find local artisans who do traditional beadwork and other Plains-style artwork.

Visitor Information: Please read more about the Arapahoe and Cheyenne under Wyoming and Montana in the Great Plains section.

Chickasaw
P.O. Box 1548
Ada, OK 74820
(405) 436-2603
Fax (405) 436-4287

Chickasaw

Location: The nation headquarters is at Arlington and Mississippi streets in Ada.

Public Ceremony or Powwow Dates: The Chickasaw Nation Annual Meeting is held the first Saturday in October five miles north of Ada at Byng School. The princess of the Chickasaw Nation is selected, there is gospel and country music, lunch is served, and the governor gives his annual address.

Visitor Information: The Chickasaw Nation is a very progressive community. Included among their enterprises are woodwork items ranging from cabinets to chests. They now have two trading post/convenience store/delicatessens, one in Ada and the other in Davis.

The Chickasaw also own and operate the Chickasaw Motor Inn, located at the gateway to the Chickasaw National Recreation Area (formerly Platt National Park) in Sulphur, Oklahoma. In addition, they have recently purchased their old capitol building, a three-story granite structure in Tishomingo, complete with its own dome.

The Chickasaw are a Muskhogean tribe, closely related to the Choctaw in language and customs, although the two tribes were mutually hostile. The earliest written history places the Chickasaw in northern Mississippi. In the eighteenth century, they were located in Pontotoc and Union counties, where the headwaters of the Tombigbee meet those of the Yazoo River and its affluent, the Tallahatchie. The de Soto narratives place them in this area in 1540 under the name Chicaza. The Chickasaw were on the Trail of Tears in the 1830s.

Choctaw of Oklahoma
P.O. Drawer 1210
16th and Locust Streets
Durant, OK 74701
(405) 924-8280
Fax (405) 924-1150

Choctaw (possibly a corruption of the Spanish *chata*, "flat," or "flattened," alluding to the custom of these people to flatten the head)

Location: The location of the nation headquarters is 16th and Locust streets in Durant. The Red River Valley Museum is in the basement. The Choctaw National Museum is located on the historic tribal capitol grounds at Tushkahoma.

Public Ceremony and Powwow Dates: The Choctaw Nation of Oklahoma Labor Day Festivities are held in Tushkahoma. From Friday through Monday, games, the princess contest, and traditional dancing are held. The stickball game is particularly interesting to watch and has its roots in the traditional game played for centuries. The parade on Monday features the State of the Nation address by the chief.

Art Forms: The museum in the old Choctaw Council House in Tushkahoma has a gift shop. Traditional Choctaw diamond pattern women's dresses and men's shirts are for sale.

The Choctaw nation is of the Muskhogean group, formerly occupying middle and southern Mississippi, their territory extending for some distance east of the Tombigbee River, probably as far as Dallas County, Georgia. They were the first tribe on the Trail of Tears when forced to move to Indian Territory from Mississippi as early as 1831.

For more information, see Mississippi, Choctaw.

Citizen Band of Potawatomi of Oklahoma
1901 S. Gordon Cooper Drive
Shawnee, OK 74801
(405) 275-3121
Fax (405) 275-0198

Location: The tribal complex is located on the south side of Shawnee at 1901 S. Gordon Cooper Drive.

Public Ceremony and Powwow Dates: The annual powwow is always held the last weekend in June. The public is welcome.

Art Forms: Members of this tribe do beautiful paintings, using both traditional subject matter and progressive styles, and ribbon work and beadwork.

Visitor Information: Tribal enterprises include the Potawatomi Tribal Store, which receives more than $1 million annually in cigarette and gas sales; the trading post operated within the tribal museum which handles artwork, jewelry, souvenirs, and craft supplies; the bingo hall, which seats 500 people and takes in $10,000 to $20,000 in monthly tribal income; the Fire Lake Golf Course in the area, with a full line pro shop and snack bar; and the swap meet, a weekend flea market held on tribal powwow grounds.

The Citizen Band Potawatomi Tribe has $5.5 million invested— approximately $3 million in grants and $2 million in enterprises and interest income. The tribe maintains jurisdiction over approximately 264 acres held in trust and has the ability to purchase and place land in trust anywhere within its old reservation boundaries, an area totaling more than 30 square miles.

For more information, see Kansas, Prairie Band Potawatomi; Wisconsin, Forest County Potawatomi.

Comanche
HC 32, Box 1720
Lawton, OK 73502
(405) 492-4988
Fax (405) 492-4981

Comanche

Location: The tribal office is located in Lawton.

Public Ceremony and Powwow Dates: The annual powwow is held in Sultan Park, Walters, Oklahoma, during July. This is a celebration of homecoming powwow that remembers the time that Comanche warriors returned to the home camp. There are Black Crow Society dances and other traditional Comanche dances as well as powwow dancing.

In April, the Comanche dance the Little Pony Society dances at Apache Park, Apache, Oklahoma. Medicine men's dances are also done during this celebration. Call the tribal office at the above number for dates and times.

Visitor Information: The people of the tribe live in the vicinity of Lawton, Cache, and Apache, Oklahoma.

The Comanche are one of the southern tribes of the Shoshone language division and the only one of that group living entirely on the Plains. Their language and traditions prove that they are a comparatively recent offshoot from the Shoshone of Wyoming, as both tribes speak practically the same dialect. Traditionally, the two tribes lived next to each other in southern Wyoming. Since that time, the Shoshone were driven back into the mountains by the Sioux and other prairie tribes, while the Comanche were driven steadily southward. In this southerly movement, the Penateka, a division of the Comanche, preceded the rest of the tribe. The Kiowa say that when they moved southward from the Black Hills region, the Arkansas River was the north boundary of the Comanche.

In 1719, the Comanche are mentioned under their Sioux name of Padouca and were living in what is now western Kansas. It must be remembered that from 500 to 800 miles and more was the ordinary range for a prairie tribe and that the Comanche were equally at home on the Platte and in the Bolson de Mapimi of Chihuahua. As late as 1805, the North Platte was still known by the Sioux name Padouca Fork. At that time the Comanche traveled over the country around the source of the Arkansas, Red, Trinity, and Brazos rivers in Colorado, Kansas, Oklahoma, and Texas. For nearly two centuries, they were at war with the Spanish of Mexico and extended their raids far down into Durango. They were usually friendly to the Americans but became bitter enemies of the Texans, by whom they were chased out of their best hunting grounds, and carried on a relentless war against them for nearly forty years. They have been close allies of the Kiowa since about 1795. In 1835, they made their first treaty with the U.S. government and by the treaty of Medicine Lodge in 1867 agreed to go to their assigned reservation between the Washita and Red rivers, in southwest Oklahoma; but it was not until after the last uprising of the southern prairie tribes in 1874-75 that they and their allies, the Kiowa and Apache, finally settled on it. They were probably never a large tribe, although they seemed to be because of their wide range. They were terribly wasted by war and disease. They numbered 1,400 in 1904 and were attached to the Kiowa Agency, Oklahoma.

The Comanche were nomadic buffalo hunters, constantly on the move and living in buffalo hide tipis. They were long noted as the finest horsemen of the plains and had a reputation for dash and courage. They considered themselves superior to the other tribes with which they were associated. Their language was the trade language of the region and more or less understood by all the neighboring tribes.

Mum-shu-kawa, Comanche, 1914
Photo by DeLancey Gill; Courtesy Museum of New Mexico, Neg. No. 86998

The clan system seems to be unknown among the Comanche. They have, or still remember, twelve recognized divisions or bands and may have had others in former times. Of these, all but five are practically extinct, and the Kwahari and Penateka are the most important.

Creek of Oklahoma
P.O. Box 580
Okmulgee, OK 74447
(918) 756-8700
Fax (918) 756-2911

Creek of Oklahoma
Alabama-Quassarte Tribal Town
P.O. Box 537
Henryetta, OK 74437
(918) 652-8708

Kialegee Creek Town
318 S. Washita, P.O. Box 332
Wetumka, OK 74883
(405) 452-3413

Thlopthlocco Creek Town
P.O. Box 706
Okemah, OK 74859
(918) 623-2620
Fax (918) 623-0419

Muskhoge
Creek (from the English because of the many creeks in their home land)

Location: The Creek Nation Tribal Capitol Complex is located on Highway 75 at Loop 56 north of Okmulgee, Oklahoma.

Public Ceremony or Powwow Dates: The Creek ceremonies are held all summer from May until September. Stomp dances are held on weekends. Dancing will often begin between 10:00 p.m. and 1:00 a.m. and then continue until dawn. Then, after some weeks of doing stomp dances, the Green Corn Ceremonial is performed according to lunar phases. Call the tribal office for dates and times.

Art Forms: The gift shop in the Creek Council House Museum at 112 West Sixth in the Town Square of Okmulgee has arts and crafts for sale. The telephone number is (918) 756-2324.

Visitor Information: The Creek Indian Nation is a very progressive tribe. The Creek Council House design of the past century inspired the design of the auditorium. The Creek Nation is organized into about nineteen towns. Many Creek people spend their weekends camping at the town's ceremonial grounds while the stomp dances are in progress. The ceremonial grounds of each town are arranged in a rectangle with brush arbors around the edge where people sit. At the center of the ground is the sacred fire, which the stomp dancing revolves around. During Green Corn time, there is fasting, drinking of the sacred drink, and ritual scratching—all for purification and health.

To make sure visitors are welcome during the stomp dances and Green Corn Ceremonial, call the tribal office for arrangements.

The Creek are a confederacy forming the largest division of the Muskhogean family. The English named the tribe "Creek" because of the numerous streams in their country. During early historic times, the Creek occupied the greater portion of Alabama and Georgia, residing chiefly on the Coosa and Tallapoosa rivers, the two largest tributaries of the Alabama River, and on the Flint and Chattahoochee rivers. They claimed the territory on the east from the Savannah to St. Johns River and all the islands, then to Apalache Bay, and from this line northward to the mountains. The southern portion of this territory was held by dispossession of the earlier Florida tribes. At an early date, they sold to Great Britain their territory between the Savannah and Ogeechee rivers, all the coast to St. Johns River, and all the islands up to Tidewater, reserving for themselves St. Catherine, Sapelo, and Ossabaw islands and from Pipemakers Bluff to Savannah. The Creek were sufficiently numerous and powerful to resist attacks from the northern tribes, such as the Catawba, Iroquois, Shawnee, and Cherokee, after they had united in a confederacy.

For more than a century before their removal to the West between 1836 and 1840, the people of the Creek Confederacy occupied some fifty towns, in which six distinct languages were spoken: Muscogee, Hitchiti, Koasati, Yuchi, Natchez, and Shawnee. About half the confederacy spoke the Muscogee language, which thus constituted the ruling language and gave name to the confederacy. The meaning of the word is unknown. Although an attempt has been made to connect it with the Algonquian *maskeg,* "swamp," a southern origin is probable. The people speaking the related Hitchiti and Koasati were contemptuously designated as "Stincards" by the dominant Muscogee. While the Seminole were still a small group confined to the extreme northern part of Florida, they were frequently spoken of as the Lower Creek. To the Cherokee, the Upper Creek were known as Ani-Kusa, from their ancient town of Kusa, or Coosa, while the Lower Creek were called Ani-Kawita, from their principal town, Kawita, or Coweta. The earlier Seminole emigrants were chiefly from the Lower Creek towns.

The history of the Creek begins with the appearance of de Soto's army in their country in 1540. Tristan de Luna came in contact with part of the group in 1559, but the only important fact that can be drawn from the record is the deplorable condition the people were in as a result of the Spanish invasion. The Creek became prominent as allies of the English in the Apalachee wars of 1703–1708 and from that period continued almost uniformly as treaty allies of the South Carolina and Georgia colonies, while hostile to the Spanish of Florida. The only serious revolt of the Creek against the Americans took place in 1813–14; this was the well-known Creek War in which General Jackson took a prominent part. This ended in complete defeat and the submission of Weatherford, the Creek leader, followed by the cession of the greater part of their lands to the United States. The extended and bloody contest in Florida, which lasted from 1835 to 1843 and is known as the Seminole War, secured permanent peace with the southern tribes. The removal of the larger part of the Creek and Seminole people and their black slaves to the lands assigned to them in Indian Territory took place between 1836 and 1840 and is today known as the Trail of Tears because of the deaths of so many along the way.

The Creek were proud and arrogant, brave and valiant in war. They were devoted to decoration and ornament and very fond of music. Ball play was their most important game. Marriage outside the clan was the rule; descent was in the female line. In government it was a general rule that where one or more clans occupied a town, they constituted a tribe under an elected chief, or miko, who was advised by the council of the town in all important matters, while the council appointed the "great warrior," or *tustenuggi-hlako.* They usually buried their dead in a square pit under the bed where the deceased had slept. Certain towns were consecrated to peace ceremonies and were known as "white towns," while others set apart for war ceremonials were designated as "red towns." They had several orders of chiefly rank. Their great spiritual ceremony was the annual puskita, of which the lighting of the new fire and the drinking of the black drink were important rituals.

The early statistics of Creek population are based on estimates. In the last quarter of the eighteenth century, the Creek population may have been about 20,000, occupying from 40 to 60 towns. Estimates made after their removal to Indian Territory place the population between 15,000 and 20,000. In 1904, the "Creeks by blood" living in the Creek Nation numbered 9,905, while Creek freedmen numbered 5,473. The number of acres in their reservation in 1885 was 3,215,395, only a portion of which was tillable; 90,000 acres were actually cultivated.

In 1904, the Creek Nation in Indian Territory was divided into 49 townships, three of which were inhabited solely by blacks. The capital was, and is, Okmulgee. Their legislature consisted of a House of Kings (corresponding to the Senate) and a House of Warriors (similar to the U.S. House of Representatives), with a head chief as executive. Several volumes of their laws have been published.

Delaware
P.O. Box 825
Anadarko, OK 73005
(405) 247-2448
Fax (405) 247-9393

Lenape
Leni-lenape ("real men," or "genuine men")

Location: The tribal office of the western Oklahoma Delaware is in Anadarko. Another group of Delaware live near Copan, Oklahoma.

Public Ceremony or Powwow Dates: The Copan community holds its powwow in late May or early June. The Anadarko community of Delaware participates in celebrations in the Anadarko, Oklahoma, area. Call the tribal office above for more information.

The original homeland of the Delaware includes New York City and much of New Jersey, Delaware, and Pennsylvania. Some of the people still live in this area, but most members of the tribe are living in Ontario, Oklahoma, and Wisconsin today.

The Delaware are a confederacy, formerly the most important of the Algonquian division. The English knew them as Delawares, from the name of their principal river; the French called them Loups, "wolves," a term probably applied originally to the Mahican on the Hudson River and afterward extended to the Munsee division and to the whole group.

To the more remote Algonquian tribes, the Delaware, together with all their related tribes along the coast far up into New England, were known as Wapanachki, "easterners," or "eastern land people," a term that also appears as a specific tribal designation, Abnaki. By virtue of admitted priority of political rank and of occupying the central home territory, from which most of the related tribes had diverged, they were accorded by all the Algonquian tribes the respectful title of "Grandfather," a recognition also accorded by the Huron as a courtesy. The Nanticoke, Conoy, Shawnee, and Mahican claimed close connection with the Delaware and preserved the tradition of a common origin.

The Lenape, or Delaware proper, were composed of three principal tribes: Munsee, Unami, and Unalachtigo. Some of the New Jersey bands may have constituted a fourth. Each of these had its own territory and dialect, with a more or less separate identity. The Munsee, in fact, were frequently considered an independent people.

For more information, see Wisconsin, Stockbridge-Munsee.

Iowa of Oklahoma
Route 1, Box 721
Perkins, OK 74059
(405) 547-2403
Fax (405) 547-5294

Iowa ("sleepy ones")

Visitor Information: The Iowa today live in two locations, here and on a reservation in northeast Kansas near the Sac and Fox.

For more information, see Kansas, Iowa.

Kaw
Drawer 50
Kaw City, OK 74641
(405) 269-2552
Fax (405) 269-2301

Black Beaver, Delaware, 1872
Photo by Alexander Gardner; Courtesy Museum of New Mexico, Neg. No. 87531

Kansa

This is a southwestern Sioux tribe. The Kansa lived along the River where Kansas is today. In 1846, they were on a reservation at Council Grove, Kansas, and in 1873, they were moved to Oklahoma.

Kickapoo of Oklahoma
P.O. Box 70
McLoud, OK 74851
(405) 964-2075
Fax (405) 964-2745

Kiwigapawa ("he stands about")

For more information, see Kansas, Kickapoo; Texas, Kickapoo.

Kiowa
P.O. Box 369
Carnegie, OK 73015
(405) 654-2300
Fax (405) 654-2188

Kiowa (Ga-i-gwu, or Ka-i-gwu, "principal people")

Location: The tribal complex is located in Carnegie, ¼ mile west of the four-way stop (Highways 9 and 58) on Highway 9.

Public Ceremony or Powwow Dates: In the fall, there is a powwow to raise funds for the museum. Traditional Kiowa dances as well as powwow dancing are featured. Over the Fourth of July weekend, the museum has an arts and crafts show with Kiowa Gourd Society dances.

Art Forms: The Kiowa are artistic people, and among their tribal rolls are listed some of the most famous painters who do traditional and contemporary Indian art.

Visitor Information: Don't miss the museum and the mural work depicting Kiowa history.

The history of the Kiowa people shows that they once resided in the area around the upper Yellowstone and Missouri, but they were more widely known to have lived near the upper Arkansas and Canadian rivers in Colorado and Oklahoma and to have a distinct language. They are found in Spanish records as early as 1732. Their oldest tradition, which agrees with the concurrent testimony of the Shoshone and Arapahoe, locates them around the junction of Jefferson, Madison, and Gallatin forks, at the extreme head of the Missouri River, in the neighborhood of the present Virginia City, Montana. They afterward moved down from the mountains and formed an alliance with the Crow, with whom they continued on friendly terms. From here they moved southward along the base of the mountains, driven by the Cheyenne and Arapahoe, with whom they finally made peace about 1840. After that, they commonly acted in concert with these tribes.

The Sioux claim to have driven them out of the Black Hills, and in 1805, they were reported by Lewis and Clark as living on the North Platte. According to the Kiowa account, when they first reached the Arkansas River, they found their passage opposed by the Comanche, who claimed all the country to the south. A war followed, but peace was finally concluded when the Kiowa crossed over to the south side of the Arkansas River and formed a confederation with the Comanche. With the Comanche, they carried on a constant war on the frontier settlements of Mexico and Texas, extending their incursions as far south as Durango.

The Kiowa made their first treaty with the U.S. government in 1837 and were put on a reservation jointly with the Comanche and Kiowa-Apache in 1868. Their last uprising was in 1874–75 in conjunction with the Comanche, Kiowa-Apache, and Cheyenne. While probably never very numerous, they were greatly reduced by war and disease. The last terrible blow came in the spring of 1892, when measles and fever destroyed more than 300 of the three confederated tribes.

The Kiowa do not have a clan system, and there is no restriction on intermarriage. The Kiowa-Apache form a component part of the Kiowa camp circle.

In the early 1900s their chief was Lone Wolf, but his title was disputed by Apiatan. Their reservation was between the Washita and Red rivers in southwest Oklahoma. In 1901, their lands were allotted and opened to settlement. The population was 1,165 in 1905.

Kishkinniequote (Jim Deer), Kickapoo, 1907
Photo by DeLancey Gill; Courtesy Museum of New Mexico, Neg. No. 59443

Apiatou, Kiowa
Courtesy Museum of New Mexico, Neg. No. 46986

Miami of Oklahoma
P.O. Box 1326
Miami, OK 74355
(918) 542-1445
Fax (918) 542-7260

Miami (Oumameg, "people on the peninsula")

Visitor Information: The Miami today live in Oklahoma and Indiana. Intertribal offices, the senior citizen's center, and a gift shop are located here just behind the Welcome Center off westbound Highway I-44. Exit at Miami on Steve Owens Boulevard and take the access road to 202 S. Eight Tribes Trail.

The Inter-Tribal Council is made up of representatives of the Eastern Shawnee, Seneca-Cayuga (Iroquois), Peoria (Illinois), Ottawa, Miami, Wyandot, Quapaw, and Modoc tribes (originally from northern California and southern Oregon).

The earliest written information is from Gabriel Druillettes in 1658. He called the Miami the Oumamik and said they were living at St. Michel at or around the mouth of Green Bay, Wisconsin. He also identified them as *outilchakouk,* which means "the crane people." The latter referred to the sandhill crane, which is about four feet in height, identified by its unusual dance of bowing and leaping in the air.

In their own language, the Miami tribe called themselves "Twa-h-twa-h," meaning "the cry of the crane," with the English version being "Twightwee." Later Americans adopted the French spelling of Miami but altered the pronunciation from Me-aw'me to Mi-am'-e.

Jacques Marquette met the Miami at the portage of the Fox River in 1673, as he journeyed with Louis Jolliet. He said their appearance, intelligence, and habits were superior to their allies and used two Oumamik warriors as guides to the Wisconsin River. Marquette also noted that the Miami were very successful warriors.

The tribe migrated to an area south of Lake Michigan, bound by the Ohio, Wabash, Maumee, and Great and Little Miami rivers in present-day southern Indiana and southwestern Ohio, at the beginning of the eighteenth century.

The Miami sided with the French during the years 1700–1763. Then they sided with the British during the next twenty years, deeply resentful of the taking of their land, after the American Rev-

olution, without consent. It was during their resistence that Chief
Little Turtle defeated two U.S. forces but was himself defeated by
General Anthony Wayne at the Battle of Fallen Timbers. This was
settled by the Treaty of Greenville in 1795.

According to tribal lawyer, Edwin A. Rothschild, "the tribe has
been involved in 75,000 transactions during 100 years of their history, and these were for 12 million acres of land in Indiana."

On November 28, 1840, at the Forks of the Wabash (present-
day Huntington, Indiana), a treaty was signed which moved the
tribe to what is now Miami County, Kansas. It took six years for
this move to be carried out. Part of the tribe was granted special
permission to remain in Indiana. The exceptions were elected
chiefs or mixed bloods.

This explains the division of the tribe into Western and Eastern
Miami. The Western Miami are a federally recognized tribe today.
The Eastern Miami are not, although they are currently seeking
this recognition. In the early days of the division, there was a great
deal of travel between the two groups. So there are many descendants of the Eastern Miami who relocated from Kansas to Ottawa
County after the Treaty of 1867. This treaty opened the way for the
tribe to join with the Peoria tribe to form a new confederation.
Contrary to some land allotment maps and history books, this was
never done.

Once in Oklahoma, the tribe came under the supervision of the
Quapaw Indian Agency of the Bureau of Indian Affairs. This was
later transferred to the Miami Agency in Miami. The Enabling Act
of Oklahoma in 1906, followed by statehood in 1907, gave U.S. citizenship to the Miami people. The Oklahoma Welfare Act of 1934
permitted the Indian tribes to form federal corporations with
constitutions and by-laws. Under the leadership of Chief Harley
Palmer, the Miami Tribe of Oklahoma constitution was prepared,
submitted, and ratified by the tribe on October 30, 1939. The tribe
received its corporate charter on April 15, 1940. The current constitution and by-laws were amended and approved on May 28, 1987.

The tribe is a member of the Illinois division of the Algonquian
linguistic family. The social structure is based on the clan system.
Historians estimate that at one time there may have been 15 to 18
different clans, each represented by an animal, such as the crane,
eagle, turtle, deer, elk, serpent, duck, fox, fish, panther, loon, wolf,
or raccoon. No one was allowed to marry outside of one's clan.

The Miami tribe did not classify according to generations. Thus,
a mother's brother and their male descendants (through males

only) were all "uncles," daughters of "uncles" were "mothers," and children of "mothers" were "brothers" and "sisters."

The Miami tribe lived in oval-shaped wigwams. The pole frames were covered with rush mats, which were in turn covered by bark or hides in the winter. By the eighteenth century, these were replaced by log structures.

Men wore simple skins most of the time. Fringed, beaded, or quilled clothing was reserved for festive occasions. Women wore skin clothing that reached their knees. Men wore their hair short, except for long locks that dangled in front of and behind their ears.

The Miami tribe relied on a mixed hunting-farming economy. After the arrival of the Europeans, the hunting was strongly oriented toward the fur trade. Unlike most of the Great Lakes tribes, they traveled on foot, using dugout canoes only if necessary.

In an interesting contrast to the flint corn of their neighbors, the Miami grew a soft white corn, which made into a superior flour. This suggested contact with Indians in the Southwest, as does the prominence of the sun-king in their religion. They also raised melons, squash, pumpkins, and beans and gathered uncultured fruits, berries, and roots.

They also believed in the overall deity called the Master of Life. They considered the soul to be a flying phantom, an image of the deceased individual, which journeyed to a world more agreeable than this one.

The earliest tribal history was lost when two chests that contained belts and pipes were burned accidentally at Kekionga during the expedition led by Colonel Josiah Harmer in 1790. These artifacts were used as memory aids to recite the oral history. Once gone, the history was lost, too. According to the constitution, one may become a member of the tribe in one of four ways: (1) be listed on the tribal roll of 1937; (2) be a child of two parents listed on the roll; (3) be born of a marriage between a member of the Miami Tribe and a member of any other Indian tribe who chooses to affiliate with the Miami Tribe; and (4) be a child born of a marriage between a member of the Miami Tribe and any other person, if such child is approved by the Council of the Miami Tribe. The roll of 1,390 names is considered an open roll since names are still being added. (The Miami were estimated to number 4,500 in 1695. On the Quapaw Agency census of the Miami Indians taken in 1887, there were 64 names listed.) There are no purebloods living. One known couple who are both tribal members are Nadiene and Hubert Mayfield of Chetopa, Kansas.

Modoc of Oklahoma
515 G SE Street
Miami, OK 74354
(918) 542-1190
Fax (918) 542-5415

Modoc (Moatokni, "southerners")

Visitor Information: The Modoc tribal complex is located in Miami, Oklahoma, and houses the office of the chief, tribal administrator, and historian as well as the tribal library and archives.

Before the coming of foreigners, Modoc territory encompassed some 5,000 square miles along both sides of what is now the California-Oregon border. In 1864, the Modoc ceded their ancestral lands to the U.S. government, agreeing to reside with the Klamath Indians on a reservation established for the tribes in southern Oregon. In 1870, "Captain Jack" (Keintepoos) led his band off the reservation and returned to the Tule Lake area in northern California. Here he demanded a reservation on Lost River from land the tribe had ceded to the United States by the Valentine's Day Treaty of 1864. His requests were refused, and later attempts to return Captain Jack and his followers to the Klamath Reservation resulted in the Modoc War.

After hostilities ended, Captain Jack and five of his warriors were tried by court martial; four were executed, and two were imprisoned at Alcatraz. The remaining rebellious Modoc were exiled to the Quapaw Agency in Indian Territory, now Ottawa County, Oklahoma. In November 1873, 153 Modoc men, women, and children arrived at the Agency as prisoners of war.

In 1909, the few remaining Modoc were allowed to return to Klamath Agency, Oregon; however, several families chose to remain in their land of exile. Today, the descendants of those who remained comprise the Modoc Tribe of Oklahoma. The Oklahoma Modoc were terminated from Federal supervision along with the Klamath and Modoc in Oregon in 1954. The Modoc in Oklahoma were reinstated to Federal recognition as the Modoc Tribe of Oklahoma in 1978.

For more information, see Oregon, Klamath.

Osage
Osage Agency Campus
Pawhuska, OK 74056
(918) 287-2495
Fax (918) 287-2257

Osage (corruption of Wazhazhe, their own name, by French traders)

Location: The museum on Grandview Avenue in Pawhuska is the oldest continuously operated tribal museum in the United States.

Public Ceremony or Powwow Dates: In June, the Osage have ceremonial dances in Hominy, Grayhorse, and Pawhuska. The Kiehkah Steh Club powwow in Skiatook is in August. Call the tribal office for dates and times.

Art Forms: Osage and American Indian arts and crafts can be found at the museum. Finger woven sashes are one of the many art forms to be found there.

The beings which ultimately became men originated in the lowest of the four upper worlds which Osage Spirituality postulates and ascended to the highest where they obtained souls. Then they descended until they came to a red oak tree on which the lowest world rests and by its branches reached our earth. They were divided into two sections, the Tsishu, or peace people, who kept to the left, living on roots, etc. . . . and the Wazhazhe (true Osage), or war people, who kept to the right and killed animals for their food. Later these two divisions exchanged commodities, and after some time the Tshihu people came into possession of four kinds of corn and four kinds of pumpkins, which fell from the left hind legs of as many different buffaloes. Still later the tribe came upon a very warlike people called Hunka-utadhantse, who lived on animals, and after a time the Wazahzhe people succeeded in making peace with them and they were taken into the nation on the war side. Originally there were seven Tsishu gentes, seven Wazhazhe gentes, and seven Hunka gentes. Ultimately the Wazhazhe and the Hunka were combined into the Hunka grand division with 15 clans. The Tsishu grand division with 9 clans completed the tribal organization. A hereditary chief was chosen from each of the grand divisions. (Taken from Osage tribal literature.)

Sho-she, Osage
Photo by DeLancey Gill; Courtesy Museum of New Mexico, Neg. No. 87005

The first written historical record of the Osage locates them on the Osage River. This was about 1673. They are a southern Siouan tribe of the western division. They are classed with the Omaha, Ponca, Kansa, and Quapaw, with whom they originally constituted a single body living along the lower course of the Ohio River.

The tribe has three bands: the Pasueli, or Great Osage; Wahakolin, or Little Osage; and Sansueli, or Arkansas Band.

Otoe-Missouria
Route 1, Box 62
Red Rock, OK 74651
(405) 723-4466
Fax (405) 723-4273

Oto (from Wat ota, "lechers")
Missouri ("great muddy," referring to the Missouri River)

Oto-Missouria

Location: The tribal office is in Red Rock.

Public Ceremony or Powwow Dates: Their annual powwow is usually in July in Red Rock. Call for exact dates and times.

The Oto are one of the Sioux tribes in the Chiwere group. The earliest written record places them above Green Bay, Wisconsin.

The Missouri are a tribe in the Chiwere group of the Sioux family. Their name for themselves is Niutachi. The most closely allied tribes are the Iowa and the Oto. According to tradition, after having parted from the Winnebago at Green Bay, the Iowa, Missouri, and Oto moved westward to the Iowa River, where the Iowa stopped.

The Missouri lived in what is now northern Missouri. After 1800, wars and epidemics greatly reduced the tribe, and by 1842, they had moved to southeastern Nebraska. In 1882, the Missouri were moved to what is now Oklahoma.

Ottawa of Oklahoma
P.O. Box 110
Miami, OK 74355
(918) 540-1536
Fax (918) 542-3214

82 / Great Plains

Ottawa (*adawe*, "to trade")

Visitor Information: The Ottawa live today in Canada and Oklahoma. Their powwow is usually in August near Miami, Oklahoma. For more information, read about them under the Miami Tribe of Oklahoma.

The Ottawa are a tribe of Algonquian language tradition, closely related to the Chippewa and the Potawatomi. The Ottawa River in Ontario is so named because these people monopolized trade along it. Their first historical location was around Georgian Bay, Lake Huron. Champlain in 1615 met 300 men of a tribe that, he said, "we call *les cheueux releuez*." He said that their arms consisted only of the bow and arrow, a buckler of boiled leather, and the club; that they wore no breechclout and their bodies were tattooed in many designs; and that their faces were painted in diverse colors, their noses pierced, and their ears bordered with trinkets. After the Iroquois victory over the Huron in 1648–49, they drove the Ottawa, along with the Huron, westward to Green Bay, Lake Michigan, Keweenaw Bay, Lake Superior, and Lake Pepin on the Mississippi River. The Ottawa wandered far and wide and are associated with many regions: Mackinac; after 1700, from Saginaw Bay to Detroit; later, eastward along Lake Erie into Pennsylvania; and into Wisconsin and Illinois. The Ottawa fought for the French, and Pontiac, their greatest known chief, was the leader of the fight against the British in 1763 with other Algonquian tribes. The Ottawa joined with the British in the American Revolution and the War of 1812. They returned to Manitoulin Island and the Canadian shore of Lake Huron, and many remain there today. A larger number are living in southern Michigan. The Ottawa were moved to a reservation in Kansas in 1833. Many became Kansas farmers and remained there until, in 1867, a new reservation was established in Oklahoma.

Pawnee
P.O. Box 470
Pawnee, OK 74058
(918) 762-3621
Fax (918) 762-2389

Pawnee (*pariki*, "horn," the dressing of the scalp-lock, by which the hair was stiffened with fat and made to stand erect and curved like a horn)

Location: The location of the tribal office is east of town on the main street in Pawnee.

Public Ceremony or Powwow Dates: The Fourth of July weekend is the time to be in Pawnee, Oklahoma, for one of the best powwows in the world. Four days of dancing, hand games, and celebrating make the trip to Pawnee worthwhile. The four bands of the Pawnee join together for this great powwow. They are the Chaui or Grand Pawnee, the Kitkehahki or Republican Pawnee, the Pitahaurat or Tapage Pawnee, and the Skidi or Wolf Pawnee.

Art Forms: The Pawnee do some fine arts and crafts, including Peyote stitch on fans, staffs, and rattles.

Visitor Information: There is a traditional-style roundhouse located one-half mile beyond the tribal headquarters.

The Pawnee call themselves Chahiksichahiks, "Men of Men." They are one of the tribes in the Caddoan language group and are closely related to the Arikara and the Wichita. They lived in earth lodges on the Platte and Republican rivers. The Pawnee raised corn, raided the Comanche for horses, and fought the Sioux and Cheyenne. In 1702, there were 2,000 families living in the central plains where western Nebraska and eastern Wyoming are today. In 1876, they were moved to present-day Oklahoma. Disease brought by settlers reduced the tribe to 649 survivors in 1906.

Peoria of Oklahoma
P.O. Box 1527
Miami, OK 74355
(918) 540-2535
Fax (918) 540-2538

Peoria (Peouarea, "carrying a pack on his back")

Visitor Information: This Illinois tribe, known today as the Peoria, live in northeast Oklahoma. They participate in Indian Heritage Days and the stomp dances after powwows. Read about the Peoria under the Miami Tribe of Oklahoma.

The Peoria are one of the principal tribes of the Illinois Confederacy. In 1688, they lived on a river west of the Mississippi above the mouth

White Horse, Pawnee, ca. 1868-69
Photo by William H. Jackson; Courtesy Museum of New Mexico, Neg. No. 31255

of the Wisconsin River, probably the upper Iowa River. The Peoria are associated with the Algonquian language group. The city of Peoria, Illinois, is named for them. In 1868, the Peoria were moved to present-day Oklahoma to live on an established reservation.

Ponca
P.O. Box 2, White Eagle
Ponca City, OK 74601
(405) 762-8104
Fax (405) 762-7436

Ponca

Location: The tribal office is located in White Eagle.

Public Ceremony or Powwow Dates: The annual powwow is usually held in August, but check with the tribal office for dates and times.

Art Forms: Call the tribal office for individuals who do arts and crafts.

Visitor Information: The White Eagle Tribal Park is the location of the powwow grounds and the fairgrounds. The museum here has information on about 12 tribes, but the Ponca, Tonkawa, Kaw, Otoe, and Osage are the prominent ones shown.

The Ponca are one of the five tribes of the so-called Dhegiha group of the Sioux language family, forming with the Omaha, Quapaw, Osage, and Kansa the upper Dhegiha or Omaha division. The Ponca and Omaha have the same language, differing only in some dialects. In 1906, the tribe totaled 833 members.

The forced removal of the Ponca to present-day Oklahoma prompted an investigation led by President Hayes. As a result of the inquiry, about 225 Ponca retained a reservation near the Niobrara River in present-day Nebraska.

For more information, see South Dakota, Ponca.

Quapaw
P.O. Box 765
Quapaw, OK 74363
(918) 542-1853
Fax (918) 542-4594

Little Soldier, Ponca, 1914
Photo by DeLancey Gill; Courtesy Museum of New Mexico, Neg. No. 87008

Quapaw (Ugakhpa, "downstream people")

Public Ceremony or Powwow Dates: The Quapaw hold their powwow over the Fourth of July weekend at Quapaw, Oklahoma. This is a real Plains-style powwow with war dancers both straight and fancy. There are round dances, rabbit dances, Plains-style stomp dancing, and even the Oklahoma two-step. After the powwow, Eastern Woodlands and Southern-style stomp dances go on all night. Read more about the Quapaw under the Miami Tribe of Oklahoma.

This tribe of the Sioux language group was also called the Arkansas tribe. When first contacted by French explorers in the late 1600s, the Quapaw lived along the Ohio River and were called the Arkansas by the Illinois people. Later, the Quapaw moved to the valley of the Arkansas River. They ceded their lands by the treaties of 1818 and 1824 and moved to the Red River, but heavy flooding forced the return to their old home. In 1833, they were moved to a reservation in present-day northeastern Oklahoma.

Sac and Fox
Route 2, Box 246
Stroud, OK 74079
(918) 968-3526
Fax (918) 968-3887

Location: The Sac and Fox Nation's tribal complex is located six miles south of Stroud, on U.S. Highway 377 (OK 99).

Public Ceremony or Powwow Dates: Their world-famous outdoor pow-wow is held the second weekend in July. The annual all-Indian Memorial Stampede Rodeo is held each summer, but you must call the tribe for exact dates and times.

Art Forms: To the Sac and Fox people, the drum is sacred, the otter is a mythical animal, and the sun and moon are considered special. Naming and adoption ceremonies are still observed. The Swan or Crane Dance is unique to the Sac and Fox and, as described by the famed warrior Black Hawk, is observed at special dances and ceremonies. The eleven ancient clans still maintained are Fish, Peace, Fox, Warrior, Bear, Wolf, Thunder, Beaver, Potato, Eagle, and Deer. The Sac and Fox are known for their fine ribbonwork, usually done in floral designs to reflect their woodland heritage.

Visitor Information: The Sac and Fox people are proud to share their rich heritage and history with all visitors and encourage guests to stop and see the old and new sites and structures in their nation's capitol. Most of the sites and buildings are open for public viewing, but some are strictly for ceremonial use by tribal members. Three historic sites, the brick vault once a part of the old agency office building, the water tower base that once served the Sac and Fox Mission School, and the old Sac and Fox Cemetery, where many tribal chiefs are buried, are all open to the public. Chief Moses Keokuk's brick home, built in 1879 and located 2½ miles west of the nation's capitol, is privately owned and listed on the National Register of Historic Sites.

One of the Sac and Fox sites to see while visiting the capitol grounds is the Sac and Fox Tribal Courthouse. Housed in the oldest building on the grounds, it was once two council houses (c. 1930), brought together for a community building (c. 1960), and dedicated as a courthouse in 1986. Open during business hours, it houses several historic tribal photographs and a 1936 wall mural painted by a tribal member as a WPA project. Court is held here regularly. The gallery at the main office building houses several exhibit cases filled with a fine collection of Sac and Fox materials, including antique beadwork and ribbonwork, old photographs, artifacts, artwork, and other memorabilia from the former museum that closed in the early 1980s. The Sac and Fox National Public Library contains the tribal archives and several display cases with changing exhibits of tribal photographs and documents. Other important buildings at the capitol are the Black Hawk Health Center, the food warehouse, and the community building. There is also an RV campground, generous campsites, a coin laundry, a children's playground, public rest rooms, and the Bark House and swimming pool where food, drink, and Indian crafts can be purchased.

Black Hawk was their famous war chief who led the last great Indian attack against the United States. He wrote eloquently of his people in an autobiography published in 1872. Moses Keokuk was the government chief who led the Sac and Fox into Indian Territory. He was well educated and a great orator. William Jones was born in Stroud and educated at the Sac and Fox Mission School, Hampton Institute, Phillips Academy, and Harvard and Columbia universities. He was a brilliant ethnologist who wrote about his tribe until his untimely death while on an expedition in the Philippines.

Mishewauk, Sac and Fox
Photo by Keystone View Co.; Courtesy Museum of New Mexico, Neg. No. 90585

Jim Thorpe was born at a Sac and Fox village south of the Agency town and educated at the Sac and Fox Mission School and at Carlisle in Pennsylvania. He won the pentathlon and decathlon at the 1912 Olympics and later played professional football and baseball. He was named the world's greatest athlete in 1950.

The story of the Sac and Fox begins in the upper peninsula of the Great Lakes region of the United States. The Sac, or Sauk (from the French word *Saukie*), or people of the yellow earth, and the Fox, or people of the red earth, were two separate but neighboring tribes. For protection and survival, they banded together in 1804. In 1869, Sac and Fox tribesmen came to Indian Territory and settled on 759,000 square miles of land they purchased in what became Lincoln, Payne, and Potawatomie counties. It was their final home-land after a succession of moves from Wisconsin through Illinois, Iowa, Missouri, and Kansas forced on them by the western migration of white settlers.

After the 500 tribesmen dispersed into several villages across the reservation, they built traditional bark houses for summer and cattail houses for winter. In 1885, they wrote and adopted a constitution and established a court system, a police department, a mission school, and a large farming operation. All of this government activ-ity was centered at the Sac and Fox Agency, a historical point dating from the time of the Civil War and a landmark in Indian Territory. The agency site marked the crossing of many trails and was a halfway point on the famous Sac and Fox Trail between Pawnee and Shawnee. It was a stagecoach stop, a military post, and a meeting place for cowboys, Indian traders, hunters, homeseekers, gamblers, and outlaws long before the opening of Indian Territory to settlers. Many colorful descriptions of life at the Sac and Fox Agency abound in Oklahoma history. The agency was really a town with many sub-stantial buildings that stood on streets running parallel to what is now the north-south highway through the capitol grounds.

The years between 1869 and 1910 saw the Sac and Fox Agency town flourish, and more than 25 businesses and dwellings are listed on the agent's inventories. A sawmill was the first structure built in 1869 and was followed by two frame houses, two large brick homes, two oak stockade buildings, a blacksmith shop, a bank, a doctor's office, a post office, a commissary, a cotton gin, a cobbler's shop, a smoke house, a church, a log calaboose (jail), a photography stu-dio, a hotel, two general merchandise stores, a drugstore, and even a little weather station. A council house stood on the ceremonial grounds near the pond and was the site of feasts, powwows, councils, and ceremonials. There were also baseball fields and a horseracing track. The Sac and Fox Mission School was begun by Quaker missionaries in 1870, on the eastern edge of the capitol grounds. Many Sac and Fox children were forced to attend and were punished for speaking their native Indian language. A handsome three-story brick classroom building was erected in 1873 at a cost of $8,500. Girls' and boys' dormitories, a laundry, a large dairy barn, horse stables, and a water tower and sewer system completed the campus. The water tower legs can still be seen on the site, but all of the buildings were torn down many years after the school closed in 1917. The Sac and Fox Agency and Mission School were moved to Shawnee in 1917 and 1919 and soon the old town was abandoned. The pews and bell of the Sac and Fox church were moved to the Only Way Church north of Stroud, the bank and cotton gin to Chandler, the post office closed, the agency office building moved to another location to become a cafe, and the other buildings demolished.

The Sac and Fox Agency office building was the center of the agency town, and inside it was a sturdy brick vault (probably constructed of brick made in a kiln on the capitol grounds) where money, supplies, and documents were kept over the years. When the office was torn down in the 1950s, the vault was saved and still stands as a testament of the strength of the Sac and Fox Nation. Despite a forced move to Indian Territory, smallpox epidemics, Deep Fork flooding, poor farm soil, drought, often cruel treatment by the government, and the white settlers that arrived in the Sac and Fox land run on September 22, 1891, the Sac and Fox Nation has endured and continues to build a modern nation on the capitol grounds on the site of the landmark Sac and Fox Agency.

For more information, see Iowa, Sac and Fox; Kansas, Sac and Fox.

Seminole of Oklahoma
P.O. Box 1498
Wewoka, OK 74884
(405) 257-6287
Fax (405) 257-5017

Sim a no le, or *Isti simanole* ("separatist," "runaway," from the Creek language)

Location: The Seminole Nation Museum is one mile southeast of the junction of U.S. Highway 270 and State Road 56 in Wewoka.

Public Ceremony or Powwow Dates: Stomp dances are held regularly, and some are open to visitors. In September, the tribe holds Seminole Nation Days in the town of Seminole. Call the tribe for dates, times, and arrangements to attend public ceremonies.

Art Forms: The museum has a good craft shop and art gallery that features traditional and contemporary Seminole work, including patchwork clothing and other arts and crafts from tribal artisans. The Seminole are a Muskhogean tribe originally from Florida. For more information, see Florida, Seminole.

Seneca-Cayuga of Oklahoma
P.O. Box 1283
Miami, OK 74355
(918) 542-6609
Fax (918) 542-3684

Seneca ("place of the stone")
Cayuga (Kweniogwen, "the place locusts were taken out")

Visitor Information: Now part of the Iroquois Confederacy, the Seneca and Cayuga are two of the Six Nations who joined together centuries ago in the East. They have managed to preserve their heritage and become progressive in today's world as well. This part of the Confederacy holds their Green Corn Ceremony in July or August in Miami, Oklahoma. Call the tribal office for dates, times, and etiquette required to attend. Also, read more about them under the Miami Tribe of Oklahoma.

The Seneca are a tribe of the Iroquois Confederacy. They lived in what is now New York and northwestern Pennsylvania. The Seneca were the westernmost tribe of the orginal Five Nations of the Iroquois Confederacy.

The Cayuga were members of the original Five Nations of the Iroquois Confederacy. The Mohawk, Oneida, Onondaga, and Seneca formed a league with the Cayuga about 1570 under the leadership of Dekanawida and Hiawatha. The poem by Longfellow was based on Ojibwa legends and only used the name of Hiawatha.

Between 1712 and 1722 the Confederacy was joined with the Tuscarora from North Carolina. The Five Nations became the Six Nations. The Tuscarora, however, were regarded as students of the Confederacy. Dutch traders supplied the Iroquois with guns, and later the English did the same. The Confederacy played an important role in Britain's war against the French. However, the Americans were victorious over the Iroquois during the American Revolution. After the war, the Mohawk and Cayuga settled in Canada.

For more information, see New York, Cayuga, Seneca, and Tonawanda.

Susquehannock
c/o The Seneca-Cayuga
P.O. Box 1283
Miami, OK 74355
(918) 542-6609

The Susquehanna people are part of the Iroquois Nation. In 1608, they were located on the lower portion of the Susquehanna River and its affluents.

Tonkawa
P.O. Box 70
Tonkawa, OK 74653
(405) 628-2561
Fax (405) 628-3375

Titskanwatitch, or Tonkaweya ("they all stay together")

This prominent tribe is of the Tonkawan linguistic family, which during most of the eighteenth and nineteenth centuries lived in central Texas. In 1778, the tribe consisted of 300 warriors besides women, old men, and children. In 1908, there were only 48 survivors of the tribe as a result of both smallpox and the massacre of 137 men, women, and children by Delaware, Shawnee, and Caddo in 1862.

Wichita
P.O. Box 729
Anadarko, OK 73005
(405) 247-2425
Fax (405) 247-2005

Kitikitish (Kirikirish)

The Wichita are in the Caddoan language group. When Coronado encountered them in 1541, the Kitikitish were living in the area around the great bend of the Arkansas River and northeastward in central Kansas. In 1772, the tribe consisted of 3,500 members. They were moved to a reservation in present-day Oklahoma in 1867 after making a treaty with the U.S. government in 1835. Smallpox reduced their numbers to 310 in 1902.

Wyandotte of Oklahoma
P.O. Box 250
Wyandotte, OK 74370
(918) 678-2297 or (918) 678-2298
Fax (918) 678-2944

Wyandot

The Wyandot live in Oklahoma today and participate in Indian Heritage Days at Miami, Oklahoma. (See the Miami Tribe of Oklahoma.)

Also known as the Huron, they are in the Iroquoian language family. About 1590, four Huron tribes formed a confederacy in the southern part of what is now called Ontario. The Huron were friendly with the French but became enemies of the Iroquois. In 1649, the Iroquois overwhelmed the Huron, and they fled to Quebec where some still live. Another group, the Wyandot, moved to present-day Detroit, Michigan, and Sandusky, Ohio. Their descendants moved to Oklahoma in the late 1800s.

Yuchi of Oklahoma
c/o The Creek Nation
P.O. Box 580
Okmulgee, OK 74447
(918) 756-8700
Fax (918) 756-3340

Yuchi ("situated yonder," probably given by some member of the tribe in answer to the inquiry, "Who are you?")

This tribe is coextensive with the Uchean family. Investigations point to the conclusion that the Westo referred to by early Carolina explorers and settlers, and for whom the Savannah River was originally named, were the Yuchi.

SOUTH DAKOTA

Sioux

The Sioux are the most populous language family north of Mexico, next to the Algonquian. The name is taken from a term applied to the largest and best-known tribal group or confederacy belonging to the family, the Sioux or Dakota, which is an abbreviation of Nadowessioux, a French corruption of Nadowe-is-iw, the name given them by the Chippewa (Ojibwa). It means "snake," "adder," and, by metaphor, "enemy."

Before contact with non-Indians, the majority of Sioux lived in an area extending from the west bank of the Mississippi River northward from the Arkansas River nearly to the Rocky Mountains, except for certain sections held by the Pawnee, Arikara, Cheyenne, Arapahoe, Blackfeet, Comanche, and Kiowa. The Dakota proper also occupied territory on the east side of the river, from the mouth of the Wisconsin River to Mille Lacs, and the Winnebago lived around Lake Winnebago and the head of Green Bay. Northern Sioux tribes extended some distance into Canada, in the direction of Lake Winnipeg. A second group of Sioux tribes, embracing the Catawba, Sara or Cheraw, Saponi, Tutelo, and several others, occupied the central part of North Carolina and South Carolina and the Piedmont region of Virginia, while the Biloxi dwelled in Mississippi along the Gulf Coast, and the Oto on the Yazoo River in Mississippi.

According to tradition, the Mandan and Hidatsa reached the upper Missouri from the northeast and, pushed by the Dakota, moved slowly upstream to their present location. Some time after the Hidatsa reached the Missouri, internal troubles broke out, and a part of that tribe, now called the Crow, separated and moved westward to the neighborhood of the Yellowstone River. The Dakota formerly inhabited the forest region of southern Minnesota and do not seem to have moved onto the Plains until hard pressed by the Ojibwa, who had been supplied with guns by the French. According to all the evidence available, traditional and otherwise, some of the so-called Chiwere tribes—Iowa, Oto, and Missouri—separated from the Winnebago and moved westward to the Missouri from the same region. Other tribes of this

group—Omaha, Ponca, Osage, Kansa, and Quapaw—undoubtedly lived together as one tribe at some time and were probably
located on the Mississippi. Those moving farther down became
known as "downstream people," Quapaw, while those who went
up were the "upstream people," Omaha. The Omaha moved
northwest along the river and divided into the Osage, Kansa,
Ponca, and Omaha proper. More remote migrations must have
taken place, but the facts are not definitely known.

The eastern Sioux were encountered by Captain John Smith in
1608, but after that time, their numbers decreased rapidly
through Iroquois attacks and European massacres. Finally, the
remnants of the northern tribes of the eastern Sioux accompanied the Tuscarora northward to the Iroquois and were adopted
by the Cayuga in 1753. On the destruction of their village in 1779,
they separated. The southern tribes of this eastern Sioux group
consolidated with the Catawba and steadily decreased in population. Some of the eastern Sioux tribes were destroyed by de Soto.

The first known meeting between any western Sioux and non-
Indians was in 1541, when de Soto reached the Quapaw villages in
eastern Arkansas. The earliest record of the main northwestern
group is probably that in the Jesuit Relation of 1640, where mention
is made of the Winnebago, Dakota, and Assiniboine. As early as
1658, Jesuit missionaries had heard of the existence of thirty Dakota
villages in the region north from the Potawatomi mission at St.
Michael, around the head of Green Bay, Wisconsin. In 1680, Father
Hennepin was taken prisoner by the same tribe.

In 1804–05, Lewis and Clark passed through the center of this
region and encountered most of the Sioux tribes. After this, there
were many expeditions into and through their country. Traders
settled among them and were followed by permanent settlers,
who illegally trespassed on the "Thieve's Road" and who pressed
the Sioux into narrower and narrower areas until they were
finally removed to Indian Territory or confined to reservations in
the Dakotas, Nebraska, and Montana. Throughout this period,
the Dakota proved themselves consistently hostile to the intruders. In 1862, there was a great Santee uprising in Minnesota
which resulted in the removal of all the eastern Dakota from that
state, and in 1876, the outbreak among the western Dakota and
the destruction of Custer's command occurred. Later still, the
Ghost Dance spread among the Sioux proper, culminating in the
massacre of unarmed men, women, and children at Wounded

Knee, South Dakota, on December 29, 1890, when their gathering for this event was misconstrued as a hostile action.

It is impossible to make general statements about the customs and habits of these people that will be true for the entire group. Nearly all of the eastern tribes and most of the southern tribes belonging to the western group raised corn, but the Dakota (except some of the eastern bands) and the Crow depended almost entirely on buffalo and other game animals, the buffalo entering very deeply into the economic and spiritual life of all the tribes of this section.

In the east, they lived in bark and mat wigwams, but on the Plains, earth lodges and buffalo hide tipis were used. Formerly, they had no domestic animals except dogs, which were used to transport tipis and all other family belongings, including children (the travois). The introduction of horses constituted a new epoch in the life of all Plains tribes, facilitating their migratory movements and the pursuit of the buffalo and doubtless contributing largely to the ultimate ability of the Sioux to conduct sophisticated warfare against the intruding non-Indians.

Taking the reports of the U.S. and Canadian Indian offices as a basis and making a small allowance for bands or individuals not counted, the total number of Sioux in 1908 was approximately 40,800.

Cheyenne River Sioux
P.O. Box 590
Eagle Butte, SD 57625
(605) 964-4155
Fax (605) 964-4151

Sioux

Location: The reservation is located in north-central South Dakota on U.S. Highway 212.

Public Ceremony or Powwow Dates: The Cultural Center in Eagle Butte is your best source of information on powwows sponsored by the Cheyenne River Sioux Tribal Council and held sometime during the summer months. Labor Day weekend provides the opportunity to hold a powwow, rodeo, buffalo feast, and celebration. Call the tribal office for dates and times.

Art Forms: Sioux arts and crafts, including dance outfits and bead-work, can be purchased in the Cultural Center.

Visitor Information: The weekly bingo enterprise holds gaming each Friday. Call the Cultural Center for time and prizes to be awarded.

In 1908, the tribes on this reservation were the Blackfeet (Sihasapa), Miniconjou, Sans Arcs, and Two Kettle (Oohenonpa) Sioux.

Crow Creek Sioux
P.O. Box 658
Fort Thompson, SD 57339
(605) 245-2221 or (605) 245-2222
Fax (605) 245-2470

Sioux

Location: The reservation is located in central South Dakota north of Interstate 90.

In 1908, the tribes on this reservation were the Lower Yanktonai, Lower Brule, Miniconjou, and Two Kettle (Oohenonpa) Sioux.

Flandreau Santee Sioux
Flandreau Field Office
Box 283
Flandreau, SD 57028
(605) 997-3891
Fax (605) 997-3878

Sioux (Isanyati)

Location: Flandreau is in extreme eastern South Dakota east of Interstate 29 on State Highway 34. Pipestone National Monument is just east of Flandreau in Minnesota.

Public Ceremony or Powwow Dates: The Santee Sioux have their annual powwow the third weekend of July at Flandreau.

Visitor Information: This is the location of the school that so many Indian young people, especially those from the Plains, have attended.

This tribe is a part of the Santee who separated from the

Mdewakanton and Wahpekute of the Santee Agency, Nebraska, in 1870 and settled in 1876 at Flandreau.

Lower Brule Sioux
Lower Brule, SD 57548
(605) 473-5561
Fax (605) 473-5606

Sioux
SichangXu

Location: The reservation is located in south-central South Dakota north of Interstate 90 on State Highway 47.

Public Ceremony or Powwow Dates: The annual powwow is usually held in August. Call the tribal office for dates and times.

Visitor Information: The tribe has a herd of buffalo and elk that may be observed by arrangement with the tribal office. Hunting and fishing permits are also available from the tribe.

In 1908, the tribes on this reservation were the Lower Brule and Lower Yanktonai Sioux.

Oglala Sioux
Pine Ridge, SD 57770
(605) 867-5821
Fax (605) 867-5659

Sioux

Location: The Pine Ridge Reservation is in southwest South Dakota southeast of Rapid City. A small part of the reservation is in northwestern Nebraska north of Rushville.

Public Ceremony or Powwow Dates: Powwows can take place at any time. May, June, and August are the most popular months, however. Call the tribal office for dates and times. The most famous Sun Dance (Offerings Lodge) in the world is in August.

Art Forms: The Sioux are known for fine beadwork and quillwork and all other traditional forms of Plains Indian art.

In 1908, the tribes on this reservation were the Brule, Oglala Sioux, and Northern Cheyenne.

Rosebud Sioux
Rosebud, SD 57570
(605) 747-2381
Fax (605) 747-2243

Sioux

Location: The Rosebud Reservation is in south-central South Dakota bordering Nebraska.

Public Ceremony or Powwow Dates: Powwows usually begin in June and continue through August. The Spotted Tail Powwow is in August, when the Rosebud Tribal Fair is held. Rosebud Powwow Days is also in August. Call the tribal office to get the exact dates and times.

In 1908, the tribes on this reservation were the Loafer (Waglukhe), Miniconjou, Oglala, Two Kettle (Oohenonpa), Upper Brule, and Wahzhazhe Sioux.

Sisseton-Wahpeton Sioux
Route 2, Agency Village
Sisseton, SD 57262
(605) 698-3911
Fax (605) 698-3708

Sioux (Lake Village)

Location: This agency is located in extreme northeast South Dakota.

Public Ceremony or Powwow Dates: The annual powwow is held in July. Call the agency for exact times and dates.

This is one of the original seven tribes of the Sioux.

Yankton Sioux
P.O. Box 248
Marty, SD 57361
(605) 384-3804
Fax (605) 384-5687

Sioux (End Village)

Not Afraid of Pawnee or Padani-Kokipi-Sni, Yankton Sioux
Photo by DeLancey Gill; Courtesy Museum of New Mexico, Neg. No. 87015

Location: This office is located in southeastern South Dakota close to Yankton.

Public Ceremony or Powwow Dates: Call the tribal office for dates and times of the powwow held at Lake Andes near Fort Randall around the first of August.

This is one of the original seven tribes of the Sioux.

TEXAS

Alabama-Coushatta of Texas
Route 3, Box 640
Livingston, TX 77351
(409) 563-4391
Fax (409) 563-4397

Alabamu (*alba ayamule,* "I open or clear the thicket")

Location: To get to the tribal complex, take Highway 190 seventeen miles east from Livingston, Texas.

Public Ceremony or Powwow Dates: At the tribe's reconstructed Indian Village and Museum of Alabama and Coushatta Culture and History, you will find traditional and other kinds of Indian dances. The dances are usually on weekends. You may find the tribe doing the Green Corn Thanksgiving Dance and the girl's basket dance. Other dances done are the buffalo, round, snake, boys' or men's hoop, and general friendship dances.

Art Forms: The Alabama-Coushatta do fine river cane baskets.

Visitor Information: The Inn of the Twelve Clans restaurant and the arts and crafts shop are the first places to visit. Then go to the Indian Chief Railroad, Indian Country and Big Thicket tours, the tribal council house, and the tribal dance square.

Guided tours of the Big Thicket Wilderness are offered by tribal members. You can canoe, camp, swim, and fish at tribal facilities. For campers, there is a grocery store, camper hookups, laundromat, and showers. Lake Tombigbee is located in the center of the camping area.

From mid-June through August, the tribe presents the outdoor drama, "Beyond the Sundown," the story of Indian history during the Texas fight for independence.

The Alabama gave the state their name but, along with the Coushatta, were driven west to Texas. Both tribes' original homeland was in Alabama, where they were members of the Creek Confederacy. Today, the Alabama and Coushatta live mostly in Texas and Oklahoma, with a few Coushatta living near Kinder, Louisiana. Over 500 members of the tribe now live near Livingston, Texas, on the reservation. For further information, please see the Coushatta of Louisiana.

This is a Muskhogean tribe of the Creek Confederacy which formerly dwelled in southern Alabama. It is clear that the Alibamu and Koasati were closely related, as their languages are practically identical. When first contacted by whites, the home of the tribe was on the Alabama River, a short distance below the junction of the Coosa and Tallapoosa rivers. Their early history is uncertain, but according to tradition, they had migrated from a westerly locality. They are mentioned in the Creek legends, under the name Atilamas, as one of four tribes contending for the honor of being considered the most ancient and valorous. The chroniclers of de Soto's expedition in 1541 locate the town of Alibamo a short distance northwest of the Chicasa, in northwest or central Mississippi. The history of the tribe begins again with the appearance of the French in Mobile Bay in 1701–02. The French soon became involved in war with the tribe, who, joining the Cherokee, Abihka, and Catawba in 1708, descended the Alabama River to attack Fort Louis and the Mobile Indians in that vicinity but retired after burning some villages. In 1713, the French established Ft. Toulouse in their country to hold them in check and to protect French traders. The site was occupied in 1812 by Ft. Jackson. After the cession in 1763 by France to Great Britain, the fort was abandoned, and at that time, a part of the tribe moved to the banks of the Mississippi and established a village 60 miles above New Orleans. This band numbered about 120, including 30 warriors. The tribe subsequently moved to west Louisiana. In 1890, some were still living in Calcasieu Parish, others lived in the Creek Nation in Indian Territory, and about 200 lived in Polk County, Texas.

Little has been recorded concerning the character and customs of the Alibamu, but it is evident from their early history that they were warlike. According to one observer, "They did not conform to the customs of the Creeks, and the Creek law for the punishment of adultery was not known to them. They cultivated the soil to some extent and had some hogs, horses, and cattle. Though hospitable, it was their custom, when a white person visited them, as soon as he had eaten, what was left was thrown away and everything which had been used by the white person was washed."

Kickapoo of Texas
P.O. Box 972
Eagle Pass, TX 78853
(512) 773-2105
Fax (512) 757-9228

For more information, see Kansas, Kickapoo; Oklahoma, Kickapoo.

WYOMING

Northern Arapahoe of Wyoming
P.O. Box 217
Fort Washakle, WY 82514
(307) 332-6120 or (307) 856-9475
Fax (307) 332-7543

Arapahoe (Inunaina, or "our people")
(Tirapihu or Larapihu or Trader from the Pawnee)
("blue sky men" or "cloud men" from the Sioux and Cheyenne)

Location: The Wind River Indian Reservation is located in central Wyoming. Communities include the following: Beaver Creek, St. Stephens, Lower Arapahoe, 17-Mile, Mill Creek, Ethete, and Big Wind.

Public Ceremony or Powwow Dates: There are several powwows and a Sun Dance (Offerings Lodge) held each year. The Wyoming Indian High School Powwow and Yellow Calf Memorial Powwow are usually held in May at Ethete. The Community Powwow is held in June at Arapahoe. The Sun Dance and Ethete Celebration are held in July at Ethete. Arapahoe Language Camp is held at Heil's Corner in July. August is the month for the Northern Arapahoe powwow at Arapahoe. During Labor Day there is a powwow at Ethete, and the Christmas holidays provide a time for powwow celebrations through the New Year in both the Lower Arapahoe and Ethete communities. Call the tribal office for dates and times.

The Sun Dance is open to the public, but extreme courtesy is required not only from the general public but from Indian people as well. Do not take any cameras, sketch pads, or food and drink close to the Offerings Lodge. Women who are on their moon are not allowed close to the Offerings Lodge. No halter tops or scanty clothing are to be worn close to the Offerings Lodge. When standing close to the lodge entrance, stand to the side and not in the center, to allow the dancers and others who are in the process of conducting the ceremony to pass in and out of the lodge. Maintain a courteous and quiet attitude.

Art Forms: There are arts and crafts available from several gift shops and galleries on the reservation. Contact the Visitors Bureau, North American Indian Heritage Center, Box 275, St. Stephens, WY 82524, (307) 856-6688, for locations to purchase fine beadwork, feather work, quill work, and other types of Plains-style art. Northern Arapahoe art designs are expressed in geometric patterns.

Visitor Information: The Wind River Indian Reservation has in operation a great natural hot springs pool near Fort Washakie, Wyoming, and the Arapahoe tribe operates the Ethete store and the Great Plains store in Arapahoe. Fishing permits are available at the tribal fish and game offices in Fort Washakie.

The tribe also operates "Singing Horse Tours." These day-long excursions into Wyoming's Indian Country give visitors to the area the opportunity to experience the rich cultures and histories of the Arapahoe and Shoshone tribes of the Wind River Indian Reservation. On the tour, you will hear the commentary of tribal members on the history and culture of the two tribes. The itinerary includes the Riverton Museum in Riverton; the Mission Heritage Center, Nature Window Gallery, Rendezvous Gift Shop, and Indian Heritage Center Gallery in St. Stephens; the Pioneer Museum in Lander; Warm Valley Arts and Crafts, Mid-West Art Gallery, Sacajawea Site, Washakie Site, Robert's Mission, and Living History Indian Village in Fort Washakie; and other historical places of interest in the area. For more information on the tours and the fine lecture series offered by the tribe, write or call the Visitors Bureau, North American Indian Heritage Center, Box 275, St. Stephens, WY 82524, (307) 856-6688.

Black Coal (Niâwâsis), Chief of Northern Arapahoe
Photo by John K. Hillers; Courtesy Museum of New Mexico, Neg. No. 37929

According to the traditions of the Arapahoe, they were once a sedentary, agricultural people, living far to the northeast of their most recent home, apparently around the Red River Valley of northern Minnesota or even as far as northeastern Canada. From this point, they moved southwest across the Missouri, apparently about the same time that the Cheyenne moved out from Minnesota, although the date of the formation of the permanent friendship between the two tribes is uncertain. The Atsina, afterward associated with the Siksika, separated from the parent tribe and moved off toward the north after their emergence onto the plains. The division into Northern and Southern Arapaho is largely geographic, originating within the last century and made permanent by the placing of the two bands on different reservations. The Northern Arapahoe, in Wyoming, are considered the nucleus or mother tribe and retain the sacred bundle.

Since they crossed the Missouri, the movement of the Arapahoe, as is true of the Cheyenne and Sioux, has been west and south. The Northern Arapahoe camped on the edge of the mountains near the head of the North Platte River, while the Southern Arapaho continued down toward the Arkansas. Around 1840, they made peace with the Sioux, Kiowa, and Comanche. They remained at war with the Shoshone, Ute, and Pawnee, however, until they were confined to reservations. They generally maintained a friendly attitude toward non-Indians. By the treaty of Medicine Lodge in 1867, the Southern Arapaho, together with the Southern Cheyenne, were placed on a reservation in Oklahoma, which was thrown open to non-Indian settlement in 1892. At the same time, Indians received allotments in severalty, with rights of American citizenship. The Northern Arapahoe leased their present reservation on Wind River in Wyoming in 1876, after having made peace with their hereditary enemies, the Shoshone, who lived on the same reservation. The Atsina division, usually regarded as a distinct tribe, is associated with the Assiniboine on the Fort Belknap Reservation in Montana. They numbered 2,283 in 1904, compared to a total of 2,638 ten years earlier.

As a people, the Arapahoe are much given to ceremonial observances. The annual Sun Dance is the greatest tribal ceremony, and they were the most active propagators of the Ghost Dance religion years ago. In arts and home life, they were a typical Plains tribe. They always buried their dead in the ground, unlike the Cheyenne and Sioux, who traditionally placed them on scaffolds or on the surface of the ground in boxes. They had warrior societies common to the Plains tribes and had no trace of the clan system.

Scabby Bull, Arapahoe, 1898
Photo by DeLancey Gill; Courtesy Museum of New Mexico, Neg. No. 86992

Shoshone of Wyoming
P.O. Box 217
Fort Washakie, WY 82514
(307) 332-3532
Fax (307) 332-3055

Shoshone (Shoshoni) (The name probably comes from the Cheyenne name Shishi-noats-hitaneo, or "snake people," without any insult intended)

Location: The Shoshone of Wyoming live on the Wind River Indian Reservation located in central Wyoming. Their agency and tribal offices are located at Fort Washakie.

Public Ceremony or Powwow Dates: The tribe conducts several powwows throughout the year, Indian Days at Fort Washakie in late June, an Indian Fair in August, and Christmas dances in December. Their Sun Dance (Offerings Lodge) is usually held in July or August. Call the tribal office for dates and times and arrangements to attend the ceremonials. At the Sun Dance, photographs, sketching, food or drink at the lodge, tape recording, and scanty clothing are prohibited. Women on their moon should not be close to the lodge.

Art Forms: The artisans of the tribe do beadwork in the traditional floral design as well as other beautiful arts and crafts. Call the tribal office for help in locating them.

Visitor Information: This tribe shares the Wind River Indian Reservation with the Northern Arapahoe, but each has its distinctive culture, language, and customs. Two famous people in the history of the exploration and settlement of the West are buried in the Fort Washakie area: Sacajawea, the Shoshone Bannock woman who helped Lewis and Clark explore the West, and Chief Washakie. A monument to Chief Washakie demonstrates the respect his people hold for him.

The most northerly division of the Shoshonean family, these people formerly occupied western Wyoming, meeting the Ute on the south; the entire central and southern parts of Idaho, except the territory taken by the Bannock; northeast Nevada; and a small strip of Utah west of Great Salt Lake. The Snake River country in Idaho is consid-

Washakie's camp, Wind River Mountains, Wyoming
Photo by William H. Jackson; Courtesy Museum of New Mexico, Neg. No. 58655

ered to be their home. The northern bands were found by Lewis and Clark in 1805, on the headwaters of the Missouri in western Montana, but they had previously ranged farther east on the Plains. They had been driven into the Rocky Mountains by the hostile Atsina and Siksika, who already possessed firearms.

The origin of the term *Shoshoni* is unknown. It apparently is not a Shoshone word, and although the name is recognized by the Shoshone as applying to themselves, it probably originated among some other tribe. The Cheyenne name for the Comanche, who speak the Shoshone language, is Shishi-noats-hitaneo, "snake people," but they have a different name for the Shoshone. The term *Snake* seems to have no etymological connection with the designation *Shoshone*.

The more northerly and easterly Shoshone were horse and buffalo Indians. The western and southern Shoshone were very different as they lived in very barren country that did not support large game. These tribes depended largely on fish as their source of food, supplemented by rabbits, roots, nuts, and seeds. These were the Indians most frequently called "Diggers." They were also called Shoshokos, or "Walkers," which simply means that they were too poor to possess horses. This term was applied to horseless Shoshone everywhere.

None of these Shoshone were agriculturists. In general, the style of homes corresponded to the two types of Shoshone. In the north and east, they lived in tipis; in the sagebrush country to the west, they used brush shelters entirely.

In 1909, there were 1,766 Shoshone and Bannock in Idaho under the Fort Hall School and about 200 not under official supervision; in Nevada, there were 243 under the Western Shoshone School and about 750 not under agency or school control; in Wyoming, there were 816 under the Shoshone School. The total Shoshone population was approximately 3,250.

For more information, see Idaho, Fort Hall; Nevada, Paiute.

MOUNTAIN AND PLATEAU

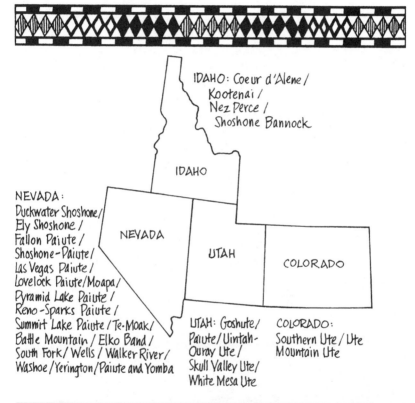

IDAHO: Coeur d'Alene /
Kootenai /
Nez Perce /
Shoshone Bannock

IDAHO

NEVADA:
Duckwater Shoshone/
Ely Shoshone /
Fallon Paiute /
Shoshone-Paiute /
Las Vegas Paiute /
Lovelock Paiute/Moapa /
Pyramid Lake Paiute /
Reno-Sparks Paiute /
Summit Lake Paiute / Te-Moak/
Battle Mountain / Elko Band /
South Fork/ Wells / Walker River/
Washoe/Yerington/Paiute and Yomba

NEVADA

UTAH

COLORADO

UTAH: Goshute/
Paiute/ Uintah-
Ouray Ute /
Skull Valley Ute/
White Mesa Ute

COLORADO:
Southern Ute / Ute
Mountain Ute

The interior of our North America is a land of basins, valleys, and great mountains. Streams rush down to the lowland river basins from springs and snow pack, and in the springtime of the year, brown cold water carries snow and ice to the warm sunlit valleys. The mountains are big. They rear their snow-capped heads above the horizons and maintain a silent vigil over all the land and all the people. And the life in the mountains and valleys and along the rivers is happy.

This is the land of the people who love the high places and the snow and winters. The mountains are their representatives to the Creator. They meet in council without demand and without being asked. The valleys that run up into the mountains are sided with steep walls, and here the people have placed prayer monuments in sacred places to the Creator. The bare faces of the tall mountains are covered with prayer shrines to our ancestors and for those that have gone on before us.

Join with the tribes on the following pages to honor their ancestors and to honor our Creator, our Mother Earth, our Moon, our Sun, and the whole of all living things in the whole of all Creation. You will find that it is good. It is very, very good.

Aho . . .

COLORADO

Southern Ute
P.O. Box 737
Ignacio, CO 81137
(303) 563-0100
1-800-876-7017
Fax (303) 563-0396

Ute

Location: Look for Ignacio south of Durango in southwestern Colorado.

Public Ceremony or Powwow Dates: The Bear Dance is held in late May, the Sun Dance is held in early July, and the Southern Ute Fair is held in early September. Remember that no photography, no sketching, no shorts or halter tops, and no food or drink are allowed near the Sun Dance Lodge. Also, women who are on their moon are not allowed at the lodge.

Art Forms: The Sky Ute Lodge has a gift shop, a museum, a 38-room lodge, and a restaurant.

Visitor Information: If you like horse racing, go to Sky Ute Downs, and if you like bingo gaming, go to Sky Ute bingo parlor. Call the office for dates and times. RV hookups are available at the Sky Ute Downs. Lake Capote offers good fishing. Navajo Lake is inside the very southern edge of the reservation, and there is a museum at the state park there.
    For more information, see Utah, Uintah and Ouray.

Ute Mountain Ute
General Delivery
Towaoc, CO 81344
(303) 565-3751
Fax (303) 565-7412

Ute Indian, ca. 1915
Courtesy Museum of New Mexico, Neg. No. 21556

Ute

Location: Drive south of Cortez, Colorado, on the highway to the four corners and watch for the pottery factory on your right, west of Highway 160/666, 15 miles from Cortez.

Public Ceremony or Powwow Dates: The annual Bear Dance is usually held in June. Go one mile east of the tribal offices in Towaoc.

Art Forms: You can buy pottery at the Ute Mountain Pottery Factory.

Visitor Information: Don't miss the spectacular scenery of the Ute Mountain Tribal Park. The cliff dwellings and ancient Anasazi ruins are in beautiful country. There are full guided tours, hiking, camping, and backpacking trips available. All trips are arranged with the Ute Tribal Office. Stop by and see the Ute people. The area is closed in the winter, so please visit from June through September.
    For more information, see Utah, Uintah and Ouray.

IDAHO

Coeur d'Alene Skitswish
Plummer, ID 83851
(208) 686-1800
Fax (208) 686-1182

Skitswish

Location: Plummer is just south and west of Coeur d'Alene, Idaho.

Public Ceremony or Powwow Dates: The tribe has three powwows each year. Call the office above for dates and times.

The Skitswish are a Salish tribe on a river and lake of the same name in northern Idaho. Coeur d'Alene (French, "Awl-heart"), the name by which they are popularly known, was originally a nickname used by some chief of the tribe to express the size of a trader's heart. The Skitswish numbered 533 in 1909.
    For more information, see Montana, Confederated Salish; Idaho, Kootenai.

Fort Hall Bannock and Shoshone
P.O. Box 306
Fort Hall, ID 83203-0306
(208) 238-3700
Fax (208) 237-0797

Bannock (Panaiti, their own name)
Shoshone

Location: The reservation is located in southeast Idaho north of Pocatello.

Public Ceremony or Powwow Dates: The Fort Hall tribe holds its annual Fort Hall Indian Days celebration in August. The Indian Day is in September and features a total celebration. Call the tribal office for dates and times.

Art Forms: The beadwork is mostly floral in design in this area. There are also other kinds of arts and crafts to be found here. Call the office for information about the type of work you wish to buy.

Visitor Information: For more information on the Shoshone, please see Wyoming, Shoshone Business Council.

The Bannock are a Shoshonean tribe whose home prior to being forced onto reservations cannot be definitely outlined. There were two geographic divisions, but references to the Bannock do not always note this distinction. The home of the chief division appears to have been southeast Idaho, and they ranged into western Wyoming. The country actually claimed by the chief of this southern division, which seems to have been recognized by the treaty of Fort Bridger, July 3, 1868, lay between lat. 42 degrees and 45 degrees and between long. 113 degrees and the main chain of the Rocky Mountains. It separated the Wihinasht Shoshone of western Idaho from the so-called Washaki band of Shoshone of western Wyoming. They were found in this region in 1859, and they asserted that this had been their home in the past. Many of this division affiliated with the Washaki Shoshone and by 1859, had extensively intermarried with them. Fort Hall Reservation was set apart by Executive Order in 1869, and 600 Bannock, in addition to a large number of Shoshone, consented to remain on it. But most of them soon left, and as late as

1874, an appropriation was made to enable the Bannock and Shoshone scattered in southeast Idaho to be moved to the reservation. The Bannock at Fort Hall were said to number 422 in 1885.

The northern division was seen in 1853 living on the Salmon River in eastern Idaho. Lewis and Clark, who passed through their country in 1805, may have included them under the general term Shoshone, unless, as is most likely, these are the Broken Moccasin Indians they mention. In all probability, these Salmon River Bannock had recently crossed the mountains from the east because of pressure from the Siksika, who claimed southwestern Montana, including the rich areas where Virginia City and Bozeman are situated, as their territory.

The Bannock were a widely roving tribe, a characteristic that favored their dispersal and separation into groups. Although their language is Shoshonean, in physical character, the Bannock more closely resemble the Shahaptian Nez Perce than other Shoshonean Indians.

The loss of hunting lands, the diminution of the buffalo herds, and the failure of the U.S. government to provide promised food led to a Bannock outbreak of 1878. During the Nez Perce war, the Bannock were forced to remain on their inhospitable reservation, to face the continued encroachments of non-Indians, and to subsist on goods provided from an appropriation amounting to 2½ cents per capita per diem. Because of the lack of food, the Bannock left the reservation in spring 1878 and went to Camas Prairie, where they killed several settlers who had confronted them. A vigorous campaign under General Howard resulted in the capture of about 1,000 of them in August, and the outbreak came to an end after a fight on September 5 at Clark's Ford, where 20 Bannock lodges were attacked and all the women and children massacred.

About 1829, the population of the southern Bannock was estimated at 8,000. In 1901, the tribe numbered 513, but it was intermixed with the Shoshone at that time. Almost all the Bannock are now living on Fort Hall Reservation.

For more information, see Wyoming, Shoshone; Nevada, Paiute.

Kootenai
P.O. Box 1269
Bonners Ferry, ID 83805-1269
(208) 267-3519
Fax (208) 267-2960

Kutenai (corrupted form, possibly by way of the language of the Siksika, of Dutonaqa, one of their names for themselves)

Visitor Information: The Kootenai hold an annual summer powwow at Fort Steele Heritage Park near Cranbrook, British Columbia, on Highway 93/95. You can call the park at (604) 489-3351 for dates and times.

These people form a distinct linguistic family who inhabited parts of southeastern British Columbia and northern Montana and Idaho, from the lakes near the source of the Columbia River to Pend d'Oreille Lake.

For more information, see the Confederated Salish and Kootenai Tribal Council, Montana.

From where the sun now sets I will fight no more forever.
— Chief Joseph (Nez Perce)

Nez Perce
P.O. Box 305
Lapwai, ID 83540-0305
(208) 843-2253
Fax (208) 843-7354

Nez Perce ("pierced nose"), a term applied by the French to a number of tribes that practiced or were supposed to practice the custom of piercing the nose for the insertion of a piece of dentalium. The term is now used exclusively to designate the main tribe of the Shahaptian family who have not, however, so far as is known, ever practiced the custom.

Location: The Nez Perce (NEZ-purse) reservation is located in northwest Idaho close to Washington and Oregon.

Public Ceremony or Powwow Dates: The Nez Perce love to powwow. There are no less than five celebrations per year, beginning with the Epethes Powwow held the first weekend in March in Lapwai. Competition war dance championships are decided at this powwow. Next comes the Mat-Al-YM'A Powwow and Root Feast at Kamiah the third weekend in May. Traditional dancing is performed there.

Tsutlim-Mox-Mox (Yellow Bull), Nez Perce, 1912
Photo by DeLancey Gill; Courtesy Museum of New Mexico, Neg. No. 87002

During the third weekend in June, at Lapwai, the tribe features dances honoring Chief Joseph and his warriors at the Warriors Memorial Powwow. The next powwow held is the Looking Glass Powwow in August at Kamiah. Great dancing and drum groups celebrate the memory of Chief Looking Glass, who lost his life in the war. Last, but not least, is the Four Nations Powwow held in October. Call the tribal office for dates and times of all the above events to confirm before traveling.

Art Forms: The Nez Perce sell arts and crafts, including their exclusive corn husk bags, during their powwows.

Visitor Information: This tribe developed the Appaloosa horse, which is honored with a museum in Moscow on Highway 8 on the way to Pullman.

The Nez Perce, or Sahaptin, were found in 1805 living in a large area in what is now western Idaho, northeastern Oregon, and southeastern Washington, on the lower Sanak River and its tributaries. They moved between the Blue Mountains in Oregon and the Bitter Root Mountains in Idaho and, according to Lewis and Clark, sometimes crossed the range to the headwaters of the Missouri. Certain writers have classed them under two geographic divisions, Upper Nez Perce and Lower Nez Perce. In 1834, the Lower Nez Perce lived to the north and west of the Blue Mountains on several of the branches of the Snake River, where they were neighbors of the Cayuse and Wallawalla. The Upper Nez Perce held the Salmon River country in Idaho in 1834 and probably also the Grande Ronde Valley in eastern Oregon, but by the treaty of 1855, they ceded a large part of this territory to the United States.

The reservation in which they were confined at that time included the Wallowa Valley in Oregon as well as a large district in Idaho. With the discovery of gold and the consequent influx of greedy miners and settlers, the Nez Perce were forced out of this region by means of a new treaty that confined the tribe to the reservation at Lapwai, Idaho. The occupants of Wallowa Valley refused to recognize the treaty, and finally, under their chief, Joseph, took active measures of resistance, resulting in the Nez Perce war of 1877. Several severe defeats were inflicted on the U.S. troops sent against the Indians. Finally, when forced to give way, Joseph conducted a masterly retreat across the Bitter Root Mountains and into Montana in an attempt to reach Canadian territory, but he and his band were surrounded and captured when within a few miles of the boundary. Joseph and his 450 followers were forced to move to Indian Territory (Oklahoma). Their loss from disease was so great there that in 1885 they were sent to the Colville Reservation in northern Washington, where a remnant of the tribe still resides.

The total population of the Nez Perce in 1805 was put at about 6,000. In 1885, they were estimated officially at 1,437. In 1906, the population was estimated at more than 1,600, 1,534 on the reservation in Idaho and 83 on the Colville Reservation in Washington.

At the time of Lewis and Clark's intrusion, the Nez Perce were reported as living in communal houses, said to contain about 50 families each. There is evidence that they used the typical underground lodge and that these seldom contained more than three or four families. A much larger dancing house was built at each permanent winter camp. Salmon constituted their most important food in early times and with roots and berries made up their entire food supply until the introduction of horses facilitated hunting expeditions to the neighboring mountains. The tribe seems to have been divided into a number of bands or villages, named according to the place where the permanent winter camp was made. Owing to the precarious nature of the food supply, the greater portion of the inhabitants of any one of these villages would often be absent for much of the year. There was no head chief of the tribe, but each band had several chiefs, one of whom was regarded as the leader. These chiefs were succeeded by their sons. Expeditions for hunting or war were led by chiefs chosen for the occasion. There are no signs of a clan system in the social organization of the Nez Perce, and marriage was apparently permitted between any couple except in the case of family relationship.

The spiritual beliefs of the Nez Perce, before the introduction of Christianity, were those characteristic of the Indians of the interior, the main feature being the belief in an indefinite number of spirits. An individual might procure a personal protecting spirit by rigorous training and fasting.

Northwestern Band of Shoshone
P.O. Box 637
Blackfoot, ID 83221
(208) 785-7401
Fax (208) 785-2206

For more information, see Wyoming, Shoshone; Idaho, Fort Hall.

NEVADA

Paiute

The word *Paiute* probably belongs to the Corn Creek tribe of southwestern Utah, but it has been extended to include many other tribes. It is used as a convenient divisional name for the tribes occupying southwestern Utah, the southwestern part of Nevada, and the northwestern part of Arizona, except the Chemehuevi.

It has been claimed that the Indians of the Walker River and Pyramid Lake reservations, who constitute the main body of those commonly known as Paiute, are not Paiute at all but another tribe, the Paviotso. The Indians of this area themselves claim the Bannock as their cousins and say that they speak the same language.

The most influential chiefs among the Paiute in modern times were Winnemucca, who died a few years before the turn of the century, and Natchez. They were generally peaceable and friendly toward non-Indians, although in the early 1860s, they sometimes came into conflict with miners and settlers, the hostility usually provoked by the non-Indians themselves. The northern Paiute were more warlike than those of the south, and a considerable number of them took part with the Bannock in the war of 1878. The great majority of the Paiute (including the Paviotso) were not on reservations. In 1906, their population could only be estimated at between 6,500 and 7,000: approximately 486 at Walker River, 129 at Moapa, 554 at Pyramid Lake, 267 at Duck Valley, 3,500 not under a reservation, and 350 in the Western Nevada School.

Traditionally, the Paiute have been closely associated with the Shoshone.

For more information, see Wyoming, Shoshone; Idaho, Fort Hall.

All Indians must dance, everywhere, keep on dancing. Pretty soon in next spring Great Spirit come. He bring back all game of every kind. The game be thick everywhere. All dead Indians come back and live again. They all be strong just like young men, be young again.

—Wovoka, the Paiute
Messiah

1826 – PIUTE INDIAN CAMP, NEVADA.

Paiute Indians, Nevada
Courtesy Museum of New Mexico, Neg. No. 43442

Duckwater Shoshone
P.O. Box 140068
Duckwater, NV 89314
(702) 863-0227
Fax (702) 863-0301

Shoshone

Location: The reservation is located in southwestern Idaho and northeastern Nevada on State Highway 51.

Public Ceremony or Powwow Dates: There is usually a rodeo during Fourth of July held at Owyhee, Nevada. This tribe participates in many activities of the Paiute. The *Native Nevadan* newsmagazine lists Western Shoshone events. Write to them at 98 Colony Road, Reno, NV 89502, or telephone (702) 329-2936.

Ely Shoshone
16 Shoshone Circle
Ely, NV 89301
(702) 289-3013
Fax (702) 289-3156

Fallon Paiute-Shoshone
8955 Mission Road
Fallon, NV 89406
(702) 423-6075
Fax (702) 423-5202

Paiute-Shoshone

Location: The Fallon Indian Reservation is located north of Highway 50 (the loneliest highway in the world), northeast of Fallon.

Public Ceremony or Powwow Dates: The most well-known of events for this area is Fallon Days, which features a parade where you may see Indian people in traditional clothing. The Fallon Chamber of Commerce has information and dates and times; telephone (702) 423-2544.

Fort McDermitt Shoshone-Paiute
P.O. Box 457
McDermitt, NV 89421
(702) 532-8259
Fax (705) 532-8913

Shoshone-Paiute

Location: The reservation is located in northwestern Nevada on Highway 95.

Las Vegas Paiute
No. 1 Paiute Drive
Las Vegas, NV 89106
(702) 386-3926
Fax (702) 383-4019

Lovelock Paiute
P.O. Box 878
Lovelock, NV 89419
(702) 273-7861
Fax (702) 273-7861

Moapa Paiute
P.O. Box 340
Moapa, NV 89025
(702) 865-2787
Fax (702) 865-2875

Moapariats (Mo-a-pa-ri-ats, "mosquito creek people")

This is a band of Paiute formerly living in or near Moapa Valley in southeastern Nevada. They numbered 64 in 1873.

Pyramid Lake Paiute
P.O. Box 256
Nixon, NV 89424
(702) 574-0100
Fax (702) 574-1008

Paiute

Location: The reservation is located northeast of Reno on State Highway 34.

Public Ceremony or Powwow Dates: Call the tribal office for more information.

Art Forms: The women continue to make the traditional baby cradleboards from woven baskets covered with leather. The decorations are very beautiful, and often you will find them for sale at powwows.

Visitor Information: The area around Pyramid Lake is very scenic, with various impressive geological features. Fishing permits are available from the tribe at the Tribal Enterprise Office in Sutcliffe, Abe and Sue's Store in Nixon, and Pyramid Lake Store in Nixon. The lake is known for large trout. Only Paiutes are allowed to fish for the cuiui, a rare fish found in the lake and still eaten by Paiute people. Camping and boating are allowed. The old Indian Trail that runs along the Truckee River between Nixon and Wadsworth can still be seen in some places.

Reno-Sparks Paiute
98 Colony Road
Reno, NV 89502
(702) 329-2936
Fax (702) 329-8710

Paiute

Location: The Paiute and Washo people of the Reno/Sparks Indian Colony own and operate the Indian Colony Mall at 2001 E. Second Street, Reno, telephone (702) 329-2573.

Public Ceremony or Powwow Dates: The Paiute people of the area sponsor many interesting events annually. Many are held around Schurz, Reno, Sparks, and Fallon. The *Native Nevadan* lists most of these events. Subscribe by writing to 98 Colony Road, Reno, NV 89502, or calling (702) 329-2936. Besides dancing there will be hand games and crafts sales.

Visitor Information: Traditional items can be found at the Earth Window Indian Arts and Crafts Shop in the Indian Colony Mall.

Shoshone-Paiute
P.O. Box 219
Owyhee, NV 89832
(702) 757-3161
Fax (702) 757-2219

See the general history of the Paiute at the beginning of this section.

Weasaw, Shoshone, 1899
Photo by Rose & Hopkins; Courtesy Museum of New Mexico, Neg. No. 4372

Summit Lake Paiute
655 Anderson Street
Winnemucca, NV 89445-3131
(702) 623-5151
Fax (702) 623-0558

The Winnemucca band was a Paviotso band under Chief Winnemucca (The Giver) which formerly lived on Smoke Creek, near Honey Lake, northeastern California, and eastward to Pyramid, Winnemucca, and Humboldt lakes, Nevada. In 1859, they were said to number 155; in 1877, they were under Malheur Agency, Oregon, and numbered 150.

Battle Mountain Shoshone
35 Mountain View Drive, #138-13
Battle Mountain, NV 89820
(702) 635-2004
Fax (702) 635-8016

Elko Shoshone
P.O. Box 748
Elko, NV 89801
(702) 738-8889
Fax (702) 753-5439

South Fork Shoshone
Box B-13
Lee, NV 89829
(702) 744-4273

Te-Moak Shoshone
525 Sunset Street
Elko, NV 89801
(702) 738-9251
Fax (702) 738-2345

Wells Shoshone
P.O. Box 809
Wells, NV 89835
(702) 752-3045

Shoshone

For more information on the Shoshone, see Wyoming, Shoshone.

Walker River Paiute
P.O. Box 220
Schurz, NV 89427
(702) 773-2306
Fax (702) 773-2585

Paiute

Location: The reservation is located east of Carson City on U.S. Highway 95.

Public Ceremony or Powwow Dates: The Walker River Paiute tribe annually holds its Pinenut Festival at Schurz in October with events including round dancing, hand games, and a barbecue. Call the tribal office for more information.

Carson Washoe
331 Paiute Street
Carson City, NV 89703
(702) 883-6431

Dresslerville Washoe
1585 Watasheamu Road
Gardnerville, NV 89410
(702) 265-5845

Woodfords Washoe
96 Washoe Boulevard
Markleeville, CA 96120
(916) 694-2170

Washoe
Rt. 2, 919 Highway 395 South
Gardnerville, NV 89410
(702) 265-4191 or 883-1446
Fax (702) 265-6240

Stewart Washoe
5258 Snyder Avenue
Carson City, NV 89701
(702) 883-7767

Washo (from *washiu,* "person," in their own language)

Location: All the above tribes are in the Carson City area.

Public Ceremony or Powwow Dates: There is an annual La Ka Le'l Ba powwow in Carson City put on by the Carson Colony. Call (702) 883-6431 for dates and times.

Art Forms: Arts and crafts are for sale at the powwow.

The Washo are a small tribe, but they form a distinct linguistic family, the Washoan, which, when first known to Americans, occupied Truckee River, Nevada, as far down as the Meadows. The Washo also occupied Carson River down to the first large canyon below Carson City, the borders of Lake Tahoe, and the Sierra and other valleys as far as the first range south of Honey Lake, California. They occupied the mountains only in summer. There is some evidence that they once were established in the valleys farther to the east, where they had been driven by the Paiute, with whom there existed a state of chronic ill feeling. Between 1860 and 1862, the Paiute conquered the Washo in a contest over the site of Carson and forbade them to own horses. In the early 1900s, they were confined to the country from Reno to a short distance south of Carson City. Study of their language indicates no linguistic relationship with any other people. In 1859, the Washo numbered about 900, but by 1905, they were reduced to about a third of that number.

Winnemucca Paiute
420 Pardee
Susanville, CA 96130
(916) 257-7093

Yerington Paiute
171 Campbell Lane
Yerington, NV 89447
(702) 463-3301
Fax (702) 463-2416

Paiute

See the general history of the Paiute at the beginning of this section.

Yomba Shoshone
HC61, Box 6275
Austin, NV 89310
(702) 964-2463
Fax (702) 964-2443

Shoshone

For more information on the Shoshone, see Wyoming, Shoshone.

UTAH

Goshute
P.O. Box 6104
Ibapah, UT 84034
(801) 234-1136
Fax (801) 234-6211

Goshute (from Gossip, their chief, plus Ute)

Location: The reservation is located in western Utah south of Ibapah. This is a Shoshonean tribe that formerly occupied Utah west of the Salt and Utah lakes and eastern Nevada.

Paiute
600 North 100 East Paiute Drive
Cedar City, UT 84720
(801) 586-1112
Fax (801) 586-7388

Skull Valley Ute
c/o Uintah and Ouray Agency
P.O. Box 130
Fort Duchesne, UT 84026
(801) 722-2406
Fax (801) 722-2406

Uintah and Ouray Ute
P.O. Box 190
Fort Duchesne, UT 84026
(801) 722-5141
Fax (801) 722-2374

Northern Ute

Location: The reservation is located in the northeast corner of Utah.

Public Ceremony or Powwow Dates: The Northern Ute Bear Dance is held in April or May. The Fourth of July and the fall are times of powwows. The Sun Dance is in July and August. Call the tribal office for dates and times. As always, the Sun Dance is restricted from cameras, tape recorders, sketch pads, and video equipment, and women should not wear halter tops or shorts. Women on their moon should not go near the lodge, and there is no food or drink allowed at the lodge.

Art Forms: The Ute do floral design beadwork and other arts and crafts that are Plains and Mountain in style.

Visitor Information: This is a beautiful part of Utah, particularly when you enter the northern part of the reservation toward the Uintah Mountains.

The Ute are an important Shoshonean division, related linguistically to the Paiute, Chemehuevi, Kawaiisu, and Bannock. They formerly occupied the entire central and western portions of Colorado and the eastern portion of Utah, including the eastern part of the Salt Lake Valley and Utah Valley. On the south they extended into New Mexico, occupying much of the upper drainage area of the San Juan. They appear to have always been a warlike people and early on possessed horses. None of the tribes practiced agriculture. Very little is known of their social and political organization, although the seven Ute tribes of Utah were at one time organized into a confederacy under Chief Tabby (Taiwi). There are dialect differences in the language, but they probably presented little difficulty in communication between the several bands. In the northern part of their range, in Utah, they appear to have intermarried with the Shoshone, Bannock, and Paiute and in the south, with the Jicarilla Apache.

The first peace treaty with the Ute was concluded December 30, 1849. By Executive Order of October 3, 1861, Uintah Valley was set apart for the Uintah tribe, and the remainder of the land claimed by them was taken without formal purchase. In a treaty of October 7, 1863, the Tabeguache band was assigned a reservation, and the remainder of their land was ceded to the United States. On May 5, 1864, various reserves, established in 1856 and 1859 by Indian agents, were ordered vacated and sold. A treaty of March 2, 1868, created a reservation in Colorado for the Tabeguache, Moache, Capote, Wiminuche, Yampa, Grand River, Uintah, and other bands, and the remainder of their lands was relinquished; but in an agreement of September 13, 1873, a part of this reservation was ceded to the United States. When it was found that a portion of this last cession was included in the Uncompahgre Valley, that part was returned to the Ute by Executive Order of August 17, 1876. By Executive

Order of November 22, 1875, the Ute Reservation was enlarged, but this additional tract was returned to public domain in 1882. In June 1878, several more tracts included in the reservations established thereunder were restored to the public domain. Under agreement of November 9, 1878, the Moache, Capote, and Wiminuche ceded their right to the confederated Ute Reservation established by the 1868 treaty, and the United States agreed to establish a reservation for them on the San Juan River. In 1880, the Southern Ute and the Uncompahgre acknowledged an agreement to settle respectively on the La Plata River and on the Grand near the mouth of the Gunnison, while the White River Ute agreed to move to the Uintah Reservation in Utah. Since sufficient agricultural land was not found at the future home of the Uncompahgre, in 1882, the president established a reserve for them in Utah. But in May 1888, a part of the Uintah Reservation was returned to public domain.

The Southern Ute lands in Colorado were in part subsequently allotted in severalty, and in April 1899, 523,079 acres were opened to settlement for non-Indians, with the remainder (483,750 acres) retained as a reservation for the Wiminuche. A large part of the Uintah Valley Reservation in Utah was also allotted in severalty, more than a million acres set aside as public forest and other public reserves, and more than a million acres more opened to non-Indian settlement. Of the Uncompahgre Reservation in Utah in June 1897, 12,540 acres were allotted and the remainder returned to public domain.

In July 1879, about 100 Ute men of the White River Agency, Colorado, left their reservation to hunt in southern Wyoming. During this time some forests were set on fire by railway tiemen, and the Ute were blamed. They were ordered to remain on their reservation. Orders were later issued for the arrest of the men charged with the recent forest fires, and a military officer was sent with a force of 190. Suspecting the outcome, the Ute procured ammunition from neighboring traders and informed the agent that the appearance of the troops would be regarded as an act of war. On September 20, the military detachment was ambushed, and their leader and thirteen men were killed. The command fell back. On October 2, a company of cavalry arrived, and three days later Colonel Merritt and 600 troops reached the scene. The conflict was soon ended, mainly through the peaceful efforts and influence of Chief Ouray.

In summer 1906, about 400 Ute, chiefly of the White River band, left their allotments and the Uintah Reservation in Utah to go to the

Pine Ridge Reservation, South Dakota, where they could live unrestricted. Although they committed no acts of aggression on the way, settlers became alarmed. Every peaceful effort was made to induce them to return to Utah, but only 45 returned there. Those who refused were charged with petty thefts while in Wyoming, and the matter was placed under the jurisdiction of the War Department. Troops were sent to the scene in October, and the Indians accompanied them peacefully to Fort Meade, South Dakota, in November. In the following spring (1907), arrangements were made whereby the absentee Ute were assigned four townships of the Cheyenne River Reservation, South Dakota, which was leased by the government at the expense of the Ute annuity fund, for five years. The Indians were removed in June to their new lands, where they remained until the following June (1908), when, at their own request, they were returned to their old home in Utah, arriving there in October.

In 1885, official reports gave 3,391 as the population of several reservations; in 1909, 2,014.

For more information, see Colorado, Mountain Ute and Southern Ute.

White Mesa Ute
P.O. Box 340
Blanding, UT 84511

For more information on the Ute tribe, see Utah, Uintah and Ouray; Colorado, Mountain Ute and Southern Ute.

NORTH

Lower Sioux /
Minnesota Chippewa /
Fond du Lac / Grand
Portage / Leech Lake /
Mille Lacs / Nett Lake /
White Earth / Prairie
Island / Red Cliff / Red
Lake / Shakopee /
Upper Sioux

MINNESOTA

The North country of North America lies in that place beyond where our plains meet the lakes and the forests of tall trees. The terrain is flat and rolling, and the lakes and streams glisten and sparkle in the sun.

This is the land of the people of the wigwam; the nomadic woodland people who hunted deer and small game and lived in tune with the spirits of all living things. They gathered wild rice and collected wild herbs for food and medicine.

They have always been there, and the spirits of their ancestors will always be over and in the land. From time immemorial, they have followed the streams in birch bark canoes and followed the paths worn through the forests.

They, too, have the drum. The ceremonials of the people act out their respect and their prayers for and to the Creator. They grew some tobacco and smoked it in pipes and rolled leaves with their intentions that the smoke would carry their prayers up to the Creator. And it did. And it does today.

There is no mystery or secret to Indian spirituality. There is only respect and natural praise composed into ceremony which defines the existence of the people.

Join with the tribes on the following pages to honor their ancestors and to honor our Creator, our Mother Earth, our Moon, our Sun, and the whole of all living things in the whole of all Creation. You will find that it is good. It is very, very good.

Aho . . .

MINNESOTA

Ojibwa (Chippewa)

Ojibwa ("to roast until puckered up," the result of wet moccasins too close to the fire)

The Ojibwa are one of the largest tribes north of Mexico. Their range was formerly along both shores of Lake Huron and Lake Superior, extending across Minnesota to the Turtle Mountains, North Dakota. Although they were numerous and occupied a large territory, the Chippewa were never prominent in history, because of their remoteness from the frontier during the period of the colonial wars. According to tradition they are part of an Algonquian body, including the Ottawa and Potawatomi, that separated into divisions when it reached Mackinaw in its westward movement, having come from some point north or northeast of Mackinaw.

They are first recorded in the Jesuit Relation of 1640 under the name Baouichtigouin (probably Bawatigowininiwug, "people of the Sault") as residing at the Sault, and it is possible that Nicolet met them in 1634 or 1639. A remnant or offshoot of the tribe resided north of Lake Superior after the main body moved south to Sault Ste. Marie, or when it had reached the vicinity of the Sault. The Marameg, a tribe closely related to if not an actual division of the Ojibwa, who dwelled along the north shore of the lake, were apparently incorporated with the latter while they were at the Sault, or prior to 1670. On the north, the Ojibwa are so closely connected with the Cree and Maskegon that the three can be distinguished only by those who are knowledgeable about their dialects and customs. On the south, the Chippewa (Ojibwa), Ottawa, and Potawatomi have always formed a sort of loose confederacy, frequently designated in the last century as the Three Fires. It is generally accepted that some of the Chippewa have resided north of Lake Superior from time immemorial. The Ojibwa cultivated some maize. Another source of food was wild rice, and the possession of wild rice fields was one of the chief causes of their wars with the Dakota, Fox, and other nations.

About 1700, the Ojibwa first came into possession of firearms and were pushing their way westward, alternately at peace and at war with the Sioux and in almost constant conflict with the Fox. In 1692, the French reestablished a trading post at Shaugawaumikong, now La Pointe, Ashland County, Wisconsin, which became an important Ojibwa settlement. In the beginning of the eighteenth century, the Ojibwa succeeded in driving the Fox, already reduced by a war with the French, from northern Wisconsin, compelling them to take refuge with the Sauk. They then turned against the Sioux, driving them across the Mississippi and south to the Minnesota River, and continued their westward march across Minnesota and North Dakota until they occupied the headwaters of the Red River and established their westernmost band in the Turtle Mountains. It was not until after 1736 that they obtained a foothold west of Lake Superior. While the main divisions of the tribe were thus extending their possessions in the west, others overran the peninsula between Lake Huron and Lake Erie, which had long been claimed by the Iroquois through conquest. The Iroquois were forced to withdraw, and the whole region was occupied by the Ojibwa bands, most of whom became known as Missisauga, although they still called themselves Ojibwa. The Chippewa (Ojibwa) took part with the other tribes of the Northwest in all the wars against the frontier settlements until the end of the War of 1812. Those living within the United States made a treaty with the government in 1815 and subsequently resided on reservations or allotted lands within their original territory in Michigan, Wisconsin, Minnesota, and North Dakota, with the exception of the small band of Swan Creek and Black River Ojibwa, who sold their lands in southern Michigan in 1836 and moved to Kansas.

Their long and successful conflict with the Sioux and Fox exhibited their bravery and determination, yet they were uniformly friendly to the French. The Ojibwa are a timber people. According to historians, the division of the tribe residing at La Pointe practiced cannibalism. (The act of eating a small particle of flesh or of an organ, such as the heart, was common practice of a victor over an enemy. This practice of the Ojibwa should not be confused with cannibalism.)

Like the Ottawa, the Ojibwa were expert in the use of the canoe and in their early history depended largely on fish for food. As is true in many tribes, polygamy was normal. Their wigwams were made of birch bark or of grass mats; poles were first placed in the ground in a circle, the tops bent together and tied, and the bark or mats thrown over them, leaving a smoke hole at the top. They knew that the shade, after the death of the body, followed a wide beaten path, leading toward the west, finally arriving in the place of spirit that abounds in everything of need. The Ojibwa believed that the spirit returns to visit the body until it is reduced to dust. Like most of our people, the Ojibwa believe that all things animate and inanimate are alive. All objects are Manitus, which in the summer are ever wakeful and quick to hear everything but in winter, after the snow falls, are in a torpid state. The Ojibwa, as most of our people do, regard dreams as revelations, and some object that appears in them is often chosen as a tutelary deity. The Medewiwin, or Grand Medicine Society, is a powerful organization of the Ojibwa, which in the past controlled the movements of the tribe and was a formidable obstacle to the introduction of Christianity. The native people of this land lived in harmony with spirituality; they did not practice it. When an Ojibwa died, it was customary to place the body in a grave facing west, often in a sitting posture, or to scoop a shallow cavity in the earth and deposit the body therein on its back or side, covering it with earth so as to form a small mound, over which boards, poles, or birch bark were placed. According to one observer, the Ojibwa of Fond du Lac, Wisconsin, practiced scaffold burial, with the body enclosed in a box. Mourning for a lost relative usually continued for a year.

Population estimates in 1764 were about 25,000. In 1905, the estimate was 30,000, with 14,144 in the United States.

Fond du Lac Ojibwa
105 University Road
Cloquet, MN 55720
(218) 879-4593
Fax (218) 879-4146

Ojibwa

Location: The tribal office address is listed above.

Public Ceremony or Powwow Dates: The Fond du Lac powwow is usually in July.

Art Forms: Arts and crafts can be purchased during the powwow.

Visitor Information: Wild rice harvesting takes place during

September. (For more about wild rice, see the general history of the Ojibwa at the beginning of this section.) This tribe owns its own construction company and a steel products company. And the bingo enterprise is doing well in Duluth.

Grand Portage Ojibwa
P.O. Box 428
Grand Portage, MN 55605
(218) 475-2279 or (218) 475-2277
Fax (218) 475-2284

Ojibwa

Location: The reservation is located in the northeastern tip of Minnesota.

Public Ceremony or Powwow Dates: Rendezvous Days is held the second weekend in August. There is traditional dancing and singing.

Art Forms: Beadwork and other arts and crafts can be found during the powwow. You can also find beadwork for sale at Crawford House in the National Monument. Also, the community arts center is an interesting place to visit.

Visitor Information: Be sure to visit Grand Portage National Monument, which is inside the reservation. Grand Portage Lodge and Conference Center on Highway 61 in Grand Portage is owned by the tribe. The marina with boat rentals, a construction company, a logging operation, a fishing company, a restaurant, an elementary school, and a cross-country skiing operation are also owned by the tribe.

Leech Lake Ojibwa
Route 3, Box 100
Cass Lake, MN 56633
(218) 335-8200
Fax (218) 335-8309

Ojibwa

Location: The powwow grounds and the convention center are located in Cass Lake.

Unidentified man, Chippewa, 1872
Photo by B. W. Kilburn; Courtesy Museum of New Mexico, Neg. No. 90556

Public Ceremony or Powwow Dates: Five annual powwows are held, on Labor Day and Memorial Day and in winter, spring, and midsummer. Call the tribal office for dates and times.

Art Forms: Birch bark baskets, paintings, moccasins, beadwork, feather work, leather work, and more are available. The gift shop and Che-Wa-Kae-Gon Restaurant and bingo parlor show some artwork.

Visitor Information: This tribe owns a logging company, a construction company, the Leech Lake Wild Rice Company, a retail grocery, service station, restaurant, bingo palace, and the Northern Lights Gaming Emporium.

Lower Sioux
Rural Route 1, Box 308
Morton, MN 56270-9801
(507) 697-6185
Fax (507) 697-6110

The Lower Sioux, as distinguished from the Upper Sioux (Sisseton and Wahpeton), are composed of the Mdewakanton and Wahpekute Sioux.

For more information, see South Dakota, Sioux.

Mille Lacs Band of Chippewa Indians
HCR 67, Box 194
Onamia, MN 56359
(612) 532-4181
Fax (612) 532-4209

Location: The tribal government center is located twelve miles north of Onamia on U.S. Highway 169.

Public Ceremony or Powwow Dates: The powwow is held in mid-August. Call the tribal office for dates and times.

Art Forms: Artwork can be found at the museum, and arts and crafts are sold at the powwow.

Visitor Information: The Mille Lacs Indian Museum and Trading Post, Grand Casino Bingo, and Anishinabe OIC are located on tribally owned land.

Minnesota Chippewa
Box 217
Cass Lake, MN 56633
(218) 335-8581
Fax (218) 335-6562

Nett Lake Ojibwa
(Bois Forte)
P.O. Box 16
Nett Lake, MN 55772
(218) 757-3261
Fax (218) 757-3166

Ojibwa

Location: The location of the powwow grounds can be obtained by calling the tribal office.

Public Ceremony or Powwow Dates: The first weekend in June is powwow time with traditional dancing and drum groups. Call the tribal office for dates and times.

Art Forms: Arts and crafts are sold at the powwow. The work will include paintings, feather work, leather work, and beadwork.

Visitor Information: The Bois Fort Wild Rice Company is doing well. For interesting information on wild rice, see the general history of the Ojibwa at the beginning of this section.

Prairie Island (Mdewakanton Sioux)
1158 Island Blvd.
Welch, MN 55089-9540
(612) 385-2554
Fax (612) 388-1576

Sioux

For information on the Sioux, see the general history of the Sioux, South Dakota.

Red Lake Ojibwa
P.O. Box 550
Red Lake, MN 56671
(218) 679-3341
Fax (218) 679-3378

Ojibwa

For more information on the Ojibwa, see the general history at the beginning of this section.

Shakopee Sioux
2330 Sioux Trail NW
Prior Lake, MN 55372-9077
(612) 445-8900
Fax (612) 445-8906

Shakopee (Shakpe, "six")

Shakopee is the name of a succession of chiefs of the Mdewakanton Sioux, who resided on the Minnesota River, not far from the present town of Shakopee, Minnesota. The first of the three chiefs met Major S. H. Long at the mouth of the Minnesota in 1817, when he came to distribute the presents that Lt. Z. M. Pike had contracted to send them twelve years earlier. Long found him very offensive. This Shakopee was succeeded by his son, who was known as Eaglehead Shakopee, and he by his son, Little Six (Shakopeela), who was a leader in the Minnesota raids of 1862.
For more information, see South Dakota, Sioux.

Upper Sioux Community
P.O. Box 147
Granite Falls, MN 56241
(612) 564-2360 or (612) 564-4207
Fax (612) 564-3264

Visitor Information: There is one Presbyterian church within the original boundaries of the reservation. Services are conducted in both Sioux and English. The native tongue will no longer exist within the next generation or two as intermarriage between the Sioux and non-Indians is diminishing Sioux blood and culture.

The original reservation for the Sioux in this area was comprised of land that was ten miles on either side of the Minnesota River from Big Stone Lake (near Browns Valley, Minn.) to what is now called St. Paul. The so-called Sioux Uprising of 1862 by the Mdewakantons (Little Crow of the Lower Sioux) virtually wiped out the reservation by an act of Congress called "the Forfeiture Act." Even though the Upper Sioux Band of Indians did not participate in the uprising, Congress confiscated all Sioux annuities and the reservation. Congress made no provision for the friendly Sisseton/Wahpeton Sioux, who were left to suffer and remain homeless wanderers.

Under the Indian Reorganization Act of the 1930s, the government did buy land that is now called the Upper Sioux Reservation. The acreage is not measured in miles as the original reservation was. It is now a mere 745 acres, held in trust by the government.

The current administration of the tribe has, in a short period, raised the funds to build a fully equipped casino building from the ground up, complete with a dining and kitchen facility. An expansion program is under consideration. The casino employs most of the available work force in the community. Although the community is small in number (approx. 150), the employment rate has historically been 85 percent. The purpose of the casino was to create employment and to supplement the dwindling contract funds from the state and federal governments.

The casino (Firefly Creek Casino) has become one of the largest employers in the area, with a complement of more than 100 employees. The surrounding area is predominantly dependent on agriculture. The community itself is comprised of several Sioux bands of Indians—the Sisseton/Wahpeton, the Santee, the Flandreau, a few Yanktons, and Devils Lake Sioux. The predominant band is the Sisseton/Wahpeton Sioux.

For more information, see South Dakota, Sioux.

White Earth Ojibwa
P.O. Box 418
White Earth, MN 56591
(218) 983-3285
Fax (218) 983-3641

Ojibwa

Location: The location of the tribal offices is in northwestern Minnesota, north of Detroit Lakes on Highway 59.

Grey Eagle and his lodge, Sioux
Photo by Keystone View Co.; Courtesy Museum of New Mexico, Neg. No. 91500

Chippewa women stir maple sap on the reservation at Cass Lake, Minnesota, 1938
Photo courtesy UPI/Bettman

Public Ceremony or Powwow Dates: The official powwow date is June 14, and the powwow takes place on the weekend of or before the 14th.

Art Forms: Members of the tribe do beautiful floral design beadwork and basket weaving.

Visitor Information: The nearest airport served by a charter airline is in Detroit Lakes, 25 miles from the reservation. A variety of lodging, restaurants, and travel services are also available there. With its numerous lakes and forest areas, the reservation has many resorts and campsites that draw large numbers of tourists/vacationers. Hunting and fishing are quite prominent, and wildlife is abundant.

Tribal Council headquarters are located right in White Earth, and the largest employer on the reservation is the White Earth Reservation Tribal Council, supporting an average of 275 employees through state and federal grants and contracts. The Tribal Council also owns the White Earth Garment Manufacturing Company, Inc., the Ojibwa Forest Products, Inc., the Ojibwa Building Supplies, Inc., and owns and operates the Golden Eagle Bingo Lodge. These enterprises employ approximately 65 people full-time and 25 part-time. The surrounding area is predominantly dependent on the agricultural and tourism industries. The main recreational areas of interest are the resorts and hunting and fishing.

Even though the current Bureau of Indian Affairs labor force report lists unemployment at 71 percent, the outlook of the people is positive, primarily because of the improvements in education.

There are two churches in White Earth which are open to the public. These are St. Benedict's Catholic Church and St. Columba's Episcopal Church.

The White Earth Band of Chippewa is the official name of the tribe, and they are of Ojibwa Indian origin. Their reservation was formed through a treaty with the government in 1867, in which 837,120 acres of land was allotted to them. Today, only 7 percent, 57,000 acres, of that land remains, which is held in trust by the Bureau of Indian Affairs.

The Chippewa were nomadic timber people, traveling in small bands, engaging primarily in hunting and fishing, sometimes settling to carry on a crude form of agriculture. Although social organization was loose, the powerful Grand Medicine Society controlled the tribe's movements and was a formidable obstacle to the Christianizing attempts of missionaries. The Chippewa today are largely of mixed blood, including French and English.

NORTHEAST

WISCONSIN: Chippewa / Potawatomi / Menominee / Oneida / Mahican / Winnebago

MICHIGAN: Chippewa

MAINE: Houlton Maliseet / Passamaquoddy / Penobscot

WISCONSIN

MICHIGAN

MAINE

NEW YORK

MASSACHUSETTS

RHODE ISLAND

CONNECTICUT

NEW YORK: Cayuga / Oneida / Onondago / Seneca / Mohawk / Tuscarora

MASSACHUSETTS · RHODE ISLAND · CONNECTICUT: Mashantucket / Pequot / Narragansett / Wampanoag / Paugusset / Mohegan / Schaghticoke / Paucatuck

DELAWARE: Nanticoke

VIRGINIA

VIRGINIA: Chickahominy / Mattaponi / Pamunkey

The Northeast of our North America lies above the Great Plains and east of the Great Waters we call the Great Lakes. The trees are pines and broadleafs that bring colors bright and warm in the fall. When the winds of winter come from the north, the leaves flutter and fall in great piles below the bare branches reaching for the sky in silent prayer. Black water, turned dark by the leaves, winds in little streams through the woods. And, on the coast, the winds and waves roar on the rocks, leaving mists of colored rainbows in the air.

This is the land of the longhouse people and the people of the sacred fire. They kept the land good and respectfully administered their responsibility as guardians.

They wore the masks of their societies, and when they prayed the drum of the heartbeat of our Mother Earth, the songs sent the message to the Creator that all life is to be praised and that all life is good and beautiful and more than mere chance. Whoever considers themselves more beautiful than the whole of life has no heart. They chant-prayed in the interiors of their sacred longhouses, and life was in tune with the heartbeat of the drum.

All of life remained in constant prayer to the Creator then. All of the people remained in always respecting the whole of all living things.

Join with the tribes on the following pages to honor their ancestors and to honor our Creator, our Mother Earth, our Moon, our Sun, and the whole of all living things in the whole of all Creation. You will find that it is good. It is very, very good.

Aho . . .

All the Indian Nations from the Sun Rise to these beyond the Lakes, as far as the Sun sets, have heard what has passed between you and me and are pleased with it.

— Teedyuscung
(Delaware)

You must lift the hatchet against them.

— Pontiac (Ottawa)

Father, be strong and take pity on us, your children, as our former father did.

— Pontiac (Ottawa)

Listen to me, fathers of the thirteen fires.

— Cornplanter (Seneca)

Brother, the Great Spirit has made us all.

— Red Jacket (Seneca)

We have borne everything patiently for this long time.

— Joseph Brant (Mohawk)

Brothers, these people never told us they wished to purchase our lands from us.

— Little Turtle (Miami)

Sleep not longer, O Choctaws and Chickasaws.

— Tecumseh (Shawnee)

Father, listen! The Americans have not yet defeated us by land.

— Tecumseh (Shawnee)

For more than a hundred winters our nation was a powerful, happy, and united people.

— Black Hawk (Sauk)

Let the Sioux keep from our lands, and there will be peace.

— Keokuk (Sauk)

CONNECTICUT

Golden Hill Paugusset
427 Shelton Road
Trumbull, CT 06611

Paugusset ("where the narrows open out")

This Algonquian tribe was a part of the Wappinger Confederacy.

Mashantucket Pequot
P.O. Box 3060
Ledyard, CT 06339-3060
(203) 536-2681
Fax (203) 572-0421

Mashantucket Pequot

Location: The reservation is located in southern New England in the state of Connecticut. The main entrance to the reservation is just off Route 214 and is centrally located between New Haven, Hartford, and Providence in Rhode Island. The Mashantucket Pequot live within the town of Ledyard.

Public Ceremony or Powwow Dates: None are being held at this time in the community.

Art Forms: The art forms of the tribe were lost when it was dispersed as a result of the massacre of 1637, which killed most of the men, women, and children.

Visitor Information: The tribe is presently selling crafts at their bingo hall and are in the process of expanding into a small gift shop. In the future, there will also be a shop in the museum which is in the planning stages.

The tribal enterprises at this time are High Stakes Bingo, the Owl's Nest Restaurant (Ohomowauke), Mashantucket Sand and Gravel,

and the Indian Health Service, which provides service to all federally recognized Indians in New London County.

The name of the tribe means "many wooded lands" in their own language. The Pequot were known as the Fox People. The tribe's logo
is a mix of four symbols reflecting the tribe's last few hundred years:
the fox, which recalls their former name; the sign of Cassassinamon,
the first leader of the Pequot to arise after the devastating attack by
John Mason against the Pequot's fort in Mystic, Connecticut, in
1637, which nearly wiped out the tribe; and the tree and rocky knoll
represent "Mashantucket, the much wooded land" in Ledyard, given
as a reservation to the remnants of the tribe in 1667.

The outlook for the future of the people of the Mashantucket
Pequot is to become more self-sufficient and to be able to provide
housing, jobs, and services so the people can come back to the reservation to live and bring back their traditions that have been lost.

Mohegan
27 Church Lane
Uncasville, CT 06382

Mohegan (from Maingan, "wolf")

Visitor Information: The Mohegan Indian Fort and Indian Cemetery
are on Highway 32 in Fort Shantock State Park four miles south of
Norwich, Connecticut.

The Mohegan belong to the Algonquian language group. They lived
along the Thames River, Connecticut, where descendants still
remain today. The Mohegan were closely associated with the Pequot,
but in the Pequot War of 1637, Uncas, the Mohegan chief, sided with
the English settlers against the Pequot chief, Sassacus, his father-in-
law. Uncas also aided the colonists in King Philip's war. As settlements encroached, some Mohegan joined the Scaticook. In 1788, a
large group joined with the Brotherton Indians in New York.

Paucatuck Pequot
935 Lantern Hill Road, RFD 7
Ledyard, CT 06339

Pawcatuck (the village name)
Pequot (Paquatauog, "destroyers")

The Pequot are in the Algonquian language group. They lived in Connecticut, east of the Connecticut River. In the Pequot War of 1637, Uncas of the Mohegan revolted against his father-in-law, Sassacus of the Pequot, and joined the English settlers. Captains John Mason and John Underhill led the attack on Fort Mystic, in which 600 Pequot were murdered.

Schaghticoke
% The Chamber of Commerce
Bristol, CT 06010

P ska tikuk ("at the river fork")

The Schaghticoke are in the process of reorganizing.

DELAWARE

Nanticoke
Route 4, Box 170B
Millsboro, DE 19966
(302) 945-7022 or 945-3400

Nanticoke (from Nentego, variation of Delaware Unechtgo, Unalachtgo, "tidewater people")

Public Ceremony or Powwow Dates: The powwow is held the weekend after Labor Day Monday.

Visitor Information: The museum is open all year, Tuesday, Wednesday, and Thursday, 9:00 a.m. to 4:00 p.m., and Saturday, noon to 4:00 p.m.

This tribe is connected linguistically and ethnically with the Delaware and the Conoy.
  For more information, see Oklahoma, Delaware.

MAINE

Houlton Maliseet
Route 3, Box 450
Houlton, ME 04730
(207) 532-4273
Fax (207) 532-2660

Malecite (Malisit, "broken talkers")
(Mahnesheets, "slow tongues")

Location: The tribal office is in Houlton.

Public Ceremony or Powwow Dates: Traditional dancing is done on occasion at Tobique and Kingsclear, New Brunswick.

Art Forms: Ash basketry is produced for sale. The tribal office can help with names and places.

Visitor Information: The Maliseet of Maine are related to the neighboring Passamaquoddy tribe. The Passamaquoddy-Maliseet Bilingual Program is trying to preserve the culture and educate the young people.

The Malecite belong to the Abenaki division of the Algonquian group. Their closest linguistic affinity is with the Passamaquoddy; the language of the two is almost identical. In 1884, they numbered 767, of whom 584 were in New Brunswick and the others in Quebec province. According to the 1904 report of Canadian Indian Affairs, their number was 805, 702 in New Brunswick and 103 in Quebec province.

Aroostook Band of Micmac Indians
P.O. Box 772
Presque Isle, ME 04769
(207) 764-1972
Fax (207) 764-7667

These people were recognized by the Bureau of Indian Affairs on 26 November 1991.

Passamaquoddy of Maine
Indian Township Reservation
P.O. Box 301
Princeton, ME 04668
(207) 796-2301
Fax (207) 796-5256

Pleasant Point Passamaquoddy
P.O. Box 343
Perry, ME 04667
(207) 853-2600
Fax (207) 853-6039

Peskedemakddi ("plenty of pollock")

Location: The tribal offices can be located by calling their respective numbers listed above.

Public Ceremony or Powwow Dates: There are still celebrations today which are traditional Passamaquoddy. The Ceremonial Day on the reservation is held between Perry and Eastport, Maine. The reservation is about two miles from Perry, five miles before Eastport. Call (207) 853-2551 for information on dates and times.

Art Forms: The artisans of the tribe still do the traditional splint and sweetgrass baskets.

Visitor Information: The Ceremonial Day Celebration should not be missed. Generally held on August 1, it features canoe races, a pageant that shows the history of the Passamaquoddy, traditional dancing and singing, the chiefs' welcome dance, the greeting dance, the peace pipe ceremonial, and social dances.
   The Indian Township Passamaquoddy also sponsor an Indian pageant in the summer. Be sure to call their tribal office for dates and times.

The Passamaquoddy belong to the Abnaki Confederacy, but they speak nearly the same dialect as the Malecite. They formerly occupied all the region around Passamaquoddy Bay and on the St. Croix River and Schoodic Lake, on the boundary between Maine and New Brunswick. Their principal village was Gunasquamekook, on the site of St. Andrews, New Brunswick. They were restricted by the pressure of the white settlements and in 1866 were settled chiefly at Sebaik, near Perry, on the south side of the bay, and on Lewis Island. They were estimated at about 150 in 1726, 130 in 1804, 379 in 1825, and from 400 to 500 in 1859.

Penobscot
Community Building-Indian Island
Old Town, ME 04468
(207) 827-7776
Fax (207) 827-6042

Penobscot, derived from Pannawanbskek, "it forks on the white rocks," or Penaubsket, "it flows on rocks"; the name applied directly to the falls at Old Town, but it has also been rendered "rock land" from *penops* (*penopsc*), "rock," and *cot* (*ot*), applied to the bluff at the mouth of the river near Castine. The aboriginal form is Penobskat, "plenty stones."

Location: The tribe is located on the river at Indian Island just north of the bridge from Old Town.

Public Ceremony or Powwow Dates: Call the tribal office for dates and times of their annual pageant.

Art Forms: The arts and crafts stores on the island have baskets, moccasins, quill work, beadwork, fish spears, carved canes, bows, war clubs, and other items.

Visitor Information: The museum is open weekdays from noon to 4:00 p.m. and contains exhibits on traditional arts of the Penobscot. The museum telephone number is (207) 827-6544.

The Penobscot are in the Algonquian language group. They are closely related to the Abnaki and Passamaquoddy and lived near Penobscot Bay and Penobscot River, Maine. The Penobscot fought against the French until 1749, when peace was made. The Penobscot and Passamaquoddy tribes send a delegate to the Maine legislature.

MASSACHUSETTS

Nipmuck
Hassanamico Indian Reservation
Grafton, MA 01519

Nipmuc (from Nipamaug, "freshwater fishing place")

Location: The Longhouse Museum, Hassanamico Indian Reservation, is located in Grafton. Their displays relate to the Nipmuck Nation.

The New England missionaries had seven villages of Christian converts among the Nipmuck in 1674. But on the outbreak of King Philip's war in the next year, almost all of them joined the hostile tribes and at its close fled to Canada or westward to the Mahican and other tribes on the Hudson. The Nipmuck are in the Algonquian language group.

Wampanoag of Gay Head (Aquinnah)
State Road, RFD Box 137
Gay Head, MA 02535
(508) 645-9265
Fax (508) 645-3790

Wampanoag ("eastern people")

Location: The people of the Wampanoag still live in this area.

Art Forms: The artisans of the tribe make pottery in colorful styles. Shops on the island have their work for sale.

This is one of the principal tribes of New England. Their proper territory appears to have been the peninsula on the east shore of Narragansett Bay now included in Bristol County, Rhode Island, and the adjacent parts in Bristol County, Massachusetts. The Wampanoag chiefs ruled all the country extending east from Narragansett Bay and the Pawtucket River to the Atlantic coast, including the islands of Nantucket and Martha's Vineyard. The Nauset of Cape Cod and the Saconnet near Compton, Rhode Island, although belonging to the group, seem to have been somewhat independent. Before the invading pilgrims, explorers visited the region and provoked the natives by bad treatment. Because of this, Champlain found those of Cape Cod unfriendly. In 1620, there were about 30 villages. They were probably more numerous before the great pestilence of 1617, which nearly depopulated the whole southern New England coast.

Their chief was Massasoit, who made a treaty of friendship with the colonists, which he faithfully observed until his death, when he was succeeded by his son, known to the English as King Philip. The bad treatment by non-Indians and their encroachment on the lands of the Indians led this chief, then the head of 500 warriors of his own tribe, to join with all the Indians from the Merrimac River to the Thames for the purpose of driving out or exterminating the non-Indians. The war, which began in 1675 and lasted two years, was the most destructive in the history of New England and was most disastrous to the Indians. Philip and the leading chiefs were killed, the Wampanoag and Narragansett were practically exterminated, and the survivors fled to the interior tribes. Many of those who surrendered were sold into slavery, and others joined the various Praying villages in southern Massachusetts. The greater part of the Wampanoag who remained in the country joined the Saconnet. The Indians of Cape Cod and Martha's Vineyard generally sided with the non-Indians and refused to join Philip in his war against them.

MICHIGAN

Bay Mills Ojibwa
Route 1, Box 313
Brimley, MI 49715
(906) 248-3241
Fax (906) 248-3283

Ojibwa ("to roast till puckered up," referring to the puckered seam on their moccasins; from Ojib "to pucker up," Ub-way "to roast")

The Ojibwa is one of the largest tribes north of Mexico. Their range was formerly along both shores of Lake Huron and Lake Superior, extending across Minnesota to the Turtle Mountains, North Dakota.
    For more information, see Minnesota, Ojibwa.

Grand Traverse Band of Ottawa and Chippewa
2605 NW Bayshore Drive
Suttons Bay, MI 49682
(616) 271-3538
Fax (616) 271-4861

The Ottawa and Chippewa are two closely related Algonquian peoples who originally occupied an area bordering on Lakes Superior, Michigan, and Huron. The upper part of Michigan's Lower Peninsula, around L'Arbre Croche, north of the Grand Traverse area, became a main seat of the Ottawa by the 1700s. Ottawa were definitely living at Grand Traverse Bay by 1740. Chippewa and possibly a few Ottawa were living in the area before that.

Hannahville Ojibwa
N14911 Hannahville Boulevard Road
Wilson, MI 49896-9728
(906) 466-2342
Fax (906) 466-2933

Keweenaw Bay Ojibwa
Center Building
Route 1, Box 45
Baraga, MI 49908
(906) 353-6623
Fax (906) 353-7540

Ojibwa

For more information, see Minnesota, Ojibwa.

LacVieux Desert Band of Chippewa
P.O. Box 249 — Choate Road
Watersmeet, MI 49969
(906) 358-4577 or 358-4578 or 358-4579
Fax (906) 358-4785

Saginaw Chippewa
7070 East Broadway Road
Mt. Pleasant, MI 48858
(517) 772-5700
Fax (517) 772-3508

Ojibwa

This Chippewa village is situated near Saginaw, Michigan. It was first occupied by the Sauk and when deserted by that tribe, it was settled by a band of Ottawa and Chippewa, known as Saginaw, who continued to live there until 1837, when they removed beyond the Mississippi. "Saginaw" was also officially employed to designate all the Chippewa of eastern lower Michigan from Thunder Bay southward.
    For more information, see Minnesota, Ojibwa.

Sault Ste. Marie Chippewa
206 Greenough Street
Sault Ste. Marie, MI 49783
(906) 635-6050
Fax (906) 632-0741

Ojibwa

For more information, see Minnesota, Ojibwa.

NEW YORK

Cayuga
P.O. Box 11
Versailles, NY 14168
(716) 532-4847
Fax (716) 532-5417

Kwenio gwe n ("the place where locusts were taken out")

Visitor Information: The Iroquois, or Six Nations, comprise the Cayuga, Mohawk, Oneida, Onondaga, Seneca, and Tuscarora tribes. These six nations joined together centuries ago and formed the well-known Iroquois Confederacy. Our U.S. Constitution was modeled after the organization of this unit. The Iroquois have done well to maintain their culture, arts, dances and songs, and spirituality within this encroaching society. Today, people from this confederacy live in New York, Wisconsin, Oklahoma, Ontario, and Quebec. They still hold special events, and there are several reconstructed villages, culture centers, and museums devoted to Iroquoian culture.

This tribe of the Iroquois Confederacy formerly occupied the shores of Cayuga Lake, New York. Its local council was composed of four clan phratries, and this form became the pattern, tradition says, of that of the confederation of the Five Nations of the Iroquois, in which the Cayuga had ten delegates. (With the later addition of the Tuscarora, it became the Six Nations.) In 1660, they were estimated to number 1,500, and in 1778, 1,100. At the beginning of the American Revolution, a large part of the tribe moved to Canada and never returned, while the rest of the people were scattered among the other tribes of the confederacy. Soon after the revolution, the latter sold their lands in New York; some went to Ohio, where they joined other Iroquois and became known as the Seneca of the Sandusky. These subsequently moved to Indian Territory. Others joined the Oneida in Wisconsin; 175 joined the Iroquois in New York; and the majority, numbering 700 or 800, moved to the Grand River Reservation in Ontario.

Iroquois of Cobleskill, Fonda, and Hunter, New York

Visitor Information: All the above towns in New York have interesting Iroquois Indian events. The annual Iroquois Indian Festival is held Labor Day weekend at the State University of New York in Cobleskill. Authentic Iroquois dancing, art exhibits, food, games, and more, are presented.

The Kateri Indian Festival in Fonda and the Mountain Eagle Indian Festival in Hunter are also events not to be missed. Call the Schoharie Museum of the Iroquois at (518) 296-8949, or write to them at Box 158, Schoharie, NY 12157, for more information.

For more information, see Oklahoma, Seneca-Cayuga.

Oneida of New York
101 Canal Street
Canastoga, NY 13032
(315) 697-8251
Fax (315) 697-8259

Oneida (Anglicized compressed form of the common Iroquois term *tiionen iote,* "a boulder standing up")

Visitor Information: See New York, Cayuga Nation.

This tribe of the Iroquois Confederacy formerly occupied the country south of Oneida Lake, New York. According to tradition, the Oneida was the second tribe to accept the proposition of Dekanawida and Hiawatha to form a defensive and offensive league of all the tribes of men for the promotion of mutual welfare and security. Like the Mohawk, the Oneida have only three clans, the Turtle, the Wolf, and the Bear.

For more information, see Oklahoma, Seneca-Cayuga.

Onondaga
RR 1, Box 270A
Nedrow, NY 13120
(315) 469-8507

Onondaga

Visitor Information: See New York, Cayuga Nation.

This is the former chief Onondaga town of central New York, whose site and name were shifted from time to time and from place to place. Within its limits formerly lay the unquenched brands of the Great Council Fire of the League of the Iroquois.
For more information, see Oklahoma, Seneca-Cayuga.

Seneca
Cattaragus Reservation
1490 Route 438
Irving, NY 14081
(716) 532-4900
Fax (716) 532-9132

Seneca ("place of the stone," the Anglicized form of the Dutch enunciation of the Mohegan rendering of the Iroquoian *Oneniute a ka,* and with a different ethnic suffix, *Oneniute ron non,* meaning "people of the standing rock")

Visitor Information: See New York, Cayuga Nation.

This is a prominent and influential tribe of the Iroquois. When first known, they occupied that part of western New York between Seneca Lake and the Geneva River. They had their council fire at Tsonontowan, near Naples, in Ontario County.
For more information, see Oklahoma, Seneca-Cayuga.

Shinnecock
% The Chamber of Commerce
Southampton, NY 11968
(516) 283-9266

Shinnecock

Location: The people of Shinnecock welcome you to Long Island, New York.

Public Ceremony or Powwow Dates: The powwow is held during Labor Day weekend.

Art Forms: Traditional arts and crafts from native people all over the east are featured at the powwow.

Visitor Information: The Shinnecock Community Center is raising funds to benefit the tribe and the church.

Seneca Iroquois National Museum
Broad Street Extension
Salamanca, NY 14779
(716) 945-1738

Location: This museum is located on the Allegany Indian Reservation and shows modern as well as traditional art. The museum shop has horn rattles, corn husk dolls, baskets, and other traditional arts and crafts for sale. Many displays of wampum belts, clothing, games, and masks are shown for informative purposes. The museum is owned and operated by the Seneca Indian Nation.

For more information, see Oklahoma, Seneca-Cayuga.

St. Regis Mohawk Akwesasne
Community Building
Hogansburg, NY 13655
(518) 358-2272
Fax (518) 358-3203

Akwesasne ("land where the partridge drums")

Location: The reservation straddles New York, Ontario, and Quebec.

Visitor Information: See New York, Cayuga Nation.

This is the most easterly tribe of the Iroquois Confederacy, and they called themselves Kaniengehage, "people of the place of the flint."
For more information, see Oklahoma, Seneca-Cayuga.

Tonawanda Band of Seneca
7027 Meadville Road
Basom, NY 14013
(716) 542-4244
Fax (716) 542-9692

Tonawanda ("confluent stream")

Visitor Information: See New York, Cayuga Nation.

This is a Seneca settlement on Tonawanda Creek in Niagara County, New York. In 1890, there were 517 Seneca and a few Iroquois on the reservation.
For more information, see Oklahoma, Seneca-Cayuga.

Tuscarora
5616 Walmore Road
Lewiston, NY 14092
(716) 297-4990

Skaru ren ("hemp gatherers," referring to *Apocynum cannabinum,* or Indian hemp, a plant of many uses among the Carolina Tuscarora)

Visitor Information: See New York, Cayuga Nation.

The Tuscarora are an important confederation of tribes, speaking languages related to those of the Iroquoian linguistic group. When first encountered by non-Indians, they lived on the Roanoke, Neuse, Taw, and Pamlico rivers, in North Carolina. The evidence drawn from writers contemporary with them, confirmed in part by tradition, makes it evident that the Tuscarora league was composed of at least three tribal constituent members, each bearing an independent and exclusive name. The names of these component members still survive in the traditions of the Tuscarora now living in western New York and southern Ontario, Canada.
For more information, see Oklahoma, Seneca-Cayuga

RHODE ISLAND

Narragansett
P.O. Box 268
Charlestown, RI 02813
(401) 364-1100 or 1-800-243-6278
Fax (401) 364-1104

People of the Small Bay

Location: The Narragansett and other Algonquin people can be found in Charlestown.

Public Ceremony or Powwow Dates: The powwow and annual meeting of the tribe is in August. Call for dates and times.

Visitor Information: The *Eagle Wing Press* is a good Indian events newspaper. You can subscribe by writing to P.O. Box 579, Naugatuck, CT 06770. Events of this area will be listed in the paper.

The Narragansett are an Algonquian group and were formerly one of the leading tribes of New England. They occupied Rhode Island west of Narragansett Bay, including the Niantic Territory, from Providence River on the northeast to Pawcatuck River on the southwest. On the northwest, they claimed control over a part of the country of the Coweset and Nipmuck, and on the southwest, they claimed by conquest of the Pequot a strip extending to the Connecticut line. In 1633, they lost 700 to smallpox, but in 1675, they could still muster 5,000 fighting men.

VIRGINIA

Chickahominy
% The Chamber of Commerce
Providence Forge, VA 23140

K'chick-aham-min-nough ("hominy people")

Visitor Information: The Chickahominy tribe holds a fall festival with many activities including dancing.

The state, not the federal government, has jurisdiction over Indian reservations in Virginia.

Mattaponi
RFD 1, Box 667
West Point, VA 23181
(804) 769-2229

Mattapony

Location: The museum is about thirteen miles west of West Point on Highway 30.

Public Ceremony or Powwow Dates: Call the tribal office for details on public ceremonies. Traditional dances are done within the membership of the tribe, and on occasion the public will be invited.

Art Forms: Traditional arts and crafts including pottery, beadwork, and miniatures are sold by the museum.

Pamunkey
Box 217-AA
King William, VA 23086

Pamunkey (from *pam,* "sloping," "slanting"; *anki,* "hill," or "rising upland," referring to a tract of land in what is now King William County, Virginia, beginning at the junction of the Pamunkey and Mattapony rivers)

WISCONSIN

Bad River Ojibwa
P.O. Box 39
Odanah, WI 54861
(715) 682-7111
Fax (715) 682-7118

Ojibwa ("to roast until puckered up, referring to the puckered seam on their moccasins; from Ojib "to pucker up," Ub-way, "to roast")

Location: The reservation is fourteen miles east of Ashland on U.S. Highway 2.

Public Ceremony or Powwow Dates: The Manomin (wild rice) Celebration is usually the weekend before Labor Day. There are feasting, dancing, and activities traditional to the Ojibwa.

Visitor Information: The history center shows the arts and crafts of this band of the Ojibwa.

The Ojibwa are one of the largest tribes north of Mexico. Their range was formerly along both shores of Lake Huron and Lake Superior, extending across Minnesota to the Turtle Mountains, North Dakota.

For more information, see North, Minnesota.

Forest County Potawatomi
P.O. Box 340
Crandon, WI 54520
(715) 478-2903
Fax (715) 478-5280

Potawatomi (Potawatamink or Potawaganink, "people of the fire")

In 1616, written record places the Potawatomi on the west shores of Lake Huron. The Potawatomi, Chippewa, and Ottawa were origi-nally one people. About 1838, the tribe was moved south toward Indian Territory. The Oklahoma Potawatomi recall this event as the "Trail of Death" due to the trail of ones lost on the way. A few remained in their homeland. This is one of those bands.

For more information, see Kansas, Prairie Band Potawatomi; Oklahoma, Citizen Band.

Lac Courte Oreilles Ojibwa
Route 2, Box 2700
Hayward, WI 54843
(715) 634-8934
Fax (715) 634-4797

Ojibwa

Public Ceremony or Powwow Dates: The Honor the Earth Powwow is held here in July. Call the tribal office for dates and times.

Visitor Information: The Ojibwa Indian Museum, Historyland, is on Highway 27 and is open during the summer.

This band of Ojibwa received their name from the lake on which they lived, at the headwaters of Chippewa River, in Sawyer County, Wisconsin. In 1852, they formed a part of the Betonukeengainubejig division of the Chippewa, and in 1854, they were assigned a reservation. In 1905, they were officially reported to number 1,214, to whom lands had been allotted in severalty.

For more information, see Minnesota, Ojibwa.

Lac du Flambeau Ojibwa
P.O. Box 67
Lac du Flambeau, WI 54538
(715) 588-3303
Fax (715) 588-7930

Ojibwa

Location: The tribal office is on Little Pine Street Road in Lac du Flambeau.

Public Ceremony or Powwow Dates: The Indian Bowl shows Indian dancing during July and August on Tuesday nights at 8:30. Drive to the lakeshore in the center of the reservation. Wonderful drumming and singing can be heard there. The annual Bear River Powwow is in July. Call the tribal office for dates and times.

Visitor Information: To see Ojibwa Indian exhibits, visit the Luc du Flambeau Chippewa Museum and Cultural Center. Their telephone number is (715) 588-3333.

For more information, see Minnesota, Ojibwa.

Menominee of Wisconsin
P.O. Box 910
Keshena, WI 54135-0910
(715) 799-5100
Fax (715) 799-4525

O-Maeh-No-Min-Ni-Wuk

Location: The reservation is located seven miles north of Shawano, Wisconsin, which is in the northeast part of the state.

Public Ceremony or Powwow Dates: The Land of the Menominee Powwow is held annually on the first weekend in August. It is considered one of the main cultural events of the year in the Midwest. No drugs or alcohol are allowed on the powwow grounds. The powwow is held in the Woodland Bowl, which is set amid giant white pines.

Art Forms: You can find embroidery work on clothing and all other forms of art of Eastern Woodland culture.

Visitor Information: Shawano, Wisconsin, provides a fine assortment of retail outlets, hotels/motels, and restaurants.

The reservation has two privately owned gift shops that sell Menominee-made crafts as well as other genuine Native American crafts. The Menominee Reservation is the home of one of the largest and most modern sawmills in the Midwest, Menominee Tribal Enterprises, Inc. There are also two privately owned raft rental outlets along the Wolf River. There is no hunting, fishing, or food gathering allowed by any nontribal members. The tribe also operates a bingo hall and gaming casino.

Early reservation days for the Menominee do not afford a pleasant story to relate. The people survived under the most trying conditions. Sickness, winters that were hard with deep snow and below-freezing temperatures, moving here and there to fuel their bodies with food, all contributed to the misery the people endured. The Menominee are proud to have survived. Each spring, those who were lucky enough to live through the winter greeted one another with, "We made it to another spring."

Summers were a little easier, but still each family worked. They planted large gardens, picked berries, and canned everything. Each family had a root cellar where they stored food to be used in the winter months. A government warehouse in Keshena issued rations (coffee, sugar, tea, and salt pork) to the elderly once a month.

Transportation, along with mail delivery, was by horse and buggy and in winter by sleigh and cutter. Roads were cleared, and ruts were made by the lumber wagons. When it rained, travel was slow, but teams of horses were sure and dependable.

There was a hospital in Keshena, but most people treated themselves with herbs, which were gathered in the fall of the year.

Education was furnished by the Franciscan Fathers and the St. Joseph Sisters in Keshena and by the Franciscan Sisters in Neopit. A government school in Keshena and a day school in Neopit provided education for those who did not want to attend a Christian school. Boys and girls also went to Tomah Indian School in Wisconsin, Flandreau Indian School in South Dakota, Pipestone Indian School in Minnesota, and Haskell Institute in Kansas where the Menominee pupils learned the three Rs and a trade.

For recreation, the Menominee played baseball and lacrosse. In the winter they ice-skated and sleighed. Those who did not have sleds made staves from hardwood barrels and used them on steep hills. Once a year, the Bureau of Indian Affairs Agency put on a fair. A merry-go-round pulled by a tractor was the only entertainment provided. The fair was mostly a time for visiting. Pony races and baseball games took up most of the afternoon.

Perhaps the people would have preferred the old life. Maybe they were slow in their endeavors, but the Menominee people have always taken their time deciding their way of life. Again today, the Menominee have to think of their young people's education. Maybe they will prefer the Waupiskayit life (white way of life) instead of going back to the blanket.

The Menominee are an Algonquian-speaking tribe (meaning wild rice gatherers) and are Wisconsin's oldest continuing residents. The original Menominee land once stretched across 9.5 million acres from the Great Lakes to the Mississippi River. A century before the Menominee were visited by Nicolet, who reached Wisconsin in 1634, the continent had already been visited by Spaniards from the south, European fishermen from the east, and French explorers and fur traders from the St. Lawrence area. The dress of Menominee men was breechclout and leggings, and blouses and skirts were worn by the women. Ornamentation consisted of quills, plant and earth colors, and beads of natural materials. Footwear consisted of soft-soled moccasins.

The Menominee lived by hunting, fishing, and gathering. The abundant wild rice was a staple food, augmented by corn, beans, and squash grown in small gardens. Part of the food supply was dried in the sun for winter use. Boiling and roasting were common methods of cooking. The land that now comprises the Menominee Reservation established by the 1854 Treaty is densely forested, dotted with clear streams, lakes, rivers, and waterfalls and rich in four kinds of resources: land, timber, water, and wildlife. There are 234,000 acres of the finest old stands of hardwood, virgin pine, and hemlock in the Great Lakes states. All of Wisconsin's timber species grow on the reservation — approximately 46 varieties of trees. The

Wolf River is the reservation's largest waterway, winding its way through 59 miles of Menominee land.

Menominee land holdings, once much more extensive, were chipped away through numerous government treaties and bargaining with the tribe. Emigrant bands of Stockbridge-Munsee and Oneida Indians from the east were the recipients of over one-half million acres of Menominee land.

"We accepted our present reservation when it was considered to be of no value by our white friends. All we ask now is that we are permitted to keep it as a home." Chief Neopit of the Menominee said these words in 1882.

This is a story about Kaku'ene, the Jumper, and the origin of tobacco. One day Ma'nabush passed by a high mountain and he detected a delightful odor coming from a crevice in the cliffs. Going to the mouth of the cavern he followed the passage that led into the very center of the mountain, where he found a large chamber occupied by a giant known as the keeper of tobacco.

The giant asked him gruffly what he wanted. Ma'nabush replied that he had come for tobacco. The giant replied that the ma'nidos had already been there for their annual smoke.

Ma'nabush saw there were many bags filled with tobacco in the cavern. He snatched one of these and darted out, pursued by the irate giant. Ma'nabush ran to the mountaintop and leaped from peak to peak with the giant in pursuit. When Ma'nabush reached a high peak, he dropped flat on the rocks. The giant leaped over him and fell into the chasm below. The giant was badly bruised, but he struggled up the face of the cliff where he hung.

Ma'nabush grasped the giant and, drawing him upward, dashed him to the ground and said, "For your meanness you shall become Kaku'ene (the Jumper Grasshopper) and you shall be known by your stained mouth. You shall become the pest of those who raise tobacco."

Then Ma'nabush took the tobacco and divided it among his brothers. He gave each some of the seed that they might never be without this plant for their use and enjoyment.

Throughout their history animals have played an important role in the lives of the people. During early times, they served as food, clothing, tools, and shelter. Early Menominee kinship divisions were based on five major totemic groups, each with subgroups named for various animals and birds. These animals were also the main subjects of each clan's creation myth.

When Menominee came in contact with non-Indians and other Indians, they depended on animal pelts as a main item of trade. Without these animals, early encounters with other people might have been more hostile. Even today, as noted in their legends, the Menominee hold in high respect the wildlife on their reservation.

Originally, temporary Menominee dwellings were made of saplings bent to form a dome-shaped structure covered with bark or mats. These dwellings were later replaced by log houses. Some of them are still standing today. The early 1900s saw Menominee progressing toward the use of modern homes as they began to build with lumber from the tribal sawmill. Recently, monies have been allocated to renovate these homes and in some cases, build new ones. In the mid-1960s, the Department of Housing and Urban Development allocated funding to build 64 new homes on the reservation. In addition, there are Menominee training programs on the reservation such as the Home Improvement Program and the Indian Technical Assistance Center where trainees are provided with valuable on-the-job training and marketable skills in carpentry, masonry, and electrical and plumbing trades in connection with home renovation and construction.

Oneida of Wisconsin
P.O. Box 365
Oneida, WI 54155-0365
(414) 869-2214
Fax (414) 869-2194

Oneida (Anglicized compressed form of the common Iroquois term *tiionen iote*, "a boulder standing up")

Location: The Oneida Business Committee, Administrative Offices, and tribal school are at the Norbert Hill Center, 3000 Seminary Road (located at the corner of Highway 54 and Seminary Road, just west of Green Bay, Wisconsin).

Public Ceremony or Powwow Dates: The annual powwow is held during the 4th of July weekend. Call tribal communications for dates and times.

Art forms: Crafts are sold at the annual powwow and also at the Oneida Nation Museum.

Visitor Information: The Oneida Nation Museum is 7 miles west of the Green Bay city limits, on the corner of E and EE roads. Museum hours are Monday through Friday 9:00 a.m. to 5:00 p.m. and Saturday and Sunday 10:00 a.m. to 2:00 p.m. Telephone: (414) 869-2768. The museum has one of the largest ongoing exhibitions of Oneida history and artifacts in the world and is taking steps toward becoming the world center and repository of Oneida heritage.

Tribal enterprises include bingo, LottOneida, tobacco outlets, a nursing home, a gift shop, printing facilities, and three convenience stores. The largest commercial venture of the tribe is the 202-room, premium-quality hotel, the Radisson Inn Green Bay. It is located in a wooded site directly across from Green Bay's Austin Straubel Airport. The newest venture of the tribe is the Oneida Research and Technology Center (ORTEC).

The Oneida tribe is a member of the Iroquois Confederacy or Five Nations, which formed in the 1500s. The Iroquois League initially was composed of Mohawk, Oneida, Onondaga, Cayuga, and Seneca nations. In the early 1700s, the Tuscarora Nation became a member of what is now known as the Six Nation Confederacy. Iroquois homelands are located in central New York State.

During the colonial period (1600s), the Iroquois traded goods and established formal treaties with the colonists. In the mid-1770s, when conflicts arose between England and the colonists, the Iroquois chose to remain neutral. However, when the Revolutionary War broke out, the Oneida and Mohawk became involved. The Mohawk sided with the English. The Oneida supported the colonists, served in General Washington's army, and even supplied the troops with food when the Continental Congress failed to do so. In retribution, the Oneida suffered the loss of their homes, crops, and animals at the hands of other Iroquois after the Revolutionary War. Meanwhile, early land developers desired the Oneida homeland because it was choice farmland and it was in the area of the Erie Canal route. The Oneida were in a difficult situation. Their lands were gradually being lost through various land deals with land companies and treaties with the State of New York. Therefore, many Oneida chose to move to Wisconsin.

In the 1820s, Oneida settled along Duck Creek about 10 miles from the city of Green Bay. The original 5,000,000 acres of land purchased by the Oneida from the Menominee tribe in the 1820s was reduced to 65,000 acres by the U.S. government. This was done by a treaty with the Menominee, without the knowledge of the Oneida, in the 1830s. In 1838, the U.S. government formally signed a treaty recognizing the present boundaries of the Oneida Tribe of Indians of Wisconsin which encompasses the township of Oneida in Outagamie County and the township of Hobart in Brown County.

The traditional form of Oneida government deteriorated after the tribe settled in Wisconsin. In 1934, the Oneida formed a constitutional government under the Indian Reorganization Act and formed an elected government under the direction of the General Tribal Council. The tribal government struggled through the years. In the 1960s, after the passage of the Indian Self-Determination Act, the Oneida tribe began to grow economically.

Red Cliff Ojibwa
P.O. Box 529
Bayfield, WI 54814
(715) 779-3701
Fax (715) 779-3704

Ojibwa

Location: Three miles north of Bayfield on Highway 13 is the location of the Buffalo Arts Center, Red Cliff Cultural Institute, and Red Cliff Indian Reservation.

Public Ceremony or Powwow Dates: The annual powwow is in August or September. Check with the tribal office for exact dates and times.

Art Forms: Red Cliff Festival of the Arts and Crafts demonstrations vary from stone pipe making to birch bark canoe building. Bark baskets, beadwork, and other arts can be found in the museum shop.

Visitor Information: The Buffalo Arts Center shows the culture and the history of the Ojibwa people with emphasis on the Lake Superior Chippewa. The exhibits show traditional Ojibwa settings such as figures in full outfits around the drum. Others show the daily life of the people. May through September is the normal season. Call for times when the center is open.

For more information, see Minnesota, Ojibwa.

St. Croix Ojibwa
P.O. Box 287
Hertel, WI 54845
(715) 349-2195
Fax (715) 349-5768

Ojibwa

For more information, see Minnesota, Ojibwa.

Sokaogon Chippewa
Route 1, Box 625
Crandon, WI 54520
(715) 478-2604
Fax (715) 478-5275

Ojibwa

For more information, see Minnesota, Ojibwa.

Stockbridge-Munsee
N. 8478 Moh He Con Nuck Road
Bowler, WI 54416
(715) 793-4111
Fax (715) 793-4299

Stockbridge are known traditionally as Mahican ("wolf")
Munsee are a branch of the Delaware (Min-asin-ink, "at the place where stones are gathered together")

Location: The reservation is located west of Green Bay on Highway 29, through Shawano, to Bowler. When you see the turnoff on County Road J, you will find Bowler. Then take County Road J three miles to Mohheconnuck Road. Go 2 miles north on Mohheconnuck Road to the log tribal office.

Public Ceremony or Powwow Dates: The powwow is held in the summer. Call the tribal office for dates and times. The powwow takes place two miles north of the library on Mohheconnuck Road in the vicinity of the campground and picnic area along the Red River.

Chief Blackhawk, wife, and child, Winnebago, ca. 1899.
Photo by T. W. Ingersoll; Courtesy Museum of New Mexico, Neg. No. 91494

Art Forms: Baskets and other old forms of art are displayed in the museum.

Visitor Information: The museum and library hold a fund-raising auction the second Saturday in October. Also, the tribe operates a bingo parlor.

The Mahican are an Algonquian tribe that occupied both banks of the upper Hudson River, in New York, extending north almost to Lake Champlain.

The Munsee originally occupied the headwaters of Delaware River in New York, New Jersey, and Pennsylvania, extending south to the Lehigh River, and also held the west bank of the Hudson from the Catskill Mountains nearly to the New Jersey line. They had the Mahican and Wappinger on the north and east and the Delaware on the south and southeast and were regarded as the protecting barrier between the latter tribe and the Iroquois.

For more information, see Oklahoma, Delaware.

Wisconsin Winnebago
P.O. Box 667
Black River Falls, WI 54615
(715) 284-4915
Fax (715) 284-1760 (call tribe before you fax)

Winnebago (*winnipig*, "filthy water" [Chippewa]; *winipyagohagi*, "people of the filthy water" [Sauk and Fox])

Location: The Wisconsin Dells Stand Rock Ceremonials are located 4 miles north of the Wisconsin Dells on Stand Rock Road.

Public Ceremony or Powwow Dates: The Ceremonials are presented every night from mid-June through Labor Day and start about 8:45 p.m. The dancers and performers of the pageant are mostly Winnebago people.

Art Forms: Dance forms from various tribes are likely to be presented at the pageant.

Visitor Information: You can get to the pageant by boat. Call the tribal office for more information.

The Winnebago are in the Sioux language family. Early French explorers found them living south of Green Bay and inland to Lake Winnebago, Wisconsin. Later the Winnebago moved to the Fox, Wisconsin, and Rock rivers. They fought on the side of the British in the War of 1812. By treaties of 1825 and 1832, they went to a reservation in Iowa. Later, they were moved to Minnesota and then again to the Omaha reservation.

For more information, see Nebraska, Winnebago.

NORTHWEST

WASHINGTON: Chehalis / Colville / Hoh / Klallam / Kalispel /
Lower Elwha / Lummi / Makah / Muckleshoot / Nisqually / Nooksack /
Port Gamble / Puyallup / Quileute /
Quinault / Tulalip / Sauk-Suiattle /
Shoalwater Bay / Skokomish /
Spokane / Squaxin / Stillaguamish /
Suquamish / Swinomish /
Upper Skagit and Yakima

OREGON: Burns-Paiute / Coos,
Lower Umpqua and Siuslaw /
Grande Ronde / Umpqua Cow Creek /
Klamath / Siletz / Umatilla /
Warm Springs

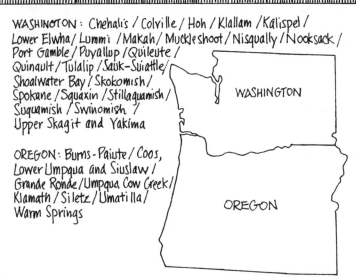

The Northwest of the continental United States lies in, and west of, that place where the great Rocky Mountains rise up out of the great water, the Pacific Ocean. It is the place of the great high trees. There are mysterious fogs and clouds over the inlets of water that invade the edge of the land and small islands jut up out of the great water to form mazes off the shore. And the mountains that are inland are snow-capped and high between deserts, trees, and lakes fed by fast-moving, crystal-clear streams.

This is the land of the People of the Totem and Longhouse and Potlatch. They are descendants of a great and proud culture that lived, in the rugged areas where land meets water, in tune with their environment and with respect for the whole of Creation.

The art of the Northwest People was, and is, steeped in symbolism, as all Indian art is. The symbol is not a mere sign for the visual satisfaction of the eye but a disguise, a mask, within which a living agent lives. It is a talisman, a charm, a key, and a revelation incorporating the wisdom of being the original inhabitants of the wilderness. Only the original people have the "medicine power" to incorporate innocence with significance into their art forms. It is through this naive, innocent, primitive art form that the Indian of the Northwest, as with all Indian people, both acts and speaks and even realizes to himself the justification of his existence. When the Northwest People masked themselves, they became no longer the natural man. They became mythic beings, embodied powers, with emblems expressing whole groups of kinships—with the animal kind, with the thunder and lightning, with the spirits of our ancestors—so that they became sacred entities, closer in touch with the Creator.

So, when we must consider that each and every movement and act was in the name of art, then all existence was in the name of the Creation and for the good of all living things. The masks of the ceremonials of the people of the Northwest act out the reality of the necessity of ceremony and project the realization that with ceremony we can become in tune with the whole of all living things and we can learn the respect necessary for the survival of the race of man in the universe. How can we respect all life without ceremony?

When you obtain an art object such as a basket or carving from the People of the Northwest, remember that the spirit of the ancestors and the spirit of the artist are embodied within it. They are inseparable and always alive. The People of the Northwest have always been there. Ask the elders of the people; they know.

Join with these tribes to honor their ancestors and to honor our Creator, our Mother Earth, our Moon, our Sun, and the whole of all living things in the whole of all Creation. You will find that it is good. It is very, very good.

Aho . . .

These shores will swarm with the invisible dead of my tribe.
—Chief Seattle
(Suquamish)
(Duwamish)

OREGON

Burns-Paiute
HC71, 100 Pa' Si' go Street
Burns, OR 97720-9303
(503) 573-2088
Fax (503) 573-2323

The Paiute people lived from the gifts the Creator provided from the fish of the lakes, jackrabbits and small game of the sage plains and mountains, and from piñon nuts and other seeds, which they grind into flour for bread. Their ordinary dwelling is the wikiup, or small rounded hut of tule rushes over a framework of poles, with the ground for a floor and the fire in the center, and almost entirely open at the top.

For more information, see Nevada, Paiute.

Confederated Coos, Lower Umpqua, and Siuslaw
455 So. 4th Street
Coos Bay, OR 97420-1570
(503) 267-5454
Fax (503) 269-1647

Coos
Umpqua
Siuslaw

Location: The tribal offices are located in Coos Bay.

Public Ceremony or Powwow Dates: The tribes continue with the salmon ceremonial traditions. Call the tribal office for dates and times.

Art Forms: Basketry has reached a particularly fine degree of quality with these native artisans.

The Confederated Tribes of Coos, Lower Umpqua, and Siuslaw Indians are the aboriginal inhabitants of the central and south-central coast of Oregon. Their homeland includes the estuaries of Coos Bay, Umpqua, and Siuslaw, a region of vast stands of forest and stretches of open beaches. The tribes, which have operated under a confederated government since the signing of the treaty of August 1855, possess a 6.1-acre reservation and tribal hall, erected for them by the Bureau of Indian Affairs in 1938 in Coos Bay, Oregon.

The Confederated Tribes were in a regular and continuous government to government relationship with the United States from 1853 until their termination by Congress in 1956. Initially, they were under the jurisdiction of the Umpqua subagency. In 1856, because of the Rogue River Indian War (in which they participated), the majority of the members of the Coos, Lower Umpqua, and Siuslaw Indians were removed from their homelands and held on a windswept spit at the mouth of the Umpqua River at Fort Umpqua.

Thus began the breakup of these large Indian families. If the women were married to non-Indians, they were allowed to remain in their homeland while their children and other Indian relatives were taken away. Some Indians hid from the soldiers who had been commissioned to lead the infamous march to Fort Umpqua. A feeling of great hopelessness settled on these people who had been forcibly removed from all that was familiar and dear to them.

In 1859, the Coos, Lower Umpqua, and Siuslaw Indians were moved from Fort Umpqua and taken to the Yachats Agency on the Siletz Reservation, where an effort was made to turn these gatherers into farmers. After clearing the land, the Indians were given simple farm tools and seed. After many of the people of these tribes died of starvation and ill treatment, the U.S. government decided to close the Yachats Agency and opened this part of the reservation to non-Indian settlement. The tribal members thus returned to their homelands only to find that this territory was settled by non-Indians, too. So the members of the Coos, Lower Umpqua, and Siuslaw tribes found themselves homeless. Again, these people were wanderers, settling wherever they could find a place.

Family, pride, homeland, and life-style were all taken away and/or changed for the members of these tribes. The subsequent feelings of low self-esteem and hopelessness set the stage for alcoholism and, later, drug addiction.

The road back was long and, indeed, seemed endless for the Coos, Lower Umpqua, and Siuslaw. Some members of these tribes left the area permanently. Others stayed and found menial employment as domestics or in the fields, as harvesters of cranberries, for example. The tribal members who stayed in their aboriginal homeland kept their sense of tribalism. They held monthly meetings and observed special celebrations throughout the years.

Then fell what appeared to many as the final blow. The federal government announced it had a new plan. It would "terminate" the Indians of western Oregon. All Indians in the area would be made American citizens. They would have all the "privileges" afforded non-Indians. They would be first-class citizens. The Indians did not fully understand that termination would deprive them of the few services they had been given because of their special status as Indians. There would be no more education in Indian boarding schools, no more Indian Health Service, no more reservations.

Some of the tribes in western Oregon approved of termination. The Confederated Tribes of Coos, Lower Umpqua, and Siuslaw, however, did not. Their protests were of no avail. In 1956, Congress passed Public Law 588, which became known as the "Termination Act." To the federal government, this meant that no Indians existed in western Oregon.

The aim of the termination act was to assimilate the Indian people into the "dominant society." It did not work. The people of the Confederated Tribes of Coos, Lower Umpqua, and Siuslaw still maintained their "Indian-ness." They continued to hold meetings and celebrations.

Early in the termination years, the tribes of western Oregon began to look for a way out of the travesty of termination. They learned that because Congress had "terminated" them, it would take an act of Congress to "restore" them if they were once again to become "federally recognized" tribes.

In 1981, buoyed by the award of a modest Campaign for Human Development (CHD) grant, the Confederated Tribes of Coos, Lower Umpqua, and Siuslaw Indians began in earnest the arduous trail leading to restoration. The restoration project was launched from donated office space in a private home with volunteer labor. There were no salaries or rents paid. All of the money from the CHD grant was used for telephone services and for essential trips to Washington, D.C.

Finally, on October 17, 1984, after setbacks, tears, frustration, and the supreme effort of tribal members, President Reagan signed Public Law 98-481, which became known as the "Restoration Act." The members of these tribes were once again "federally recognized" Indians.

With the restoration of the tribes in 1984, the relationship with the Bureau of Indian Affairs was reestablished. The tribal council began the implementation of education and housing programs. The tribal constitution was approved, and the tribes are electing council members again.

The tribal government, with aid from the Oregon Endowment for the Humanities, is involved in cultural preservation efforts. The tribe is active in providing services that include education, employment, housing, alcohol and drug counseling, and health care. Economic development plans will provide self-sufficiency.

Confederated Grande Ronde
9615 Grand Ronde Road
Grande Ronde, OR 97347-0038
(503) 879-5211
Fax (503) 879-5964

Visitor Information: The people of this reservation comprise several tribes. They were terminated as members of Indian tribes by the federal government in 1954. As of 1974, they have reorganized as a non-profit organization and are in the process of rebuilding an economy and rebuilding their feeling of tribal community.

In 1908, the tribes placed on this reservation were the Kalapuya, Clackamas, Cow Creek, Lakmiut, Mary's River, Molala, Nestucca, Rogue River, Santiam, Shasta, Tumwater, Umpqua, Wapato, and Yamhill.

Confederated Siletz of Oregon
P.O. Box 549
Siletz, OR 97380-0549
(503) 444-2513 or (503) 444-2532
Within Oregon 1-800-922-1399
Fax (503) 444-2307

Siletz

Location: The Confederated Tribes are located in the town of Siletz, approximately fifteen miles inland from the central Oregon coast town of Newport. The tribal center is located on Government Hill. The remaining reservation occupies small parcels of timberland scattered within Lincoln County.

Public Ceremony or Powwow Dates: The Nesika Illahee Powwow is held the second weekend in August of each year. Restoration Day is November 18 of each year, but sometimes the celebration is moved to the Saturday following the 18th for ease of attendance. Everyone is welcome. It is good to ask permission prior to taking pictures. No pictures are allowed during traditional ceremonies, for example, the Eagle Feather Ceremony.

Art Forms: You will find traditional design work in beading and basketry. Call the tribal office for details on where to purchase artwork.

Visitor Information: There are many motels, restaurants, and services located in the nearby town of Newport, Oregon.

The close proximity to the Pacific Ocean draws many people to the Newport area (15 miles away) each year. Several local events occur. The Siletz tribe is located among some of the best sportfishing rivers and streams for steelhead, salmon, and trout. The ocean provides opportunities for clam digging, crabbing, and ocean fishing.

The Siletz tribe is actually a confederation of tribes, comprised of 24 separate tribes and bands. A terminated tribe from 1954 to1977, the Siletz, through an act of Congress, was restored to federal recognition in 1977.

The Siletz Tribal Council established the Siletz Tribal Economic Development Corporation (STEDCO), which is responsible for economic development enterprises on and off the Siletz Reservation. Because the Siletz tribe only received approximately 3,600 acres of reservation land in 1980, most of which is timberland and not suitable for development or housing, an eight-county service area was established. Recently, the service area was increased to include eleven counties in the state of Oregon. STEDCO is currently working on building an evergreen management industry. They plan to market fern, salal, and other evergreen products.

Possible future development for the Siletz tribe includes a health clinic in Siletz to service both tribal and nontribal members, a minimall in the city of Siletz, and possibly, office buildings for rent.

Confederated Tribes of Warm Springs
P.O. Box C
Warm Springs, OR 97761-0078
(503) 553-1161
Fax (503) 553-1924

Des Chutes
John Day
Paiute
Tenino
Warm Springs (Tilkuni)
Wasco

Location: The reservation is located in north central Oregon.

Public Ceremony or Powwow Dates: The biggest powwow here is probably the one held in June, but there are dances during the Fourth of July also. The traditional Root Festival is held in mid-April. Call the tribal office for dates and times. Also, dances are held Sundays, May through October.

Art Forms: Some arts and crafts are sold during the celebrations. The gift shop at the Warm Springs Information Center is on Highway 26 at the east end of Warm Springs. The cradleboards, baskets, beadwork, feather work, and tule mats are all of good quality.

Visitor Information: You can rent tipis from the tribe at their nice campground. Also, visit the Kah-Nee-Tah Resort for swimming, hot springs, tennis, saunas, and other enjoyable activities.

Des Chutes: This Shahaptian group lived formerly on and around the Deschutes River, Oregon. The term probably included remnants of several tribes.

John Day: This Shahaptian tribe, speaking the Tenino language, formerly lived on John Day River, Oregon, and had their principal village four miles above the mouth. In 1909, there were 50 survivors of the tribe at Warm Springs, Oregon.

Paiute: See Nevada, Paiute.

Tenino: This Shahaptian tribe formerly occupied the valley of Des Chutes River, Oregon. The Tenino dialect was spoken on both sides of the Columbia from The Dalles to the mouth of the Umatilla. In 1855, they joined in the Wasco treaty and were placed on the Warm Springs Reservation, since which time they have usually been called Warm Springs Indians, a term embracing a number of tribes of other groups that were included in the treaty. In 1909, there were 30 survivors on this reservation.

Tilkuni (Warm Springs): This Shahaptian tribe is said to have spoken the Tenino language and to have claimed the territory between Tygh and Warm Springs rivers in Wasco County, Oregon. They were classed Warm Springs Indians by the U.S. government.

Wasco (from the Wasco word *wadalo*, "cup or small bowl of horn," the reference being to a cup-shaped rock a short distance from the main village of the tribe; from the tribal name Galasq!o, "those that belong to Wasco," or "those that have the cup"): This is a Chinookan tribe formerly living on the south side of the Columbia River, in the neighborhood of The Dalles, in Wasco County, Oregon. This tribe with the Wishram on the north side of the river were the easternmost branches of the Chinookan family. These two tribes were practically identical in language and culture, though they were removed to different reservations. On the north, east, and south they bordered the Shahaptian tribes; on the west, closely related Chinookan tribes (White Salmon and Hood River Indians, Chiluktkwa and Kwikwulit). In 1822, the population estimate was 900. About 200 joined in the Warm Springs Reservation treaty in 1855.

Coquille Umpqua
P. O. Box 1435
Coos Bay, OR 97420-0330
(503) 276-4587
Fax (503) 269-2573

Cow Creek Band of Umpqua
2400 Stewart Parkway, Suite 300
Roseburg, OR 97470-1563
(503) 672-9405
Fax (503) 673-0432

Umpqua

See Oregon, Confederated Tribes of Coos, Lower Umpqua, and Siuslaw Indians, for more information. This is the Nahankhuotana group of the Umpqua Indian tribe.

Klamath
Box 436
Chiloquin, OR 9762-0436
(503) 783-2219

1-800-524-9787
Fax (503) 783-2029
Klamath (possibly from Maklaks, the Lutuami term for Indians,
"people," "community," the encamped)

Location: The Klamath Indian Reservation is in southern Oregon,
north of Klamath Falls.

Public Ceremony or Powwow Dates: Memorial Day weekend is the holiday for celebrating in Klamath Falls, Oregon, with the Chief
Schonchin Days Powwow. You will find a powwow, Indian rodeo,
parade, and arts and crafts at the fairgrounds.

Art Forms: The tribe is restoring the art of basket making from tule.
These and other arts and crafts will be found at the powwow.

Visitor Information: This reservation was "terminated" in 1954, and with
the land base gone, the people were in a state of culture shock. Cash
payments cannot replace the feeling of belonging to a tribe when it
has been that way for hundreds of years. Many people became alco-
holics, and as a result, death rates were on the rise. The government
treaties guaranteed health and education benefits in exchange for the
tribe's land; with "termination" these benefits were lost. In August
1986, the Klamath tribe was restored to full federal recognition as a
result of years of work by the people. It is good to be a tribe again.

The Klamath call themselves Eukshikni or Auksni, "people of the
lake," referring to the fact that their principal residences were on
Upper Klamath Lake. There were also important settlements on the
Williamson and Sprague rivers. The Klamath, unlike the other
branch of the family, the Modoc, have always lived at peace with the
invading non-Indians. In 1864, they joined the Modoc in ceding the
greater part of their territory to the United States and settled on the
Klamath Reservation, where they numbered 755 in 1905. This
included, however, many members of other tribes who had become
more or less assimilated with the Klamath since the establishment of
the reservation.

For more information, see Oklahoma, Modoc.

Umatilla
P.O. Box 638
Pendleton, OR 97801-0638

(503) 276-3165
Fax (503) 276-9060

Umatilla

Location: Look for Pendleton in the northeast corner of your map of Oregon.

Public Ceremony or Powwow Dates: Local celebrations are held here occasionally. Call the tribal office for dates and times.

Art Forms: The tribe offers arts and crafts that include beadwork, moccasins, cradleboards, and traditional clothing, all at Mission Market.

Visitor Information: The Umatilla, Walla Walla, and Cayuse tribes share this reservation.

Umatilla: This Shahaptian tribe formerly lived on Umatilla River and the adjacent banks of the Columbia in Oregon. They were included under the Walla Walla by Lewis and Clark in 1805, though their language is distinct. In 1855, they joined in a treaty with the United States and settled on the Umatilla Reservation in eastern Oregon.

Wallawalla ("Little River"): This Shahaptian tribe formerly lived on the lower Wallawalla River and along the east bank of the Columbia from Snake River nearly to the Umatilla in Washington and Oregon. While a distinct dialect, their language is closely related to the Nez Perce. Their number was estimated by Lewis and Clark as 1,600 in 1805, but it is certain this figure included other bands now recognized as independent. By treaty of 1855, they were removed to the Umatilla Reservation in Oregon.

Cayuse: This Waiilatpuan tribe formerly occupied the territory around the heads of the Wallawalla, Umatilla, and Grande Ronde rivers and from the Blue Mountains to Deschutes River in Washington and Oregon. The tribe was closely associated with the neighboring Nez Perce and Wallawalla and was regarded by the early explorers and writers as belonging to the same stock. So far as the available evidence goes, however, they must be considered linguistically independent.

Wishram

See this section, Confederated Tribes of Warm Springs.

WASHINGTON

Chehalis
P.O. Box 536
Oakville, WA 98568
(206) 273-5911
Fax (206)273-5914

StsEe lis

Location: Chehalis is in the southwest corner of Washington, on Interstate 5.

Public Ceremony or Powwow Dates: The tribe has its Tribal Day Celebration in late May. Call the office for dates and times.

The Chehalis are a Salishan tribe on the Chehalis River and its affluents and on Grays Harbor, Washington. There were five principal villages on the river and seven on the north and eight on the south side of the bay; there were also a few villages on the north end of Shoalwater Bay. Many historians divided the tribe into Upper Chehalis or Kwaiailk, dwelling above Satsop River, and the Lower Chehalis, from that point down. In 1806, Lewis and Clark estimated their population at 700 in 38 lodges. In 1904, there were 147 Chehalis and 21 Humptulips under the Puyallup School Superintendent, Washington.

Colville
P.O. Box 150
Nespelem, WA 99155
(509) 634-4711
Fax (509) 634-4116

Colville

Skitswish (Coeur d'Alene [French, Awl-heart])
Kalispel (popularly known as Pend d'Oreilles, "ear drops")
Okinagan
Senijextee
Methow (Met-how, etymology unknown)
Nespelim
Pend d'Oreilles ("ear drops")
Sanpoil
Spokan

Location: The Colville Reservation is located in northeast Washington state, northwest of Spokane.

Public Ceremony or Powwow Dates: The joint tribes of the Colville Reservation hold powwows, Indian fairs, and other varied activities during the late spring, summer, and fall. During Stampede Days in Omak, Washington, you can see the great tipi encampment. Call the tribal office for dates and times.

Art Forms: There are varied art forms to be found here. Call the tribal office for the names of individuals who do the kind of work you want to buy.

The following is a short synopsis of each tribe listed above.

Colville: A division of the Salish between Kettle Falls and the Spokane River, eastern Washington; it is said to have been one of the largest of the Salish tribes. Lewis and Clark estimated their number at 2,500 in 130 houses in 1806. There were 321 under the Colville Agency in 1904.

Skitswish: This is a Salish tribe on a river and lake of the same name in northern Idaho. The name Coeur d'Alene (French "Awlheart"), by which they are popularly known, was originally a nickname used by some chief of the tribe to express the size of a trader's heart.

Kalispel (popularly known as Pend d'Oreilles, "ear drops"): This is a Salish tribe around the lake and along the river of the same name in the extreme northern part of Idaho and northeastern Washington. The Lewis and Clark expedition found three divisions: Upper Pend d'Oreilles, Lower Pend d'Oreilles, and Micksuck-sealton. Lewis and Clark estimated their number at 1,600 in 30 lodges in 1805. In 1905, there were 640 Upper Pend d'Oreilles and 197 Kalispel under the Flathead Agency, Montana, and 98 Kalispel under the Colville Agency, Washington.

Okinagan: This name originally applied to the confluence of the Similkameen and Okanogan rivers but extended first to include a small band and afterward to a large and important division of the Salishan family. They formerly inhabited the west side of the Okanogan River, Washington, from Old Ft. Okanogan to the Canadian border, and in British Columbia the shores of Okanogan Lake and the surrounding country. Later they displaced an Athapascan tribe from the valley of the Similkameen. In 1906, there

Colville Indians, 1914
Photo by Paul Standar; Courtesy Museum of New Mexico, Neg. No. 121219

were 527 Okinagan on Colville Reservation, Washington, and 824 under the Kamloops - Okanagan Agency, British Columbia.

Senijextee: This is a Salish tribe formerly residing on both sides of the Columbia River from Kettle Falls to the Canadian boundary; they also occupied the valley of the Kettle River, the Kootenay River from its mouth to the first falls, and the region of the Arrow Lakes, British Columbia. In 1909, those in the United States numbered 342, on the Colville Reservation in Washington.

Methow: This Salishan tribe of eastern Washington was formerly living in the area of the Methow River and Chelan Lake. As of 1909, they were mostly living on the Colville Reservation and their population was not recorded.

Nespelim: This Salish tribe is from a creek of the same name, a north tributary of the Columbia River, about 40 miles above Ft. Okinakane, Washington. As of 1906, they numbered 653 on Colville Reservation, Washington.

Pend d'Oreilles: See Kalispel.

Sanpoil: This body of Salish people on the Sans Poil River and on the Columbia below Big Bend, Washington, are classed as one of the eight bands of Spokan and also as one of the six bands of Okinagan. No treaty was ever made with these Indians for their lands; the government simply took possession of their country except for those portions set apart by executive order for their occupancy.

Spokan: This name has been applied to several small bodies of Salish on and near the Spokane River in northeastern Washington. The name was originally employed by the Skitswish to designate a band at the forks of the river, called also Smahoomenaish. The whites extended the name to cover eight other groups. The population was estimated by Lewis and Clark in 1805 at 600 in 30 houses. In 1908, the entire number of Spokan on Coeur d'Alene Reservation, Idaho, was 634. In 1909, the entire number of Spokan in Washington was 509, while those in Idaho numbered 104.

Hoh
HC 80, Box 917
Forks, WA 98331-9304
(206) 374-6582
Fax (206) 374-6549

Hoh

Location: The boundary of the reservation is determined by the Hoh River on two sides and the Pacific Ocean on the other—with a total of one square mile in area. Look on your map in northwest Washington State where Federal Highway 101 connects with the Pacific Ocean south of Forks.

Art Forms: Some members of the tribe still do basket weaving.

Visitor Information: There is a camping spot at the lower village. Some of the members of this tribe participate in the motorized canoe races using traditional canoes outfitted with high-powered engines. They race in the rivers, which can be dangerous because of snags and boulders. The Hoh can be seen racing against the Quinault and Quileute at Chief Taholah Days on Fourth of July weekend.

Jamestown Band of S'Klallam
1033 Old Blyn Highway
Sequim, WA 98382-9342
(206) 683-1109
Fax (206) 683-4366

Clallam ("strong people")

This Salish tribe lived on the south side of Puget Sound, Washington, formerly extending from Port Discovery to the Hoko River, bounded at each end by the Chimakum and Makah. Subsequently, they occupied Chimakum Territory and established a village at Port Townsend. A comparatively small number found their way across to the south end of Vancouver Island, and there was a large village on Victoria harbor. They are said to be more closely related to the Songish than to any other tribe. The population was 800 in 1854 and 336 in 1904.

Kalispel
Box 39
Usk, WA 99180-0039
(509) 445-1147
Fax (509) 455-1705

Kalispel Pend d'Oreilles (popularly known as "ear drops")

Location: The reservation is located north of Spokane near Usk.

Public Ceremony or Powwow Dates: The tribe sponsors an annual pow-wow and potlatch. Call the office above for dates and times.

Art Forms: The arts and crafts of the people can be found by calling the tribal office and by attending the powwow.

See Washington, Colville, for more information on the Kalispel.

Lower Elwha
2851 Lower Elwha Road
Port Angeles, WA 98362-9518
(206) 452-8471
Fax (206) 452-4848

Elwha (a Clallam village at the mouth of the river of the same name in Washington state)

See Washington, Jamestown Klallam Tribal Council, for more information on the Clallam people.

Lummi
2616 Kwina Road
Bellingham, WA 98226-9298
(206) 734-8180
Fax (206) 384-4737

Ca-Choo-Sen
Nuh-Lummis

Location: The 12,000-acre Lummi Indian Reservation is located 12 miles south of the Canadian/U.S. border on a peninsula with water to the west, south, and east. The reservation begins 3 miles to the west of Interstate 5, which connects Vancouver, British Columbia, one hour away, and Seattle, Washington, which is an hour and a half away.

Public Ceremony or Powwow Dates: During the month of June, the annual Stommish Festival is held at the reservation (Stommish means warrior or veteran). The celebration is patterned after the old potlatches, still fresh in the memories of tribal elders. Activities include exciting war canoe races, the Princess contest, Sla-hal bone games (gambling), authentic Indian music, and Lummi Spirit dances. Genuine Indian art and craft booths, traditional Indian foods, and the world-famous Lummi barbecued salmon, cooked slowly in front of alder-fired pits, add to this once-in-a-lifetime experience. Call the tribal office for exact dates. No drugs or alcohol are allowed. No fireworks are allowed. Any eagle or prayer feather that is found is not to be picked up; instead, you should inform the closest elder for proper retrieval.

Art Forms: The art of basketry has been reintroduced to the younger generation recently through the Heritage Program in conjunction with Lummi Community College. The students are taught all phases of gathering and preparing traditional materials that go into the Lummi baskets. Students are encouraged to do only the style of work that was traditionally done by their ancestors. The types of baskets the students make include clam baskets, cooking baskets, and food storage baskets. The Heritage Program has produced many fine new artists in a number of areas.

The Lummi Indians were known for knitting Indian sweaters made of wools. These sweaters are known around the world for their fine quality, warmth, and durability. In the past few years, the art of Salish weaving has been revived, and a few people are doing this type of work. Some women knit ski socks and hats for the local shops using only the natural colored wools and spinning their yarns by hand.

Carving is another art being taught to a few people by the elders of the tribe. There are those who do small carvings for retail sale. These carvings include canoe paddles, canoes, masks, feast bowls, totem poles, and rattles, in cedar. A select few artists carve in the mediums of soapstone, antler, and bone. There are some who specialize in two-dimensional paint design.

Visitor Information: Fisherman's Cove Restaurant is located at the southern tip of the Lummi Reservation. Tribally owned and operated, it provides a spectacular view of Lummi Island and Hales Pass. The restaurant specializes in seafood that is obtained fresh daily, locally. One of the specialties of the house is their well-known oyster omelet. Delicious salmon dishes are prepared in many different ways.

Adjacent to the restaurant is the Hyas Gift Shop, which features articles made by Lummi and other Indian artists and craftspersons.

The wide variety of handicrafts includes wood carvings, leather work, beadwork, silverwork, and different kinds of sketches and paintings.

The tribe operates a charter boat on which visitors can take a cruise through the surrounding waters for an unforgettable experience. The boat is operated by personnel with wide experience in the local waters. The sunsets are magnificent and can only be appreciated fully when seen reflecting on the crystal clear waters.

Overwhelming views of Lummi Bay, Hales Pass, Lummi Island, Bellingham Bay, and the majestic 10,000-foot-high snow-capped Mount Baker await the visitor to the Lummi Reservation. The breathtaking multicolored sunsets cannot be found elsewhere due to the unique combination of latitude and local geography. For those who enjoy strolls along the beach, certain areas have been retained in their natural state so that visitors can enjoy these simple pleasures from the past.

When the white man arrived, the Lummi Chief was Chow-Its-Hoot. In 1875, he was succeeded by Chief Kwina, who ruled the Lummi for over 50 years. Kwina was succeeded in 1926 by August Martin who was followed by Norbert James in 1950, and by the present chief, James McKay, in 1958.

In 1855, Isaac I. Stevens, Governor and Superintendent of Indian Affairs for the Territory of Washington, negotiated the Point Elliott Treaty with western Washington tribes north of the present city of Seattle. In this treaty, the Indians ceded land between Olympia and the Canadian border for annual payments of money, protection of certain hunting and fishing rights, and for implements, smithies, carpenters, doctors, and schools. The island called Ca-Choo-Sen (the home of the Lummi) became the home of the Huh-Lummi or the combined tribes of Lummi, Samish, Skagit, Semiahmoo, and Nooksack.

The Lummi people, along with many others, lived in this territory from the beginning of time. They lived in huge buildings made from ancient cedar trees, carved into beams and planks. These homes were known as longhouses. There were up to ten families living in these homes. An average compartment inside the longhouse and lining the walls would be 6 fathoms by 6 fathoms square (1 fathom equals 6 feet). These homes were occupied in the winter. The longhouses were built to provide the warmth needed during the cold winter months.

There were many social gatherings in one of these longhouses, one of which was known as the potlatch. During the potlatch, large meals were prepared. Many people gathered from all parts of the country. Gifts were exchanged. The people at this time were very generous. It was the ability to give that determined a wealthy man, village, clan, or tribe. At these gatherings, beautiful handwoven blankets were given away. These blankets were made from the split roots and from other parts of the young cedar tree. There were different kinds of animal furs and bird feathers mixed into this material to make it soft and colorful.

The Lummi have always depended on fishing as their main source of subsistence. In warm weather, they moved from place to place, camping along riverbanks and beaches, fishing, and gathering clams, oysters, berries, and wild roots. The men hunted extensively and caught wild fowl in nets. The tribal knowledge required that no overharvesting take place; thus, the harvest site of the tribes was always rotated.

The Lummi fishing fleet currently is the largest in the Northwest and employs over 600 Lummi. Approximately 500 make their sole source of income from fishing. There are 447 fishing boats in the Lummi fleet: 32 seine boats, 165 gill net boats, and 250 skiffs. Total annual harvest value of the fleet exceeds $13,000,000. Lummi fishermen landed 5.8 million pounds of seafood in 1986. Salmon species dominate the landings.

The largest employer on the reservation is the Lummi Indian Business Council, which has 167 people on its payroll. The Indian Health Service employs 37, the Tribal Agriculture Program employs 21, and the Lummi Water and Sewer Department employs 8. The Fishermen's Cove employs over 30 people in the summer and 15 in the winter; the Lummi Seafood Processing Venture employs over 45 in the summer and 15 in the winter. Other economic development plans include entry into the recreational field through the operation of card and bingo games. The Lummi have been approved to operate a Foreign Trade Zone. They are currently seeking businesses to locate in this zone. Development of a commercial marina is being planned. The salmon enhancement program has been a tremendous success, with millions of salmon added to the fishery catch that is enjoyed by both Indian and non-Indian fishermen alike.

The overriding mission of the Lummi Indian Business Council is to realize economic self-sufficiency for its tribal members, tribal government, and tribal institutions. In the pursuit of having new business and industry locate on the reservation, it is also a goal of the tribe to assist and train members to be capable of owning and managing them. The Lummi Community College has established a training program to assure that the businesses and industries have the trained personnel they require.

Makah
P.O. Box 115
Neah Bay, WA 98357
(206) 645-2201, ext. 36
Fax (206) 645-2323

Makah ("cape people")

Location: The Makah Cultural Center and Museum are on the east side of Highway 112 in Neah Bay.

Public Ceremony or Powwow Dates: In late August, you will find the Makah people participating in one of the best celebrations in the Northwest with dancing and other activities.

Art Forms: The artwork of this area includes woodcarvings and baskets. Other types of artwork will also be found at the powwow.

Visitor Information: The museum is operated by the Makah Nation and includes some artifacts from a village buried by a mudslide some 500 years ago.

The Makah are the southernmost tribe of the Wakashan group, the only one within the United States. They belong to the Nootka branch. In 1905, there were two reservations, Makah and Ozette, Washington, on which there were, respectively, 399 and 36 people. In 1806, they were estimated by Lewis and Clark to number 2,000. By treaty of January 31, 1855, the Makah ceded all their lands at the mouth of the Strait of Juan de Fuca except the immediate area. This reservation was enlarged by Executive Order of October 26, 1872, superseded by Executive Order of January 2, 1873, and in turn revoked by Executive Order of October 12 of the same year, by which the Makah Reservation was established and defined. The Ozette Reservation was established by order of April 12, 1893. It is no wonder that Indian people were confused by the U.S. government.

Muckleshoot
39015 172nd Street SE
Auburn, WA 98002-9763
(206) 939-3311
Fax (206) 939-5311

Nisqually
4820 She-Nah-Num Drive SE
Olympia, WA 98503-9199
(206) 456-5221
Fax (206) 407-0125

This Salish tribe lived on and around the Salish River, which flowed into the south extension of Puget Sound, Washington. The Nisqualli Reservation is on the Nisqualli River between Pierce and Thurston counties. The name has also been extended to apply to those tribes of the east side of Puget Sound speaking the same dialect. The Nisqualli made a treaty with the United States at Medicine Creek, Washington, December 26, 1854, ceding certain lands and reserving others. The Executive Order of January 20, 1857, defined the present Nisqualli Reservation.

Nooksack
P.O. Box 157
Deming, WA 98244
(206) 592-5176
Fax (206) 592-5753

Nooksak ("mountain men")

This name was given to a Salish tribe, said to be divided into three small bands, on the Salish River in Whatcom County, Washington. About 200 Nooksak were officially counted in 1906, but they speak the same dialect as the Suquamish, from whom they are said to have separated.

Port Gamble S'Klallum
31912 Little Boston Road NE
Kingston, WA 98346
(206) 297-2646
Fax (206) 297-7097

Puyallup
2002 East 28th Street
Tacoma, WA 98404-4996
(206) 597-6200
Fax (206) 848-7341

Puyallup ("shadow," from the forest shade)

This important Salish tribe is of the Puyallup River and Commencement Bay. By treaty of December 26, 1854, the Puyallup and other tribes at the head of Puget Sound ceded their lands to the United States and agreed to go to a reservation set apart for them on the sound near Shenahnam Creek, Washington. In 1901, there were 536 on Puyallup Reservation, Washington; in 1909, 469.

Quileute
P.O. Box 279
LaPush, WA 98350-0279
(206) 374-6163
Fax (206) 374-6311

Visitor Information: In July of each year, the tribe celebrates "Quileute Days." This is a celebration of their culture, both past and present, which involves canoe races, bone games, fish bakes, softball tournaments, tug-of-war, and much more.

The Quileute Reservation was established on February 19, 1889, and is located on the Olympic Peninsula of Washington State. The reservation is approximately one square mile (surrounded on three sides by Olympic National Park and by the Pacific Ocean on the fourth side). They have a resident population of over 400 and an enrollment of over 750. Historically, the Quileute people were whalers and fishermen; however, hunting and gathering were also important. Presently, the Quileute are still dependent on salmon and other resources from the sea.

Although the Quileute have always been few in number, they successfully resisted all the attempts of neighboring tribes to dislodge them. Their most active enemy was the Makah tribe of Neah Bay.

Quinault
P.O. Box 189
Taholah, WA 98587-0189

(206) 276-8211
Fax (206) 276-4682

Quinaielt

Location: This reservation borders the Pacific Ocean and is located north of Aberdeen.

Public Ceremony or Powwow Dates: Chief Taholah Days is the event to attend during the Fourth of July weekend in Taholah.

Art Forms: A few arts and crafts will be offered for sale during the celebration. If you consider delicious salmon cooked over an open fire art, then you are in the right place, also.

Visitor Information: The tribe operates a cannery on the Quinault River.

Lewis and Clark found this Salish tribe along the coast between the Quileute and the Quaitso on the north and the Chehalis on the south. They described them in two divisions, the Calasthocle and the Quiniilt, with 200 and 1,000 in population, respectively. In 1909, they numbered 156, under the Puyallup School Superintendency. For their treaty with the United States, see Washington, Quileute.

Sauk-Suiattle Skokomish
5318 Chief Brown Lane
Darrington, WA 98241-9421
(206) 435-8366
Fax (206) 436-1511

Shoalwater Bay Skokomish
P.O. Box 130
Tokeland, WA 98590-0130
(206) 267-6766
Fax (206) 267-6778

Skokomish
N. 80 Tribal Center Road
Shelton, WA 98584-9748
(206) 426-4232
Fax (206) 877-5148

Skokomish ("river people")

This body of the Salish forms one of three subdivisions of the Twana. They lived at the mouth of the Skokomish River, which flows into the upper end of Hoods Canal, Washington, where a reservation of the same name was set aside for them. They officially numbered 203 in 1909, but this figure included the two other subdivisions of the Twana.

Spokane
P.O. Box 100
Wellpinit, WA 99040-0100
(509) 258-4581 or (509) 838-3465
Fax (509) 258-9243

Spokan

Location: This reservation is located north and west of Spokane.

Public Ceremony or Powwow Dates: The tribe holds its annual Labor Day Celebration at Wellpinit each year. There is a war dance competition as well as intertribal dances of all kinds.

Art Forms: There are many arts and crafts and other kinds of booths featured at the powwow. Food is an art, also, and there are many Indian food booths there.

Visitor Information: Contact the Spokane Community Center for other arts and crafts that might be available on a daily basis.

Spokan has been applied to several small tribes of Salish on and near the Spokane River in Washington. The name was originally employed by the Skitswish to designate a band at the forks of the river, called also Smahoomenaish. The population in 1805 was 600 in 30 houses, and in 1853 the population was 450. In 1909, the Spokan in Washington numbered 509, while those in Idaho numbered 104.

Squaxin Island
SE 70 Squaxin Lane
Shelton, WA 98584-9200

(206) 426-9781
Fax (206) 426-3971

Squaxon

This is a division of the Salish on the peninsula between Hoods
Canal and Case Inlet, Washington. The population in 1909 was 98.

Stillaguamish
P.O. Box 277
Arlington, WA 98223-0277
(206) 652-7362
Fax (206) 435-2204

Stillaguamish

There was an attempt to put the Stillaguamish on a reservation.
However, the Stillaguamish refused to remain there and returned to
their river, where they still live today.

Suquamish
P.O. Box 498
Suquamish, WA 98392-0498
(206) 598-3311
Fax (206) 598-4666

Suquamish

Location: The Port Madison Indian Reservation is located west of
Seattle, at Suquamish.

Public Ceremony or Powwow Dates: Chief Seattle Days are held August
18–20, or the third weekend in August. The Native American Art
Fair is held in mid-April. Call the tribal office for exact dates and
times. No alcohol or drugs are allowed on the reservation.

Art Forms: Basketry and carving are the main art forms on the reservation today.

Visitor Information: The Suquamish Museum is located forty minutes
from downtown Seattle, via the Winslow ferry. For visitors to the

Olympic Peninsula, the Suquamish Museum is located on Highway 305, the gateway to and from the peninsula.

The museum staff will be happy to assist you in making arrangements for transportation and tours. Picnics, traditional salmon dinners, and special luncheons at nearby Kiana Lodge are available to museum visitors. For information, call (206) 598-3311. Hours are 10:00 a.m. to 5:00 p.m. daily, April through September; Tuesday-Friday, 11:00 a.m. to 4:00 p.m., and Saturday and Sunday, 10:00 a.m. to 5:00 p.m., October through March.

Quotes from tribal elders give a powerful voice to the Suquamish Museum experience:

"It was my grandmother that taught me how to make the baskets. She used to make clam baskets. She used to make me sit down and do it. She says `You got to learn how. You're going to get old, too, like I am, so you better learn how to make this.'" (Ethel Sam)

"My earliest recollection of living in the village first five or six years of my life. . .the children were always playing there and the village run for about a mile along the shore of Suquamish. There's where we always seemed to gather, elders and children, sometime through the day. . .and the life of the people at that time wasn't too complicated. . . get up and do whatever chores or work they had to." (Lawrence Webster)

Here you can experience the history of the Pacific Northwest from the perspective of Chief Seattle and his descendants, the Suquamish people. In a forested setting on the shores of Agate Passage, the Suquamish Museum reveals the world of Puget Sound's original inhabitants. Sights and sounds from the past bring life to the museum's premier exhibition, "The Eyes of Chief Seattle," which received international acclaim when it traveled to Nantes, France, as part of Seattle's Sister City exchange. The museum's award-winning media production, "Come Forth Laughing: Voices of the Suquamish People," provides a firsthand account of life over the past one hundred years.

Spend time at the museum, and then walk along their beautiful beach, have a picnic lunch overlooking Agate Pass, stop in the gift shop, and tour the nature trail. Their guides can direct you to other spots on the Port Madison Indian Reservation, including Chief Seattle's grave, Old Man House, the site of the original Suquamish village and the largest longhouse in the Pacific Northwest, and the Suquamish Fish Hatchery.

660 – CHIEF SEATTLE.

Chief Sealth (or Seattle), Dwamish, 1865
Photo by E. M. Sammis; Courtesy Museum of New Mexico, Neg. No. 88464

Chief Seattle, head of the Suquamish and Duwamish tribes, has been given honors that few other Indians have received. The City of Seattle, Washington, was named for him; there is a bronze statue in Seattle commemorating this. Each year, the Boy Scouts of America hold a memorial ceremony at his tomb at Suquamish.

Seattle and his father before him were both friendly to the white settlers and eagerly helped them. After Seattle became a Catholic in the 1830s, he demonstrated his beliefs in the way he lived. He was the first to sign the Port Elliott Treaty in 1855 whereby the Suquamish and other Washington tribes received reservations. Seattle was born in 1786 and died June 7, 1866.

The speech that follows on these pages was taken down by Dr. Henry Smith, a man who mastered the Suwamish language in about two years. Dr. Smith did us a great service in preserving this address, which may cause some present-day citizens to wonder at his predictions. The Washington Territory was organized in 1853. A plat for the town of Seattle was filed, and the first post office was put into use. Governor Stevens soon visited Seattle and on the occasion, made an address to the settlers and Indians gathered in the small community. After his talk, Seattle made his reply, which was delivered through an interpreter. Dr. Smith carefully wrote it down on the spot.

Yonder sky that has wept tears of compassion upon my people for centuries untold, and which to us appears changeless and eternal, may change. Today is fair. Tomorrow it may be overcast with clouds. My words are like the stars that never change. Whatever Seattle says the great Chief at Washington can rely upon with as much certainty as he can upon the return of the sun or the seasons. The White Chief says that Big Chief at Washington sends us greetings of friendship and goodwill. This is kind of him for we know he has little need of our friendship in return. His people are many. They are like the grass that covers vast prairies. My people are few. They resemble the scattering trees of a storm swept plain. The great, and I presume, good White Chief sends us word that he wishes to buy our lands but is willing to allow us enough to live comfortably. This indeed appears just, even generous, for the Red Man no longer has rights that he need respect, and the offer may be wise also, as we are no longer in need of an extensive country.

There was a time when our people covered the land as the waves of a wind ruffled sea cover its shell paved floor, but that time long since passed away with the greatness of tribes that are now but a mournful memory. I will not dwell on, nor mourn over, our untimely decay, nor reproach my paleface brothers with hastening it as we too may have been somewhat to blame.

Youth is impulsive. When our young men grow angry at some real or imaginary wrong, and disfigure their faces with black paint, it denotes that their hearts are black, and that they are often cruel and relentless, and our old men and old women are unable to restrain them. Thus it has ever been. Thus it was when the white man first began to push our forefathers westward. But let us hope that the hostilities between us may never return. We would have everything to lose and nothing to gain. Revenge by young men is considered gain, even at the cost of their own lives, but old men who stay at home in times of war, and mothers who have sons to lose, know better.

Our good father at Washington, for I presume he is our father as well as yours, since King George has moved his boundaries further north, our great and good father, I say, sends us word that if we do as he desires he will protect us. His brave warriors will be to us a bristling wall of strength, and his wonderful ships of war will fill our harbors so that our ancient enemies far to the northward, the Hydas and Tsimpsians, will cease to frighten our women, children and old men. Then in reality will he be our father and we his children. But can that ever be? Your God is not our God! Your God loves your people and hates mine. He folds his strong protecting arms lovingly about the paleface and leads him by the hand as a father leads his infant son, but He has forsaken His red children, if they really are His. Our God, the Great Spirit, seems also to have forsaken us. Your God makes your people wax strong every day. Soon they will fill all the land. Our people are ebbing away like a rapidly receding tide that will never return. The white man's God cannot love our people or He would protect them. They seem to be orphans who can look nowhere for help. How then can we be brothers? How can your God become our God and renew our prosperity and awaken in us dreams of returning greatness. If we have a common heavenly father He must be partial, for He came to His paleface children. We never saw Him. He gave you laws but had no word for his red children whose teeming multitudes once filled this vast continent as stars fill the firmament. No; we are two distinct races with separate origins and separate destinies. There is little in common between us.

To us the ashes of our ancestors are sacred and their resting place is hallowed ground. You wander far from the graves of your ancestors and seemingly without regret. Your religion was written upon tables of stone by the iron finger of your God so that you could not forget. The Red Man could never comprehend nor remember it. Our religion is the traditions of our ancestors, the

Angelina, Chief Seattle's daughter, Dwamish
Courtesy Museum of New Mexico, Neg. No. 73091

dreams of our old men, given them in the solemn hours of night by the Great Spirit; and the visions of our sachems, and is written in the hearts of our people.

Your dead cease to love you and the land of their nativity as soon as they pass the portals of the tomb and wander way beyond the stars. They are soon forgotten and never return. Our dead never forget the beautiful world that gave them being. They still love its verdant valleys, its murmuring rivers, its magnificent mountains, sequestered vales and verdant lined lakes and bay, and ever yearn in tender, fond affection over the lonely hearted living, and often return from the Happy Hunting Ground to visit, guide, console and comfort them.

Day and night cannot dwell together. The Red Man has ever fled the approach of the White Man, as the morning mist flees before the morning sun.

However, your proposition seems fair and I think that my people will accept it and will retire to the reservation you offer them. Then we will dwell in peace, for the words of the Great White Chief seem to be the words of nature speaking to my people out of dense darkness.

It matters little where we pass the remnant of our days. They will not be many. The Indians' night promises to be dark. Not a single star of hope hovers above his horizon. Sad-voiced winds moan in the distance. Grim fate seems to be on the Red Man's trail, and wherever he goes he will hear the approaching footsteps of his fell destroyer and prepare stolidly to meet his doom, as does the wounded doe that hears the approaching footsteps of the hunter.

A few more moons. A few more winters, and not one of the descendants of the mighty hosts that once moved over this broad land or lived in happy homes, protected by the Great Spirit, will remain to mourn over the graves of a people, once more powerful and hopeful than yours. But why should I mourn at the untimely fate of my people? Tribe follows tribe, and nation follows nation, like the waves of the sea. It is the order of nature, and regret is useless. Your time of decay may be distant, but it will surely come, for even the White Man whose God walked and talked with him as friend with friend, cannot be exempt from the common destiny. We may be brothers after all. We will see.

We will ponder your proposition and when we decide we will let you know. But should we accept it, I here and now make this condition that we will not be denied the privilege without molestation of visiting at any time the tombs of our ancestors, friends, and children. Every part of this soil is sacred in the estimation of my people. Every hillside, every valley, every plain and grove, has been hallowed by some sad or happy event in days long vanished. Even the rocks, which seem to be dumb and dead as they swelter in the sun along the silent shore, thrill with memories of stirring events connected with the lives of my people, and the very dust upon which you now stand responds more lovingly to their footsteps than to yours, because it is rich with the blood of our ancestors and our bare feet are conscious of the sympathetic touch. Our departed braves, fond mothers, glad, happy-hearted maidens, and even our little children who lived here and rejoiced here for a brief season, will love these somber solitudes and at eventide they greet shadowy returning spirits. *And when the last Red Man shall have perished, and the memory of my tribe shall have become a myth among the White Men, these shores will swarm with the invisible dead of my tribe,* and when your children's children think themselves alone in the field, the store, the shop, upon the highway, or in the silence of the pathless woods, they will not be alone. In all the earth there is no place dedicated to solitude. At night when the streets of your cities and villages are silent and you think them deserted, they will throng with the returning hosts that once filled them and still love this beautiful land. The White Man will never be alone.

Let him be just and deal kindly with my people, for the dead are not powerless. Dead, did I say? There is no death, only a change of worlds.

Suquamish
P.O. Box 498
Suquamish, WA 98392-0498
(206) 598-3311
Fax (206) 598-4666

Suquamish

This Salish division claimed their homeland on the west side of Puget Sound. According to records, they claimed the land from Appletree Cove in the north to Gig Harbor in the south. Seattle, who gave his name to the city, was chief of this tribe and the Dwamish in 1853. The population was 441 in 1857, 180 in 1909.

See Suquamish, above, for more information.

Swinomish
P.O. Box 817
La Conner, WA 98257-0817
(206) 466-3163
Fax (206) 466-4047

This tribe is a subdivision of the Skagit, formerly on Whidbey Island, northwest Washington. The Skagit and Swinomish together numbered 268 in 1909.

Tulalip
6700 Totem Beach Road
Marysville, WA 98271-9715
(206) 653-4585
Fax (206) 653-0255

Visitor Information: The Tulalip today live north and west of Everett, Washington. They operate a bingo parlor and have other economic development programs.

The Tulalip are one of three divisions of the Twana, a Salish tribe on the west side of Hoods Canal, Washington. This branch lived on a small stream, near the head of the canal, called Dulaylip. In 1909, the name was also given to a reservation on the west side of Puget Sound.

Upper Skagit
2284 Community Plaza
Sedro Woolley, WA 98284-9739
(206) 856-5501
Fax (206) 856-3175

Skagit

This body of the Salish lived on a river of the same name in Washington. In 1853, the population of the Skagit proper was about 300. They moved to the Swinomish Reservation, Washington, in 1909.

Yakama
P.O. Box 151
Toppenish, WA 98948-0151
(509) 865-5121
Fax (509) 865-5528

Yakama (Ya-ka-ma, "runaway")
Waptailmin ("people of the narrow river")
Pa kiut lema ("people of the gap")

Location: Look on your map of Washington, near Yakima, for the location of the Yakama Reservation.

Public Ceremony or Powwow Dates: The Yakama Nation Summer Encampment and the Toppenish Powwow are both held over the Fourth of July weekend. Traditional dancing and a powwow competition are featured along with intertribal dancing. The common name of this area's celebrations is White Swan. The Yakama Powwow is usually held in September. Call the tribal office for dates and times.

Art Forms: Arts and crafts of many kinds are offered during the powwows. There are also hand games.

Visitor Information: The Cultural Center at Highway 97 and Fort Road, Toppenish, is preserving some of the most important aspects of Yakama culture. Arts and crafts—beadwork, silverwork, and other interesting items—are offered for sale at the gift shop. The Heritage Inn Restaurant has ordinary food as well as Indian food.

This important Shahaptian tribe, formerly living on both sides of the Columbia River and on the northerly branches of the Yakima (formerly Tapteal) and the Wenatchee, in Washington, are mentioned by Lewis and Clark in 1806 under the name Cutsahnim and estimated as 1,200 in number. In 1855, the United States made a treaty with the Yakima and thirteen other tribes of Shahaptian, Salishan, and Chinookan groups, by which they ceded the territory from the Cascade Mountains to the Palouse and Snake rivers and from Lake Chelan to the Columbia. The Yakima Reservation was established, on which all the participating tribes and bands were to be confederated as the Yakima Nation under the leadership of Kamiakan, a distinguished Yakima chief. Before this treaty could be ratified, the Yakima war broke out, and it was not until 1859 that the provisions of the treaty went into effect. The Paloos and certain other tribes never recognized the treaty or moved to the reservation. In 1909, the total population on the reservation was 1,900. There is little reason to believe that the customs of this tribe differed from the Nez Perce and other Shahaptian people. See Idaho, Nez Perce, for more information. In 1992, the Yakama Nation changed the spelling of its name from Yakima to the traditional spelling, Yakama.

SOUTH

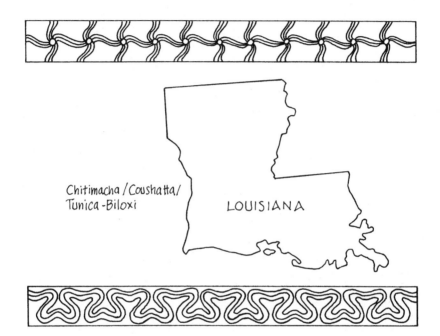

Chitimacha / Coushatta / Tunica -Biloxi

LOUISIANA

The South of North America is above that place where the waters of the Gulf of Mexico meet the great river, the Mississippi, from the north. The terrain is largely flat and rolling, with some swamps and bogs and trees and streams. There are grasses and the land is green.

This is the land of the people of the towns; the houses lined the rivers. Often, houses lined both sides of the river for miles. In the larger towns, there were squares like plazas in the center. This is where the people gathered to dance pray the ceremony of keeping tradition alive.

The sacred fire was always kept alive and burning, and the people danced around it with dedication and steadfastness. Then, the seasons brought the greater ceremonies of hope and thanks. The dances around the fire always culminated in the seasonal blessings.

Join with the tribes on the following pages to honor their ancestors and to honor our Creator, our Mother Earth, our Moon, our Sun, and the whole of all living things in the whole of all Creation. You will find that it is good. It is very, very good.

Aho . . .

LOUISIANA

Chitimacha
P.O. Box 661
Charenton, LA 70523
(318) 923-7215
Fax (318) 923-7791

Chuti Masha ("they have cooking vessels")

Location: The tribal office is in Charenton.

Art Forms: The Chitimacha are known for their fine baskets made of cane.

This tribe is of the Chitimachan linguistic family, whose earliest known home was the shore of Grand Lake, formerly Lake of the Shetimasha, and the banks of Grand River, Louisiana. Some 16 or 18 members of the tribe were living on the Grand River in 1881, but the majority, about 35, lived at Charenton, on the south side of Bayou Teche, in St. Mary's Parish, about ten miles from the Gulf of Mexico. This tribe's name for itself is Pantch-pinunkansh, "men altogether red," a designation apparently applied after they came into contact with non-Indians. The Chitimacha were known soon after the French settled Louisiana, through the death by one of their men of St. Cosme, a missionary, on the Mississippi in 1706. This was followed by protracted war with the French, who compelled them to sue for peace. It was granted on condition that the head of the Indian be brought to him; this was done and peace was made. It is believed the tribe was then reduced to a small number of warriors.

Little is known about their traditional customs. Fish and the roots of native plants constituted their food, but later they planted maize and sweet potatoes. They were strict monogamists, and women had considerable authority in their government. The men wore their hair long, with a piece of lead at the end of the queue, and tattooed their arms, legs, and faces. The noonday sun is said to have been their principal celebration representative. The dead of the tribe were buried in graves, and after the flesh had decayed, the bones were taken up and reinterred.

Coushatta
P.O. Box 818
Elton, LA 70532
(318) 584-2261
Fax (318) 584-2998

Koasati

This is an upper Creek tribe that speaks a dialect almost identical with the Alibamu. The name contains the word for "cane" or "reed," and it may signify "white cane."

During the middle and latter part of the eighteenth century, the Koasati lived, apparently in one principal village, on the right bank of the Alabama River, three miles below the confluence of the Coosa and Tallapoosa, where the modern town of Coosada, Alabama, perpetuates their name; but soon after western Florida was ceded to Great Britain, in 1763, "two villages of Kosati" moved over to the Tombigbee and settled below the mouth of Sukenatcha Creek. A "Coosawda" village existed on the Tennessee River, near the site of Langston, Alabama, in the early part of the nineteenth century, but it is uncertain whether its occupants were true Koasati. In 1805, some members of the tribe settled in Louisiana. From there, they spread over much of eastern Texas as far as the Trinity River, while a portion, or perhaps some of those who had remained in Alabama, obtained permission from the Caddo to settle on the Red River. Those who stayed in their original homes and subsequently moved to Indian Territory also largely remained near the Alibamu, although they are found in several places in the Creek Nation, Oklahoma. Two towns in the Creek Nation are named after them.

Houma
Star Route Box 95A
Golden Meadow, LA 70357

Visitor Information: There is an Indian Crafts Co-op based in Dulac, Louisiana, for the Houma Nation.

Tunica-Biloxi
P.O. Box 331
Marksville, LA 71351
(318) 253-9767
Fax (318) 253-9791

Tunica ("people")
Biloxi (Taneks haya, "first people")

Location: The tribal office is in Marksville, Louisiana.

Tunica

This tribe is from a distinct language family known as Tonikan that formerly lived on the lower Mississippi. The Tunica are prominent in the early history of the lower Mississippi region because of their attachment to the French and their aid as allies in fights with neighboring tribes. When first visited by non-Indians, they lived in Mississippi on the lower Yazoo River. In 1699, the number of their cabins was estimated at 260, scattered over four leagues of countryside. At that time, they lived entirely on Indian corn and did no hunting. In 1700, they occupied seven hamlets containing 50 or 60 small cabins. In 1706, the Tunica were driven from their villages by the Chickasaw and Alibamu and joined the Houma; it is said that subsequently they killed more than half that tribe and occupied its territory. In 1730, the Natchez, who had taken refuge among the Chickasaw, burned their village and a large number of them were killed. In 1760, they occupied three villages, the largest of which was on a lake at Tunica Bayou. In 1802, the population was estimated at 120 men, a total of about 450 people altogether. In 1908, the Tunica consisted of about 30 people in eastern and southeastern Marksville, the parish seat, on what is called Marksville Prairie. At that time, they spoke Tunica, Creole, and English.

A description of the Tunica in 1700 indicates that the women made an excellent fabric of mulberry cloth. There was fair division of labor between the sexes; the men cultivated the soil, planted and harvested the crops, cut the wood and brought it to the cabin, and dressed the deer and buffalo skins; the women performed the indoor work and made pottery and clothing.

Biloxi

This is a tribe of Siouan origin which formerly lived in southern Mississippi. The first direct notice of the Biloxi was in 1699 around Biloxi Bay, on the gulf coast of the Mississippi area, in connection with two other small tribes, the Paskagula and Moctobi, the three altogether numbering only about 20 cabins. In 1828, there were 20 families of the tribe on the east bank of the Neches River, Texas. In 1829, approximately 65 were living with the Caddo, Paskagula, and other small tribes on the Red River, near the Texas frontier, and in 1846, a Biloxi camp was seen on Little River, a tributary of the Brazos in Texas. After this, little was heard of them until 1886, when a few Biloxi were seen among the Choctaw and Caddo. Prior to the coming of non-Indians, the men wore breechcloths, belts, leggings, moccasins, and garters and wrapped skin robes around their bodies. Feather headdresses and necklaces of bone and the bills of a long-legged redbird, possibly the flamingo, were worn, as were nose rings and earrings. The dwellings of the people resembled those found among the northern tribes of the same family, one kind similar to the low tipi of the Osage and Winnebago and the other like the high tipi of the Dakota and Omaha. It is said they formerly made pottery, wooden bowls, horn and bone implements, and baskets. Tattooing was practiced to a limited extent. Descent was through the female line, and there was an elaborate system of kinship.

SOUTHEAST

The Southeast of our North America lies in that place toward where the sun rises and all the days of men begin. It is a land of rolling hills, valleys, mountains rounded by time, streams and coastlines with bright sands. There are forests of broadleaf trees and pine. There are swamps and bogs and rivers running to the Great Water, the Gulf of Mexico.

This is the land of the people of the thatched houses. The floors are raised above the often-rising water caused by storms from the coast. The people lived by the gifts from deer, small animals, herbs, and vegetable gardens and the corn.

There was beauty in the path of the people, and they acted out the goodness of the gift from the Creator with sacred ceremonies. The most perfect time of Creation was the time of the people living in harmony with all living and natural things. There was no need for machines. No need for things that polluted and ruined the earth. There was no need to live in unnatural ways. Man had reached the best of his culture.

Join with the tribes on the following pages to honor their ancestors and to honor our Creator, our Mother Earth, our Moon, our Sun, and the whole of all living things in the whole of all Creation. You will find that it is good. It is very, very good.

Aho . . .

We do not take up the warpath without a just cause and honest purpose.

—Pushmataha (Choctaw)

ALABAMA

Poarch Band of Creek
HCR 69 A, Box 85B
Atmore, AL 36502
(205) 368-9136
Fax (205) 368-4502

Muscogee

This confederacy forms the largest division of the Muskhogean family. They received their name from the English on account of the numerous streams in their country. During early historic times, the Creeks occupied the greater portion of Alabama and Georgia, residing chiefly on the Coosa and Tallapoosa rivers, the two largest tributaries of the Alabama River, and on the Flint and Chattahoochee rivers. The tribes at the time of the confederation were Abihka (or Kusa), Kasihta, Kawita, and Oakfuskee. Before 1540, there may have been another tribe at the Coosa and Tallapoosa rivers. In the last quarter of the eighteenth century, the Creek population may have been about 20,000, occupying from 40 to 60 towns. In 1775, the whole confederacy, without the Seminole, was 11,000 in 55 towns. In 1785, there were 5,400 men and a total population of 19,000. In 1789, there were 6,000 warriors and 24,000 inhabitants in 100 towns. In 1904, after removal to Indian Territory, the population was 9,905.

For more information, see Oklahoma, Creek.

Lo-cha-ha-jo (The Drunken Terrapin), Treaty-making chief of the Creeks, pre-1877
Courtesy Museum of New Mexico, Neg. No. 87530

FLORIDA

Bobby Henry's Seminole Indian Village
5221 N. Orient Road
Tampa, FL 33610
(813) 626-3948

Seminole ("runaways," from the Creek language)

Location: Leave Interstate 4 on the eastern outskirts of Tampa at Orient Road (Exit 5). Drive north on Orient Road a quarter-mile to the Seminole Cultural Center, which is now Bobby Henry's Seminole Indian Village.

Visitor Information: In the nineteenth century, the Seminole fought for their homeland in one of history's most lethal guerrilla wars. The swamps and forests of Florida were their home after being forced out of their native Georgia and Alabama by the encroaching non-Indian settlers. General Andrew Jackson with 3,000 federal troops invaded Florida in 1818. His victory not only claimed the land for the United States but also confined the Seminole to Florida's swamps. Then, in May 1830, President Jackson signed into law the Indian Removal Act. It called for the removal of all the Indians of the so-called Five Civilized Tribes from their southeastern homelands to Indian Territory (what we know as Oklahoma today). The Seminole proudly refused to move, and thousands were killed in the second Seminole War of 1835–1842. Medicine Man Bobby Henry has preserved the arts, crafts, history, and way of life of the Seminole in this traditional village. Hours are Monday through Saturday, 9:00 a.m. to 5:00 p.m.; Sunday, noon to 5:00 p.m.

Miccosukee
P.O. Box 440021
Tamiami Station
Miami, FL 33144
(305) 223-8380 or (305) 223-8383
Fax (305) 223-1011

Mikasuki

Location: The tribal complex is 25 miles west of Miami on the Tamiami Trail, which is Highway 41.

Public Ceremony or Powwow Dates: Call for the dates of the Green Corn Ceremonies and stomp dances. The Arts Festival featuring dancing, arts, and crafts is held the week after Christmas.

Art Forms: The Miccosukee museum shows traditional Miccosukee life in exhibits, films, photos, and paintings. There is a reconstructed village with open-sided Miccosukee "chickees," the old-fashioned houses of the tribe. Here you can find traditional colorful Miccosukee clothing, dugout canoes, and arts and crafts demonstrations and sales.

Visitor Information: Don't miss the alligator wrestling. Across the street from the village is the Miccosukee restaurant serving Miccosukee and regular fare. Adjacent to the restaurant are the Miccosukee airboat rides, which fly you through the Everglades. Your guides will be happy to take you to a small tree-covered island to show you a real old-time Miccosukee camp that is still in use.

The Mikasuki are a former Seminole division. They spoke the Hitchiti dialect and were partly emigrants from the Sawokli towns on the lower Chattahoochee River, Alabama. At this time, they had 300 houses, which were burned by General Jackson. There were then several villages near the lake, known also as Mikasuki towns, which were occupied almost wholly by blacks. In the Seminole War of 1835–1842, the people of this town became famous for their courage and audacity.

Seminole
6073 Stirling Road
Hollywood, FL 33024
(305) 584-0400
Fax (305) 581-8917

Sim a no le or Isti simanole ("separatist," "runaway," from the Creek language)

Location: The Seminole Okalee Village is on the Seminole Reservation west of Dania, near Hollywood, Florida.

Public Ceremony or Powwow Dates: The annual powwow is usually held in February. The Seminole Fair is generally held the fourth weekend in December.

Cora Osceola Seminole Indian Camp, Tamiami Trail
Photo by Doubleday; Courtesy Museum of New Mexico, Neg. No. 88478

Art Forms: The Arts and Crafts Center, 6073 Sterling Road, in Hollywood, is at Highway 441 and Sterling Road, 4 miles west of Dania, telephone (305) 583-3590. Many traditional arts and crafts are sold. There are beautiful patchwork clothes, baskets, and carvings for sale.

Visitor Information: The Florida Seminole are very traditional in some aspects of their life-style in the Everglades of Florida. They wear colorful clothing and practice traditional ceremonial ways. For a tour of the area, call the tribal office.

This is a Muskhogean tribe of Florida, originally made up of immigrants from the lower Creek towns on the Chattahoochee River, who moved into Florida following the destruction of the Apalachee and other native tribes. They were at first classed with the lower Creeks but began to be known under their present name about 1775. Those still residing in Florida call themselves Ikaniuksalgi, "peninsula people."

Before the removal of the main body of this tribe to Indian Territory, the Seminole consisted chiefly of descendants of Muscogee (Creeks) and Hitchiti from the lower Creek towns, with a considerable number of refugees from the upper Creeks after the Creek war, together with remnants of Yamasee and other conquered tribes, Yuchi, and many blacks who were runaway slaves. While still under Spanish rule, the Seminole became involved in hostility with the United States, particularly in the War of 1812 and again in 1817-18, the first Seminole war. This war was quelled by General Andrew Jackson, who invaded Florida with a force of about 3,000 men, as the result of which Spain ceded the territory to the United States in 1819. By the treaty of Ft. Moultrie in 1823, the Seminole ceded most of their lands, except for a central reservation. Because of pressure from the bordering non-Indian population for their complete removal, another treaty was negotiated at Paynes Landing in 1832, by which they were bound to move beyond the Mississippi within three years. The treaty was repudiated by a large proportion of the tribe who, under the leadership of the great Osceola, at once prepared to resist. Thus began the second Seminole War in 1835, with the killing of Emathla, the principal signer of the removal treaty, and of General A. R. Thompson, who had been instrumental in applying pressure to those who opposed the arrangement. The war lasted nearly eight years, ending in August 1842 with the practical expatriation of the tribe from Florida to the west, but at the cost of the lives of nearly 1,500 American troops and the expenditure of $20 million. Blacks took an active part throughout the war on the side of the Seminole. Those removed to Oklahoma were subsequently organized into the "Seminole Nation," as one of the so-called Five Civilized Tribes. With the other tribes, they signed the agreement for the opening of their lands in Oklahoma, Indian Territory, to settlement. In 1908, they were officially reported as numbering 2,138, largely mixed with blacks in addition to 986 "Seminole Freedmen." At this time, a refugee band of Seminole lived on the Mexican side of the Rio Grande in Eagle Pass, Texas. The Seminole still residing in the southern part of Florida were officially estimated at 275.

For more information, see Oklahoma, Seminole.

MISSISSIPPI

Mississippi Band of Choctaw
P.O. Box 6010—Choctaw Branch
Philadelphia, MS 39350
(601) 656-5251
Fax (601) 656-1992

Chata Hapia Hoke

Location: Tribal headquarters are located in the Pearl River Community, which is also the site of the bustling Choctaw Industrial Park, east of Philadelphia, Mississippi. Visitors will find the Choctaw Museum, Arts and Crafts Shop, and the Choctaw Indian Fair in Pearl River. Nanih Waiyah, Mother Mound of the Choctaw, is near Bogue Chitto (Preston). Bogue Homa is the southernmost community.

Public Ceremony or Powwow Dates: The annual four-day Choctaw Indian Fair begins in the early morning of the first Wednesday after the Fourth of July. In olden times, it was the Green Corn Ceremony. Now, as traditionally, it is the grand gathering of the Okla, the people. Here you can participate in the world of the Indian: dances, crafts, entertainers, and pageantry. You can also see the incomparable granddaddy of games, the Choctaw Stickball World Series, the oldest field sport in America.

Art Forms: Members of the tribe do basket weaving, beadwork, and needlepoint on traditional styles of clothing.

Visitor Information: Every year in midsummer since 1949, the Mississippi Band of Choctaw Indians has presented the Choctaw Indian Fair as a major social gathering to revive and preserve Choctaw heritage and to promote public relations with surrounding communities. It has grown into a major tourist attraction. The fair attracts over 20,000 people a year in four days. These visitors come from nearby and faraway, even Europe, where there is considerable interest in Indian cultures.

The Choctaw were once one of the largest of tribes in what is now the southeastern United States, with strong democratic governmental institutions and a productive, agriculture-based community. The colonial powers vying for Choctaw Country (Britain, France, Spain, and later the United States) destroyed the tribal economy and forced the tribal government into a series of treaties making economic and land cessions. Although the tribe had developed sophisticated educational and law enforcement systems on the lands it administered, the last 10,423,130 acres of Choctaw Country were ceded to the United States under the Treaty of Dancing Rabbit Creek (1830), a treaty endorsed by only a minority of tribal members.

The members of the Choctaw tribe now living on a 21,000-acre reservation in east central Mississippi are the descendants of those tribal members who elected to remain in the original homeland when faced with removal to Indian Territory in the nineteenth century and who struggled with poverty and segregation in their homeland in order to preserve and enhance their traditional culture.

With the establishment of the tenant farming system after the Civil War, the Choctaw became sharecroppers. In the late nineteenth century, the Catholic church established a mission and school in the Tucker community. In 1918, the Congress, reacting to hearings that revealed the dire living conditions endured by the members of the tribe, established a Bureau of Indian Affairs agency at Philadelphia and schools in each of the seven Choctaw communities and began buying the land that today forms the reservation.

In 1945, the tribe adopted a Constitution and By-laws that provided for establishment of a Tribal Council. In the 1960s, the council and other tribal governmental institutions began to develop rapidly under the tribal goal of Choctaw self-determination. Reources for social programs to improve the tribal standard of living and health status were obtained, and an effort to develop the reservation economy was begun. This effort paid off in 1979, when, under the aegis of Chief Phillip Martin, the first tribal enterprise opened its doors. Since then, five additional industrial plants have been built. The Mississippi Band of Choctaw Indians is now the largest employer in Neshoba County and one of the largest in the state.

Choctaw people have been on their land so long that their origin is known only through legends. These legends focus on Nanih Waiya, the Mother Mound, located near Preston, Mississippi. This mound is connected by legend with both the creation and migration of the tribe. The center of the Choctaw before the advent of non-Indians, it was considered by Indians to be the birthplace of their race. Out of the mound ages ago, they believe, came first the Creek, Cherokee, and Chickasaw, who sunned themselves until dry to settle around the mound, their Great Mother, who told them that if ever they left her side they would die.

Another legend relates Nanih Waiya to Choctaw migration in the tribe's search for a new homeland. A tribal elder gives one account:

"Many years ago, the ancestors of our people lived in the northwest. In time their population became so large that it was difficult to exist there. The prophets of the tribe announced that a land of fertile soil and abundant game lay in the southeast and that the people could live there in peace and prosperity forever. Under the leadership of Chahta, our people set forth.

"At the end of each day's journey, a sacred pole was planted erect in front of the camp. The next morning the pole would be found to be leaning one way or another; in that direction the tribesmen were to travel for that day. For months our people followed the sacred staff. One day when the tribe stopped on the west side of a creek, Chahta planted the pole; heavy rain began to fall. The next day, the staff which had burrowed itself deeper in the ground stood straight and tall for all to see. Chahta proclaimed that the long sought land of Nanih Waiya had been found. Here, we would build our homes and a mound as the sacred burial spot for our ancestors."

Today Nanih Waiya is surrounded by fields and pasture. Nature's wind and water erosion and man's farming have reduced the mound to a fraction of its former size. Several years ago, the state of Mississippi developed a small state park at the site which included a trail to the legendary Nanih Waiya cave, a picnic area, and a small meeting hall. Although figuring in the Choctaw legends, Nanih Waiya as it exists today is not under the ownership or control of the Mississippi Band of Choctaw Indians.

Gold seekers were the first Europeans to come to Choctaw Country. The Choctaw lands stretched from offshore islands in the Gulf of Mexico to north-central Alabama and central Mississippi and from the Mississippi River to eastern Alabama. A Spaniard, Alonzo Pineda, was the first known European to enter Choctaw territory, although before his arrival in 1519, the coastline had been charted by an unknown cartographer.

In 1540, Hernando de Soto, a cruel and powerful man, came to the Choctaw land. He brought about 600 well-armed men, 200 of them on horseback. They enslaved, looted, and killed Indian people as they traveled through the Southeast. Thousands were killed, but finally the Choctaw drove the Spanish from the territory. They left behind the booty stolen from the Indians.

About 1700, the French came and were soon followed by the Spanish and English. Choctaw Country became pivotal in the struggle of the three powers to gain economic and political control of the vast Mississippi Valley. For over 100 years, the Choctaw were caught up in the struggle for occupation of their lands by the three powers. Finally, the Choctaw were recognized as an independent nation by the United States and a treaty was signed in 1786. This treaty aligned the Choctaw with the United States against the other nations. But their determined efforts to gain friendship and fair treatment from the United States eventually failed.

Thomas Jefferson's 1803 message to Congress urging that the huge Louisiana Territory be purchased from France included the proposal that Indian nations be moved to less desirable lands west of the Mississippi. Accordingly, the Louisiana Territorial Act of 1804 empowered the president to move tribes off their land to make way for American settlers. But removal was delayed for a generation during which Choctaw people sought to accept non-Indian customs. For thirty years, the Choctaw people made an effort to please the United States by adapting their governmental and social institutions and were successful, until the tragedy at Dancing Rabbit Creek.

The succession of treaty agreements had restricted Choctaw land to east-central Mississippi. In 1829, encouraged by President Andrew Jackson, the State of Mississippi declared all members of the tribe to be citizens of the state and attempted to obliterate the tribal government through laws that imposed severe punishment on any Choctaw who accepted tribal office. Spokesmen for Jackson claimed the federal government, in spite of treaties, could not prevent the State of Mississippi from enforcing its new laws. In 1830, the Choctaw were coerced into accepting the terms of the Treaty of Dancing Rabbit Creek. The treaty was signed, however, only after many of the tribal negotiators had left in disgust. The last of the Choctaw land was lost. Provision was made for individuals to stay and claim the land, but strong inducement was given the tribe to move to lands set aside for them in Oklahoma. The trek to Oklahoma was marked with hardship, heartbreak, and disease. Many died.

Over 8,000 Choctaw remained in Mississippi, relying on the promise of allotments of land and other considerations. For them, treachery came soon and hope died fast. Those few who acquired allotted land were forced out with the approval, often with the active support, of state and federal governments. In the years after 1830, harsh, constant pressure was placed upon Mississippi Choctaw to move west. From a preremoval population of 19,200, 1,253 remained in 1910. During this period, concerted federal efforts to remove the tribe to Oklahoma took place in 1831, 1846, 1849, 1853, 1854, 1890, and 1903.

From the beginning of removal until after the American Civil War, the Choctaw lived as squatters and sharecroppers on the land that was once theirs. Finally in 1918, the U.S. government acknowledged that this tribe was not going to leave Mississippi.

It is ironic that the Choctaw had allied themselves with the young United States, seeing their future as part of the new experiment in democracy. Indeed, Benjamin Franklin and others of the founding fathers drew heavily on the Native American confederacy pattern as they shaped the Union. Franklin said, in effect, if the Indians can do it, so can we. A great confederacy in the South, the Choctaw were composed of many subtribes, allies, and satellite groups.

In 1824, Pushmataha and other chiefs journeyed to Washington City to call on the president. His opening speech was to the Secretary of War. At that time, the Indian Service was in the War Department. This speech was to be his last. In it, he reaffirmed the alliance of the Choctaw Nation with the United States: "I can boast and say, and tell the truth, that none of my fathers, or grandfathers, nor any Choctaw, ever drew bows against the United States. They have always been friendly. We have held the hands of the United States so long that our nails are long like the talons of a bird and there is no danger of their slipping out."

Pushmataha was buried in the Old Congressional Cemetery in Washington, D.C. He was a warrior of great distinction. He was wise in council, eloquent in an extraordinary degree; and on all occasions, and under all circumstances, the white man's friend. For more information, see Oklahoma, Choctaw.

NORTH CAROLINA

Eastern Band of Cherokee
Cherokee Council House
P.O. Box 455
Cherokee, NC 28719
(704) 497-2771
Fax (704) 497-2952

Cherokee

Location: The Cherokee Reservation is in western North Carolina, south of Interstate 40, with State Highway 19 running through it.

Public Ceremony or Powwow Dates: Many festivals are held from April through December, including the ongoing festival "Unto These Hills." Please call or write Cherokee Tribal Travel and Promotion at P.O. Box 465, Cherokee, NC 28719, (704) 497-9195 or 1-800-438-1601, for a beautiful full-color kit with *everything* you need to know for a great travel experience with the whole family in Cherokee country.

Art Forms: Nearly all the people spend some of their time doing arts and crafts, producing some of the very finest Native American baskets, pottery, beadwork, finger weavings, stone carvings, and wood carvings.

Visitor Information: Your visit to the Cherokee Indian Reservation will be an adventure in fun and learning. Visit the Oconaluftee Indian Village, a replica of a 1700s Cherokee community featuring guided tours, demonstrations by craftworkers, and the traditional seven-sided Council House. The Museum of the Cherokee Indian tells the story of the Cherokee through the magic of electronics, audiovisual displays, and priceless artifacts. The Qualla Arts and Crafts Mutual next door is nationally known for handmade quality arts and crafts.

Other popular Cherokee attractions include the Cherokee Heritage Museum and Gallery located in Saunooke's Village, the

Cyclorama Cherokee Indian Wax Museum, the Museum of the American Indian, and the Pioneer Farmstead Visitor Center located at the Cherokee entrance to the Great Smoky Mountains National Park. A guided visit into the back roads and contemporary life of the Cherokee is available through Smoky Mountain Tours.

In addition, the Cherokee have Santa's Land theme park as well as one of the largest trout farms in the Southeast. They also stock three huge ponds and 30 miles of mountain streams with over a quarter of a million trout per year. Horseback riding, rafting, tubing, and miniature golf are also available.

At night from mid-June through late August, the outdoor drama, "Unto These Hills," portraying the history of the Eastern Band of Cherokee Indians, is presented.

Cherokee forefathers had a very thought-provoking way of looking at life. They believed that the universe was made up of three separate worlds, the Upper World, the Lower World, and the world we live in. This world, a round island resting on the surface of the waters, was suspended from the sky by four cords attached to the island at the four cardinal points of the compass.

Each direction of this world was identified by its own color. According to Cherokee doctrine, east was associated with the color red because it was the direction of the sun, the greatest deity of all. Red was also the color of sacred fire, believed to be directly connected with the sun, with blood, and, therefore, with life. Finally, red was the color of success.

The west was the moon segment. It provided no warmth and was not life-giving as the sun way. So its color was black, which also stood for the region of the souls of the dead and for death itself. North was the direction of cold, and so its color was blue, representing trouble and defeat. South was the direction of warmth. Its color, white, was associated with peace and happiness.

This world hovered somewhere between the perfect order and predictability of the Upper World and the total disorder and instability of the Lower World. Mankind's goal, according to the Cherokee, was to find some kind of halfway path, or balance, between the Upper World and the Lower World while living in this world today. It is not surprising that many Cherokee still believe in an Upper World and a Lower World. The Upper World is called Heaven, the religion is called Christianity, and many denominations are very active on this reservation, both Protestant and Catholic. If you are visiting the reservation on a Sunday, you are welcome to join the Cherokee for Sunday worship at any of their many churches.

Years ago, around the campfires, men and women took their turn telling stories and entertaining the whole tribe. Some stories had serious meanings and others were just for fun. For instance, if you were a young Cherokee boy you would learn that the bears in the Great Smokies were once men, who were transformed into bears by the Great Spirit because they were so lazy. You would learn that the Buzzard is a highly respected bird and that a huge Buzzard formed the Great Smoky Mountains by flying too close to the ground. The valleys of the mountains are where the giant Buzzard's wings hit, pushing the ground down and the mountains up.

If you were sick, your Cherokee Indian mother would explain why. "Man made the animals of the woods angry by killing them. One day, the bears, fishes, deer, reptiles, and birds got together for a meeting and decided to punish man by giving him diseases. When the plants, who were friendly to Man, heard what had been done by the animals, the plants decided to defeat the animal's evil diseases. Each tree, shrub, and herb agreed to furnish a cure for one of the diseases for man. Man had only to figure out which type of plant cured which diseases."

Because the early Cherokee really believed this story, they discovered many useful medicines. In fact, some modern-day doctors believe that many of these long-lost Cherokee remedies would be just as effective as, and in some cases more effective than, modern medicines commonly used today.

The Cherokee were once a mighty and powerful nation. At the time when the Cherokee first came into contact with the white man (de Soto in 1540), they claimed 135,000 square miles of territory covering parts of eight states: North Carolina, South Carolina, Georgia, Alabama, Tennessee, Kentucky, Virginia, and West Virginia. By the end of the revolution, the Cherokee had lost about half their land. Between 1785 and 1835, the Cherokee lands had shrunk to a few million acres. By the Treaty of New Echota in 1835, all lands east of the Mississippi were ceded to the federal government. (Of the 40 treaties executed with the Cherokee, the federal government chose to break each and every one.) Article 12 of this treaty, as amended, provided that Cherokee who were adverse to removal (about 1,200) could become citizens and remain in the state of North Carolina.

The status of those who remained in the state was anomalous. Their connection with the main body of the Cherokee Nation, which had removed to lands west of the Mississippi, was severed. They became subject to the laws of the state of North Carolina although they were not admitted to the rights of citizenship. Any interest in the lands formerly held by the Nation in North Carolina had been divested by the treaty, and even their right to self-government had ended. North Carolina later granted a charter to the Cherokee authorizing them to exercise limited powers of self-government.

Pressure to force removal of this remnant of Cherokee continued. Funds due them were withheld by the U.S. government unless they would remove to the Indian Territory or would secure an act of the Legislature of North Carolina permitting them to remain permanently within the state.

Through purchase by an agent, the Eastern Band of Cherokee Indians acquired the right to possession of tracts of land in North Carolina, and by a North Carolina statute of 1866, they acquired, with the approval of the U.S. government, permission to remain in the state. Cherokee possession of their lands was conveyed to the United States to be held in trust for the Eastern Band. Taking the land into trust status had the effect of establishing Cherokee lands as an Indian reservation and recognizing them as such by the federal government. Although the manner in which the Cherokee Reservation was established is different from the ways in which other reservations were established, the Cherokee Reservation is subject to the same general federal laws and regulations that apply on other Indian reservations.

The lands now held in trust by the U.S. government for the Eastern Band of Cherokee Indians comprise 56,572.8 acres scattered over five counties. It consists of 52 tracts or boundaries, which are contained in 30 completely separated bodies of land. All of the land is held in common by the tribe; possessory holdings are issued to individuals. The Council of the Eastern Band of Cherokee Indians determines the management and control of all real and personal property belonging to the Band, subject to the trust responsibility of the United States.

For the most part, the lands are mountainous with small valleys along the rivers and streams suitable for farming, business, and recreational sites. The elevation varies from 1,718 feet to over 5,000 feet.

The latest official enrollment was conducted in 1982. There were 8,822 enrolled members, with 5,971 living on Eastern Band of Cherokee Indian lands and 2,851 residing off the reservation.

As a federally recognized tribe, the Eastern Band of Cherokee Indians possesses sovereignty over its territory and its members. Like other tribes, the Eastern Band is a sovereign unit of government in its own right. It is neither an instrumentality of the federal government nor a political subdivision of the state government.

Much of the old culture remains, consisting principally of non-material elements. Most, if not all, Cherokee speak or understand English, but the Cherokee language is taught in the homes and elementary schools. Sequoyah's syllabary, which uses symbols of sounds instead of letters or words, has made it possible for this language to be written and taught from text.

Bean dumplings, bean bread, chestnut bread, and ramps are a few native foods that are still commonly eaten in Cherokee homes. Many still cling to the ancient lore and customs. They sing old hymns in their own musical language. Some of the older women wear long full dresses and a bright kerchief tied on their heads. Occasionally, one can see a baby tied on the back of a Cherokee woman.

In earlier times, the Cherokee had their own set of laws, they farmed, and they lived in log houses. They made clothing from a type of cloth and did not wear feather headdresses. They introduced corn and tobacco to the white man and used salicylic acid (aspirin) for headaches and had caffeine in their drinks for a "pick-me-up" before Bayer or Coca-Cola was even thought of.

For more information, see Oklahoma, Cherokee.

Lumbee
Lumbee Regional Development Association
P.O. Box 68
Pembroke, NC 28372
(919) 521-8602
Fax (919) 521-8625

Location: Most members of the Lumbee tribe live in Robeson and the adjoining counties of North Carolina. Tribal offices are located in Pembroke, North Carolina.

Public Ceremony or Powwow Dates: The Lumbee Regional Development Association sponsors Lumbee Homecoming, an annual tribal festival held in Pembroke the first week of July. An annual powwow is held in the fall. Call the tribal office for dates and times.

Art Forms: Members of the Lumbee tribe practice a variety of traditional and modern art forms including basketry, wood carving, beadwork, leathercrafts, and silversmithing. Lumbee arts and crafts are available at local stores and at the annual powwow and public events.

Visitor Information: Pembroke is 10 miles west of Lumberton, which is located on Interstate 95 in southeastern North Carolina. Visitors to the area will find lodging, restaurants, and many other attractions. The Native American Resource Center on the campus of Pembroke State University in Pembroke has a fine museum collection of artifacts of the Lumbee and other Indian tribes. Also being developed nearby are the Indian Education Resource Center and the North Carolina Indian Cultural Center. "Strike at the Wind," an outdoor drama based on the history of the Lumbee, is performed in the area during July and August. The Lumber River is a natural and scenic river which flows through the area.

More than 40,000 Lumbee Indians live in Robeson and the surrounding counties. According to the 1990 Census, the Lumbee are the ninth largest tribe in the country and the second largest tribe east of the Mississippi. The Lumbee take their name from the Lumbee River, known as the Lumber River today, which flows through their homeland. They consider the town of Pembroke to be their Indian education and trade center.

The present-day Lumbee tribe is descended from an Indian community composed largely of Cheraw Indians and related Siouan-speaking people. Both are known to have inhabited the area of what is now Robeson County since the 18th century. Documents exist to substantiate this statement. It is also substantiated by oral tradition.

The Lumbee have been recognized by the state of North Carolina since 1885, when they were given their own separate school system that operated under the authority of tribal leaders. The school system was exclusively for Lumbee tribal members. Two years later, in 1887, the state established the Indian Normal School for the training of Indian teachers. This institution is known today as Pembroke State University and is one of 16 institutions that make up the North Carolina University System.

The tribe has had a relationship with the federal government since 1888. At that time approximately 54 tribal members petitioned for federal educational aid. Since 1888 more then 10 bills that would recognize the Lumbee as an Indian tribe have been introduced by Congress. The tribe was denied recognition because of money issues or the government's policy toward Indians. However, in 1956 a bill passed that recognized the Lumbee as Indians but denied the tribe full status as a federally recognized Indian tribe.

Haliwa-Saponi
P.O. Box 99
Hollister, NC 27844
(919) 584-4017

Location: Tribal Pottery and Arts is located on Highway 561, 20 miles west of Hollister. Call for hours they will be open.

Art Forms: Pottery, quilts, beadwork, and stonework are offered for sale.

The Saponi are one of the eastern Siouan tribes, formerly living in North Carolina and Virginia. The Saponi were at war with Virginia settlers as early as 1654–1656, the time of the attack by the Cherokee and probably in alliance with them.

SOUTH CAROLINA

Catawba
P.O. Box 11106
Rock Hill, SC 29731
(803) 366-4792
Fax (803) 366-9150

Catawba (probably from the Choctaw *katapa,* "divided," "separated," "a division")

Visitor Information: The artisans of this tribe still make pottery and welcome inquiries at their address or phone above.

SOUTHWEST

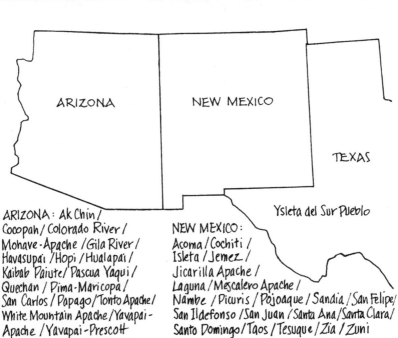

ARIZONA

NEW MEXICO

TEXAS

ARIZONA: Ak Chin /
Cocopah / Colorado River /
Mohave-Apache / Gila River /
Havasupai / Hopi / Hualapai /
Kaibab Paiute / Pascua Yaqui /
Quechan / Pima-Maricopa /
San Carlos / Papago / Tonto Apache /
White Mountain Apache / Yavapai-
Apache / Yavapai-Prescott

NEW MEXICO:
Acoma / Cochiti /
Isleta / Jemez /
Jicarilla Apache /
Laguna / Mescalero Apache /
Nambe / Picuris / Pojoaque / Sandia / San Felipe /
San Ildefonso / San Juan / Santa Ana / Santa Clara /
Santo Domingo / Taos / Tesuque / Zia / Zuni

Ysleta del Sur Pueblo

The Southwest of North America lies in, and south of, that place where the great Rocky Mountains slope down to meet the mesas and deserts. The combination of plains, valleys, mesas, and mountains creates breathtaking visual experiences, and the sunsets and cloud formations often combine to create indescribable beauty.

This is the land of the People of the Villages, the Pueblo People. And it is the land of the nomadic and mysterious Apache. And it is the land of those people who live in hogans in the desolate and isolated deserts and mesas, the Navajo.

The Southwest People are descendants of a proud and great culture. The ruins of villages can be found throughout the area, and sacred prayer sites are found in the mountains, valleys, and mesas. These people are now, as they have always been, spiritually attuned with their environment and respectful of the natural ways of life.

You can feel the spirit of the old ones in this land. Stand on a mesa and lift up your arms and your heart to the Creator and a feeling of awe for the Creation will overwhelm your being. This is the land of original life.

Before the coming of the European, this land was unspoiled and untouched by pollution. The Southwest People planted their crops with prayers and respect for the Creator of all life. They hunted for food with prayers and respect for the spirits of the animals that gave their lives for food. And they gathered food and herbs for medicine with offerings and thanks for these blessings from the Creator. Religion was not a part of their life; spirituality was their whole life. The old ones taught the young ones in ceremony, in the deserts, in the village kivas, and in the mountains by sacred lakes and streams, the wisdom of the goodness of life and that life is valuable only when it is good.

They developed one of the greatest cultures ever to exist on our Mother Earth. Their art forms were beautiful and functional. Pottery, turkey feather quilts, cotton cloth and buckskin for clothing, weavings, and stone jewelry were all refined to a fine degree. They utilized their resources without waste and gave thanks with every breath for the goodness provided to them by the Creator. They traded their artworks with the Plains People for buffalo meat and horses.

And they played the drum, the heartbeat of our Mother Earth, in their ceremonies while the people danced in honor of the Creator and all living things. They danced in thanks for good crops and good harvest and all the things the Creator provides through respect and love.

The sacred winds blow even today in the Southwest. The Southwest People still celebrate life in ceremony and praise of the Creator and the Creation.

You are welcome to join with the Southwest People and attend sacred ceremonies. As visitors, you are asked to stay in public areas only. Photographing, videotaping, tape recording, and sketching are not allowed unless specifically permitted by the people you are visiting. Always ask tribal officials before ceremonies begin for the proper etiquette to follow.

Join with the tribes on the following pages to honor their ancestors and to honor our Creator, our Mother Earth, our Moon, our Sun, and the whole of all living things in the whole of all Creation. You will find that it is good. It is very, very good.

Aho . . .

You must speak straight so that your words may go as sunlight to our hearts.

—Cochise (Apache)

There is one God looking down upon us all.

—Geronimo (Apache)

ARIZONA

Ak-Chin Pima and Tohono O'odham
42507 W. Peters and Nall Road
Maricopa, AZ 85239
(602) 568-2227

Pima
Tohono O'odham

Location: The Ak-Chin community is located straight south of Phoenix at Maricopa.

Public Ceremony or Powwow Dates: The Feast of St. Francis is held annually on October 4. It is a major holiday on many reservations because it honors St. Francis, who loved nature. Chile stew, flour tortillas, beans, fry bread, corn, and kool-aid are served. The afternoon and evening are filled with traditional dances, in which more than 500 dancers usually participate.

Art Forms: The Pima are outstanding basket weavers, and the pottery of the Maricopa is ranked with the best in the Southwest. Look for their work at the Gila River Arts and Crafts Museum at Sacaton, Arizona. Take Interstate 10 and Exit 175, at Casa Blanca; telephone (602) 963-3981.

Visitor Information: The Ak-Chin EcoMuseum (602-568-2221/2) was established recently after the discovery of valuable artifacts that relate to the early Ak-Chin people during the course of a land clearance and archaeological project. These artifacts contributed to a renewed interest by community members in their past as well as a greater sense of self-esteem. The EcoMuseum provides an opportunity to communicate Tohono O'odham culture and history to future generations of Ak-Chin and to non-Indians as well. The EcoMuseum is distinguished from a traditional museum in that land and territory

Unidentified man and woman, Pima, ca. 1883
Photo by Ben Wittick; Courtesy Museum of New Mexico, Neg. No. 102058

replace the museum building, the residents of the area take on the role of curator and public, and the decentralized organization encourages each and every family to create, maintain, and enjoy exhibits they have developed. The Ak-Chin EcoMuseum serves the community that owns it and shares the spirit of the community with the museum visitor.

The Pima are of the Piman language group, which is a subdivision of the Uto-Aztecan language family. They are closely related to the Nevome and Papag tribes. Since prehistoric times they have lived in the Gila and Salt River valleys, near what is now Phoenix, Arizona. Non-Indian settlers have depleted their water, but they still farm with the aid of irrigation. The Pima were first encountered by non-Indians in 1697. The Apache were their chief enemies. Early in the 1800s, the Maricopa joined with the Pima, and the two tribes have lived in harmony.

For more information, see Arizona, Gila River.

Cocopah
P.O. Box Bin "G"
Somerton, AZ 85350
(602) 627-2102
Fax (602) 627-3173

Cocopah

Location: The reservation is located south of Yuma at Somerton.

Public Ceremony or Powwow Dates: The annual Cocopah Festivities Day is held in March or April. There is traditional dancing and singing, including the Rabbit Dance and Round Dances.

Art Forms: You can find good beadwork and fine gourd rattles at the festival. Also, the Cocopah Elderly Center on Cedar Street on the reservation has a small gift shop that sells ribbon shirts, beadwork, and other arts and crafts. Telephone (602)627-2632 for more details. The traditional singers from this community often sing at memorial services, but there are also occasions when they do sing for the public.

Visitor Information: There are plans for a museum at the Yuma Territorial Mall.

Big Frank (Frank Tehanna), Cocopa, 1900
Photo by DeLancey Gill; Courtesy Museum of New Mexico, Neg. No. 59448

Colorado River Mojave, Chemehuevi, Navajo, and Hopi
Route 1, Box 23B
Parker, AZ 85344
(602) 669-9211
Fax (602) 669-5675

Mojave
Chemehuevi
Navajo
Hopi

Location: To find the museum, go two miles south of Parker, and at 2nd and Mojave streets turn off toward the hospital.

Art Forms: Baskets and modern arts and crafts are offered for sale in the gift shop.

Visitor Information: The first two tribes, the Mojave and Chemehuevi, are the original people of this area. The museum offers a collection of ancient and modern arts and crafts, a library, a gift shop, and cultural collections.

These tribes are in the process of developing commercial enterprises and currently are operating the Blue Water Marine Park, a mobile home park, a charter air service, and large-scale farming.

The Mojave are of the Yuman language group of the Hokan language family. They preferred living on both sides of the Colorado River. Although they never signed a treaty, the Colorado River Reservation was established in 1865. The early Mojave used rafts made of bundles of reeds in fishing but preferred a diet of corn, pumpkins, melons, and beans. The Mojave lived in huts covered with brushwood and sand. The Yavapai, another tribe in the Yuman language group, are often called the Apache Mojave.

Fort McDowell Mohave-Apache
P.O. Box 17779
Fountain Hills, AZ 85268
(602) 837-5121
Fax (602) 837-1630

Mohave-Apache

Location: This reservation is a suburb of the city of Phoenix and is located in the northeast part of the city.

For more information, see Arizona, Colorado River.

Gila River Pima and Maricopa
P.O. Box 97
Sacaton, AZ 85247
(602) 562-3311 or (602) 963-4323
Fax (602) 562-3422

Pima
Maricopa

Location: This reservation is located south of Phoenix. Take Interstate 10 south and Exit 175 at Casa Blanca, to Sacaton.

Public Ceremony or Powwow Dates: There is usually a festival held the second weekend in March. There is traditional Pima dancing with crafts demonstrations, foods, and other interesting events. Call the Gila River Arts and Crafts Museum at (602) 963-3981 for dates and times.

Art Forms: The Pima make fine baskets, and the Maricopa make some of the best pottery to be found in the Southwest. The gift shop at the Gila Arts and Crafts Museum sells arts and crafts from over 30 tribes in the Southwest, California, and Mexico.

Visitor Information: There is a great restaurant here which serves Indian food. The outdoor museum displays reconstructed houses of the Pima, Maricopa, Apache, and Papago.

For more information, see Arizona, Ak-Chin.

Havasupai
P.O. Box 10
Supai, AZ 86435
(602) 448-2961
Fax (602) 448-2551

Havasupai

Location: The tribal offices are in Supai, which is located in the bottom of the Grand Canyon. Drive from Peach Springs to the canyon rim and leave your vehicle. Hike the 8 miles down to the reservation or call from the phone at the rim to make arrangements for mules or horses available for rent from the tribe. This is the most advisable way because the hike back up and out of the canyon can be a challenge.

Public Ceremony or Powwow Dates: The Peach Festival is held in August, and dances are often held on Memorial Day. Call the tribal office for dates and times.

Visitor Information: This is an unusual opportunity to experience a place that is not accessible by modern means. Arrange your visit ahead of time with the tribally owned Havasupai Tourist Enterprise in Supai. You will enjoy the beauty of the area. If you've seen the Grand Canyon and liked it, you will love the trip to Havasupai country.

Hopi
P.O. Box 123
Kykotsmovi, AZ 86039
(602) 734-2445
Fax (602) 734-2435

Hopi

Location: The mesa villages are located on State Highway 264 in northeast Arizona.

Public Ceremony or Powwow Dates: Kachina dances are held from late winter to midsummer, but the dates are usually not set more than two or three weeks in advance. Inquiries about dates and places may be addressed to the Hopi Cultural Center, P.O. Box 67, Second Mesa, AZ 86043; telephone (602) 734-2401. Remember, no alcohol or drugs are permitted, and no photographs or tape-recordings can be made without the approval of the tribal office. Be respectful of the ceremonies and the people.

Art Forms: The Hopi have never faltered in their respect for the arts. They create pottery, baskets, jewelry, paintings (both traditional subject matter and very progressive), and cottonwood root carvings of

Kachina dolls. Traditional Hopi people do not approve of the sale of Kachina dolls, so you may not wish to purchase any yourself. However, the artists feel that they are preserving the culture and they need the income, so it is a matter of your own heart.

Visitor Information: I recommend that you stay with the tribe in their Cultural Center Motel and Restaurant. There is traditional Indian food, and the lodging is excellent. A guide is required to visit Walpi, on First Mesa, along State Route 264 at Polacca. Drive to the top of the mesa (leave motor homes and buses) and arrange for a guide at the Village Information Office, at the entrance to Walpi village (9:00 a.m. to 5:00 p.m. daily, no telephone). No fee will be charged to enter the reservation, but a donation is always appreciated.

The Hopi have lived in the Southwest for more than 2,000 years; their ancestors were called the Anasazi. When Coronado entered the Southwest in 1540, the Spanish, with their guns and horses, enslaved the Hopi and their spiritual ceremonial life was altered.

They were forced to close their kivas (circular underground cere-monial chambers), and their sacred Kachina dances were prohib-ited. The Hopi, normally pacifist in nature, then joined with the other New Mexico pueblos in a successful revolt in 1680 which drove the Spanish from the country. About twenty years later the mission at Awatovi was rebuilt by the Spanish, but, as before, the mission was ultimately destroyed by tribal members. During the next two hun-dred years, serious droughts diminished their crops. Raids by the Navajo, Apache, and Ute slowly reduced the membership of the tribe. Then smallpox, brought by the Europeans in the 1800s, almost destroyed them entirely.

Today, the tribe has over 9,000 members, and the Hopi reservation covers over one and a half million acres of high plateau country, completely surrounded by the gigantic Navajo Reservation. Most of the people of the tribe live on three mesas near the center of the reservation. Three long fingers of land several miles apart stick up from the valley floor, and they are named from east to west, First Mesa, Second Mesa, and Third Mesa. On the top of the mesas are the three ancient Hopi villages, and at their bases are the three modern communities.

The people are friendly and courteous, but please contact the tribe for a guide before entering. The Hopi Mesa villages are constructed of stone, not adobe as most of the New Mexico pueblos. Many Hopi pre-

Da-wa-uni-ci, Mishongnovi Pueblo, Hopi, Arizona, 1901
Photo by Carl N. Werntz; Courtesy Museum of New Mexico, Neg. No. 37536

fer to live in the traditional villages despite the inconveniences. The people still use wood and coal for cooking and heating, but some homes have electricity. Many Hopi still farm the valleys below by hand with a planting stick as did their ancestors. Corn can be seen growing out of sand along hillsides and along dry creek beds. The power of prayers and ceremony cannot be overlooked. The corn is typical "Indian corn" in shades of blue, gold, maroon, and yellow. It is dried in the sun and ground into meal. Some of the fields are irrigated from springs, but most Hopi farmers practice dry farming. Small fields of corn, melons, beans, and squash flourish in almost impossible places. Again, the power of prayer and ceremony is the power of growth.

While they retain many ancient traditions, the Hopi have faced many changes over the years, as have all Indian people. Arts and crafts provide more personal income than any other source on the reservation. Jobs are hard to find, and the young people often move to urban areas to obtain work or more education. Many return to Hopiland to take part in ceremonies or to stay. The HUD houses below the mesas are typical of housing in rural communities.

The old stone pueblo villages on the mesas endure the passage of time, and sacred places are undisturbed. Prayer feathers and eagle feathers awaiting some upcoming ceremonial are tied in crevices among the dwellings. Stacks of gray dry cedar from juniper trees are waiting to be burned in outside ovens to bake traditional Indian bread.

Hopi ceremonials are intertwined with the everyday life of the people. One will not exist without the other. Kachina ceremonies are conducted to maintain the harmony of the world and satisfy the spirits of man, animals, rocks, trees, and all living things in the whole of all the Creation. The Kachinas are the embodiment of the spirits, and all Hopi life revolves around the proper performance and completeness of these spiritual ceremonies. The dancers who portray the Kachinas do ancient rituals after days of fasting and secret ceremony in the Kiva. The dances, in the end, are always offered to the Creator in praise and thanks and celebration for good crops, good health, well-being, and the welfare of all living things.

The Kachinas live in the San Francisco peaks near Flagstaff and only come to Hopiland for the ceremonials. The Hopi, being among the most spiritually oriented of people, celebrate in a regular fashion. The Wuwuchim, or New Year, is held on the eve of the new moon in November. It is among the most important rituals because it establishes the rhythms for the year to come. For four days, prayers, songs, and dances for a prosperous and safe new year are led by the priests (Hopi Medicine People) before the Kivas in their respective villages. The men of the tribe dance bare-chested, dressed in embroidered Hopi cotton kilts. Priests, from the Bear Clan, chant about the time before there were Hopi people, the time of Creation. It is a re-creation of the Creation; the time of the Creator's introduction of Hopi into the world.

The winter solstice celebration, December 21 and 22, is in ceremonial fashion the creation of the Hopi universe. The priests of the Bear Clan bless prayer feathers for the protection of the people. Traditionally, eagle feathers were used, but now, to protect the endangered species, turkey feathers are used instead.

The Hopi people follow a matrilineal society. The Basket Dances are held from late October through November. These dances remember the time when all the men were gone from the villages and the women kept the spiritual life of the people whole.

There are three different societies, each with their own dance and outfits. The Mamzaw is the group that represents the Hopi Spirituality. The women wear the headdress and costume, but not the mask of the Kachinas, representing various spirits that are in Hopi ceremonies. These ceremonies that take place in the plazas of the villages are the most popular of the year because the women throw little gifts from the baskets when they dance.

Each individual village sponsors "social dances." They are held from August to mid-October, to celebrate the good harvest and to give the young people the opportunity to mingle. The dances are open to young women, as long as they are not married and have no children, and even young children of both sexes. Among the most popular of the dances is the Butterfly, for which the men are outfitted in embroidered kilts and velvet shirts with ribbons. The dances usually take place on weekends, from about 10:00 a.m. until about 6:00 p.m. Competition dancers from neighboring villages often drop by, and the dancing can be fierce.

Enjoy your visit in Hopiland.

Hualapai
P.O. Box 179
Peach Springs, AZ 86434
(602) 769-2216
Fax (602) 769-2343

Walapai

Location: Peach Springs is located northeast of Kingman on old Route 66.

Public Ceremony or Powwow Dates: There are traditional dances held, but you must check with the tribal office for dates and times. The women are beautiful as they dance to Bird Songs. There is also a powwow in August.

Art Forms: The women wear long traditional dresses with beaded collars.

Visitor Information: The tribe is engaged in cattle raising and lumbering, and they operate Hualapai Grand Canyon Outfitters, which will take you on an exciting rafting trip down the Grand Canyon. Call the number above for more details.

Kaibab-Paiute
Tribal Affairs Building
HC 65, Box 2
Fredonia, AZ 86022
(602) 643-7245
Fax (602) 643-7260

Kaibab Paiute

Location: The Kaibab Indian Reservation is in the northwest corner of Arizona, 14 miles west of Fredonia.

Visitor Information: The tribe owns and operates an RV park for visitors to the reservation. It is a modern facility that includes a laundromat and a store. Pipe Springs National Monument is located on the reservation. It is the site of a fort from the days of the Indian wars. The tribe plans to build a museum of Paiute culture and history.

For more information, see Nevada, Paiute.

Navajo
P.O. Box 9000
Window Rock, AZ 86515

(602) 871-6352
Fax (602) 871-4025

Dene

Location: The Navajo Indian Reservation is in the Four Corners area of the United States (where Utah, Arizona, Colorado, and New Mexico have a common corner). Tribal headquarters are located in Window Rock. Navajo Community College is located in Tsaile. Monument Valley Navajo Tribal Park is north of Kayenta. Navajo Nation Visitor Centers are located in Cameron, Chinle, and Monument Valley. Kinlichee Navajo Tribal Park is eight miles east of Ganado.

Public Ceremony or Powwow Dates: The Northern Navajo Fair in Shiprock, New Mexico, is one of three major Navajo fairs that take place during the year. Indians from all over the whole of Turtle Island gather for this powwow, which features competitions in traditional song and dance. This one is usually the first weekend in October. Other powwows are held throughout the year, and you can find one somewhere on this huge reservation almost any weekend. Call the tribal office for places and times.

Traditional dances are also held regularly all over this reservation. Most are healing ceremony dances, and visitors may be allowed with the family's permission. Again, no pictures or sketching or tape recordings are allowed without the express permission of the medicine people or family involved in the ceremony.

Art Forms: Of course, the Navajo are famous for their fine rugs and jewelry and sand paintings, but they also do fine pottery and other traditional forms of functional arts. The Navajo Nation Arts and Crafts Enterprise is just east of Window Rock, at the junction of Highway 264 and Navajo Highway 12. Owned by the Navajo Nation, this is the home of authentic Indian arts and crafts. Also, the people sell their fine arts at the Four Corners area and along the highways throughout the reservation.

Visitor Information: Contact the Navajo Tourism Office, P.O. Box 663, Window Rock, AZ 86515, (602) 871-6436, for more information about lodging, restaurants, arts and crafts, dances, powwows, and other activities. Their fax number is (602) 871-7381.

Ralph Gray and family, Navajo, September 1935
Courtesy Museum of New Mexico, Neg. No. 42219

The Navajo Nation is the largest Indian tribe in the country. The majority reside in Arizona, roughly one-third live in New Mexico, and a few make their homes in southern Utah. Window Rock, near the Arizona-New Mexico border northwest of Gallup, is the Navajo government and business center.

The portion of the reservation lying in New Mexico is in the northwestern corner of the state and contains magnificent land formations and good fishing lakes. Sixteen lakes offer trout, channel catfish, bass, northern pike, and bluegill. Hunting for deer, turkey, bear, and small game is permitted. The Washington Pass picnic area and campground on N.M. 134 is very popular. For camping, fishing, and hunting information and permits, contact the Navajo Fish and Wildlife Deparment, Box 1480, Window Rock, AZ 86515 (602-871-6451).

Sand painting is a delicate art form done by the Navajo. But it is much more than an art form. It is a cleansing and healing ceremony. When it is used for the healing of one that is ill, the Hataali, or singer, who conducts the ceremony may direct several others who are his helpers. When it is done as an art form for demonstrations with the public present, these are the steps taken in the process: First, the ground is brushed clean and flattened if necessary. Then the layer of sand that is used for the base or foundation is spread. Finely ground charcoal, corn meal, pollen, mudstone, gypsum, and turquoise run like small streams through the artist's fingers to form the spirits of animals, plants, sunbeams, and rainbows. Working from the center out in circles in the ways of Creation, he creates the intricate painting, leaving the east side open for the spirit people to enter. The painting will not be correct in form and style as a healing painting would be in order not to offend the spirits. If he did a healing painting for demonstration purposes, he would lose the ability to do the real thing when it was needed. But only the medicine people notice what is missing and what may have been added. With the commercialization of sand paintings, the art is no longer confined to the singer; anyone can do the art.

Even before sand paintings were being done for commercial purposes, there were about 1,200 designs used in a wide range of ceremonies that varied with the illness being treated. With the Dene, illness in a person's body means that there is disharmony in the universe. The cleansing and healing ceremony of the sand painting calls the spirits to heal the patient and puts things back in an orderly way.

Sam Yazzie, Navajo, Pine Springs, Arizona, 1938
Courtesy Museum of New Mexico, Neg. No. 29934

The sand painting may be as small as a foot in diameter or as large as 12 feet in diameter, but most are about 6 by 6 feet, approximately the floor area of the average hogan (house). Often the painting will take hours to complete, even with several helpers. When the painting is finished, the ill person sits on it and the singer transforms the orderly, clean, goodness of the painting into the patient and puts the illness from the patient into the painting. The sand painting is discarded afterward. The whole ceremony can last from three to nine days, depending on the illness, accident, or catastrophe being treated.

Both commercial and sacred sand paintings use natural pigments on a tan sand base, resulting in pictures largely composed of earth tones, with some black, white, red, and yellow for strength. Both feature angular figures, made of straight lines and zigzags. Both are traditionally bordered on at least three sides, either with a straight or circular design. Subject matter, in addition to the Navajo spirits and scenery, is animals, the sun, the sky, and rainbows.

The most popular design includes sticklike figures (the spirits) adorned with belts, jewelry, skirts, and carrying bows and arrows. Sacred spirit animals like bears, coyotes, deer, and eagles frequently are drawn, as are plants such as corn, beans, squash, and tobacco. Although snakes are sacred, they are usually not found in Dene artwork because they represent danger. All the figures are geometric in design.

Some of the dances conducted in Navajo land are the Yei-Bei-Chei dances. These are for healing and are prescribed by a medicine man; therefore, they are sporadic in nature and scheduled only about two weeks in advance. These dances most often occur in fall and continue through the winter and spring months. They are rarely performed in summer. The patient is placed within the ceremonial hogan with the singer and his helpers chanting prayers, while dancers, usually 15 or 16 teams of 11 members each, dance throughout the night. The dancing is done in everyday clothes until the final two nights, when full outfits with special headgear and rattles are used to represent various spirits.

The Fire Dance Ceremony, like the Yei-Bei-Chei, is also a nine-day healing ceremony and also largely restricted to tribal members. This dance is rarely performed. It is important to note that the sponsoring family must give permission to attend the dances described here. If you happen to be on the site, you could be asked to leave.

Pascua Yaqui
7474 S. Camino de Oeste
Tucson, AZ 85746
(602) 883-2838
Fax (602) 883-7770

Yaqui

Location: The Yaqui were originally Mexican Indians, but many have resettled in Arizona and are recognized by the U.S. government. Most live in or near Tucson or Phoenix. The reservation address is listed above.

Public Ceremony or Powwow Dates: During Holy Week, the Yaqui perform a selection of dances. Some are influenced by the Spanish, but their Deer Dance is very Indian.

Art Forms: The Yaqui produce Deer Dance statues and paintings of their culture.

Visitor Information: The tribe operates a landscape nursery, charcoal packing business, and a bingo enterprise on their reservation.

The Lenten Ceremonies at the Pascua-Yaqui Reservation are a hybrid of Christian and Yaqui beliefs. Accepting the crucifixion and resurrection of Jesus while rejecting the dogma of the evangelizing Jesuits, the Yaqui tribe has fashioned an annual Passion Play that expresses their faith.

Every Friday, beginning after Ash Wednesday and continuing to Holy Week, the community makes the Stations of the Cross in 14 venues outside the church and with people playing the parts in each complex tableau under the leadership of an Indian priest, called the maestro. This continues until the Saturday night before Palm Sunday when groups of Indian societies, numbering 300 or 400, converge and dance until dawn, whereupon palms are distributed to the participants. This intertribal ceremony begins a Holy Week whose key events are again reenacted, with effigies of the Roman soldiers and Judas being burned in bonfires that light up the countryside on Holy Saturday and burn until Easter Sunday dawns over the rocky landscape.

Ceremonies are open to visitors in Guadalupe Village, near Phoenix, and at Old Pasqua Village, Barrio Libre, and the Pasqua-Yaqui Reservation, all in or around Tucson.

Quechan
P.O. Box 1352
Yuma, AZ 85364
(619) 572-0213
Fax (619) 572-2102

Euqchan

Location: The Quechan Indian Reservation is actually located in California. To get there from Yuma, take the old bridge across the river. Obtain a map from the Chamber of Commerce at 377 Main, Yuma, AZ 85364, telephone (602) 782-2567.

Art Forms: In the museum there are displays of Quechan clay dolls, pottery, bows, arrowheads, cradleboards, and other arts and crafts.

Visitor Information: Fishing permits are available from the tribal office, and there is a bingo enterprise for those who like to gamble.

The Quechan or Yuma (they prefer Euqchan) people have been in control of the river crossing here for centuries, and this relationship with both the Spanish and United States military is explained in the museum.

Salt River Pima-Maricopa
Route 1, Box 216
Scottsdale, AZ 85256
(602) 941-7277
Fax (602) 949-2909

Pima ("no," in the Nevome dialect, a word incorrectly applied through misunderstanding by the early missionaries)

Maricopa (they call themselves Pipatsji, "people," Maricopa being their Pima name)

The Pima are a division of the Piman family living in the valleys of the Gila and Salt in southern Arizona. The Pima call themselves A-a tam, "the people." According to tradition, the Pima tribe had its genesis in the Salt River Valley, later extending its settlements into the valley of the Gila; but a deluge came, leaving a single survivor, a specially favored chief named Ciho, or Soho, the progenitor of the present tribe. One of his descendants, Sivano, who had 20 wives, erected as his own residence the now ruined adobe structure called Casa Grande (called Sivanoki, "house of Sivano") and built other massive pueblo groups in the valleys of the Gila and Salt.

The Maricopa, an important Yuman tribe, have lived with and below the Pima since the early nineteenth century. They joined the Pima for mutual protection against the Yuma, and the two have lived together in peace.

For more information, see Arizona, Ak-Chin; Gila River.

San Carlos Apache
P.O. Box 0
San Carlos, AZ 85550
(602) 475-2361
Fax (602) 475-2566

Apache (probably from *apachu* "enemy," the Zuñi name for the Navajo, who were designated "Apaches de Nabaju" by the early Spaniards in New Mexico)

Location: The reservation is located at San Carlos.

Public Ceremony or Powwow Dates: The girls' rites and mountain spirit dances are held throughout the summer. Call the tribal office for those that are open to the public. The tribal fair is held over Veterans Day weekend, and this will also include traditional dancing.

The tribe numbered 1,172 in 1909. The name Apache has little ethnic significance, having been applied officially to those Apache living on the Gila River in Arizona and sometimes referred to also as Gilenos, or Gila Apache.

For more information, see Arizona, White Mountain Apache.

San Juan Southern Paiute
P.O. Box 2656
Tuba City, AZ 86045
(602) 283-4583 or (602) 283-4587
Fax (602) 283-5761

For more information, see Nevada, Paiute.

Na-tu-ende, Apache
Photo by Ben Wittick; Courtesy Museum of New Mexico, Neg. No. 15910

Tohono O'Odham
P.O. Box 837
Sells, AZ 85634
(603) 383-2221
Fax (602) 383-3379

Papago (from *papah* "beans," *ootam*, "people": "beansmen," "bean-people"; hence, Spanish *Frijoleros*)

Location: The tribal office is located in Sells.

Public Ceremony or Powwow Dates: The Papago dance at the O'Odham Tash Indian Celebration at Casa Grande, Arizona, in February. Memorial Day weekend will find them dancing at the Morongo Indian Reservation in California. Easter provides the opportunity for them to dance at Mission San Xavier del Bac on the Friday following Easter Sunday.

Art Forms: Arts and crafts are sold during the O'Odham Tash at Casa Grande.

Visitor Information: There is also a rodeo, contemporary Indian bands, parade, barbecue, and dancing at the O'Odham Tash. To find Mission San Xavier del Bac, drive 10 miles south of Tucson on San Xavier Road, just off I-19. The mission telephone number is (602) 294-2624; they can give you more information.

The Papago are a Piman tribe, closely allied to the Pima, whose original home was the territory south and southeast of the Gila River, especially south of Tucson, in the main and tributary valleys of the Rio Santa Cruz and extending west and southwest across the desert known as the Papagueria, into Sonora, Mexico. Because of the harshness of their land, they did not live in villages. The Papago subsisted by agriculture, and maize, beans, and cotton were their chief crops, which they cultivated using irrigation. Many desert plants also contributed to their diet, especially mesquite, the beans of which were eaten, and the saguaro, pitahaya, or giant cactus, from whose fruit they made preserves and a syrup. The tribe once traded extensively in salt, taken from the great inland lagoons. They also raised stock. Later, many earned a livelihood by working as laborers, especially on railroads and irrigation ditches.

The Papago are tall and dark complexioned. Their dialect is close to the Pima, and their habits and customs are generally similar except that the men wear their hair only to the shoulders. Like the Pima, the Papago women are expert basketmakers, and the designs and patterns of the pottery and the basketry are the same as those of the Pima. One of their favorite games, played with four sticks, was that known as kings (Spanish, *quince*, "fifteen"), which they called *ghin-skoot* (probably derived from the same word).

Traditionally, their typical dwelling was dome shaped, consisting of a framework of saplings, thatched with grass or leafy shrubs, with an adjacent shelter or ramada. These lodges were from 12 to 20 feet in diameter, and sometimes the roof was flattened and covered with earth.

In 1906, the Papago in the United States numbered 4,981. In addition, 859 Papago were officially reported in Sonora, Mexico, in 1900, but this was probably a low estimate

Tonto Apache
Tonto Reservation #30
30 Payson, AZ 85541
(602) 474-5000
Fax (602) 474-9125

Public Ceremony or Powwow Dates: The people of this tribe have joined together and are presenting public dances during the Fourth of July at the Flagstaff, Arizona, Coconino Center for the Arts. The Camp Verde Apache, (602) 567-5276, are also participating in these presentations. They are from Camp Verde, Arizona.

For more information, see Arizona, White Mountain Apache.

White Mountain Apache
P.O. Box 700
Whiteriver, AZ 85941
(602) 338-4346
Fax (602) 338-4778

Apache (probably from *apachu*, "enemy," the Zuñi name for the Navajo, who were designated "Apaches de Nabaju" by the early Spaniards in New Mexico)

Location: The reservation is south of Show Low.

*Nalte, Coyotero Apache, on left; Gudi-ze-eh, San Carlos Apache, on right; ca. 1883
Photo by Ben Wittick; Courtesy Museum of New Mexico, Neg. No. 15900*

Public Ceremony or Powwow Dates: The Apache Tribal Fair is usually held over Labor Day weekend and features mountain spirit dances. Other dances and girls' puberty rites are held most weekends during July and August. Call the tribal office for celebrations that are open to the public.

Art Forms: Traditional arts and crafts can be found by telephoning the tribal office.

Visitor Information: The reservation is in the most scenic part of southeast Arizona. It is great for skiers, hunters, fishermen, and campers. The tribe operates the Sunrise Ski Resort, which is open year-round. This resort is 3 miles south of McNary, telephone (602) 334-2144. Less expensive accommodations can be found at the White Mountain Apache Motel and Restaurant at Whiteriver, telephone (602) 338-4927. Be sure to contact the tribal office for hunting and fishing permits. Other attractions include the ancient Kinishba Ruins, Geronimo's Cave, and the fish hatchery.

This is a tribe of the Athapascan language family. The name has been applied also to some unrelated Yuman tribes, as the Apache Mohave (Yavapai) and Apache Yuma. The Apache call themselves N'de, Dine, Tinde, or Inde, "people." Their numbers have increased since the beginning of the seventeenth century, apparently because they took captives from other tribes, particularly the Pueblo, Pima, and Papago. They were first mentioned as Apache in 1598, although Coronado, in 1541, met the Querecho (the Vaqueros of Benavides, and probably the Jicarilla and Mescalero of modern times) on the plains of eastern New Mexico and western Texas. Apparently, the Apache did not reach Arizona until after the middle of the sixteenth century. From the time of the Spanish colonization of New Mexico until the late 1800s, they were noted for their warlike disposition, raiding both non-Indian and Indian settlements and extending their territory as far southward as Jalisco, Mexico. Although most of the Apache have been hostile since they have been known to history, the most serious outbreaks in modern times have been attributed to mismanagement on the part of civil authorities. The most important hostilities in the 1800s were those of the Chiricahua under Cochise, and later Victorio, who, together with 500 Mimbreno, Mogollon, and Mescalero, were assigned, about 1870, to the Ojo Caliente reserve in western New Mexico. Cochise, who had repeatedly refused to be confined within reservation limits, fled with his band but returned in 1871, at which time 1,200 to 1,900 Apache were on the reservation.

Complaints from neighboring settlers resulted in their removal to Tularosa, 60 miles to the northwest, but 1,000 fled to the Mescalero reserve on Pecos River, while Cochise went out on another raid. In accordance with the wishes of the Indians, they were returned to Ojo Caliente in 1874. Cochise died soon afterward. In the following year, the Chiricahua reservation in Arizona was abolished. Three hundred twenty-five Indians were removed to the San Carlos Agency; others went to Ojo Caliente; and some either remained on the mountains of their old reservation or fled across the Mexican border. This removal of Indians from their ancestral homes was a matter of government policy. In April 1877, Geronimo and other chiefs, with the remnant of the band left on the old reservation, and evidently the Mexican refugees, began raiding in southern Arizona and northern Chihuahua, but in May, 433 were captured and returned to San Carlos.

At the same time, the policy of removal was applied to the Ojo Caliente Apache of New Mexico. But when the plan was put in action, only 450 of 2,000 Indians were found, the remainder having formed bands under Victorio. After considerable conflict, in February 1878, Victorio surrendered in the hope that he and his people might remain on their former reservation, but another attempt was made to force the Indians to go to San Carlos, with the same result. Just when arrangements were finally made for them to settle there, the local authorities indicted Victorio and others for murder and robbery. With his few immediate followers and some Mescalero, Victorio fled from the reservation and resumed marauding. There were numerous skirmishes, and even when he was outnumbered, Victorio held his own. Victorio eluded capture and fled across the border, where he continued his victorious campaign. Pressed on both sides of the international boundary, and at times harassed by U.S. and Mexican troops combined, Victorio finally suffered severe losses and his band became divided. In October 1880, Mexican troops encountered Victorio's party, comprising 100 warriors, with 400 women and children, at Tres Castillos; the Indians were surrounded and attacked in the evening, and the fight continued throughout the night. In the morning, the Indians' ammunition was exhausted. Although rapidly losing strength, the remnant refused to surrender until Victorio, who had been wounded several times, finally fell dead.

Victorio was succeeded by Nana, who collected the divided force, received reinforcements from the Mescalero and the San Carlos

*Cha-si-to (son of Bonito) with mescal fiddle, Warm Springs Apache, ca. 1883
Photo by Ben Wittick; Courtesy Museum of New Mexico, Neg. No. 15899*

Chiricahua, and continued the Indian campaigns against the whites. Geronimo participated in these hostilities until he and his band finally surrendered September 4, 1886, and with a number of friendly Apache, were sent to Florida as prisoners. They were later taken to Mt. Vernon, Alabama, and then to Ft. Sill, Oklahoma. Apache hostility in Arizona and New Mexico had ceased by 1902.

A nomadic people, the Apache practiced agriculture only to a limited extent before their permanent establishment on reservations. They subsisted chiefly by hunting and on roots (especially that of the maguey) and berries. Although fish and bear were found in abundance in their country, eating them was taboo. Their dwellings were shelters of brush, which were easily erected by the women and were well adapted to their arid environment and constant shifting.

Yavapai-Apache
P.O. Box 1188
Camp Verde, AZ 86322
(602) 567-3649
Fax (602) 567-3994

Yavapai

Location: The Yavapai-Apache Visitor Center is in central Arizona on Interstate 17. Take the middle Verde exit, then go one-quarter mile east.

Public Ceremony or Powwow Dates: The Camp Verde Apache began dancing for the public recently, and they sometimes perform the Mountain Spirit Dance. Call the tribal office for more details.

Visitor Information: The exhibits in the visitor center offer traditional and modern styles of life of the people of this tribe. A film offers interesting examples of their past and present life. Call the Yavapai Community College at Prescott for more details.

For more information, see Arizona, White Mountain Apache and Yavapai-Prescott.

Yavapai-Prescott
530 E. Merritt Street
Prescott, AZ 86301-2038

(602) 445-8790
Fax (602) 778-9445

Yavapai (said to be from *enyaeva*, "sun," *pai*, "people": "people of the sun")

Location: The reservation is on the edge of Prescott.

The Yavapai are a Yuman tribe, popularly known as Apache Mojave and Mojave Apache, that is, "hostile or warlike Mojave." Before its removal to the Rio Verde Agency in May 1873, the tribe claimed as its territory the valley of the Rio Verde and the Black Mesa from the Salt River as far as Bill Williams Mountain in western Arizona. They then numbered about 1,000. Earlier, they ranged much farther west, appearing to have had rancherias on the Rio Colorado. In spring 1875, they were placed under San Carlos Apache Agency. In 1890, most of the tribe drifted from the San Carlos Reservation and settled in part of their old home on the Rio Verde, including the abandoned Camp McDowell military reservation. By 1903, there were said to be between 500 and 600 (but probably including Yuma and Apache) scattered in small bands from Camp McDowell to the head of the Rio Verde. By Executive Order of September 15, 1903, the old reservation was set aside for their use, the claims of the white settlers being purchased under the act of April 21, 1904. In 1905, tuberculosis was responsible for many deaths. In 1910, there were about 550 Mojave Apache and Yavapai.

For more information, see Arizona, Colorado River.

NEW MEXICO INDIAN EVENTS

	Event	Pueblo
January		
1	Turtle, Corn, and various other dances	Most pueblos, or Taos, Santo Domingo, San Felipe, Cochiti, Santa Ana, Picurís
6	King's Day and installation of new governors and officials; Deer, Buffalo, Eagle, and Elk Dance	Most northern and southern pueblos
23	Annual feast day in honor of San Ildefonso; Comanche, Buffalo and Deer Dance	San Ildefonso
25	Various dances	Picurís
27	Basket Dance	San Juan
February		
1st week	Governor's Feast, various dances	Ácoma
2	Candelaria Day Celebration; Buffalo and various dances	San Felipe and other pueblos
4-5	Los Comanches Dance	Taos
Date set each year	Deer Dance	San Juan
Date set each year	Deer and Buffalo Dance	Santa Clara
Date set each year	Evergreen Dance	Isleta

March

19	St. Joseph's Feast Harvest and Social Dance	Old Laguna Village
Easter	Various dances	Most pueblos

April

19-20	Eight Northern Indian Pueblos Spring Arts and Crafts Show	De Vargas Mall, Santa Fe

May

1	Annual Feast Day in honor of St. Phillip, Green Corn Dance	San Felipe
3	Santa Cruz Day (Coming of the Rivermen), Green Corn Dance and traditional foot races	Cochiti, Taos
Date set each year	Blessing of the fields, Corn or Flag Dance	Tesuque

June

13	Annual feast day of St. Anthony	Sandia
	Corn Dance	Cochiti
	Grab Day, St. Anthony's Day; Corn, Comanche, or various other dances	San Ildefonso, San Juan, Santa Clara, Taos, Picurís
23-24	Annual Feast for St. John the Baptist, Buffalo Dance on evening of the 23rd, War Dances and foot races	San Juan

24	St. John the Baptist Feast Day, Corn Dance	Taos
	St. John the Baptist Feast Day, Grab Day	Cochiti
29	San Pedro's Day, Rooster Pulls	Ácoma, San Felipe
	San Pedro's Day, Corn Dance	Santa Ana, Santo Domingo

July

1-4	Mescalero Apache Gahan Ceremonial	Mescalero
4	Nambe Falls Ceremonial	Nambe
14	Annual Feast Day of St. Bonaventure, Corn Dance	Cochiti
18-20	Annual Eight Northern Pueblos Arts and Crafts Show	San Juan
20	Annual Pope foot race	San Juan
25	Santiago's Day, various dances	San Ildefonso, Taos
	Celebration of St. James, Grab Day	Ácoma, Cochiti, San Felipe, Laguna, Santo Domingo
26	Annual Feast Day in honor of St. Anne, Corn Dance	Santa Ana
Last weekend	Puye Cliff Ceremonial, various dances	Santa Clara

August

2	Old Pecos Bull and Corn Dances	Jémez
4	Annual Feast Day in honor of St. Dominic, Corn Dance	Jémez, Santo Domingo
5-10	Symbolic Relay Run	All Pueblos
9-10	Annual Feast Day in honor of St. Lawrence, Sunset Dance on 9th, dances and foot races on 10th	Picurís
10	St. Lawrence Day, Corn Dance	Acomita Village, Ácoma
	St. Lawrence Day Grab Day	Laguna, Cochiti
12	Annual Feast Day in honor of St. Clara; Corn, Harvest, Comanche, or Buffalo Dances	Santa Clara
Mid-August	Intertribal Indian Ceremonial	Gallup
15	Annual Feast Day in honor of Our Lady of Assumption, Corn Dance	Zia
	Feast of St. Anthony, Harvest and Social Dances	Mesita Village, Laguna
28	Spanish and Indian Fiestas	Isleta

September

2	Annual Feast Day in honor of St. Stephan, Harvest Dance	Ácoma
4	Annual Feast Day in honor of St. Augustine, Harvest Dance	Isleta

8	Honoring the nativity of the Blessed Virgin Mary, Harvest and Social Dances, Corn Dance	Encinal Village, Laguna
14-15	Jicarilla Apache Fair, rodeos, powwows, foot races, dances	San Ildefonso, Stone Lake, Dulce
Date set each year	Window Rock Navajo Fair	Window Rock, AZ
19	Annual Feast Day in honor of St. Joseph, Harvest Dance	Old Laguna
25	Annual Feast Day in honor of St. Elizabeth, Harvest and Social Dances	Paguate Village, Laguna
29-30	Annual Feast Day in honor of San Jerome, Sundown Dance on evening of 29th, war and various dances, trade fair, races and pole climbing on 30th	Taos
Last week	Harvest Dance	San Juan

October

1st week	Annual Navajo Fair	Shiprock
4	Annual Feast Day in honor of San Francisco de Assisi, Elk and various dances	Nambe
17	Celebrations of St. Margaret Mary's Day, Harvest and Social Dances	Paraje Village, Laguna

November

12	Annual Feast Day in honor of San Diego, Corn Dance	Jémez

	Annual Feast Day in honor of San Diego, Flag, Buffalo, Deer or Comanche Dance	Tesuque

December

Date set each year	Shalako Ceremonial, blessing of new homes	Zuñi
Date set each year	Navajo Nightway and Mountain Topway Ceremonies	Navajo (Window Rock)
12	Celebration in honor of Our Lady of Guadalupe, Matachina Dance	Jémez
	Annual Feast Day in honor of Our Lady of Guadalupe, Comanche or Buffalo and Bow and Arrow Dances	Pojoaque
24-25	Matachina Dance, Religious Procession	San Juan
	Sundown Torchlight Procession of the Virgin after vespers on 24th, Deer or Matachina Dance on 25th	Taos
	Matachina Dances	Picurís
25	Matachina Dances	San Ildefonso, Santa Clara
	Matachina or Deer Dance	Tesuque
	Buffalo, Deer, Harvest, Basket, Rainbow, Matachina and various other dances	Jémez, Santa Ana, San Felipe, Santo Domingo, Cochiti
26	Turtle Dance	San Juan
28	Holy Innocence Day, various children's dances	Santa Clara

Ácoma Pueblo, 1904
Photo by Edward S. Curtis; Courtesy Museum of New Mexico, Neg. No. 144511

NEW MEXICO

The New Mexico Pueblos

The term "Pueblo" applies to all people living in compact villages in southern Colorado, central Utah, and New Mexico. The Pueblo people of the historical period lived in an area extending from northeastern Arizona to the Rio Pecos in New Mexico and from Taos on the Rio Grande, New Mexico, in the north, to a few miles below El Paso, Texas, in the south.

The ancient domain of the Pueblo people, however, covered a much greater territory, extending approximately from western Arizona to the Pecos and into the Texas panhandle and from central Utah and southern Colorado southward into Mexico, where the remains of their homes have not yet been clearly distinguished from those of the northern Aztec.

Of the Pueblo tribes, the first to become known to non-Indian people were the Zuñi. After reports of their wealth in 1539, an expedition into their territory was led by Coronado. Exploring parties were sent in various directions—to the Hopi villages of Tusayan, the Grand Canyon of the Colorado, the Rio Grande Valley, and the buffalo plains, nowhere finding the expected wealth but always encouraged by news of what lay beyond. Many Indians were killed by the Spanish. In spring 1542, Coronado's force started on their return to Mexico. Two missionaries were left behind, Fray Juan de Padilla, who went to Quivira, and Fray Luis, a lay brother, who remained at Pecos. Both were killed by the native people whom they expected to convert. In Coronado's time, the Pueblo were said to occupy 71 towns, and there may have been others. The Pueblo people were visited successively by several other Spanish explorers. Francisco Sanchez Chamuscado, in 1581, escorted three Franciscan missionaries to the Tigua country of the Rio Grande, but they were killed soon after. Antonio de Espejo, late in 1582, started with a small force from San Bartolome in Chihuahua for the purpose of determining the fate of the missionaries. He traversed the Pueblo country from the Hopi villages of northeast Arizona to Pecos in New Mexico and returned to San Bartolome by way of the Pecos River. Espejo's estimates of the population are greatly exaggerated. One of the most important of all the expeditions was that of Juan de Oñate, the colonizer of New Mexico in 1598 and founder of Santa Fe seven years later. This is when the Pueblo tribes were first definitely influenced by "civilization."

Active missionary work among the Pueblo people was begun early in the seventeenth century. Toward the middle of the century, difficulties arose between Spanish civil officials and Spanish missionaries, in which the Indians became involved. The Pueblo Revolt of 1680 drove the Spanish back to Mexico. Many of the Pueblo people abandoned their settlements and took refuge in new ones on less vulnerable sites, leaving the former villages to crumble. For 12 years, the Pueblos remained independent of the Spaniards but not free from dissension among themselves or from attacks by their old enemies, the Navajo and the Apache. In 1692, Diego de Vargas reconquered the province after severely punishing many of the natives and destroying some of their towns. Of all the Pueblo people of New Mexico at the beginning of the revolt (at which time there were 33 active missions, while others were mere visitas), only Ácoma and possibly Isleta continued to occupy their former sites after the conquest. In 1696, some of the Pueblo people once more rebelled, killing several missionaries, but they surrendered after again being severely punished by de Vargas.

Ácoma Pueblo
P.O. Box 309
Acomita, NM 87034
(505) 552-6604 or (505) 252-1139
1-800-747-0181
Fax (505) 552-6600

Ácoma

Location: Ácoma, the "Sky City," is located west of Albuquerque and 12 miles south of Interstate 40 on Highway 23.

Public Ceremony or Powwow Dates: The annual feast day is on September 2.

Charles Dixon, Ácoma Pueblo, 1914
Courtesy Museum of New Mexico, Neg. No. 41662

Art Forms: Arts and crafts are sold at the visitors center at the base of the mesa.

Visitor Information: Ácoma is situated atop a 367-foot mesa that rises abruptly from the valley floor. Ácoma Pueblo well deserves its nickname, Sky City. Ácoma is dominated by the massive mission church of San Estevan del Rey. Both the church and the pueblo are national historic landmarks.

Established in the twelfth century, Ácoma is the oldest continuously inhabited community in America. Today, there are only about 50 year-round residents in this Keresan village without electricity or running water. During feast days and celebrations, however, Ácoma people from neighboring Ácomita, Anzac, and McCarty's return to their ancestral home.

The fine, thin-walled pottery for sale on the mesatop and from stalls at the visitor center below is characterized by "op art" patterns and Mimbres designs. A restaurant, crafts shop, and museum are located in the visitor center. There is a bingo hall nearby.

Ácoma may be seen by guided tour only. Hours of tour operation are from 8:00 a.m. to 4:30 p.m. in fall and winter and 8:00 a.m. to 7:00 p.m. in spring and summer. The last daily tour departs from the visitor center one hour before closing. There is a fee for cameras, when permitted.

Cochití Pueblo
P.O. Box 70
Cochití, NM 87072
(505) 465-2244
Fax (505) 465-2245

Cochití

Location: This village is located south of Santa Fe, west of Interstate 25.

Public Ceremony or Powwow Dates: The Corn Dance is usually performed on July 14.

Visitor Information: Men and women continue to farm and make jewelry, pottery, and much-prized storyteller figures. They also produce the famed Cochití drums.

Cooka boy, Cochití Pueblo, ca. 1935
Photo by T. Harmon Parkhurst; Courtesy Museum of New Mexico, Neg. No. 3516

The church built in 1628 still stands. Although it has been rebuilt and remodeled, it contains sections of the original structure.

The pueblo leases land to the town of Cochití Lake and operates services for it. In addition, Cochití Lake boasts an 18-hole golf course, tennis courts, a swimming pool, marina and commercial center.

No admission fee is charged; cameras are not allowed. The language is Keresan.

Isleta Pueblo
P.O. Box 1270
Isleta, NM 87022
(505) 869-3111 or (505) 869-6333
Fax (505) 869-4236

Isleta

Location: This pueblo is located 13 miles south of Albuquerque just off Interstate 25.

Public Ceremony or Powwow Dates: The annual feast day is on September 4.

Art Forms: Jewelry and pottery and other arts and crafts can be found here.

Visitor Information: Isleta is the largest of the Tiwa-speaking pueblos. It is composed of several settlements, the largest of which is Shiaw iba, on the west side of the Rio Grande.

With the 1680 Pueblo Revolt against the Spanish, many members of the community fled to Hopi. After the uprising, the Isleta people returned home, some bringing Hopi mates and children.

While the majority of Isleta's residents work in Albuquerque, some operate grocery stores or are employed at the bingo hall and fishing and camping areas at Isleta Lakes. Others farm and ranch. In addition, some women make traditional polychrome pottery, using black and red designs on a white background.

Isleta Pueblo does not charge an admission fee. No cameras are allowed. Camping, picnicking, and fishing permits may be acquired at Isleta Lakes.

Jémez Pueblo
P.O. Box 100
Jémez Pueblo, NM 87024
(505) 834-7359 or (505) 834-7525
Fax (505) 834-7331

Jémez

Location: Take Interstate 25 north from Albuquerque to Bernalillo; go northwest on Highway 44; turn north on Highway 4 to Jémez Pueblo.

Public Ceremony or Powwow Dates: The annual feast day is on November 12.

Art Forms: Many Jémez artisans produce pottery and other arts and crafts.

Visitor Information: This village is located at the place where the Jémez Mountains slope down to meet the desert. It is worth the drive to go on up to the village of Jémez to see the old mission there which has many items from centuries past. Originally on Indian land, the mission now sits on land owned by the state.

With the abandonment of Pecos Pueblo in the 1830s, Jémez was left the sole remaining Towa-speaking pueblo. A handful of Pecos survivors resettled in Jémez. On August 2, the feast of Our Lady of the Angels is celebrated with the Old Pecos Bull Dance.

Wilderness surrounds Jémez Pueblo. Visitors might want to stop at the Holy Ghost Spring or the Sheep Spring Fish Pond, a recreation area on N.M. 4 near the pueblo. Fishing licenses for both areas can be purchased from the Jémez game warden. Hunting permits also are available.

Many Jémez residents maintain gardens, and there are some excellent vineyards. The women are known for their weaving, especially of fine baskets made from yucca fronds. In addition, traditional polychrome pottery is making a comeback.

There is no admission fee to the pueblo. Cameras are not permitted.

Jicarilla Apache
P.O. Box 507
Dulce, NM 87528
(505) 759-3242
Fax (505) 759-3005

Augustine, Head Chief, Jicarilla Apache, ca. 1886
Courtesy Museum of New Mexico, Neg. No. 56149

Jicarilla

Location: Take Highway 64 from Taos or Highway 84 from Española and go north past Chama where the two highways split. Turn left, staying on Highway 64, at the Broken Butt Saloon.

Public Ceremony or Powwow Dates: The Little Beaver Rodeo and Powwow is usually held in late July. The tribe conducts Gojiiya Feast Day on September 14–15 each year. Girls' rites, bear dances, and other ceremonials are held regularly. Call the tribe for exact dates and times for all events.

Art Forms: The Jicarilla Apache are encouraging a return to traditional arts and crafts, including basketry, buckskin tanning, leather work, beadwork, and feather work. The Jicarilla museum has arts and crafts on display. The gift shop there has local artisans' work for sale.

Visitor Information: This is a very beautiful and scenic area. The gravel road north out of Dulce to Ignacio, Colorado, is wonderful for unspoiled scenery, but be sure the roads are dry before attempting the drive.

The reservation in northern New Mexico extends from the Colorado border south for some 64 miles. The Continental Divide crosses the Jicarillas' homeland twice.

The tribe has a large fishing and hunting operation, with eight lakes open to the public. Permits also are available for fishing in the Navajo River. There are also campgrounds around the lakes. For information and permits, contact the tribal Game and Fish Department, P.O. Box 546, Dulce 87528, or call the Jicarilla tourism office. In the winter months, the tribe has a cross-country skiing program, with trails and equipment rentals. Dulce is the location of the Best Western Jicarilla Inn. No fees are charged for cameras or admission to the reservation.

Laguna Pueblo
P.O. Box 194
Laguna, NM 87026
(505) 552-6654 or (505) 243-7616
Fax (505) 552-6941

Laguna

Location: Take Interstate 40 west from Albuquerque. The highway passes right through the reservation.

Public Ceremony or Powwow Dates: The annual feast day is held on September 19.

Art Forms: Call the tribal office for details on where to purchase arts and crafts.

Visitor Information: The largest of the Keresan pueblos, Laguna is a community of six villages scattered over many acres. Centered at Old Laguna, the pueblo also includes Paguate, Mesita, Paraje, Encinal, and Seama.

Each town has its own feast day. Celebrated with a fair, the feast draws other Pueblo and Navajo peoples, as well as Anglos and Hispanics.

One of the world's richest uranium mines was located at Laguna, and until its closing, many pueblo men worked as miners. The ongoing Laguna Reclamation Project is dedicated to restoring the mining site.

In the 1970s, the traditional craft of pottery making was revived, Today, Laguna potters produce fine work with geometric designs similar in style to that of neighboring Ácoma.

The tribe also has several businesses, including Laguna Industries Inc., which manufactures communication shelters for the U.S. Army. In addition, there is a residential center for the Indian elderly, a large grocery store, and a filling station.

A guide service is available. Fishing permits for Paguate Reservoir may be obtained at Paguate. Camera regulations vary from village to village, and visitors should check with officials to see whether photography is allowed (243-7616).

Mescalero Apache
P.O. Box 176
Mescalero, NM 88340
(505) 671-4495
Fax (505) 671-9191

Mescalero

Location: The reservation is in south-central New Mexico on Federal Highway 70, just northeast of Alamogordo.

*Domingo, Mescalero Apache, standing left; Nallt' Zilli, Mescalero Apache Chief,
seated; ca. 1886
Photo by J. R. Riddle; Courtesy Museum of New Mexico, Neg. No. 2131*

Public Ceremony or Powwow Dates: This is the place to go if you are in the area on the Fourth of July. The Apache girls' ceremony is held honoring the young women of the tribe who are now of age. There are Mountain Spirit Dancers, rodeo, arts and crafts, and celebrating.

Art Forms: Go to the Inn of the Mountain Gods for Apache arts and crafts.

Visitor Information: The Mescaleros are leaders in recreation and sporting enterprises, which the mountains and clear streams on their 460,000-acre reservation in southern New Mexico favor. Lake and stream fishing is permitted from about mid-May through mid-September at Eagle Creek Lakes, Silver Springs, and Rio Ruidoso recreation areas. Camping is available at some sites. For information about fees and seasons, write to the Mescalero Apache Tribe.

The Inn of the Mountain Gods has a number of amenities, including lodging, several restaurants, a gift shop, and an 18-hole golf course. Tennis, bingo, horseback riding, skeet and trap shooting, and fishing by permit in Mescalero Lake are among the activities available at the resort.

In addition, Ski Apache offers excellent skiing and employs many members of the tribe. A visitor center and museum are located in the town of Mescalero on U.S. 70. Tipis sprout from the hillsides during the first weekend in July, when the Apache Maidens' Puberty Rites and rodeo take place. No cameras are allowed at the ceremonial.

Nambe Pueblo
Route 1, Box 117 BB
Santa Fe, NM 87501
(505) 455-2036/37/38/39
Fax (505) 455-2038

Nambe

Location: This reservation is located north of Santa Fe east of Highways 84 and 285. Turn east after crossing the bridge over the river at the Nambe turnoff. Follow the paved road, being careful on the many curves, to Nambe.

Public Ceremony or Powwow Dates: The annual feast day is on October 4. Traditional dances are held on July 4.

Art Forms: Call the tribal office for information on where to purchase local arts and crafts.

Visitor Information: This is enchanted land in the Land of Enchantment. Very scenic land formations are just beyond the last turnoff to the village on the highway to Chimayo. Many tribal members work at Los Alamos National Laboratory, in Santa Fe, in Española, or for the Eight Northern Indian Pueblos Council. Others farm or work at the pueblo's recreational complex.

Fishing is allowed for a fee from March to November, and permits are available for picnicking, camping, and boating. Photography permits may be purchased as well.

Picurís Pueblo
P.O. Box 127
Peñasco, NM 87553
(505) 587-2519 or (505) 587-2957
Fax (505) 587-1071

Picurís

Location: The village is located 7 miles northwest of Peñasco off Highway 75.

Public Ceremony or Powwow Dates: Please see the calendar at the beginning of the New Mexico section.

Art Forms: Local artisans produce very nice undecorated pottery and other arts and crafts. Call the tribal office for more details.

Visitor Information: Picurís, the smallest of the Tiwa-speaking pueblos, retains its sovereign status. The people still govern themselves by a traditional form of government consisting of a governor, tribal council, and officers.

Settled in the late 1200s, Picurís blossomed in the fifteenth century, when its inhabitants lived in large six- and seven-story buildings similar to those still standing at Taos. The pueblo was abandoned in the wake of the Pueblo uprising. It was reestablished in the early 1700s.

Mica-flecked pottery is available for sale at the Pueblo Cultural Center, which houses a store, a restaurant, and a museum. Artifacts from recent excavations may be seen at the Picurís Pueblo Museum,

An offering at the waterfall, Nambé Pueblo, 1925
Photo by Edward S. Curtis; Courtesy Museum of New Mexico, Neg. No. 132696

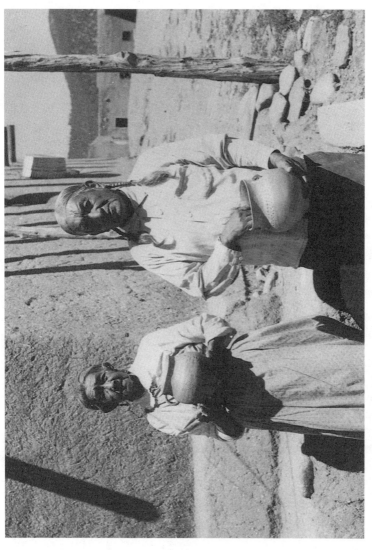

Ramita and Juan Jose Martinez, Picurís Pueblo, August 1959
Photo by Flavia Champ; Courtesy Museum of New Mexico, Neg. No. 31053

open from 8:00 a.m. to 7:00 p.m. daily. The Hidden Valley Restaurant serves Native American and American food from 11:30 a.m. to 7:00 p.m. daily.

Picurís Pueblo Enterprise Cultural Center offers guided tours, some of which include a traditional Indian meal. The pueblo has two stocked trout lakes. Fishing and overnight camping permits may be obtained at the Picurís Market. Camera permits are available at the visitor center. In recent years, the Picurís have revived the pole-climbing celebration held in the late fall. Call the tribal office for more information.

Pojoaque Pueblo
Route 11, Box 71
Santa Fe, NM 87501
(505) 455-2278 or (505) 455-2279 or (505) 455-3460
Fax (505) 455-2950

Pojoaque (P'o-Zuang-Ge, "drinking place")

Location: The pueblo is located 16 miles north of Santa Fe on Highways 285 and 84.

Public Ceremony or Powwow Dates: This tribe is in the process of reviving ceremonials with the help of other tribes in the area. They are now doing the Comanche, Buffalo, and Bow and Arrow dances. Our Lady of Guadalupe is honored with a dance held annually on December 12.

Art Forms: Local artisans produce pottery and other arts and crafts. Ask at the tribal office for more information.

Visitor Information: Of the original pueblo of Pojoaque, only low mounds scattered in fields and among houses remain. The tribe was almost destroyed by a smallpox epidemic in the late nineteenth century. "New Pojoaque" was founded in the 1930s.

Since then, Pojoaque has become one of the more well-to-do pueblos, largely because of revenues generated by a commercial strip on tribal land fronting U.S. 84/285. A professional building, supermarket, and mobile home park are among the businesses on Pojoaque property.

Pueblo Indian girl, Pojoaque Pueblo, ca. 1900
Photo by Kaadt & Whitlock; Courtesy Museum of New Mexico, Neg. No. 46151

The pueblo also operates an official state tourist center, where local arts and crafts are sold. Pottery, embroidery, silver jewelry, and beadwork are some of the items made by Pojoaque artisans.

Tradition remains important to this Tewa pueblo. In 1973, after a hiatus of more than 100 years, Pojoaque tribal members performed Indian ceremonial dances.

On the first Saturday in August, Pojoaque hosts the Plaza Fiesta, a multicultural celebration that features Indian, western, and international folk dancing as well as food and hot-air balloon rides.

Pojoaque is the smallest of the pueblos. Around the Pojoaque of today cluster ancient recollections. The Tewa claim that this pueblo marks the center of the range of their people and that the division into two branches took place in Pojoaque in ancient times.

Pojoaque was inhabited when the invaders, led by Oñate, occupied New Mexico in 1580. After the Pueblo Rebellion of 1680, it was abandoned and only resettled in 1706 by order of Governor Don Francisco Cuerbe y Valdez. There are numerous prehistoric remains in the area.

Two other pueblos or villages that were abandoned in 1696 were Jacona or Socona and I'Ha'Mba on the south side of Pojoaque. To the southeast was Cuyamunge, another Tewa pueblo that was also abandoned in 1696 after the Pueblo Rebellion against the Spanish in which its inhabitants took part. This land was then granted to a Spaniard in 1699, and Cuyamunge passed from native to Spanish hands. This pueblo was closely associated with Pojoaque in the pre-Rebellion period. Through archaeological studies, it is believed that some part of Pojoaque's ancestors came from the pueblo of Cuyamunge. Pojoaque is reputed among Tewa to have been large and important in what archaeologists group as Pueblo III and Pueblo IV, from A.D. 1200 to 1540.

Pojoaque was resettled in 1706 with five families under the name of Nuestra Señora de Guadalupe de Pojoaque. In 1749, it was known as San Francisco de Pojoaque, which indicates that the people of the settlement were mixed. This mixture was of Tehua from other Tehua pueblos and other tribes including Navajo, Apache, Ute, and Comanche (previously known as Geniserors).

In 1712, the population of Pojoaque was 79. In 1790, it was 53, and in 1870, it was 32. In 1890, there was a low of 20 members.

In 1852, John Greiner spoke of the Pojoaque Indians as having been crowded out by the "Mexicans." Indian agent Pedro Sanchez in

1883 commented that Pojoaque's best lands had been sold to whites, and the few remaining Indians were very poor. The date of the death of the last cacique (Pedro Martinez) is not known. The last capitanes (Manuel Abeyta and Francisco Tapia) died before 1900. By the early 1900s, the number of official positions to be filled was more than the adult male population of Pojoaque Pueblo. Only those of governor and sacristan were maintained. Most of the remaining Indians moved to other pueblos, particularly Santa Clara and Nambe, either because of marriage or to live with relatives.

In 1934, Commissioner John Collier published a call for Pojoaque families to move back to their lands. José Antonio Tapia had returned from a period of work in Lumberton, New Mexico, and was living in Nambe. He persuaded his two daughters, Feliciana, along with her Chimayo husband, Fermin Viarrial, and Maria Duran, to return to Pojoaque with him. Thus, with these two families, the Romeros and the Tapias, 14 members altogether, Pojoaque was born again. Today, there are approximately 160 members.

Intermarriage with non-Indians has been extensive, and there are only a few, if any, full-blooded Pojoaque Indians. Most Pojoaque Indians are a mixture of Indian and Spanish descent and take great pride in both cultures.

Ramah Navajo
Rt. 2, Box 13
Ramah, NM 87321
(505) 775-3383
Fax (505) 775-3538

For more information, see Arizona, Navajo.

Sandia Pueblo
Box 6008
Bernalillo, NM 87004
(505) 867-3317
Fax (505) 867-9235

Location: Sandia Pueblo is a small community located 15 miles north of Albuquerque on U.S. Highway 85 and two and a half miles south of the Spanish-American town of Bernalillo. The pueblo itself occupies approximately 26 acres within a total reservation area of 24,034 acres. The pueblo is situated near the center of the reservation with a clear view of the mountains.

Mariano Carpentero, Governor of Sandía Pueblo, 1899
Photo by DeLancey Gill; Courtesy Museum of New Mexico, Neg. No. 87010

Public Ceremony or Powwow Dates: The Pueblo of Sandia celebrates its annual feast day to honor its patron saint, Saint Anthony de Padua, on June 13th every year. This is open to the public. There are Indian Corn Dances all day. The feast begins with mass in the morning. Then St. Anthony is carried down from the church in a procession to an altar erected by tribal members, located in the plaza where the Corn Dances are held. Concession stands are open all day selling various kinds of food.

Other dances held during the year are on January 6th, or King's Day, when the new governor is installed. Dances are also held early Christmas morning.

No cameras, sketching, or recorders of any kind are allowed.

Art Forms: There are various tribal members who still do traditional arts and crafts. There is pottery making, silversmithing, and beautiful beadwork available.

Visitor Information: Albuquerque is located south of Sandia Pueblo, and there are motels, hotels, restaurants, campgrounds, and other facilities available there.

Located right on the Sandia Reservation and tribally owned are Sandia Indian Bingo Parlor, one of the largest in New Mexico with the highest payouts; Bien Mur Indian Market Center, offering quality handmade Indian arts and crafts, which includes jewelry, rugs, kachinas, pottery, moccasins, original art and prints, baskets, and beadwork; and Sandia Lakes Recreation Area, offering fishing, tackle rental, picnicking, and nature trails.

Located on the southern boundary of the reservation is the Los Amigos Stables, where you can enjoy horseback riding, picnics, hayrides, private parties, and music and dancing. All the food is prepared right there.

Sandia Pueblo prepared a display of photographs and text on its history and culture which will be traveling to community centers, museums, and libraries throughout the nation. For information on the traveling display, contact the pueblo.

San Felipe Pueblo
P.O. Box A
San Felipe Pueblo, NM 87001
(505) 867-3381
Fax (505) 867-3383

Unidentified girl, San Felipe Pueblo, ca. 1935
Photo by T. Harmon Parkhurst; Courtesy Museum of New Mexico, Neg. No. 47427

San Felipe

Location: This reservation is located on Interstate 25 north of Albuquerque, about halfway to Santa Fe.

Public Ceremony or Powwow Dates: The annual feast day is held on May 1.

Art Forms: There is still some jewelry being produced here as well as other arts and crafts. Call the tribal office for more details.

Visitor Information: There are several Kivas in this village, and they have very powerful dances. I enjoy the feast days here as well or more than those of any other village.

San Felipe is one of the most conservative of the Keresan pueblos, struggling to retain its customs in face of pressure from the outside world. Known among the Rio Grande pueblos for its beautiful ceremonials, San Felipe has a spectacular Green Corn Dance with hundreds of participants.

The dances take place in a sunken bowl of a plaza, which was worn away to 3 feet below the surrounding ground level by centuries of ceremonials. Neither cameras nor sketching or recording are permitted. Information is available at the community center.

San Ildefonso Pueblo
Route 5, Box 315 A
Santa Fe, NM 87501
(505) 455-2273
Fax (505) 455-7351

San Ildefonso

Location: To get to the village, take Highways 84/285 north from Santa Fe and turn off at Pojoaque on State Highway 502 to Los Alamos; turn off to the right after about 8 miles.

Public Ceremony or Powwow Dates: The annual feast day is on January 23.

Art Forms: This is the home of the famous potter, Maria Martinez, who has been gone to the other side for some years now. The black pottery here is some of the best you will find. The work can be found in artisans' homes as well as two shops in the plaza.

Florentine Martinez, San Ildefonso Pueblo, 1908
Photo by Jesse L. Nusbaum; Courtesy Museum of New Mexico, Neg. No. 61769

Eliseo Trujillo, Margurita Trujillo, and baby Pedro, San Juan Pueblo, ca. 1932-34
Photo by T. Harmon Parkhurst; Courtesy Museum of New Mexico, Neg. No. 31856

Visitor Information: This Tewa-speaking pueblo remains home to many well-known potters and painters. The pueblo also hosts the annual Eight Northern Indian Pueblos Artist and Craftsman Show, the largest Indian-operated arts and crafts fair in the country.

There are several trading posts and a museum and visitor center. The pueblo also has several fishing ponds and a picnic area. Permits are available at the sites. No cameras are permitted either at the dawn feast day dance or on Easter.

San Juan Pueblo
P.O. Box 1099
San Juan Pueblo, NM 87566
(505) 852-4400 or 852-4210
Fax (505) 852-4820

San Juan

Location: Drive north of Española on Highway 68 (the Taos Highway), and turn left at the signs to the village.

Public Ceremony or Powwow Dates: The annual feast day is on June 23–24.

Art Forms: To buy traditional arts and crafts from local tribal artisans, go to Oke Oweenge Crafts Cooperative. They sell red pottery, embroidery, beadwork, and other arts.

Visitor Information: San Juan, the largest and northernmost of the Tewa pueblos, was the site of the first Spanish capital in New Mexico, founded in 1598.

To do photography or sketching, go to the tribal office for a permit. To find when the Eight Northern Pueblos Indian Artist and Craftsman Show will be held, check with the Eight Northern Indian Pueblos Council here in San Juan. Don't forget the bingo parlor here, also. They do have high payouts.

The tribe has fishing ponds open in the spring and summer, with permits available on site. There is no admission fee to the pueblo.

Santa Ana Pueblo
2 Dove Road
Bernalillo, NM 87004
(505) 867-3301
Fax (505) 867-3395

Three dancers, Santa Ana Pueblo, ca. 1935
Photo by T. Harmon Parkhurst; Courtesy Museum of New Mexico, Neg. No. 4884

Santa Ana

Location: Drive north of Albuquerque to Bernalillo and take Highway 44 northwest to Santa Ana Pueblo.

Public Ceremony or Powwow Dates: The annual feast day is on July 25.

Art Forms: Arts and crafts are available at the Ta Ma Myia on Tuesdays and Thursdays from 10:00 a.m. to 4:30 p.m.

Visitor Information: The ceremonies are very much alive at Santa Ana. The landscape is beautiful here where the desert meets the end of the Jémez Mountains. Most members of Santa Ana Pueblo live outside the village. Residing in houses scattered throughout the nearby farmland, they return on ceremonial feast days.

This Keresan pueblo is open to the public on January 1 and 6, Easter, June 24 and 29, the annual feast day on July 25 and 26, and December 25-28. At other times, the gate to the village is likely to be closed.

Santa Ana craftsmen began to revive their ancient arts during the 1970s. Pottery and woven belts and headbands are among the items they produce.

The tribe is in the process of rehabilitating its agricultural land and developing other property. Businesses include the Prairie Star Restaurant and a new 27-hole golf course.

Santa Clara Pueblo
P.O. Box 580
Española, NM 87532
(505) 753-7326 or 753-7330
Fax (505) 753-8988

Santa Clara

Location: The easiest way to find Santa Clara Pueblo is to go to Española and take the Los Alamos Highway to the reservation.

Public Ceremony or Powwow Dates: The annual feast day is on August 12.

Art Forms: There are many potters in the village, and other arts and crafts may be purchased there also. Call the tribal office for more information.

Florentino, Santa Clara Pueblo, ca. 1920
Photo by T. Harmon Parkhurst; Courtesy Museum of New Mexico, Neg. No. 12444

Francisco Abeita and Victorano Gachupin, Santo Domingo, August 4, 1907
Photo by Milton E. Porter; Courtesy Museum of New Mexico, Neg. No. 7923

Visitor Information: The people at Santa Clara are friendly. If you like to camp and fish, go to Santa Clara Canyon on the highway past Puye Cliffs. The rangers there will sell you a permit to picnic, camp, or fish. There is no hiking allowed, however, off the floor of the canyon.

The pueblo offers both self-guided and guided tours of its ancestral home, the 740-room Puye Cliff Dwellings. Cameras are allowed by permit.

Santo Domingo Pueblo
P.O. Box 99
Santo Domingo Pueblo, NM 87052
(505) 465-2214 or 465-2215
Fax (505) 465-2688

Santo Domingo

Location: The reservation is on Interstate 25, south of Santa Fe.

Public Ceremony or Powwow Dates: The annual feast day is on August 4.

Art Forms: The people here make fine turquoise and silver jewelry. Many of them sell their work on the portal on the plaza in Santa Fe.

Visitor Information: This area is beautiful, with lava formations along the edge of the mountains and above the Rio Grande. Travelers to Santo Domingo Pueblo will see roadside ramadas offering shell and turquoise jewelry, silverwork, and pottery. Traditionally a farming community, the pueblo is now developing commercial property along the interstate. This largest of the eastern Keresan pueblos also operates a small museum on I-25.

The pueblo does not permit photographs, nor are sketching or tape recording allowed. Alcoholic beverages are prohibited.

Taos Pueblo
P.O. Box 1846
Taos, NM 87571
(505) 758-9593
Fax (505) 758-4604

Taos

Unidentified men on horses, Taos Pueblo, ca. 1915
Courtesy Museum of New Mexico, Neg. No. 21531

Location: The village is located just northeast of the downtown plaza in Taos.

Public Ceremony or Powwow Dates: The annual feast day is September 30. In recent years, also, there has been a powwow close to the area where the buffalo pasture is located. Call the tribal office for dates and times.

Art Forms: There are several arts and crafts stores on the road into the village, and some are located in the village. The craftsmen in Taos make wonderful drums.

Visitor Information: The multistoried mud-plastered dwellings of Taos Pueblo have long inspired painters and photographers. Indeed, these golden-brown structures led Spanish conquistadors who arrived 400 years ago to believe they had discovered one of the lost cities of gold.

During its volatile history, Taos Pueblo weathered ordeals ranging from the Pueblo Revolt in 1680 to the backlash following the Taos Rebellion against the U.S. government in 1847. In many ways, Taos has changed little in the past several centuries. For tradition's sake, members of this Tiwa-speaking pueblo choose to do without electricity and indoor plumbing. They can still be seen carrying water in tin buckets from the Rio Pueblo de Taos, a stream that bisects the village.

However traditional, Taos Pueblo is one of the most heavily visited of the northern villages. A National Historic Site, the pueblo has been nominated by the World Heritage Commission in Geneva as the 15th American site in the World Heritage Convention.

Visitors are welcome to attend numerous ceremonials conducted throughout the year. Admission is charged. Cameras are not allowed on feast days. Signs mark pueblo dwellings that offer jewelry, pottery, drums, and other arts and crafts for sale. A map of the pueblo is available; it marks off zones prohibited to the public. There are a few trading posts on the reservation, as well as a horseback-riding and guided-tour business that operates during the summer months (758-4604).

Tesuque Pueblo
Route 11, Box 1
Santa Fe, NM 87501
(505) 983-2667
Fax (505) 982-2331

Tesuque

Location: Tesuque Pueblo is just north of Santa Fe on Highways 285/84.

Public Ceremony or Powwow Dates: The annual feast day is November 12.

Art Forms: Arts and crafts, including pottery, are all available here. Call the tribal office for more information.

Visitor Information: Excavations have uncovered evidence that this site was inhabited as early as 1250. The pueblo is listed on the National Register of Historic Places. Despite its proximity to Santa Fe, Tesuque has the reputation for being one of the most culturally conservative of the northern pueblos. (This may account for the spirited opposition Tesuque mounted against the Spanish. The first blood shed during the Pueblo Revolt was at Tesuque.)

The Tesuque tribe operates the Camel Rock Campground, with a swimming pool and nice RV spaces, on the highway north of the village. They also have horses for rent for riding, hayrides, and cookouts, on the east side of the highway. Don't miss the bingo parlor, if you enjoy gaming.

Cameras are allowed by permit only.

Zía Pueblo
135 Capitol Square Drive
Zía Pueblo, NM 87053-6013
(505) 867-3304
Fax (505) 867-3308

Zía

Location: Drive north from Albuquerque and take Highway 44 at Bernalillo northwest to Zía.

Public Ceremony or Powwow Dates: The annual feast day is August 15.

Art Forms: The orange-on-white pottery is distinctive at Zía, and there are other arts and crafts as well.

Unidentified man, Zía Pueblo, ca. 1935
Photo by T. Harmon Parkhurst; Courtesy Museum of New Mexico, Neg. No. 3773

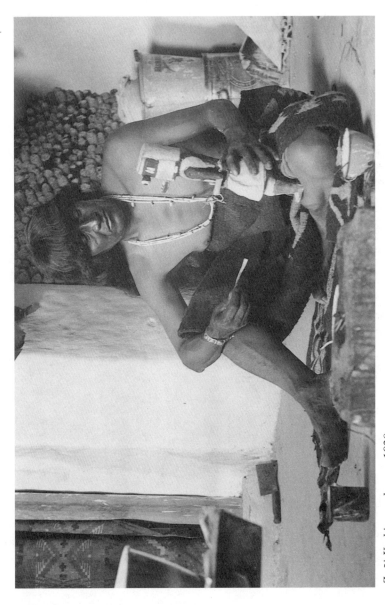

Zuñi Kachina maker, ca. 1920
Courtesy Museum of New Mexico, Neg. No. 68770

Zuñi Pueblo, 1903
Photo by Edward S. Curtis; Courtesy Museum of New Mexico, Neg. No. 143701

Visitor Information: It is an inspiring drive up to Zía, which overlooks the Jémez River. This is the land where the desert meets the mountains.

Zía is a Keresan-speaking pueblo best known for its ancient sun symbol, which was adopted as the official emblem by the state of New Mexico and appears on the state flag. Neither cameras nor sketching or recording are allowed. Fishing is available at Zía Lake, 2 miles west of the pueblo. Permits may be purchased on site.

Zuñi Pueblo
P.O. Box 339
Zuñi, NM 87327
(505) 782-4481
Fax (505) 782-2700

Zuñi

Location: Drive south from Grants on Highway 53 or from Gallup on Highway 602 and then west on Highway 53.

Public Ceremony or Powwow Dates: See the calendar at the beginning of the New Mexico section.

Art Forms: The Zuñi Craftsmen Cooperative Association, Box 426, Zuñi, NM 87327, offers silver and turquoise jewelry. They are located on State Highway 53 at the pueblo. The Zuñi excel in various kinds of jewelry craftsmanship.

Visitor Information: There are stores, restaurants, gas stations, and a tribal campground. If you are in an adventurous mood, take a guided tour from the Zuñi Tribal Office and visit Hawikuh ruins, 12 miles south of Zuñi Pueblo. This was an active pueblo when first visited by the black explorer Esteban and Spanish priest Fray Marcos in 1539. Some sort of conflict took place and Esteban was killed. Fray Marcos returned to Mexico, and the following year Coronado returned with armed men and attacked Hawikuh. The pueblo then lived with Spanish influence for a century. It was abandoned after the Pueblo Revolt of 1680 when the Pueblo people drove the Spanish out of New Mexico.

Rock art paintings dating from early in this century can be viewed at the Village of the Great Kivas. And more Zuñi art can be viewed in the mission church at the village. Coronado was wrong when he found Zuñi and thought it was one of the Seven Cities of Cibola, but mythical gold cities are hard to find.

TEXAS

Ysleta del Sur Pueblo
P.O. Box 17579 Ysleta Stn.
El Paso, TX 79917
(915) 859-7913/14/18
Fax (915) 859-2988

Ysleta

Location: The Tigua Indian Reservation is south on I-10; 12 miles south to Exit 32 (Avenue of the Americas); then 2½ miles south on Zaragosa Road. Turn on Alameda Road one block east to 119 South Old Pueblo Road, Ysleta. If you get lost, ask for directions, like I did.

Public Ceremony or Powwow Dates: Call the tribal office for exact times when dances are held which are open to the public.

Art Forms: There are traditional arts and crafts in the center, and there is a display in the museum.

Visitor Information: Don't miss the tribal restaurant. They generally have dancing in the plaza, also. These people moved here sometime after the Pueblo Revolt of 1680 from the northern areas of the Rio Grande. They were forgotten by the other Pueblo people, but they have now regained recognition.

WEST

Smith River/ Soboba / Susanville / Sycuan /Table Bluff /Table Mountain / Torres -Martinez / Trinidad /Tule River / Tuolumne /Twenty nine Palms/ Upper Lake / Utu Utu Gwaitu Paiute/Viejas/ Yurok/Chemehuevi / Fort Mojave / Woodfords /Agua Caliente /Alturas / Barona/ Berry Creek/ Big Bend / Big Lagoon / Big Pine / Big Sandy / Big Valley / Bishop / Blue Lake / Bridgeport/Buena Vista / Cabazon/ Cahuilla / Campo /Cedaryille /Chicken Ranch/Cloverdale / Cold Springs/ Colusa/Cortina/Covelo/ Coyote /Cuyapaipe/ Death Valley/ Dry Creek/Elem / Elk Valley/Enterprise/ Fort Bidwell / Fort Independence /Greenville /Grindstone/ Hoopa /Hopland/Inaja and Cosmit /Jackson / Jamul / Karok /Kashia / La Jolla / La Posta / Laytonville / Lone Pine / Lookout / Los Coyotes/Mancheria - Fort Arena /Manzanite./Mesa Grande/ Middletown/Montgomery Creek/Mooretown/Morongo/North Fork/Otter Valley / Pala/

CALIFORNIA

Pauma/ Pechanga /Picayune/ Pinoleville / Pit River/ Quartz Valley /Ramona Band/ Redding / Redwood Valley/ Resighini / Rincon / Robinson / Rohnerville / Rumsey / San Manuel / San Pasqual / Santa Rosa/ Santa Ynez / Santa Ysabel / Sherwood Valley / Shingle Springs

The land slopes down to meet the Great Water, the Pacific, and the land slopes up to meet the Grandfather Mountains, the Sierras. In between, there are deserts and forests and lakes and rivers. It is beautiful land, and it is our land.

The people are not known by others. The Spanish missionary influence in the last part of the eighteenth century and the beginning of the nineteenth century and the gold miners in the mid-nineteenth century took over the land, and the people.

The people lived from the land, and they lived from respect. With great skill, they made baskets and built their houses. They used tule, grasses, brush and/or bark, and they covered their houses with earth to protect themselves in winter. In the northwest, they hewed planks to form their houses, and canoes were made from the great trees there. Tules were made into rafts, and the rivers were their highways. Agriculture and breaking the skin of our Mother Earth was not necessary. Deer and small game and fish and vegetables gave themselves to the people for food. Acorns, seeds, grasses, herbs, roots, and berries were plentiful.

The people practiced their spiritualism within societies, and ceremony acted out their heart and mind to a fine degree.

Join with the tribes on the following pages to honor their ancestors and to honor our Creator, our Mother Earth, our Moon, our Sun, and the whole of all living things in the whole of all creation. You will find that it is good. It is very, very good.

Aho . . .

I have said yes, and thrown away my country.
—Captain Jack (Modoc)

CALIFORNIA

Readers, note: California Indian people are all listed by tribal affiliation, with the reservation address and telephone numbers listed for information only.

Alturas Achomawi
P.O. Box 1035
Alturas, CA 96101
No telephone number
Fax (916) 233-3055

Pit River Achomawi
P.O. Drawer 1570
Burney, CA 96013
(916) 335-5421
Fax (916) 335-5241

Achomawi (Pit River), *adzuma, achoma,* "river"

Visitor Information: The Pit River Home and Agricultural Society is located in Alturas. Their telephone number is (916) 263-2584.

This division of the Shasta family occupied the Pit River country of northeastern California, except Burney, Dixie, and Hat Creek valleys, which were inhabited by the Atsugewi. A principal village was near Fallriver Mills, Shasta County. The languages of the Achomawi and the Atsugewi, while unquestionably related, are strikingly unlike.

Lassen Volcanic National Park
P.O. Box 100
Mineral, CA 96063-0100
(916) 595-4444

Atsugewi

Location: The park is 50 miles east of Redding on Highway 44.

Visitor Information: The park employs local Atsugewi Indian people as cultural historians. Demonstrations include basket weaving and a display of an Atsugewi wickiup.

There are only 200 Atsugewi Indians today. Their ancestors hunted and gathered food for centuries in what is now Lassen Volcanic National Park 180 miles northeast of San Francisco.

The lakes and mountains in Lassen Park were the spiritual lakes and mountains of the Atsugewi. There were about 2,000 Atsugewis when non-Indian intruders came to this area about 150 years ago.

Blue Lake Cabazon
P.O. Box 428
Blue Lake, CA 95525
(707) 668-5101
Fax (707) 668-4272

Buena Vista Cabazon
4650 Coalmine Road
Ione, CA 95640
(916) 455-7652

Cabazon
84-245 Indio Springs Drive
Indio, CA 92201
(619) 342-2593
Fax (619) 347-7880

Cabazon

Location: The Cabazon Band of Mission Indians' 1,700-acre reservation is divided into three parcels located adjacent to the cities of Indio, Coachella, and Mecca in the eastern section of the Coachella Valley.

Visitor Information: The Cabazon Indian Reservation has been a federally recognized reservation since 1876. The 26 enrolled members own and operate the Indio Bingo Palace and Gaming Center. The full-service gambling facility, just off Interstate 10 at the Auto

Center Drive Exit, consists of $500,000 High Stakes Bingo seven nights a week; a 24-hour card casino featuring poker, pan, and pai gau; and the newest addition, a live via satellite horse racing off-track betting parlor. There are also two full-service restaurants on the reservation.

Laytonville Cahto
P.O. Box 1239
Laytonville, CA 95454
(707) 984-6197

Cahto

Visitor Information: The Cahto live on their reservation just west of Laytonville.

This Kuneste tribe or band formerly lived in Cahto and Long valleys, Mendocino County, California. They belong to the Athapascan group and are closely related to the Wailaki, although culturally they resemble the Pomo.

Agua Caliente Cahuilla
960 E. Tahquitz Way, #106
Palm Springs, CA 92262
(619) 325-5673
Fax (619) 325-0593

Cahuilla
P.O. Box 391760
Anza, CA 92539-1760
(909) 763-5549

Los Coyotes Cahuilla
P.O. Box 249
Warner Springs, CA 92086
(619) 782-3269

Morongo Cahuilla
11581 Potrero Road
Banning, CA 92220
(909) 849-4697
Fax (909) 849-4698

Ramona Band Cahuilla
3940 Cary Road
Anza, CA 92539-0439
(909) 763-0371

Santa Rosa Cahuilla
325 N. Western Avenue
Hemet, CA 92343
(619) 741-5211

Torres-Martinez Desert Cahuilla
66-725 Martinez Road
Thermal, CA 92274
(619) 397-8144
Fax (619) 397-0300

Cahuilla

Location: The Morongo Indian Reservation is located at Banning, California. To go to the museum, take Interstate 10 east to the Fields Road exit.
The Torres-Martinez Indian Reservation is located in the Coachella Valley.

Public Ceremony or Powwow Dates: The annual Malki Museum Fiesta is held on Memorial Day weekend. There are Cahuilla bird singers, Papago Chelkona dancers, Apache Mountain Spirit dancers, Luiseño singers, and Aztec dancers.

Art Forms: The arts and crafts sold are likely to include jewelry, beadwork, baskets, cradleboards, and gourd rattles.

Visitor Information: The museum of the Cahuilla and Serrano tribes is named the Malki, and it displays pottery, baskets, and traditional items from the tribes. The gift shop also carries arts and crafts. During the Fiesta there will also be hand games.
The name Kawia is of uncertain origin, but the people are affiliated linguistically with the Agua Caliente, Juaneño, and Luiseño. They lived in the northern Colorado Desert from Banning southeast at least as far as Salton and on the headwaters of Santa Margarita River, where the Kawia Reservation was located. They

were first visited in 1776 by Fray Francisco Garces. At this time they lived around the northern slopes of the San Jacinto Mountains and to the north and roamed east to the Colorado, but their principal seat was near San Gorgonio pass. There were 793 Indians assembled under the name "Coahuila" at all the Mission Reservations in 1885. The Indians on Cahuilla Reservation under the Mission Tule River Agency in 1894 numbered 151, and in 1902, 159. This reservation consists of 18,240 acres of unpatented land.

Chemehuevi
P.O. Box 1976
Havasu Lake, CA 92363
(619) 858-4301
Fax (619) 858-5400

Chemehuevi

Location: The reservation is located south of Needles and across the river from Lake Havasu City, Arizona.

Visitor Information: The tribe is in the process of developing the recreation potential of their river location. Since they are across the river from an already developing tourist attraction, they will undoubtedly succeed.

For more information, see Arizona, Colorado River.

Chicken Ranch Chumash
P.O. Box 1699
Jamestown, CA 95327
(209) 984-3057

Santa Ynez Chumash
P.O. Box 517
Santa Ynez, CA 93460
(805) 688-7997
Fax (805) 688-8005

Woman basket maker with her baskets, Chimehuevis
Courtesy Museum of New Mexico, Neg. No. 82624

Chumash

Location: The members of this tribe reside primarily in Santa Barbara County. The new tribal office building, their bingo enterprise, and many new homes are located on their reservation.

Public Ceremony or Powwow Dates: The Santa Ynez Dolphin dancers are doing traditional Chumash dances and songs. Call the tribal office for dates and times to attend some of their ceremonies.

Visitor Information: The Chumash are striving to retain their culture and are trying to preserve their sacred Point Conception.

Cloverdale Miwok
4555 Redwood Hwy. South
Petaluma, CA 94952
(707) 766-9758

Coast Miwok

The Miwok of the coast are the people who lived where Marin and Sonoma counties are today. They were taken to Mission San Rafael where the population was reduced by disease. Some of the people survive, and their songs are heard with the Kashaya Pomo.

Barona Diegueño
1095 Barona Road
Lakeside, CA 92040
(619) 433-6612 or (619) 433-6613

Campo Diegueño
1779 Campo Truck Trail
Campo, CA 91906
(619) 478-9046
Fax (619) 478-5818

Cuyapaipe Diegueño
2271 Alpine Blvd.
Alpine, CA 91901
(619) 478-5289

Inja and Cosmit Diegueño
P.O. Box 491
Santa Ysabel, CA 92070

La Posta Diegueño
1064 Barona Road
Lakeside, CA 92040
(619) 561-9294

Manzanita Diegueño
P.O. Box 1302
Boulevard, CA 91905
(619) 766-4930

Mesa Grande Diegueño
P.O. Box 270
Santa Ysabel, CA 92070
(619) 282-9650

San Pasqual Diegueño
P.O. Box 365
Valley Center, CA 92082
(619) 749-3200

Santa Ysabel Diegueño
P.O. Box 130
Santa Ysabel, CA 92070
(619) 765-0845
Fax (619) 765-0320

Sycuan Diegueño
5459 Dehesa Road
El Cajon, CA 92021
(619) 445-2613
Fax (619) 445-1927

Diegueño

Visitor Information: The Tipai and Ipai people live primarily in San Diego County on reservations established by the federal government. Some of these hold annual fiestas that include dancing and food. The other coastal southern California tribes include the Luiseño, Cahuilla, Juaneño, Gabrieliño, and Cupeño.

Diegueños is probably a collective name synonymous with Comeya, applied by the Spaniards to Indians of the Yuman group who formerly lived in and around San Diego (and still do). It included representatives of many tribes and has no proper ethnic significance. In 1909, there were about 400 Indian people included under this name as attached to the Mission Agency of California, but they are now officially recognized as a part of the "Mission Indians."

Dry Creek Pomo and Wappo
P.O. Box 607
Geyserville, CA 95441
(707) 857-3842

Pomo
Wappo

Visitor Information: The Wappo Indian people of central California have intermarried with the Pomo. The Warm Springs Dam Visitor Center, 3333 Skaggs Springs Road, Geyserville, CA, (707) 433-9483, shows the work of Laura Fish Somersall, a Wappo speaker and consultant on scholarly studies of the tribe.

Wappo is from Spanish *quapo*, "brave." This small detached portion of the Yukian family of northern California, separated from the Huichnom, the nearest Yuki division, by 30 or 40 miles of Pomo territory, are the residents of the mountains separating Sonoma from Lake and Napa counties, between Geysers and Calistoga. A portion of them, called Rincons, occupied the Russian River Valley in the vicinity of Healdsburg.

Elk Valley Yurok, Hoopa, and Talawa
P.O. Box 1042
Crescent City, CA 95531
(707) 464-4680
Fax (707) 464-4519

Elk Valley Rancheria is an independent American Indian Organization made up of members of the Yurok, Hoopa, and Talawa

Indian tribes. It is located in northern California, in Del Norte County, just outside of Crescent City. These tribes occupied areas of California from the Oregon border south as far as Eureka and east of the city of Redding.

There is no connection with the Gabrieliño or Shoshone tribes or with southern California tribes near Los Angeles.

Hoopa

Hoopa Valley
P.O. Box 1348
Hoopa, CA 95546
(916) 625-4211
Fax (916) 625-4594

Location: The museum is located inside the shopping center, which is next to the market in the town of Hoopa on Highway 96.

Public Ceremony or Powwow Dates: Call the tribal office for dates and times of public ceremonies.

Visitor Information: The Hoopa Tribe has the Six Rivers Bingo Enterprise in the shopping center at Hoopa.

The Hoopa are an Athapascan tribe formerly occupying the valley of Trinity River from the South Fork to its junction with the Klamath, including Hoopa Valley. In August 1864, a 12-mile-square reservation was established. The population in 1888 was 650; in 1900, 430; and in 1905, 412.

Jamul
P.O. Box 612
Jamul, CA 91935
(619) 669-4785
Fax (619) 669-4817

Karuk of California
P.O. Box 1016
Happy Camp, CA 96039
(916) 493-5305
Fax (916) 493-5322

Karuk

Location: Some ceremonies are held near Somes Bar.

Public Ceremony or Powwow Dates: Odd-number years have more events than do even-number years as the Karuk calendar is on a two-year cycle. There are brush dances, white deerskin dances, jump dances, and more. Call the tribal office for dates and times and etiquette.

Visitor Information: You will often find Karuk dance groups performing at Indian celebrations and at colleges in northern California.

Luiseño

La Jolla Luiseño
Star Route, Box 158
Valley Center, CA 92082
(619) 742-3771
Fax (619) 742-3772

Pala Luiseño
P.O. Box 43
Pala, CA 92059
(619) 742-3784
Fax (619) 742-1411

Pauma Luiseño
P.O. Box 86
Pauma Valley, CA 92061
(619) 742-1289
Fax (619) 742-3422

Pechanga Luiseño
P.O. Box 1477
Temecula, CA 92593
(714) 676-2768
Fax (714) 699-6983

Rincon Luiseño
P.O. Box 68
Valley Center, CA 92082
(619) 749-1051
Fax (619) 749-8901

Soboba Luiseño
P.O. Box 487
San Jacinto, CA 92581
(714) 654-2765
Fax (714) 654-4198

Twenty Nine Palms Luiseño
555 Sunrise Hwy., Suite 200
Palm Springs, CA 92264
(619) 320-8168

Visitor Information: The Luiseño office sponsors a fiesta with festivities and peon games (hand games) and other interesting events. Call the tribal office for dates and times.

This is the southernmost Shoshonean division in California which received its name from San Luis Rey, the most important Spanish mission in the territory of these people.

Maidu

Berry Creek Maidu
1779 Mitchell Avenue
Oroville, CA 95966
(916) 534-3859

Round Valley Maidu
P.O. Box 448
Covelo, CA 95428
(707) 983-6126
Fax (707) 983-6128

Greenville Maidu
645 Antelope Blvd., Suite 15
Red Bluff, CA 96080
(916) 528-9000
Fax (916) 529-9002

Susanville Maidu
Drawer U
Susanville, CA 96130
(916) 257-6264
Fax (916) 257-6983

Location: The Maidu do the Bear Dance at Janesville and Greenville.

Public Ceremony or Powwow Dates: The dates and times of the Bear Dance can be determined by calling the Greenville and/or Susanville offices above. Traditional dancing and singing are performed during the Bear Dances.

Art Forms: During the dances, arts and crafts are offered for sale.

Visitor Information: There is a Maidu dance group that performs traditional dancing and singing at Indian Grinding Rock State Park's Chaw-Se Big Time and other events. Call California State University, Sacramento, for more information.

Maidu ("man," "Indian"). The Maidu are a tribe of the Penutian language group. Their original home was in a valley of California east of the Sacramento River and west of the Sierra Nevadas. They lived in conical-roofed earthen lodges and were very skilled at basket making. Prospectors discovered gold in the valley, and the Maidu were displaced after 1848.

Miwok

Jackson Miwok
P.O. Box 429
Jackson, CA 95642
(209) 223-1935
Fax (209) 223-5366

Shingle Springs Miwok
P.O. Box 1340
Shingle Springs, CA 95682
(916) 676-8010
Fax (916) 626-8010 (call first)

Tuolumne Me-Wuk Miwok
P.O. Box 699
Tuolumne, CA 95379
(209) 928-3475
Fax (209) 928-1677

350 / West

Location: The California State Indian Museum, which is adjacent to Sutter's Fort, 2618 K Street, in Sacramento, (916) 324-0971, is the location of an annual California Indian Days Celebration. The Kule Loklo Miwok Indian Village is a half-mile northwest of Olema, and the Miwok dance here during the Kule Loklo Celebration in July or August. Call (415) 663-1092 for dates and times.

Public Ceremony or Powwow Dates: The spring of the year features Pomo and Miwok dancing at the museum in Sacramento. Call for dates and times of the dances.

Art Forms: The arts and crafts of the Miwok are available at the Chaw-Se Big Time Celebration.

Visitor Information: The Mi-Wuk Indian Acorn Festival is also held annually at Tuolumne Indian Rancheria near Tuolumne. September is the time to watch Miwok dancing and eat California Indian foods such as acorn bread and acorn soup.

Miwok ("man"). This is one of the two divisions of the Moquelumnan family in central California, the other being the Olamentke. With a small exception in the west, the Miwok occupied territory bounded on the north by Cosumnes River, on the east by the ridge of the Sierra Nevada, on the south by Fresno Creek, and on the west by the San Joaquin River. The exception on the west is a narrow strip of land on the east bank of the San Joaquin occupied by Yokuts Indians beginning at the Tuolumne and extending northward to a point not far from the place where the San Joaquin bends to the west. Their language was so uniform that the Miwok could travel from the Cosumnes to the Fresno and make themselves understood.

Fort Mojave
500 Merriman Avenue
Needles, CA 92363
(619) 326-4591
Fax (619) 326-2468

Mojave

Location: The reservation is located north and northeast of Needles.

For more information, see Arizona, Colorado River.

Mono (Monache)

Big Sandy Mono
P.O. Box 337
Auberry, CA 93602
(209) 855-4003

Cold Springs Mono
P.O. Box 209
Tollhouse, CA 93667
(209) 855-8187
Fax (209) 855-8359

North Fork Mono
3027 Clement #2
San Francisco, CA 94121
(415) 752-9085

Sierra Mono Museum
North Fork, CA
(209) 877-2115

Visitor Information: The museum shows the history and culture of the Sierra Mono Indian people.

This tribe forms one of the three great dialect groups in which the Shoshone of the great plateau are distinguished. It includes the Mono of southeastern California, the Paviotso, or "Paiute," of western Nevada, and the "Snakes" and Saidyuka of eastern Oregon. Part of the Bannock may be related to them. In 1903, there were about 5,400 people in this division.

Mooretown Concow-Maidu
P.O. Box 1842
1900 Oro Dam Boulevard, Suite 8
Oroville, CA 95965
(916) 533-3625
Fax (916) 533-3680

Visitor Information: This is a recently reorganized Concow-Maidu tribe, just recognized in 1988. They are in the process of acquiring a land base and housing at the time of this writing. They have established a Tribal Roll and are continuing to enroll both lineal descendants and adoptees.

Ohlone (Costanoan). These are the original inhabitants of San Francisco Bay south to Monterey Bay. The mission system reduced their culture, but they are recovering.

Potter Valley
755 B. El Rio Street
Ukiah, CA 95482
(707) 468-7494
Fax (707) 468-0874

Paiute and/or Shoshone

Big Pine
P.O. Box 700
Big Pine, CA 93513
(619) 938-2003
Fax (619) 938-2942

Bishop
P.O. Box 548
Bishop, CA 93515
(619) 873-3584
Fax (619) 873-4143

Bridgeport
P.O. Box 37
Bridgeport, CA 93517
(619) 932-7083
Fax (619) 932-7846

Cedarville
P.O. Box 126
Cedarville, CA 96104
Message Fax (916) 233-2439

Fort Bidwell
P.O. Box 127
Fort Bidwell, CA 96112
(916) 279-6310
Fax (916) 279-2233

Fort Independence
P.O. Box 67
Independence, CA 93526
(619) 878-2126 (Recording)
Fax (619) 878-2311

Lone Pine
P.O. Box 747
Lone Pine, CA 93545

Timbisha Shoshone
P.O. Box 206
Death Valley, CA 92328
(619) 786-2374
Fax (619) 786-2344

Utu Utu Gwaitu Paiute
Benton Paiute Reservation
Star Route 4, Box 56A
Benton, CA 93512
(619) 933-2321 (Recording)

For more information on the Paiute, see Nevada, Paiute. For more information on the Shoshone, see Wyoming, Shoshone.

Paiute Shoshone Indian Cultural Museum
2300 West Line Street
Bishop, CA 93514
(619) 873-4478

Visitor Information: This is an Indian owned and operated museum that features interesting Paiute and Shoshone cultural displays. Contact the museum for dates and times of special events that benefit the museum.

For more information, see Nevada, Paiute; Wyoming, Shoshone.

Picayune
P.O. Box 269
Coarsegold, CA 93614
(209) 683-6633
Fax (209) 683-0599

Pomo

Big Valley Pomo
P.O. Box 955
Lakeport, CA 95453
(702) 262-0629

Coyote Valley Pomo
P.O. Box 39 or 7901 Hwy. 10 North
Redwood Valley, CA 95470-0039
(707) 485-8723
Fax (707) 468-1247

Elem Pomo
Sulphur Bank Rancheria
P.O. Box 618
Clearlake Oaks, CA 95423
(707) 998-2549

Hopland Pomo
P.O. Box 610
Hopland, CA 95449
(707) 744-1647
Fax (707) 744-1506

Kashia Pomo
Stewarts Point Rancheria
P.O. Box 38
Stewarts Point, CA 95480
(707) 528-4267

Manchester/Point Arena Pomo
P.O. Box 623
Point Arena, CA 95468
(707) 882-2788
Fax (707) 882-4142

Middletown Pomo
P.O. Box 1035
Middletown, CA 95461
(707) 987-3670
Fax (707) 987-9615

Pinolville Pomo
367 N. State Street, Suite 204
Ukiah, CA 95482
(707) 463-1454

Robinson Pomo
P.O. Box 1119
Nice, CA 95464
(707) 257-0527
1-800-445-3385
Fax (707) 275-0235

Scotts Valley Pomo
149 N. Main #200
Lakeport, CA 95453
(707) 263-4771
Fax (707) 263-4773

These people were recognized by the Bureau of Indian Affairs on 6 September 1991.

Sherwood Valley Pomo
190 Sherwood Hill Drive
Willits, CA 95490
(707) 459-9690
Fax (707) 459-6936

Upper Lake Pomo
P.O. Box 245272
Sacramento, CA 95820
(916) 371-2576

Location: The Kashaya Pomo, Elem Pomo, Big Valley Pomo, Coyote Valley Pomo, and Point Arena Pomo listed above have dance groups.

Public Ceremony or Powwow Dates: In August, the City of Cotati, California, sponsors an Indian Day at which the Pomo dance. Telephone the City of Cotati at (707) 795-5478 for dates and times. The Elem Pomo dance, and it is possible to book them for special events. Call (707) 998-1666 for more details. Along the Soda Bay Road between Lakeport and Kelseyville, off Highway 29, is the Big Valley or Mission Rancheria. The Pomo hold traditional dances here periodically. Pomo dance groups also sometimes hold dances at Ft. Ross on Highway 1, 11 miles north of Jenner, California.

Indian Grinding Rock State Park, off Highway 88 on the Pine Grove-Volcano Road near Pine Grove is the site of the Chaw-Se Big Time Celebration, usually the last weekend in September. Often you will find the Pomo dancing here. No pictures or videotapes are allowed inside the roundhouse. Also, the costumes of the dancers are not to be touched because of spiritual rules against doing so.

There are two Pomo communities near Point Arena, the Point Arena and the Manchester rancherias. This is the home of the Coastal Pomo Indian Dancers, among the best in the country. You may write Box 423, Point Arena, CA 95468, or call (707) 882-2218 and ask for Jackie Frank, for more details.

There is an annual Kule Loklo Celebration in July or August at Kule Loklo Miwok Indian Village. Call (415) 663-1092 for more information. Often there will be Point Arena Pomo, Kashaya Pomo, and other dance groups performing here. The Strawberry Festival in the spring and the Acorn Harvest Festival also find Pomo dancers at Kule Loklo.

The Jesse Peter Memorial Museum, Santa Rosa Junior College Campus, 1501 Mendocino Avenue, Santa Rosa, California, (707) 527-4479, is the location of the Day Under the Oaks Celebration featuring Coastal Pomo Indian dancers. Pomo dancing also takes place on occasion at Lake Mendocino Cultural Center at Ukiah, California, (707) 462-7581.

Art Forms: The Elem Pomo have a tribal office decorated with traditional basketry designs. Lakeport Historical Museum, Main and Third streets in Lakeport, has a collection of Pomo baskets, (707) 263-4555. Arts and crafts are sold during the Big Time Celebration. The Kule Loklo Celebration has basket weaving, fire making, crafting of musical instruments, and sales of arts and crafts. The Lake Mendocino Cultural Center displays arts and crafts, and the Mendo-Lake Indian Council operates a gift shop here with Pomo crafts, books, and classes in traditional Pomo arts such as basketry.

The name of the Indian linguistic group known as Pomo is the Kulanapan, living in parts of Sonoma, Lake, Mendocino, Colusa, and Glenn counties. In the northern Pomo dialect, Pomo means "people" and added to a place-name, forms the name for a group of people. Although Poma is almost as frequently heard as Pomo, the latter has come into general use.

Quartz Valley Salinan
P.O. Box 737
Etha, CA 96027
(916) 467-3307 or (916) 467-5409
Fax (916) 467-3466

Redwood Valley Salinan
P.O. Box 499
Redwood Valley, CA 95470
(707) 485-0361

Rohnerville Salinan
P.O. Box 108
Eureka, CA 95502-0108
(707) 443-6150
Fax (707) 442-6403

Salinan

The Salinan are the people of Monterey and San Luis Obispo counties. They were in Missions San Antonio and San Miguel. Their descendants are living in central California.

San Manuel Serrano
P.O. Box 266
Patton, CA 92369
(909) 864-8933

Serrano

Serranos (Spanish, "highlanders," "mountaineers")

Visitor Information: The Serrano Cultural Center is on the beautiful San Manuel Indian Reservation in the tribal hall. Archaeological and ethnological displays are presented.

This is a Shoshonean division with a common dialect, centering in the San Bernardino Mountains in southern California, north of Los Angeles, but extending down the Mohave River at least to Daggett and north across the Mohave desert into the valley of Tejon Creek.

Shasta

Not many of the original people are left here in California and Oregon. In 1967, "termination" policies of the U.S. government took the last of their land. The Siskiyou County Museum in Yreka, California, has some of their history.

Howonquet
Smith River Rancheria
P.O. Box 239
Smith River, CA 95567
(707) 487-9255
Fax (707) 487-0930

Tache Yokuts

Santa Rosa Tache Yokuts
325 North Western Avenue
Hemet, CA 92343
(909) 849-4761

Table Mountain Tache Yokuts
P.O. Box 445
Friant, CA 93626
(209) 822-2587
Fax (209) 822-2693

Tule River Tache Yokuts
P.O. Box 589
Porterville, CA 93258
(209) 781-4271
Fax (209) 781-4610

Location: The Lemoore celebration is held on the reservation; call for dates and times. The Tule River Reservation is east of Porterville, California. Call (209) 781-4271 for dates and times and etiquette required to attend their celebrations and ceremonies.

Public Ceremony or Powwow Dates: In late August, the Lemoore people sponsor an annual celebration that features traditional Yokuts songs. Also in late August, the Tule River Yokuts hold a spiritual gathering for their community and guests. Call for information.

The Tachi are one of the larger tribes of the Yokuts family, living on the plains north of Tulare Lake in south central California.

Tolowa

The Tolowa have a cultural program that includes dance in traditional form. The College of the Redwoods sponsors a program at Redwood National Park. For more information, contact Redwood National Park at 1111 Second Street, Crescent City, CA 95531, (707) 464-6101.

Tygh

The Indian people of Tygh Valley hold the Tygh Valley Indian Celebration north of Warm Springs, Oregon, in May. See this section, Warm Springs Tribal Office, for more information. Call the tribal office for dates and times.

Viejas Kumeyaay
P.O. Box 908
Alpine, CA 91903
(619) 445-3810
Fax (619) 445-5337

Kumeyaay

Location: The Viejas Indian Reservation is in south San Diego County, 35 miles east of San Diego adjacent to Interstate 8.

Visitor Information: San Diego, just 35 minutes west of the reservation, has all services and accommodations.
   The Viejas tribe operates the Ma-Tar-Awa Park with a gift shop where you will find beautiful basketry, basketry design in textiles, beadwork, and clothing. There is an RV park with all hookups.

The people of Viejas are progressive and modern Americans who have contributed substantially to fire ecology, irrigation, highway transportation systems, and the building of the San Diego County Mission system established by the Spanish missionaries when they first arrived from Spain. They are independent people who make significant contributions to our world society.

Wailaki

These Indian people live on the Round Valley Indian Reservation at Covelo, California. They have recently revived their beadwork in a new arts and crafts program. Call the tribal office at (707) 983-0612 for details.

Wintun (Indian, "people")

Colusa Wintun
P.O. Box 8
Colusa, CA 95932
(916) 458-8231 (Recording)
Fax (916) 787-4006

Cortina Wintun
P.O. Box 7470
Citrus Heights, CA 95621-7470
(916) 726-7118
Fax (916) 726-3608

Grindstone Wintun
P.O. Box 63
Elk Creek, CA 95939
(916) 968-5365
Fax (916) 968-5366

Redding Wintun
2000 Rancheria Road
Redding, CA 96001
(916) 225-8979
Fax (916) 241-1879

Rumsey Wintun
P.O. Box 18
Brooks, CA 95606
(916) 796-3400
Fax (916) 796-2143

Visitor Information: The Cach Creek Bingo Enterprise is located at Rumsey Rancheria, telephone (916) 796-3182.

Wintun territory was bounded on the north by Mt. Shasta and on the south by a line running from the eastern boundary, about 10 miles east of the Sacramento River, due west through Jacinto and the headwaters of Stoney Creek, Colusa County. The eastern boundary began at the headwaters of Bear Creek, bearing south some miles east of the parallel to McCloud River. From Pit River to the neighborhood of Redding, the Wintun occupied a triangular area east of the Sacramento.

Table Bluff Wiyot
P.O. Box 519
Loleta, CA 95551
(707) 733-5055
Fax (707) 733-5601

Wiyot

Location: The Table Bluff Reservation is located 15 miles southwest of Eureka, California, by way of U.S. 101. It is near the southwest corner of Humboldt Bay, 5 miles west of Loleta, using Copenhagen Road.

The Wiyot tribe's aboriginal territory extended from Little River (south of Trinidad, California, some 5 miles) south to the Bear River Ridge (approximately 15 miles south of Ferndale, California) and from the Coast inland for about 20 miles. Located deep in the heart of the redwood belt, the redwood tree was one of the Wiyots' most valuable assets. It was used to build their houses and canoes.

Their diet consisted mostly of seafood (clams, eels, salmon, and fish of all types on the North Coast), many types of berries, and meat from various animals and waterfowl. Basket weaving was very important. Soapstone was used in constructing pottery. Deer and elk horn were used to construct various tools, as were flint and animal bones.

The Wiyot tribe was all but annihilated on February 26, 1860, by non-Indians in several massacres around Humboldt Bay and on Indian Island. Most of the Wiyot artifacts were removed from the area after the massacres or were destroyed. Little remains in the local museum to remind visitors of the Wiyot Indians. The Table Bluff Reservation was established in 1908, consisting of 20 acres, one-half mile from the Pacific Ocean at sea level. By law (P.L. 85-671 passed by Congress in 1958), the Table Bluff Reservation (one of 41 named rancherias) was terminated from federal jurisdiction in 1960. The reservation filed suit against the federal government in 1975. By a court decision, the reservation became, once again, federally recognized in 1981.

Because of very serious health and safety hazards on the reservation which are not correctable, the Wiyot are now in the process of relocating to a site that offers a healthier environment. The reservation purchased 102 acres of land approximately one-half mile above the existing reservation. The master plan calls for 25 to 35 new homes, community buildings, playgrounds, a traditional Wiyot Indian village, a health clinic, a museum, and a workshop.

The tribe is governed by a tribal constitution and by-laws established in 1982. The tribal council consists of six members serving staggered terms. The annual meeting date is the first Saturday in April.

Yahi

This is a branch of the Yana tribe. They are known for their member, Ishi, the last Indian person living in his original state. Ishi died in 1916.

Round Valley Yuki
Covelo, CA

Yuki

The Yuki were almost exterminated by greedy land grabbers in the area of their reservation near Round Valley, California. There is a book about the story of this disgraceful American episode of manifest destiny, Virginia Miller's *Ukomno'm: The Yuki Indians.*

The Yuki occupied the Round Valley area as well as an area along the coast and south in the mountains dividing Sonoma from Napa and Lake counties.

Yurok

Big Lagoon Yurok
P.O. Drawer 3060
Trinidad, CA 95570

(707) 826-2079
Fax (707) 826-1737

Hoopa Valley Yurok
P.O. Box 1348
Hoopa, CA 95546
(916) 625-4211

Resighini Yurok
P.O. Box 529
Klamath, CA 95548
(707) 482-2431
Fax (707) 482-3425

Trinidad Yurok
P.O. Box 630
Trinidad, CA 95570
(707) 677-0211
Fax (707) 677-3921

Yurok
517 Third Street, Suite 18
Eureka, CA 95501
(800) 848-8765
(707) 444-0433
Fax (707) 444-0437

Yurok (from Karok *yuruk*, "downstream")

The Yurok live on the lower Klamath River, California, and the adjacent coast. They have no name for themselves other than Olekwo'l, "persons," sometimes written Alikwa. The territory of the Yurok extended from Bluff Creek, six miles above the mouth of the Trinity, down the Klamath River to its mouth, and on the coast from beyond Wilson Creek, six miles north of the mouth of the Klamath, to probably Mad River.

In 1870, the population was 2,700. In 1909, they numbered 500 or 600 along the Klamath River.

Conclusion

The land is plowed up and fenced and paved over. There are giant buildings reaching up to the sky where there were springs and meadows and trees. Trash dumps and pollution and housing areas cover over the Sacred Land. Indian America is reduced to about one-half of one percent in land area, and the population of the people compared to the non-Indian population is about the same. Native American aboriginal people were the residents and caretakers of this land.

You can still walk the sacred places. All of Mother Earth is sacred. But you have to pay or ask permission or trespass on another one's property. How can you own the Earth? The Earth is our Mother.

And when the U.S. government makes another settlement or condemns the Sacred Earth for their ownership, Native American people are paid for that land with the value it was when the treaty was signed. Usually that means 1860s prices. Is this fair? Many people believe that Indian people receive money from the government like a handout. I often hear people say that they wish they were Indian so they could receive money and a free ride. The fact is that Indian people do not have a free ride. What they receive is dividends from their own resources. And medical care and education were guaranteed by the government in the treaties for as long as the water flows and the grass grows. This stipulation was the only benefit Native American tribes received in exchange for their land. Usually the treaties were arranged and signed by Indians who did not have the authority and consent of the people, but they often did have the welfare of the people at heart. What could they do against "civilized" armies and weapons and the hordes of encroaching intruders? As the administration of the government changes, the benefits that Indian people receive change with it. There are cutbacks in education and medical benefits. Cutbacks in the only benefits Indian people traded their Sacred Earth to receive.

What has been lost can never be regained. The population of the Earth will not allow it. The attitude and greed of the people will not allow it. When man had reached the height of his perfect state, that time in his culture just before the Industrial Revolution, it was the center of the world, and it was in balance and the tree flowered and filled with singing birds. The air was clean, and the sky was always blue, and fresh air blew across the land. It was good. It was very, very good. Buffalo herds were wide as day, and the earth stayed young. The original people of the land were innocent and without the need of machines. There were reasons to celebrate with ceremony and dance and songs. Man had a love affair with natural things, and all living things rejoiced and were in love with mankind. The spirit of the whole of all living things was happy.

Now the people of the Earth who live on Turtle Island still celebrate that time of the past when they were free. Tribes still hold pow-wows and celebrations and conduct ceremonies that are filled with prayers and hope. It is our responsibility to make sure that their prayers and hope are answered and fulfilled.

Sitting Bull was murdered by members of his own people who had been hired by the government as policemen. A few days before he died, he said, "There are no Indians left but me. And soon, too, I will be gone."

Sitting Bull was a medicine man. Our culture may be smothered by this society, but Indian people have maintained their society, under the most adverse conditions, as well as any other native people on Mother Earth. He must be proud.

Glossary

Absentee: A division of the Shawnee tribe which about 1845 left the rest of the tribe, then in Kansas, and removed to Indian Territory. In 1904, they numbered 459, under the Shawnee School Superintendent in Oklahoma.

Agency: The Bureau of Indian Affairs office established on the reservation is called the "agency."

Algonquian family: The linguistic group that occupied a larger area than any other in North America.

Altar: In Indian ceremonial usage, it is the place of the offerings to the spirit or the place of the cleansing of the particular article placed there.

Athapascan family: The linguistic group that is most widely distributed in North America.

Awl: The sharpened stick, bone, stone, or piece of metal used as a perforator in sewing.

Beadwork: Belts, hair ties, earrings, and other jewelry made by stringing beads is called beadwork. Among the types of beadwork are loomwork, lazy stitch, and peyote stitch.

Casa Grande: The principal structure of an extensive ruined pueblo one-half mile south of the Gila River, Pinal County, Arizona.

Ceremony: The performance in a prescribed order of a series of formal acts constituting a drama that has an ultimate object; usually, the expression of spiritual emotion.

Civilization: The overturning of the aboriginal idea of government, the abolition of many of the aboriginal social beliefs, the readjustment of aboriginal ideas of property and personal rights, and the changing of aboriginal occupation.

Confederation: The political league of two or more tribes.

Coup ("blow"; "stroke"): To touch an enemy was more honorable than to kill him.

Cradleboard: The device made to hold an infant while in the early months of life.

Dance: The prodigal nature of life and energy. It is universal and instinctive. The physical expression of spiritual joy.

Dreams and visions: The revelation of spiritual inspiration from the Creator.

Earth lodge: A dwelling partly underground, circular in form, from 30 to 60 feet in diameter, with walls about 6 feet high, on which rested a dome-shaped roof with an opening in the center to afford light within and to permit the egress of smoke.

Ethics and morals: The rules of the community adapted to its mode of life and surroundings. The primitive aboriginal had more rigorous and demanding moral systems than so-called civilized man.

Family clans: An American Indian clan or gens is an intratribal exogamic group of persons either actually or theoretically consanguine, organized to promote their social and political welfare, the members being usually denoted by a common class name derived generally from some fact relating to the habitat of the group or to its usual tutelary being.

Fasting chants: As with other chanting, this is the expression of prayer verbalized into song. It may or may not be within the language. Often, it is song verbalized with rhythmic sounds from spiritual inspiration.

Featherwork: The art of using feathers in costumes; spiritual objects for prayers, decoration, and rewards.

Five Civilized Tribes: The Cherokee, Chickasaw, Choctaw, Creek, and Seminole tribes in Indian Territory were so called because of their rapid advancement into "civilization."

Gaming; hand games: Indian games today are games of chance: (1) games in which implements corresponding with dice are thrown at random to determine a number or numbers, the counts being kept by means of sticks, pebbles, etc., or on an abacus or counting board or circuit; (2) games in which one or more of the players guess in which of two or more places an odd or particularly marked counter is concealed, success or failure resulting in the gain or loss of counters. Also games of dexterity: archery, darts, shooting at a moving target, ball games in many forms, and racing games.

Ghost Dance: The ceremonial spiritual dance connected with the messiah Wovoka ("Cutter"). The massacre of so many men, women, and children at Wounded Knee, South Dakota, on December 29, 1890, was undertaken because of the mistaken notion of the U.S. Army that the people were gathering for a violent exchange with them. They were actually gathering for the performance of the Ghost Dance.

Great Spirit: The Creator, God, Jehovah.

Hogan: A Navajo house, constructed of logs with dirt thrown and piled against the sides.

Iroquoian family: A linguistic group of the northeastern United States and Canada.

Kachina: A supernatural being impersonated by men or statuettes.

Keresan family: A linguistic family of Pueblo Indians.

Kiva: Sacred ceremonial and assembly chamber of the Pueblo Indians.

Maize: Corn.

Medicine; Medicine Man: The scope of spiritual agents that are medicinal, magical, prayerful, symbolical, and empirical. The one that interprets and administers and conducts the ceremony surrounding such agents is a Medicine Man.

Metalwork: The art of converting metals into adornments and jewelry.

Metate: The name given to stones for grinding grains, seeds, chile, dried meats, and so forth.

Missions: The southern California and coastal Spanish settlements that employed forced Indian labor to construct, maintain, and operate. Other missions were common across the Americas and were conducted by a variety of groups, usually religious in nature.

Moccasin: A shoe, usually made of deerskin.

Muskhogean family: A linguistic group comprising the Creeks, Choctaw, Chickasaw, Seminole, and other tribes.

Powwow: A social gathering of the tribes with intertribal singing and dancing. Usually there is also competition dancing in many styles.

Pueblo: A town or village built in a permanent manner. In the Southwest, the term has come to signify all Indian villages built from stone or adobe.

Quill work: The embroidery work that includes the quills of porcupines or bird feathers.

Reservation: A tract of land that is held in trust by an Indian tribe, nation, or community. The U.S. government set aside these areas as a result of treaties that were often signed by people of the tribe who did not have authority to do so. The reservation was a device that allowed the government to bring Indian people under control and to take the greater portion of the land area. Ironically, much of the poor land that was set aside for the reservations also was the land that contained mineral deposits.

Salinan family: A linguistic group of California.

Sand painting: An art existing among Indian people, especially those of the southwestern part of the United States. Some tribes use the painting in a ceremonial and healing way.

Shoshonean family: The linguistic group that occupied most of the Mountain and Plateau all the way to the southwest coast of the United States.

Shrine: The place where sacred offerings are deposited in prayers to the Creator.

Sinew: The tendonous animal fiber used for sewing purposes.

Siouan family: The most populous linguistic family north of Mexico, next to the Algonquian.

Snake Dance: The ceremony of the Hopi people in which live snakes are carried.

Soul: The concept of spiritual life residing in the body.

Sun Dance: The Offerings Lodge, misnamed the Sun Dance by observers who believed the dancers were worshiping the sun. This is the most sacred of ceremonies of the Plains tribes, especially the Arapahoe, Cheyenne, Siksika, Cree of Algonquian stock, the Dakota, Assiniboine, Mandan, Crow, Ponca, Omaha of Siouan stock, Pawnee of Caddoan stock, Kiowa, Shoshone, and the Ute of Shoshonean stock. The ceremony does not involve self-inflicted torture as many writers have postulated in the past. This is the giving and offering of one's self to the Creator with fasting and praying and, in some tribes, piercing of the pectoral muscle.

Sweat lodge: The ceremony of prayer in a sweat lodge built with a willow frame and covered with buffalo robes (blankets, carpet, canvas or combinations of these today). Hot stones are brought into the lodge, and water is poured over them to produce steam. It is a rigorously prescribed ceremony in which rules and observances are followed.

Symbol: An object or action that conveys a meaning distinct from the actual concept corresponding to the object or to the action.

Tattooing: The act of affixing a permanent symbol or design on the body. This is very common among many Indian tribes. The act of signing for Arapahoe was a tapping of the upper chest because they usually tattooed one or more dotted circles in that area.

Tewa: A linguistic family of the Pueblo people in the Southwest.

Tipi: From the Siouan root *ti* "to dwell," *pi* "used for." This is the spelling approved by the Sioux Nation. A tipi is the conical skin dwelling of the Plains tribes and by some of the tribes of the Northwest. Constructed with buffalo hides sewn to form a single piece and held in place by lodgepoles, the average tipi was about 16 feet in diameter in the days when people were free to roam the plains.

Tribe: The body of persons who are bound together by ties of consanguinity and affinity and by certain esoteric ideas or concepts derived from their philosophy concerning the genesis and preservation of the environing cosmos and who by means of these kinship ties are thus socially, politically, and spiritually organized through a variety of ritualistic, governmental, and other institutions, and who dwell together occupying a definite territorial area, and who speak a common language or dialect.

Walum Olum: The sacred tribal chronicle of the Lenape or Delaware. The name signifies "painted tally."

Wickiup: The popular name for the brush shelter or mat-covered house of the Paiute, Apache, and other tribes of the Nevada and Arizona regions.

Wigwam: An arborlike or conical structure covered with bark or whatever the local area dictated.

Yuman family: A linguistic group of southern California and southern Arizona.

Bibliography

Brown, Dee. *Bury My Heart at Wounded Knee.* Holt, Rinehart, Winston, New York, 1970.
——*Wounded Knee: An Indian History of the American West,* Dell, New York, 1975.
Brown, Joseph Epes. *The Sacred Pipe.* University of Oklahoma Press, Norman, Oklahoma, 1953.
Capps, Benjamin. *The Indians.* Time-Life Books, Alexandria, Virginia, 1973.
Eagle/Walking Turtle. *Keepers of the Fire.* Bear and Co., Santa Fe, New Mexico, 1987.
Formen, Werner, and Norman Bancroft-Hunt. *The Indians of the Great Plains.* Orbis Publishing Limited, London, 1981.
Hardt, Athia L. "The Art of Navajo Sand Paintings." *New York Times,* October 2, 1988.
Hillinger, Charles. "Tribe's Single Survivor Passes Along Knowledge." *Los Angeles Times, Albuquerque Journal,* September 25, 1988.
Hodge, Frederick W. *Handbook of American Indians North of Mexico.* Pageant Books, Inc., New York, 1959.
Jacka, Lois Essary. "On the Mesas of the Hopis." *New York Times,* October 2, 1988.
Karr, Jane Alice. Courtesy Note. *New York Times,* October 2, 1988.
Mails, Thomas E. *Dog Soldiers, Bear Men and Buffalo Women.* Prentice-Hall, Inc., Englewood Cliffs, New Jersey, 1973.
Marquis, Arnold. *A Guide to America's Indians.* University of Oklahoma Press, Norman, Oklahoma, 1974.
Neihardt, John G. *When the Tree Flowered.* University of Nebraska Press, Lincoln, 1951.
Pacheco, Patrick. *Rites of Passage. New York Times,* October 2, 1988.
Schmitt and Brown. *Fighting Indians of the West.* Chas. Scribner's Sons, Bonanza Books, New York, 1948.
Shakespeare, Tom. *The Sky People.* Vantage Press, New York, 1971.
Shanks, Ralph. *The North American Indian Travel Guide.* Petaluma, California, 1986, 1987.
Snyder, Fred. *National Native American Directory.* San Carlos, Arizona, 1982.
Trenholm, Virginia Cole. *The Arapahoes, Our People.* University of Oklahoma Press, Norman, Oklahoma, 1970.
Vanderwerth, W. C. *Indian Oratory.* University of Oklahoma Press, Norman, Oklahoma, 1971.

Appendix

Indian Moons

January

Sioux:	Moon of strong cold
Zuni:	Moon when the limbs of trees are broken by snow
Omaha:	Moon when the snow drifts into the tipis
Ojibwa:	Spirit moon

February

Sioux:	Raccoon moon
Omaha:	Moon when the geese come home
Tewa Pueblo:	Moon of the cedar dust wind
Kiowa:	Little bud moon
Winnebago:	Fish-running moon
Ojibwa:	Sucker moon

March

Sioux:	Moon when the buffalo cows drop their calves
Omaha:	Little frog moon
Tewa Pueblo:	Moon when the leaves break forth
Cherokee:	Strawberry moon
Ponca:	Water stands in the ponds moon
Ojibwa:	Crust on the snow moon

April

Sioux:	Moon of greening grass
Cheyenne:	Moon when the geese lay eggs
Winnebago:	Planting corn moon
Kiowa:	Leaf moon
Mandan-Hidatsa:	Moon of the breaking up of the ice
Ojibwa:	Snowshoe breaking moon

May

Sioux:	Moon when the ponies shed
Creek:	Mulberry moon
Osage:	Moon when the little flowers die
Cheyenne:	Moon when the horses get fat
Winnebago:	Hoeing-corn moon
Ojibwa:	Flowers moon

June

Sioux:	Moon of making fat
Omaha:	Moon when the buffalo bulls hunt the cows
Tewa Pueblo:	Moon when the leaves are dark green
Ponca:	Hot weather begins moon
Ojibwa:	Strawberry moon

July

Sioux:	Moon when the wild cherries are ripe
Omaha:	Moon when the buffalo bellow
Kiowa:	Moon of deer horns dropping off
Creek:	Little ripening moon
Winnebago:	Corn-popping moon
Ojibwa:	Raspberry moon

August

Sioux:	Moon when the geese shed their feathers
Cherokee:	Drying up moon
Ponca:	Corn is in the silk moon
Creek:	Big ripening moon
Osage:	Yellow flower moon
Ojibwa:	Blueberry moon

September

Sioux:	Moon of drying grass
Omaha:	Moon when the deer paw the earth
Tewa Pueblo:	Moon when the corn is taken in
Cherokee:	Black butterfly moon
Creek:	Little chestnut moon
Ojibwa:	Wild rice moon

October

Sioux:	Moon of falling leaves
Zuni:	Big wind moon
Ponca:	Moon when they store food in caches
Cheyenne:	Moon when the water begins to freeze on the edge of streams
Kiowa:	Ten-colds moon
Ojibwa:	Falling leaves moon

November

Creek:	Moon when the water is black with leaves
Kiowa:	Geese-going moon
Mandan-Hidatsa:	Moon when the rivers freeze
Tewa Pueblo:	Moon when all is gathered in
Winnebago:	Little bear's moon
Ojibwa:	Freezing moon

December

Sioux:	Moon of popping trees
Cheyenne:	Moon when the wolves run together
Creek:	Big winter moon
Arikara:	Moon of the nose of the great serpent
Winnebago:	Big bear's moon
Ojibwa:	Little spirit moon

Powwow Dance Styles and Clothing

If you have never attended a Native American powwow, you are in for an exciting experience. Be sure to be there for the beginning, the Grand Entry, when all the dancers dance single-file into the arena. The colors, sounds, and contrasting dance styles of the participants will truly bring happiness into your spirit.

For hundreds of centuries Native Americans have held social gatherings to celebrate success in battle or hunting, or just to celebrate the goodness of life. Even though the United States Government did try to suppress Native American culture, the Indian Citizenship Act of 1924 and the returning Native American veterans from America's wars helped to revitalize the social gathering we today call the intertribal powwow. And because dance styles have always been changing, it is not odd that they continue to change today. You are welcome to powwow, too. Indian and non-Indian people alike are joining in the fun throughout the United States and Canada. Many dancers travel on a powwow circuit and compete from New York to California and from Canada to Mexico.

The Native American events calendar in this edition of Indian America is your guide to celebrations that are open to the public. For a small entrance fee, you can spend all day at a powwow, sampling the great food, buying arts and crafts, and enjoying the beautiful music and dancing.

Powwow etiquette is necessary, but easy. Some pointers:

1.   Be aware of Indian time. Powwows begin when everyone is ready. Relax and enjoy the food and the arts and crafts booths.
2.   Don't take pictures without permission from the officials.
3.   Follow the lead of Indians when special ceremonies are in process. You should stand and remove headwear.
4.   Bring your own chairs and leave the front row open for the dancers.
5.   You are welcome to dance when special dances, such as the round dance, are done.

The following descriptions of dancers and their styles will help you enjoy the powwow to the fullest.

Men's Northern Traditional Dance
Plains Indians performed this dance after they were successful in battle or a raid. The warriors would re-enact the story of their experiences as they danced.

For this event, dancers interpret what "traditional dress" means to them personally, but may still wear real traditional elements. The basic dress usually includes a porcupine roach with two eagle feathers, which is mounted on a spinner worn on the head. War bonnets, and buffalo, wolf, and other bird and animal headdresses are still seen.

The dancer may wear a breastplate made from bone, a mirrored otter sash, a bustle, a heavy belt, leggings, and a loincloth or apron. Moccasins and heavy sleigh bells or cow bells are also often worn.

Dancers often hold eagle wing fans, beaded pipes or tobacco bags, or beaded coup sticks ("to touch the enemy" sticks) with feathers of different kinds. Battle gear such as clubs and spears are often seen as well.

The dance is very dignified, with movements that keep the head feathers rotating continuously. The dancer's head movements often imitate a bird in search of prey. Since a warrior must always keep his enemy in sight, the dancer never completes or rotates in a complete circle. During hard drum beats the dancer raises the hand holding the eagle feather fan.

Men's Southern Traditional (or Straight) Dance
This dance style originated on the Southern Plains. One distinctive feature of this dancer is that he wears a long otter hide down his back. The featherwork is not as elaborate as it is for the other men's-dance styles, and the circular, feathered tailpieces (bustles) are not usually worn by straight-dancers. The dancer could be carrying an eagle feather fan and dance stick or staff. He may wear an eagle feather attached to a porcupine roach on his head, two decorated scalp feathers hanging from the side of his head, long German earrings, a bone breastplate and/or metal pectoral necklace, a scarf wrapped around his neck, leg drops or garters, and brass bells or sleigh bells.

The dancer keeps a stately posture. He dances with dignity and smoothness, and without aggressive movements. When strong drum beats, the honor beats, are played (in about the middle of the song), many dancers yell while others point their staffs and mirror boards as if they are tracking the enemy.

Ladies' Northern Traditional Dance
The style of the dancer in this category depends on the individual's tribe. Some dancers perform in a heel and toe step style that is similar

to that of the Southern Plains dancers, while others use an in-place bobbing motion and at the same time slowly rotate their bodies from side to side.

Either buckskin dresses or cloth dresses can be worn. Some of these dresses feature fully beaded yokes, and the dancers wear either a fluffy plume in their hair or a single feather in their headband. Breastplates and otter mink are often worn. A loose or stiff feather fan is often carried, along with a shawl or a beaded purse.

Dignity and modesty are necessary to perform well in this dance. Those who walk with the drum beat must be graceful and pause on the "up" beat of the drum. During the honor beats, dancers raise their fans.

Ladies' Southern Traditional Dance

This style dance emphasizes grace and elegance, as the dancers step to every other beat of the drum. The southern dancer steps in a fluid, continuous motion. With each step the dancer rises slightly, so that there is a kind of ebb and flow to the movement.

Traditionally, southern dancers wore two-piece leather dresses, but one-piece dresses are often seen in intertribal powwows. Eagle feathers and plumes, breastplates, loose or stiff fans, beaded purses or fringed shawls, and princess headbands are typical apparel.

During honor beats dancers raise their fans.

Gourd Dance

This is a dance for society members that originated among Southern Plains tribes. The Kiowa, Comanche, and Cheyenne have, in recent years, given the dance and its songs to a number of other tribes. It is frequently performed by "gourd dance clubs" around the United States. The dancers face a central drum and bounce on their heels in time to the spirited songs. Many wear cowboy boots and hats along with sashes and more traditional Native American garb. The "salt shaker" rattle is also distinctive with gourd dancers.

Men's Fancy Dance

This dance style probably originated on the Southern Plains, but now it is done throughout the United States and Canada. Usually it is done by younger men and boys because it is a very active dance, but I have seen young women and older men in contest.

The dancers twirl around frequently and use a double step. Each dancer has a style of his own but must stay in step with the drum beat. Stopping exactly with the last beat of the drum is very important.

Two vertical eagle feathers in porcupine roaches are worn on the head, and they are mounted so that they rock back and forth and spin in a circle. Very elaborate designs of beadwork, ribbons, sequins, and feathers decorate the entire body and the bustles. On the dancers' legs are angora leggings and sheep bells. Most dancers wear matching bustles, one on the back of the neck and one on the lower back.

Don't try this at home! It is very strenuous.

Grass Dance
This dance is the most popular of the old warrior-society dances. In the early days, the dancers of the Northern Plains, especially those from North Dakota, carried braids of sweet grass on their costumes, hence the name "grass dance." To some traditionalists this is the main dance of the powwow.

The most distinctive part of this dancer's costume is the chain fringe, made of cloth or leather strips, or yarn, that covers the entire outfit. Yarn is preferred because it looks like prairie grass blowing in the wind. Formerly these dancers were called "ribbon dancers" or "sway dancers" because they had many ribbons or chainette fringes sewn to their fabric outfits. Nowadays yarn in vivid colors is used as fringe.

Two types of spreaders (to flatten the porcupine roach) or a headpiece of stretched porcupine are worn. Eagle feathers spin on top.

The grass dancer performs as if he is a warrior searching for a ceremony site. Once he finds a site, he lays down in the grass, first with one foot, then with the other. These movements resemble swaying prairie grass. The term "sway" refers to the style of the dancer, which is often a swaying, shoulder-shaking motion, done very close to the ground. The drum pace is medium and the dancers never wear bustles.

Jingle Dress Dance
In the mid-1980s, after more than 30 years of absence, the jingle dress dance became popular again at powwows. Some say that this style of dancing originated in the dream of a Canadian Indian woman.

Distinct to this dancer's outfit are the hundreds of metal cones sewed to her dress. The cones are constructed by cutting and bending tobacco can lids or other metal lids. More than 200 cans are used.

The outfit can include a wide leather belt with conchas or tacks. Eagle wings or tail fans are used by most dancers, as are hand purses, scarves, and other items. Dancers do not wear or carry a shawl. The left hand usually rests on the hip, and right hand carries the feather fan.

The dancer must keep the jingle sound and movement in sync with the drum beat, as is true of all styles of powwow dancing. Fancy and uneven movements are minimized. Special songs have been created for a rapid, side-stepping style of jingle dress dancing. Dancers lift their fans during the drum's honor beats.

Ladies' Fancy Shawl
The ladies' fancy shawl is equivalent to the men's fancy dance. The style is fairly modern and is seen at most powwows. Because the dance is very strenuous, mostly younger women and girls participate. The drum tempos can be very fast. The dance steps involve many change-ups, or quick steps from one foot to the other, and there is much twirling.

As the name implies, "fancy shawlers" wear a colorful fringed shawl that is decorated with embroidery, sequins, ribbon applique, or felt applique.

At powwows today, the dancing has evolved from a traditional, strict nature to a competitive, complex one in which participants compete in specific categories and by age groups for prize money.

The dancers are free to use their own styles in dancing and dress and they are awarded points for these aspects. Dancers also earn points based upon their attendance, participation, and the place they earn during contest dancing.

Dancers must abide by certain registration rules. Usually registration is limited to one category, and all dancers know they will be automatically disqualified if they fail to stop on the last drum beat during a contest.

Pick out your favorite dancers at your next powwow and see how close you can come to the choices of the professional judges.

Native American Events Calendar for North America

Dec. 31–Jan. 1
Porcupine New Year's Powwow
Porcupine, SD
(605) 455-2995, Cedec Young Bear

Dec. 31–Jan. 1
Bright and Morning Star
New Year's Eve Powwow
Meadowbrook Center
Nathan Hale High School
Seattle, WA

Dec. 31–Jan. 2
New Year's Indoor Contest Powwow
Amigos Indoor Sports Arena
South Tuscon, AZ
(602) 622-4900

Dec. 31–Jan. 2
Annual AIM On the Red Road
MAIC
1530 E. Franklin Ave
Minneapolis, MN
(612) 724-3129

Dec. 31–Jan. 2
Annual New Year's Powwow
Cerritos Par
Cerito, CA
(909) 864-7425, Brigette DeCora

Jan. 3–5
N11-J11 Sobriety Powwow
LDF Community Center
Lac du Flambeau, WI
(715) 588-3371

Jan. 6–8
Santa Monica Indian
Show–Sale–Powwow
Civic Auditorium
1855 Main Street
Santa Monica, CA
(310) 430-5112, Alicia & Don Bullock

Jan. 7
SACNAS Conference
El Paso, TX
(602) 965-2230, Lee Williams

Jan. 8
American Indianist Society
Powwow Benefit
Quinsigamond Village
Community Center
16 Greenwood St.
Worchester, MA
(508) 852-6271

Jan. 11–15
Napi Friendship Association Annual
Cross Cultural Conference
Annual Napi Powwow
Pincher Creek, AB CANADA
(403) 627-4224

2nd Saturday Jan.
Algonquin Intertribal Society Social
Trinity United Methodist Church
375 Broad St.
Providence, RI
(401) 421-0888

2nd Saturday Jan.
Mason School Powwow
2819 N. Madison
Tacoma, WA
(206) 596-1139

Jan. 15
Massachusetts Center for Native
American Awareness
Native American Awareness
Day Powwow
Cambridge, MA
(617) 884-4227

Jan. 21
Greater Lowell Indian Cultural
Association Midwinter Powwow
VA Hospital
Bedford, MA
(508) 453-7182

Jan. 21
Mashpee Wampanoag Winter
Social & Potluck
Mashpee United Church
Village Community Center
Mashpee, MA
(508) 477-0208

Jan. 21–22
Indian Summer Festival Winter
Powwow
Mecca Arena
Milwaukee, WI
(414) 774-7119

3rd Saturday Jan.
TIHA Powwow
San Antonio, TX
(817) 498-2873

3rd weekend Jan.
Powwow
Fort Alex, MAN CANADA
(204) 367-4504

Jan. 28
Thunderbird American Indian
Dancers Powwow
McBurney YMCA
215 W. 23rd St.
New York, NY
(201) 587-9633, Louis Mofsie

Last weekend Jan.
Dakota–Ojibway Tribal Days
Winnapeg, MAN CANADA
(204) 729-3682

Feb. 1–3
Sinte Gleska College Founders
Day Powwow
Sinte Gleska College
Rosebud, SD
(605) 747-2263

Feb. 3–5
American Indian Exposition & Sale
San Mateo Expo Center
Oak Hall
San Mateo, CA
(209) 221-4355

Feb. 4
Hosaga Annual Powwow
Springfield College Dana Gym
Springfield, MA
(413) 783-3428

Feb. 4–5
Red Earth Native American Fair
Kirkpatrick Center
Oklahoma City, OK
(405) 427-5228

1st Saturday Feb.
Mason School Powwow
2812 N. Madison
Tacoma, WA
(206) 596-1139

Feb. 10–11
GIIWEBIBOON Annual Midwinter
Powwow
Bay de Noc Community College
Escanaba, MI
(906) 789-0505

Feb. 10–12
American Indian Exposition
& Sale
Alameda Fairgrounds
Hall of Commerce
Pleasanton, CA
(209) 221-4355

Feb. 10–12
Lincoln's Birthday & Self-
Government Sovereignty Celebration
Warm Springs, OR
(503) 553-3393, Anna Clements

Feb. 11
North Carolina School of Sciences
& Mathematics Powwow
Charles R. Eilber Phys. Ed. Center
Durham, NC
(919) 286-3366

Feb. 11
Joliet Jr. College Powwow
Joliet, IL
(815) 436-4950

Feb. 11
Citizen Band of Potowatomi
Annual Meeting
Mercer Middle School
Seattle, WA
(800) 722-8055, Suzanne Campbell

Feb. 11
Cherokee Nation Housing Authority
Annual Winter Powwow
Community Building
Tahlequah, OK
(918) 456-5740

Feb. 11
Valentines Powwow
Indian Heritage School
1330 N. 90th
Seattle, WA
(206) 298-7895, Amy Markishtum

2nd weekend Feb.
Honor Our Ancestors Traditional
Powwow
Negaunee Community Center
Negaunee, MI
(906) 249-3153

2nd weekend Feb.
Annual Council of Indian Students
Traditional Winter Powwow
Bemidji State University
Bemidji, MN
(218) 755-2094, Tony Troyer

2nd weekend Feb.
Seminole Tribal Fair & Rodeo
Hollywood Reservation
Hollywood, FL
(305) 584-0400

2nd weekend Feb.
Annual Brighton Field Day & Rodeo
Brighton Reservation, FL
(813) 763-4128

2nd Saturday Feb.
Algonquin Intertribal Social
Trinity United Methodist Church
375 Broad St.
Providence, RI
(401) 421-0888

Feb. 16–18
Advisory Council on California
Indian Policy Conference
(Powwow on 18th)
Holiday Inn
Sacramento, CA
(909) 654-2781

Feb. 17–19
Mid Winter Wacipi
Marty Indian School
Marty, SD
(605) 384-5431

Feb. 17–19
Tulsa Indian Art Festival & Powwow
Tulsa, OK
(918) 838-3875, Sam Jones

Feb. 18 (tentative)
Annual Ira H. Hayes Recognition
Day & Powwow
Veteran's Park
Sacaton, AZ
(602) 562-3310 ext. 13, Shirley Lewis

Feb. 18
Blanket Supper & Social
in Honor of Late Chief Red
Christ Congregational Church
Brockton, MA
(617) 884-4227

Feb. 18–19
Annual Michigan State University
Powwow
West Lansing, MI
(517) 353-5255 ext. 113

Feb. 18
Gathering of Tribes Powwow
University of California–Riverside
Riverside, CA
(909) 787-4143

Feb. 18–19
Namebini Giizis Gathering
Keweenaw Bay
Big Bucks Bingo Hall
Marquette, MI
(906) 942-7126

**Weekend before
President's Day Feb.**
Annual O'Odham Tash
Casa Grande, AZ
(602) 836-4723

3rd weekend Feb.
Annual Native American Heritage
Association of Radford University
Powwow
Peters Gym
Radford, VA
(703) 633-1871

3rd weekend Feb.
Casa Grande Outdoor
Indian Market
Casa Grande, AZ
(602) 762-5266, Rosalie & Bob Baker

Washington's Birthday weekend
Washington's Birthday Celebration
Toppenish Community Center
Toppenish, WA
(509) 865-5121

Feb. 25
Mashpee Wampanoag Winter
Social & Potluck
Mashpee United Church
Village Community Center
Mashpee, MA
(508) 477-0208

Feb. 25
Thunderbird American Indian
Dancers Powwow
Mc Burney YMCA
215 W. 23rd St.
New York, NY
(201) 587-9633

Feb. 25–26
American Indian Exposition & Sale
Scottish Rites Hall
San Diego, CA
(209) 221-4355

Feb. 25–26
Chippewa Cultural Presentation
Northland Pines High School
Eagle River, WI
(715) 479-7428

4th Saturday in Feb.
Annual Stanley Purser Powwow
Port Gamble Tribal Center
"Little Boston"
Port Gamble, WA
(206) 297-2253

Last full weekend in Feb.
Lima Council For Native American
Indians Traditional Powwow
UAW Hall 1440 Bellefontaine Ave.
Lima, OH
(419) 228-1097

March 3–5
American Indian Exposition & Sale
Monterey Fairgrounds
Salinas Room
Monterey, CA
(209) 221-4355

1st weekend March
Carmel American Indian Festival
Carmel, CA
(408) 623-2379, Sonny or
Elaine Reyna

1st weekend March
Annual College Park Powwow
The Armory Building
University of Maryland Campus
College Park, MD
(301)270-2991

1st Saturday March
Indian Education Annual Powwow
Gaiser Middle School
3000 NE 99th St.
Vancouver, WA
(206) 693-1369, Angela Johnson
(206) 892-5684, Clark Tierney

1st weekend March
Annual Benefit Powwow
Miami Valley Council for Native
Americans
Dayton, OH
(513) 275-8599, James J. Cain

1st weekend March
Annual Heard Museum Guild Indian
Fair & Market
The Heard Museum
Phoenix, AZ
(602) 252-8840

1st weekend March
Annual Central Wisconsin Indian
Center Powwow
Rothchild Pavilion
Rothchild, WI
(715) 845-2613

1st weekend March
WA AK Powwow
Ball Park St. Xavier Mission
Tuscon, AZ
(602) 294-5727

1st Saturday March
Mason School Powwow
2812 N. Madison
Tacoma, WA
(206) 596-1136

March 4
Mass Center for Native American
Awareness Day Celebration
South Shore, MA
(617) 884-4227

March 4
Annual Trails Powwow
Sokaogan Chippewa Tribal Hall
Mole Lake, WI
(715) 478-5115
(715) 478-2709

March 4–5
Annual Indian Festival Bazaar
St. John Indian School
Laveen, AZ
(602) 550-2400

March 4–5
Hawks Flight Intertribal Powwow
Perris, CA
(909) 923-3553, Chuck Reddich

March 4–5
Rimrock Rendezvous
"A Celebration of Contemporary &
Traditional Native American Arts"
Chico Mall
Chico, CA
(916) 873-4834

March 4–5
Spring Craft Fair
Vancouver Aboriginal
Friendship Centre
1607 Hastings St.
Vancouver, BC CANADA
(604) 251-4844, Phil L'Hirondelle
(604) 251-1986, FAX

March 5–11
Arctic Winter Games
Slave Lake, AB CANADA
(403) 849-1994

2nd weekend March
Speelyi Mi Arts & Crafts Fair
Yakima, WA
(509) 865-5121

2nd weekend March
E-Peh-Tes Powwow
Lapwai, ID
(208) 843-2253

2nd weekend March
Annual North American Indian
Student Alliance Powwow
Montezuma Hall Aztec Center
San Diego State University
San Diego, CA
(619) 594-6991 or 594-4251

March 10–11
Fife Indian Education Powwow
Surprise Lake Middle School
Milton, WA
(206) 922-6697, Phyllis Covington
(206) 922-3316, Gloria Bean

March 10–12
Annual Ormond Beach Indian
Festival
Historical Casements
Ormond Beach, FL
(404) 735-6275

March 10–12
Annual Friendship Powwow
Lummi Indian Reservation
Bellingham, WA
(206) 734-8180

March 11
Algonquin Powwow
1505 Broad St.
Providence, RI
(401) 421-0888

March 11–12
Powwow
Shoal Lake, ONT CANADA
(807) 226-5411

March 16–19
Annual Great Falls Native American
Art Association Exhibit & Sale
Ponderosa Inn
Great Falls, MT
(406) 791-2212 or
(406) 761-6251, Gladys Cantrell

March 17
Native American Awareness Day
Northland College
Ashland, WI
(715) 682-4531

March 17–18
Annual American Indian Festival
& Market
Museum of Natural History of
Los Angeles County
900 Exposition Blvd.
Los Angeles, CA
(213) 964-6327, Susan Snellgrove

March 17–18
Annual Denver March Powwow
Denver Coliseum
Denver, CO
(303) 936-4826, Grace Gillette

March 17–19
Annual Celebration of Sobriety
& Powwow
College of Great Falls
MacLaughlin Center
Great Falls, MT

March 17–19
NAY AH SING Powwow
Nay Ah Sing Upper School
Mille Lacs, MN
(612) 532-4695

3rd Weekend March
Annual Powwow
Cal State University–Long Beach
1250 Bellflower
Long Beach, CA
Robert or (714) 990-5873

3rd weekend March
Florida Indian Hobbyist
Association Powwow
Indian River Community College
Ft. Pierce, FL
(407) 464-4973
(407) 336-0807, Nan

3rd weekend March
United Indians of Milwaukee
Traditional Annual Powwow
State Fair Park
Milwaukee, WI
(414) 384-8070

March 18
St. Joseph's Feast Day
Laguna Pueblo Plaza
Laguna Pueblo, NM
(505) 552-6654

March 18
Annual Birthday Celebration for
Slow Turtle
National Guard Armory
Middle Burrow, MA
(617) 884-4227

March 18
Carolina Indian Circle Powwow
Great Hall
University of North Carolina
Chapel Hill, NC
(919) 929-0883

March 18
NASA Spring Contest Powwow
Oklahoma State University
Animal Science Arena
Stillwater, OK
(405) 744-5481

March 18
Annual University of Tulsa
Spring Contest Powwow
State Fairgrounds
Tulsa, OK
(918) 446-5116

March 18
Annual Homestead Intertribal
Powwow
Homestead High School Gym
Cupertino, CA
(408) 749-9758, Pavatea or
(408) 241-7999, Gwen Steirer

March 18
Potawatome Trails Powwow
Pearce Campus
Zion, IL
(708) 746-9086
(708) 249-3182

March 18–19
United Natives Indian Education
Powwow
Poulson High School Gym
Poulson, WA
(206) 598-3311, Ronda Jones

March 19
Honor the Elders Powwow
St. Gertrude
Chicago, IL
(312) 561-6155

4th weekend March
Traditional Intertribal Annual
Powwow
Armed Forces Armory
Rochester, MN
(507) 281-4772

4th weekend March
Edisto Indian Cultural Festival
Summerville, SC
(803) 871-3453

4th weekend March
Annual Heart of the Earth Contest
Powwow
Minneapolis Convention Center
Minneapolis, MN
(612) 331-8862

4th weekend March
American Indian Students
Association Powwow
University of Massachusetts Gym
Amherst, MA

4th weekend March
Natchez Annual Powwow
Grand Village of the Natchez Indians
Natchez, MS
(601) 442-0200 day
(601) 446-5117 p.m, Chuck Borum

March 23–25
Annual Statewide Conference on
American Indian Education &
Powwow
Sacramento, CA
(916) 657-2745, Peter Dibble

March 24–25
United Tribes All Nations Powwow
UTTC Campus
Bismark, ND
(701) 255-3285

March 24–26
Annual Powwow for American Indian
Cultural Society of North Florida
Tom Brown Park
Tallahassee, FL
(904) 574-9552

March 24–26
American Indian Exposition & Sale
Fresno Fairgrounds Art Building
Fresno, CA
(209) 221-4355

March 24–26
Annual Ann Arbor Contest Powwow
Chrysler Arena
Ann Arbor, MI
(313) 763-9044

March 25
Waila Annual Festival
Arizona Historical Society Museum
Tucson, AZ
(602) 622-8080, Angelo Joaquin

March 25
Sugar Run Powwow
Laconia Indian Historical Association
VFW Court St.
Laconia, NH
(603) 783-9922

March 25
SACNAS Traditional Powwow
Fairmont Hotel
Chicago, IL
(602) 965-2230

March 25
American Indian Annual Powwow
Cal State University
Stanislaus-Gym
Turlock, CA
(800) 828-7733

March 25
Tri-College Powwow
Moorhead High School
Moorhead, MN
(701) 237-8204

March 25
Annual University of Tulsa Powwow
Exchange Center
Tulsa Fairgrounds
Tulsa, OK
(918) 631-3215

March 25
Salem Area Spring Powwow
Polk County Fairgrounds
Richreal, OR
(12 mi. west of Salem)
(503) 623-8971, Cookie Spencer
(503) 581-4900, Tim-Vendors Info

March 25
Sucker Ceremony
Chiloquin High School
Chiloquin, OR
(503) 783-2219 ext. 162
Gordon Beetles, Mary Gentry

March 25
Mashpee Wampanoag Winter
Social & Potluck
Mashpee United Church
Village Community Center
Mashpee, MA
(508) 477-0208

March 25–26
PAH-LOOTS-PU Celebration
WSU Bohler Gym
Pullman, WA
(509) 335-8676

March 25–26
Annual Indigenous Peoples'
Cultural Festival
Munn Park
Lakeland, FL
(813) 683-2893

March 25–26
Annual Natchez Powwow
Grand Village Natchez
Natchez, MS
(601) 446-5117

March 26
Traditional Powwow
Dominic Jacobetti Center
Michigan University Campus
Marquette, MI
(906) 227-2138

March 31–April 1
Toronto International Powwow
Skydome
Toronto, ONT CANADA
(519) 751-0040

March 31–April 1
American Indian Heritage Powwow
Collier County Museum
Naples, FL
(813) 455-5066

March 31–April 1
Title 5 Youth Powwow
Reeds Chapel Elementary School
Mcantosh, AL
(205) 944-2422

March 31–April 1
Chief Little Wolf Powwow
Powwow Grounds
Lame Deer, MT
(406) 477-6241

Late March or early April
UC Davis Native American Cultural
Days & D-Q University Powwow
Davis, CA
(916) 758-0470

April 1
San Francisco State University
Annual Powwow
Main Gym
19th & Holloway
San Francisco, CA
(415) 338-1929

April 1
Northern Virginia Powwow
Gelston/White Oak Armory
12200 Cherry Hill Rd.
White Oak, MD
(703) 451-8617

April 1
Annual Wildflower Festival
Tule River Indian Reservation
Porterville, CA
(209) 784-3155, Leona Dabney
after 5 p.m.
(209) 784-3155, Peggy Christman

April 1
Native American Annual Spring
Festival
Virginia Wesleyan College
1518 Wesleyan Dr.
Norfolk, VA
(804) 481-7342

April 1
Annual Native American Festival
Ocean Stables
Virginia Beach, VA
(804) 481-7342

April 1
Nighthawk Dancers Annual Powwow
Little Falls High School
Little Falls, NY
(315) 823-2570

April 1
Northeastern State University
Simpossium Powwow
Union Ballroom
Tahlequah, OK

April 1
American Indian Day
Boston Children's Museum
300 Congress St.
Boston, MA
(617) 426-6500 ext. 261

April 1-2
Annual Spring Powwow
Montana State University
Bozeman, MT
(406) 994-4880

April 1-2
Hawks Flight Intertribal Powwow
Perris, CA
(909) 923-3553, Chuck Reddich

April 1-2
Austin Indian Market & Southwest
Arts Festival
East 6th St.
Austin, TX
(512) 448-1797, Britt Kimball

1st weekend April
Tulsa Indian Annual Art Festival
Expo Square Pavilion
Tulsa, OK
(918) 838-3875, Monetta Trepp

1st weekend April
Annual Powwow
Field House
Humboldt State University
Arcata, CA
(707) 826-4994

1st weekend April
Central Michigan University Annual
Powwow
Finch Field House
Mt. Pleasant, MI
(517) 772-5700

1st weekend April
Annual Indian Creek Traders Expo
Midlands Mall
Council Bluff, IA
(712) 325-1770

1st weekend April
Native American Cultural Awareness
Annual Weekend
North Carolina State University
Raleigh, NC
(919) 839-2214, Reggie Oxedine

1st weekend April
North Florida Indian Cultural
Association Powwow
Chamber Farm
(21 miles north of Silver Springs)
Orange Springs, FL
(904) 799-7981

1st weekend April
Annual Spring Powwow
University of Wyoming
Laramie, WY
(307) 766-6189

April 7–9
Indian Art Market & Southwest
Showcase
Overland Park, KS
(806) 355-1610 Randy Wilkerson

April 7–9
Southern Eagle Powwow
Mescalero Gym
Mescalero, NM
(505) 671-4494

April 7–9
American Indian Exposition & Sale
Santa Clara County Fairgrounds
Fiesta Hall
San Jose, CA
(209) 221-4355

April 7–9
Annual Honoring of the Elders
& Annual SANAI Powwow
West Fieldhouse
University of Santa Cruz
Santa Cruz, CA
(408) 459-2296

2nd weekend April (tentative)
Bitterroot Valley Mini Powwow
High School Gym
Corvalis, MT
(406) 961-4705
(406) 642-3769

2nd weekend April
Cocopah Indian Patent Day
Tribal Offices
Sommerton, AZ
(602) 627-2102

2nd weekend April
Navajo Community College Powwow
Tsaile, AZ
(605) 724-3311 ext. 219

2nd weekend April
Davis Lake Annual Powwow
Davis Lake Camp
Suffolk, VA
(804) 539-1191

2nd weekend April
University of Iowa Powwow
Iowa City, IA
(319) 335-8298

2nd weekend April
Celilo-Wyam Salmon Feast
Celilo, OR
(503) 298-1559

2nd weekend April
1st Peoples Annual International
Trade Expo & Powwow
Macomb Community College
South Campus
Warren, MI
(313) 756-1350

2nd weekend April
Tewaquchi American Indian Club
Annual Powwow
Cal State University–Fresno
Fresno, CA
(209) 278-3277

2nd weekend April
Southwest Nations Annual Powwow
New Mexico State University
Las Cruces, NM
(505) 646-4207, Lydia

April 8
Indian Awareness Day Annual
Powwow
Morningside College Campus
Sioux City, IA
(712) 274-5147

April 8
University of Wisconsin–Superior
Indian Awareness Annual Powwow
Central Jr. High
Superior, WI
(715) 394-8358

April 8
Native American Awareness Day
Celebration
Wellesley Middle School
Wellesley, MA
(617) 884-4227

April 8
Algonquin Intertribal Winter Social
Trinity Methodist Church
Providence, RI
(401) 421-0888

April 8
Annual Traditional Powwow
Itasca Community College
Mullins Hall
Grand Rapids, MN
(218) 327-4491

April 8
Native American Ponatom
National Guard Armory
Natick, MA
(617) 884-4227

April 8
Cultural Awareness Powwow
Napa Valley College
Napa, CA
(707) 253-3060, Ann Grant
(707) 226-5075, Charlie Toledo

April 8
Spring Contest Powwow
Northwestern OK A&M
Miami, OK
(918) 673-2533

April 8
Oyate/AISES Spring Powwow
University of Colorado–Boulder
Solar Hogan Area
Boulder, CO
(303) 492-8874 or
(303) 447-5074

April 8–10
Annual Traditional Powwow
University of South Dakota
Vermillion, SD
(605) 624-4825

April 14–15
Annual San Diego University Powwow
Montezuma Hall
San Diego, CA
(619) 594-6991

April 14–15
Keeper of the Plains Celebration
Enid, OK
(405) 237-2494

April 14–15
Cheyenne Arapaho
Downtown Square
Crodell, OK
(405) 832-3538

April 14–16
ASU Annual Spring
Competition Powwow
Band Practice Field
Arizona State University
Tempe, AZ
(602) 965-5224, Lee Williams

April 14–16
Grand Moccasin Festival
Bacone College Campus
Muscogee, OK
(916) 682-2586

April 14–16
Rattlesnake Festival
Apache, OK
(405) 588-2880

April 14–16
Annual Chilliwach Intertribal
Powwow
Exhibition Grounds
Chilliwach, BC CANADA
(604) 858-3366, Gwen Point

3rd week April
Annual Powwow
Western Washington University
Bellingham, WA
(206) 650-7273

3rd week April
Saskatchewan Indian Federated
College Powwow
Agridome Exhibition Park
Regina, SASK CANADA
(306) 584-8333, 8334

3rd week April
"Art Under the Oaks" Indian Market
Five Civilized Tribes Museum
Muskogee, OK
(918) 683-1701

3rd week April
American Indian Powwow
West Valley College
14000 Fruitvale Ave.
Saratoga, CA
(408) 867-2200 ext. 5601

3rd week April
Annual Northern Dance
Arlington High School
Indianapolis, IN
(317) 356-1006

3rd week April
American Indian Days Powwow
Chico State University
Chico, CA
(916) 895-5396

3rd week April
Octagon American Indian
Preservation Society Annual Powwow
Lee Civic Center
Ft. Myers, FL
(813) 543-1130

3rd week April
Annual Haliwa–Saponi
Haliwa School
Hollister, NC
(919) 586-4017

3rd week April
Rock Creek Annual Salmon Feast
Rock Creek, WA
(509) 773-3787

3rd week April
Annual Native Arts & Crafts Show
Suquamish Tribal Center
Suquamish, WA
(206) 598-3311

3rd Saturday April
TIHA Powwow
San Antonio, TX
(817) 498-2873

April 15
Annual NASA Powwow
Eastern Washington University
Special Events Pavilion
Cheney, WA
(509) 359-2441

April 15
Powwow/Walk-a-thon
Lynnwoods
Lynnwoods, MA
(617) 844-4227

April 15
ITSC Powwow
University of California–Berkeley
Berkeley, CA
(510) 642-6613, Ruth Hopper

April 15
Annual South Beach Sobriety
Powwow
Ocosta School Gym
Westport, WA
(206) 267-6766, Rose Shipman
(206) 267-6212, Ben or Joan Taylor

April 15–16
Anishinabe Club Powwow
Hedgecock Field House
Marquette, MI
(906) 227-1554

April 15–16
Annual Lakota Omnicyi
Black Hills State University
Spearfish, SD
(605) 642-6003

April 17–23
Annual American Indian Week
Indian Pueblo Cultural Center
Albuquerque, NM
(800) 288-0721

April 20–23
Tennessee Powwow & Cultural Expo
Municipal Auditorium
Nashville, TN
(615) 532-0745

April 21–22
Gathering of Nations Powwow
The Pit at the
University of New Mexico
Albuquerque, NM
(505) 836-2810

April 21–22
Texas Gulf TIA-PIAH Powwow
Sallas County Park
New Carey, TX
(713) 523-0583, Janelle Walker

April 21–23
Tut Mountain Indian Festival
Tut Mountain Wildlife Preserve
Clayton, GA
(800) 621-1768
(404) 735-6275

April 21–23
Annual Raleigh Powwow
State Fairgrounds
Raleigh, NC
(919) 257-5383

April 22
Keeper of the Earth Spring Powwow
Fullerton Union High School
Stadium
Fullerton, CA
(800) 428-3872

April 22
Winter Social & Potluck
VA Hospital
Bedford, MA
(508) 453-7182

April 22
East Carolina University Powwow
Campus
Greenville, NC
(919) 752-5294

April 22
CT. River Society
Earth Day Celebration & Social
Town Green
Rocky Hill, CT
(203) 684-5407

April 22
Annual Powwow
Mills College
Oakland, CA
(510) 430-2080

April 22
"Lords of the Plains" Powwow
Whitely Baseball Field
Cromwell, TX
(817) 684-1557, Janelle Manard

April 22
South Umpaqua Powwow
Myrtle Creek, OR
(503) 863-4942

April 22
Annual Eau Claire Traditional
Powwow
Eau Claire, WI
(715) 836-3367

April 22
WUNK-SHEEK Powwow
Fieldhouse
Madison, WI
(608) 263-2048

April 22-23
Aqua Caliente Heritage Festival
Palm Springs, CA
(619) 325-5673

April 22-23
Native American Festival
Little Rock Zoo
Little Rock, AZ
(800) 228-0936

April 22-23
Annual La Crosse Powwow
Mitchell Hall Gym
La Crosse, WI
(608) 785-8225

April 23-24
Annual New England
NAI Powwow
Boxboro Host Hotel
Boxboro, MA
(508) 791-5007

4th weekend April
A.I.R.O. Powwow
University of Wisconsin–Stevens Point
Stevens Point, WI
(715) 346-3576

4th weekend April
Annual KYI-Yo Youth Conference
& Powwow
Missoula, MT
(406) 243-5831

4th weekend April
GLICA: Maple Syrup Festival
Tyngsborough State Forest
Lowell, MA
(508) 453-7182

4th weekend April
University of Minnesota–Duluth
Annual Powwow
Sports Arena
Duluth, MN
(218) 726-8141

4th weekend April
Annual NASA Powwow
Loy Student Center
Colorado State University
Ft Collins, CO
(303) 491-8946, Debra Wadena

4th weekend April
Annual Spring Traditional Powwow
UAW 933 Hall
Indianapolis, IN
(317) 545-5057

4th weekend April
Celebrating Life Not Genocide
Powwow
Ohio State University
Columbus, OH
(614) 443-6120

April 28-30
Annual Harrisburg Powwow
Harrisburg Farm Shop Complex
Harrisburg, PA
(919) 257-5383

April 28-30
American Indian Exposition & Sale
Airport Convention Center
San Antonio, TX
(209) 221-4355

Last weekend April
Annual Powwow
Weber State University
Ogden, UT
(801) 626-7330

Last weekend April
Indian Festival
Talihina, OK
(918) 567-2539

April 29
Annual Powwow
Native American Indian Association
Metrolina Indian Center
Charlotte, NC
(704) 331-4818

April 29
Powwow Celebrating Life
University of Wisconsin
Stout Field House
Menominee, WI
(715) 235-1625
(715) 232-8769

April 29
Annual University
Wisconsin–Superior
Superior Armory
Superior, WI
(715) 394-8358

April 29
University of Wisconsin–Oshkosh
Traditional Powwow
Oshkosh, WI
(414) 424-1246

April 29
Annual North High School Indian
Club Powwow
East Side Football Field
Phoenix, AZ
(602) 277-2959

April 29–30
Annual AIC Spring Powwow
Boone City 4-H Grounds
Lebanon, IN
(317) 482-3315

April 29–30
Ohio Indian Movement
OSU Campus
Columbus, OH
(614) 292-2324

April 29–30
Annual Northern Colorado
Intertribal Powwow
Northside Aztlan Community Center
Ft. Collins, CO
(303) 498-8323

April 29–May 1
American Indian Festival
LaFleur State Park
Jackson, MS
(601) 371-8242 or 847-5482

May (date TBA)
Indian Festival
Carthage, MS
(601) 267-8322

May (date TBA)
U.W. Spring Powwow
Hec Edmundson Pavilion
University of Washington
Seattle, WA
(206) 685-4147

May (date TBA)
Native American Awareness Day
Grays Harbor Community College
Aberdeen, WA
(800) 562-4839 ext. 211

May 4
Annual Fond Du Lac Ojibwe
School Powwow
Ojibwe School Gym
Cloquet, MN
(218) 879-4593 ext. 48

May 4–7
Annual Tannehill State Park Powwow
McCalla, AL
(205) 477-5711

May 5–6
Louisiana Indian Heritage
Association Powwow
Spring Contest Powwow
Folsom, LA
(504) 241-5866

May 5–6
Northern Montana College Powwow
NMC Armory Gym
Havre, MT
(406) 265-3700 ext. 3040

May 5–7
East Tennessee League Powwow
World's Fair State Park
Knoxville, TN
(615) 693-0079

May 5–7
Annual Intertribal Gathering
& Powwow
Mary Vagle Nature Center
11501 Cypress Ave.
Fontana, CA
(714) 984-6215

May 5–7
American Indian Exposition & Sale
The Terrace
Austin, TX
(209) 221-4355

1st weekend May
Annual UCLA Contest Powwow
UCLA Intermural North Field
Los Angeles, CA
(310) 825-7315 or 206-7315

1st weekend May
Cupa Days
Pala Cultural Center
Pala Reservation, CA
(619) 742-1590

1st weekend May
Southern Ute Bear Dance
Ignacio, CO
(303) 563-4525

1st weekend May
American Indian Annual Spring
Market
Mission San Juan Bautista
San Juan Bautista, CA
(408) 623-2379, Sonny or
Elaine Reyna

1st weekend May
Abenaki Celebration Powwow
Highgate, VT
(802) 748-8477, Mark Mitchell
(802) 748-2559, Tribal Council

1st weekend May
Annual Powwow at the Turtle Center
for Living Arts
Niagara Falls, NY
(716) 284-2427

1st weekend May
Wampanoag New Year Ceremony
& Indian Gathering
Wampanoag Indian Reservation
Freetown, MA
(508) 947-7466

1st weekend May
Annual Winona State University
Intertribal Powwow
Maxwell Football Field
(rain Talbot Gym)
Winona, MN
(507) 457-5345 or 5230

1st Saturday May
Feather River Festival
Native American Village
Heritage Park
Oroville, CA
(916) 538-7986

1st Saturday May
Annual Powwow
Dartmouth College
Hanover, NH
(603) 646-2110

1st Saturday May
Palomar College Powwow
Student Union
San Marcos, CA
(619) 744-1150 ext. 2425

1st Saturday May
LIHA 5th Annual Auction & Powwow
VFW Court St.
Laconia, NH
(603) 783-9922

1st Saturday May
Nipmuck Council Planting Moon
Ceremony & Potluck
Nipmuck Reservation
Webster, MA
(508) 943-4569

1st Saturday May
Friends of Native Americans & Mystic
River Association Powwow
Sandy Beach Park Upper Mystic
Lake Winchester, MA
(617) 646-0743

1st Sunday May
Corn Planting Ceremony
Lenni Lenape Historical Society
Allentown, PA
(215) 797-2121

May 6
Annual Spring Powwow
Quim Coliseum
La Grande, OR
(503) 962-3672

May 6
Marshall Powwow
Gym
Marshall, MN
(507) 537-6018

May 6
Annual Mt. Senario American
Indian Program
Mt. Senario College
Ladysmith, WI
(715) 532-5511 ext. 242

May 6–7
Intertribal Riverland Powwow
Celebration '95
Riverland River Resort
Freeway 99
Visalia, CA
(800) 564-3325

May 6–7
Moon When the Ponies Shed
Traditional Powwow
Ohio State University
Canton, OH
(614) 443-6120

May 6–7
Annual Traditional Wacipi Honoring
All Mothers
Simmons Jr. High School
1300 South 3rd St.
Aberdeen, SD
(605) 225-4485
Ramona Saul (weekends)
(605) 226-2533
Stella Pretty Sounding Flute
(605) 226-3026
Mary Spears (evenings)

May 6–7
Hawks Flight Intertribal Powwow
Perris, CA
(909) 923-3553, Chuck Reddich

May 6–7
Annual Heal Mother Earth Powwow
Fairgrounds
York, PA
(804) 929-6911, George Whitewolf

May 6–7
Powwow
Portage La Prairie, MAN CANADA
(204) 239-6333

May 6–7
Annual United Indians Powwow
State Fair Park
Milwaukee, WI
(414) 384-8070

May 6–7
GLICA-Stone Zoo Powwow
Stoneham, MA
(508) 453-7182

May 10–12
Annual Cherokee County Powwow
Boling Park
Canton, GA
(404) 735-6275

May 12–13
Heritage Festival
Occaneechi State Park
Clarksville, VA
(919) 732-8512

May 12–13
Annual Dilkon Powwow
Dilkon School Gym
Dilkon, AZ
(602) 686-6258

May 12–13
Tuscarora Nation Annual Powwow
Tribal Grounds
Maxton, NC
(919) 844-3352

May 12–13
Takini Skyhawk Stampede & Wacipi
Takini School
Howes, SD
(605) 538-4399

May 12–13
Annual H. V. Johnston Cultural
Center Powwow
Eagle Butte, SD
(605) 964-2542, Matt Uses Knife

May 12–13
August a Powwow
4-H Club Camp (on Hwy 56)
Augusta, GA
(706) 771-1221, Bill Medeiros
(general info)
(706) 560-9593, Pam Crews
(trader info)

May 12–14
Buffalo Feast
St. Ignatius Indian Center
St. Ignatius, MT
(406) 745-2951

May 12–14
Lumbie Spring Powwow
Robeson County Fairgrounds
Lumberton, NC
(910) 521-8602

May 12–14
American Indian Exposition & Sale
City Auditorium
Colorado Springs, CO
(209) 221-4355

May 12–14
Annual Lake Powell Rodeo &
"Cowboy Days & Nights" Powwow
Page, AZ
(602) 645-5018

May 12–14
Sedona Hopi Show
Sedona, AZ
(602) 282-6428 or 282-7722

2nd weekend May
Annual Powwow
Stanford University
Palo Alto, CA
(415) 725-6944

2nd weekend May
Spring Powwow
Portland State University
Portland, OR
(503) 725-4452

2nd weekend May
Mother's Day Powwow
Lassen Community College
Susanville, CA
(916) 257-5222

2nd weekend May
Root Festival
Lapwai, ID
(208) 843-2253

2nd weekend May
TSE-HO-TSO Intertribal Powwow
Window Rock High School
Fort Defiance, AZ
(602) 729-5704

2nd weekend May
CSRIHA Mother's Day Powwow
Augusta, GA
(404) 863-6931, Grady Burnett

2nd weekend May
Claremore State Dance Powwow
& Stomp
Old Fairgrounds
Claremore, OK
(918) 341-2818

2nd weekend May
Mother's Day All Indian Rodeo
Browning, MT
(406) 338-7406

2nd weekend May
In Honor of Our Children Powwow
Kelso, WA
(206) 577-2451, Dena Taylor
(206) 577-1970, Tina Shadiow

May 13
Prairie Band Potawanami Powwow
Horton, KS

May 13
Nisenan–Maidu Big Time
Maidu Park
Roseville, CA
(916) 782-7957, Lillian Medina-Zidro
(916) 785-5144, Mary Orr

May 13
Annual Permian Basin Native
American Powwow
UT P B Campus
Odessa, TX
(915) 964-4166

May 13–14
GLICA Spring Planting Festival
Tyngsborough State Forest
Tyngsboro, MA
(508) 453-7182

May 13–14
New Jersey Indian Center Annual
Powwow
Old Bridge Ice Arena
Old Bridge, NJ
(908) 525-0066

May 13–14
Annual Spring Powwow
McArthur Court
University of Oregon
Eugene, OR
(503) 346-3723

May 13–14
Annual Eagle Point Powwow
Las Casitas
Ojai, CA
(805) 494-1558 or 646-7433

May 13–14
Mankato State University Powwow
Mankato, MN
(507) 389-5230

May 13–14
AISA University of Minnesota
Annual Powwow
East Phillips Park
Minneapolis, MN
(612) 624-2555

May 13–14
Massachusetts Center for Native
American Awareness Annual Powwow
Pratt Farm Rte. 105
Middleboro, MA
(617) 884-4227

May 13–14
Aurora University Powwow
Aurora University
Aurora, IL
(708) 844-5402

May 13–14
Annual St. Croix Casino Spring
Powwow
Hwy 63 & 8 (west of Turtle Lake)
Turtle Lake, WI
(800) 846-8946

May 13–14
East Texas Native American Annual
Powwow of Champions
(off Hwy 80)
Wills Point, TX
(903) 873-4315

May 14
Ben Calf Robe Annual Powwow
Ben Calf Robe School
11833 64th St.
Edmonton, AB CANADA
(403) 471-2360

May 18
Elders Week Powwow
2 Eagle River School
Pablo Mont
(406) 675-0292

May 18–19
Powwow
North Seattle Community College
Seattle, WA
(206) 527-3722, office
(206) 323-9105, home–Ron
Alexander

May 19
Abenaki Midwinter Winter Mini
Powwow
Annunciation Catholic Church
87 Broad St.
Akron, OH
(216) 628-5796, Curt Baltzer

May 19–20
University of Utah Annual Powwow
Jon Huntsman Center
Salt Lake City, UT
(801) 581-8151

May 19–20
Haskell Indian Jr. College Powwow
Lawrence, KS
(913) 749-8428

May 19–21
Pyramid Lake Powwow
Nixon, NV
(702) 574-0311, Billy

May 19–21
Odawa Annual Powwow
Nepean Tent & Trailer Park
Nepean, ONT CANADA
(613) 238-8591
(613) 238-6106, FAX

May 19–21
Heart of the Circle Powwow
St. Croix Tribal Center
Hertel, WI

May 19–21
Call to Cream Ridge Powwow
Cream Ridge Winery
Cream Ridge, NJ
(908) 475-3872

May 19–21
Annual Celebration of Sobriety
Clearwater County
Red Lake, MN
(218) 679-3392

May 19–21
Annual Spring Juried Arts Festival
Rancocas Indian Reservation
Rancocas, NJ
(609) 261-4747

May 19–21
Indian Powwow
Rockome Gardens
(5 miles west of Arcola, IL)
(217) 268-4106, Jean Lambeth

May 19–21
Annual Ute Legacy Celebration
& Powwow
Glenwood Springs, CO
(303) 945-6644, Kenny Frost

May 20
Penn Cove Water Festival
Coupeville
Whidbey Island, WA
(206) 679-7327, Susan Berta

May 20
Upper Mattaponi Spring Festival
Sharon School
King William, VA
(804) 769-2408

May 20–21
Annual Veterans Memorial Powwow
Woodland Bowl
Keshena, WI
(715) 799-5168

May 20–21
Annual Texas Gulf Coast
Championship Powwow
Traders Village
(off NW Hwy 290)
Houston, TX
(713) 890-5500

May 20–21
Powwow
Sioux Valley, MAN CANADA
(204) 885-2671

May 20–21
AIS May Dance
4-H Campo Marshall
(off Rte. 31)
Spencer, MA
(508) 852-6271

May 20–21
Massachusetts Center for Native
American
Awareness Powwow
Topsfield Fairgrounds Rte. 1
Topsfield, MA
(617) 884-4227

May 20–21
Mohawk Trail Powwow
Indian Plaza Mohawk Trail
Charlemont, MA
(413) 339-4096 or
(603) 882-6607

May 20–21
Unity of the Peoples 3rd Annual
Powwow
Flathead High School Gym
Kalispel, MT
(406) 755-0302, Jack Azure
(406) 862-9201, Lillian Smith

May 20–21
Annual Richmond Community
College Powwow
Hamlet, NC
(910) 582-7071

3rd weekend May
Chehaw National Indian Festival
Albany, GA
(912) 436-1625

3rd weekend May
San Diego American Indian
Cultural Days
Balboa Park
San Diego, CA
(619) 281-5964

3rd weekend May
Red Mountain Powwow &
Indian Rodeo
Fort McDermitt, NV
(702) 532-8259

3rd weekend May
Mat'Alyma Root Festival
Kamiah, ID
(208) 935-2144

3rd weekend May
De Anza College Powwow and
Arts & Crafts Fair
21250 Steven Creek Blvd.
Cupertino, CA
(408) 864-8963

3rd weekend May
Tygh Valley All Indian Rodeo
Tygh Valley, OR
(503) 553-1161 ext. 214
Ginger Smith

3rd weekend May
Kiowa Blacklegging Ceremonial
Indian City USA
Anadarko, OK
(405) 247-3987

May 22
Oneida Vietnam Veterans Powwow
Norbert Hill Center
Oneida, WI
(414) 869-1261

May 23–27
Native American Festival
Orange Park High School
Orange Park, FL
(904) 269-8865

May 25–29
Annual Powwow in the Poconos
Fernwood Resort
Bushkill, PA
(717) 588-9500

May 26–27
Annual Spavinaw Powwow
Spavinaw, OK
(918) 968-3526, Deborah Smoke

May 26–28
Eastern Shore Native American
Powwow
Rt. 50 West Flea Market
Mardela Springs, MD
(410) 543-4189

May 26–28
Honoring All Veterans
Ft. Hayes
Plymouth, OH
(614) 443-6120

May 26–28
North Bay Clan Spring Powwow
Lower Creek Muscogee Tribe
3733 Co. Rd 2321
Lynn Haven, FL
(904) 763-6717, Chief Woods
(904) 265-3345

May 26–29
DE-UN-DA-GA Powwow
Yellow Creek State Park
Penn Run, PA
(814) 944-5116, Dallas Luke

May 27
Annual Tribal Elder Day Celebration
Ghost Hawk Park
Rosebud, SD
(605) 747-2381

May 27
Honoring Powwow for American
Indian Children
Rancho Santiago Community College
Santa Ana, CA
(714) 360-1025 or 674-7361

May 27
Annual First Peoples Cultural Festival
Capilano Longhouse
Squamish Reserve
North Vancouver, BC CANADA
(604) 873-3761, Lillian

May 27–28
Ohio Valley Memorial Day Powwow
Hocking College
Nelsonville, OH
(513) 753-4388, Roy Baver

May 27–28
Annual Seabird Island Indian Festival
BC CANADA
(604) 796-2177, Don Davis
(604) 796-3729, FAX

May 27–28
Choctaw–Apache Powwow
Ebarb Community
Zwolle, LA
(318) 645-2744

May 27–28
Klamath Memorial Powwow
Klamath Falls, OR
(503) 884-2917

May 27–28
Gissiwas Creek Annual Powwow
Tribal Building
Marion, MI
(616) 281-3640

May 27–28
Annual Delaware Contest Powwow
& Stomp Dancing
Copan, OK
(918) 336-4925 or 531-2526

May 27–28
Annual NAC Powwow
Lake County Fairgrounds
Grays Lake, IL
(708) 740-9270

May 27–28
Abenaki Nation & State Parks
Department Powwow
Salisbury State Park
Salisbury, MA
(508) 682-4511

May 27–29
Annual Memorial Day Powwow
Columbus, OH
(614) 443-6120

May 27–29
Georgetown Annual Powwow
Nowal, ONT CANADA
(905) 873-6200, Ed Cochrane

May 27–29
Drums Along Rock Powwow
The Rock County 4-H Fairgrounds
Janesville, WI
(414) 473-7748

May 27–29
Native American Church Powwow
McHenry Fairgrounds
Woodstock, IL
(414) 862-6742

May 27–30
Annual Wacipi
Fort Hayes Vocational School
Columbus, OH
(614) 443-6120

4th weekend May
YA-KA-AMA Spring Festival
6215 Eastside Rd.
Forrestville, CA
(707) 887-1541

4th weekend May
Burnt Corn Rodeo & Powwow
Pinon, AZ

4th weekend May
Annual Zuni Artists Exhibition
Museum of Northern Arizona
Flagstaff, AZ
(602) 774-5211

4th weekend May
Spavinaw Days
Spavinaw, OK
(918) 598-2758

May 28
Annual Ft. Garland Powwow
The Old Fort
Ft Garland, CO
(719) 384-4850, Sherry Manyik

Memorial Day weekend (tentative)
Medicine Ways Conference &
Powwow
University of California–Riverside
Riverside, CA
(909) 787-4143

Memorial Day weekend
Annual Red Nations Memorial
Weekend Celeb-Nation
Movieland Frontiertown
Colton, CA
(909) 864-7425, Brigette DeCora

Memorial Day weekend
Memorial Day Powwow
Ceremonial Grounds
Cherokee, NC
(800) 438-1601

Memorial Day weekend
Annual Memorial Weekend
Celebration
Cecil B. DeMille Middle School
7025 Parkcrest Ave.
Long Beach, CA
(714) 785-4377 or 883-1815

Memorial Day weekend
Red Road Annual Powwow
Casa de Fruta (near
Hollister, CA)
(408) 426-8211, Tina

Memorial Day weekend
Omaha Memorial Day Celebration
Macy, NE
(402) 837-5391

Memorial Day weekend
Gathering of Boarding School
Powwow
White Swan Ceremonial Grounds
White Swan, WA
(509) 865-5121 ext. 448

Memorial Day weekend
Choctaw Annual Rodeo
Jones Academy
Hartshome, OK
(405) 924-8280

Memorial Day weekend
Kenel Powwow
Kenel, SD
(701) 854-7231

Memorial Day weekend
Fredericksburg Powwow
Fredericksburg, VA
(410) 675-3535

Memorial Day weekend
American Indian Arts & Crafts
Festival
Indian Canyon Way
Palm Springs, CA
(619) 329-3407, Raymond Kingfisher

Last weekend May
Santa Fe Powwow & Indian Art
Market
Pojoaque Pueblo
(13 mi. north of Santa Fe, NM)
(505) 983-5220

Last weekend May
Otsiningo Indian Powwow
Appalachia, NY
(607) 625-2221

Last weekend May
Annual Championship Dance
Contest
Pierre Indian Learning Center
Pierre, SD
(605) 224-8661

May 31–June 4
Annual Dreamspeakers Festival, Film
Festival & Symposium
University of Alberta
Edmonton, AB CANADA
(403) 439-3456
(403) 439-2066, FAX

June 2–3
A Celebration of the Native
People of the Americas
North Park Village
Chicago, IL
(312) 463-0301

June 2–3
Traditional Powwow Honoring
1995 Graduates
Indian Heritage School
1330 N. 90th
Seattle, WA
(206) 298-7895, Amy Markishtum

June 2–4
Santa Monica Indian Ceremonial
Show–Sale–Powwow
Civic Auditorium
1855 Main Street
Santa Monica, CA
(310) 430-5112, Alicia & Don Bullock

June 2–4
NAIA Spring Powwow
Loretta Lynn's Ranch
Hurricane Mills, TN
(615) 726-0806

1st weekend June
Ute Mountain Bear Dance
Ute Mountain
Towaoc, CO
(303) 565-3751 ext. 200, 221, 201

1st weekend June
Annual Winds of The Northwest
Contest Powwow
11110 Corrine Ave. SE
(exit 114–Nisqually–off I-5)
Olympia, WA
(206) 456-1311, 8-3

1st weekend June
Worchester Intertribal Center
Powwow
Rutland, MA
(508) 754-3300

1st weekend June
Day of the Eagle Annual Powwow
East Jordan, MI
(616) 536-7583

1st weekend June
Annual Powwow
Collier Pavilion
Siskiyou County Fairgrounds
Yreka, CA
(916) 842-9200, Florine Super
(916) 436-2243, after 5

1st weekend June
Annual Indian Intertribal Agency
Committee Powwow
Bishop, CA
(619) 938-2122, Cheryl

1st weekend June
Tulalip Veteran's Annual Powwow
Tulalip Tribal Center
Marysville, WA
(206) 659-5385, David C. Fryberg

1st weekend June
Morton Powwow
Morton, MN
(507) 697-3250

1st weekend June
Four Moons Powwow
California Steel & Arts Foundation
9600 Cherry Ave.
Fontana, CA
(714) 822-8302, 624-1072, Ray Wade

1st weekend June
Alabama Coushatta Powwow
(17 miles east of
Livingston, TX)
(409) 563-4391, Roland Poncho

1st weekend June
Honoring of Elders Gathering
Mt. Madonna Santa Clara
County Park
(Hecher off Hwy 129)
Santa Clara, CA
(408) 638-2179

1st weekend June
Otsinigo Powwow & Indian Craft Fair
Watermam Conservation Education
Center
Appalachian, NY
(607) 625-2221

1st weekend June
YA-KA-AMA Annual Spring Festival
6215 Eastside Rd.
Forestville, CA
(707) 887-1541, Joe 9-5

1st weekend June
LCO Ojibwe School Contest Powwow
Hayward, WI
(715) 634-8924

1st weekend June
Tiinowit Annual International
Powwow
Yakima Sundome
Yakima, WA
(509) 452-6566, office or
(509) 877-4093, Hazel Olney

1st weekend June
NIYC Annual Powwow
Southwestern Indian Polytechnic
Institute
Albuquerque, NM
(505) 247-2251

June 2–4
Red Elk Powwow
(east of city on Hwy 66)
Elk City, OK
(405) 664-5901

June 2–4
Annual Tulsa Powwow
Fairground Pavillion
Tulsa, OK
(918) 835-8699

June 3
Trail of Tears Commemorative Walk
Skullyville, OK
(405) 924-8280 ext. 249, Judy Allen

June 3
Indian Heritage Day
Grass Valley, CA
(916) 273-6887
(916) 274-9735, Zula Galsh

June 3
Richmond Title V Indian Program
Powwow
DeAnza High School
Richmond, CA
(510) 237-1643, Mac Thiemar
(510) 233-4981, Judy Perry

June 3–4
Coree, Machapunga & Tuscarora
Intertribal Heritage Powwow
Moratok Park
(on the Roanoke River)
Williamston, NC
(919) 975-1473

June 3–4
Kitigan Zibi Anishinabe Kijigon
Powwow
Kitigan Zibi School Grounds
Maniwaki, QUE CANADA
(819) 449-5449

June 3–4
Annual Kingston Powwow
Kataroki Native Friendship Centre
Kingston, ONT CANADA
(613) 548-7094

June 3–4
Brandywine Annual Powwow
Tribal Grounds
Brandywine, MD
(301) 372-1932

June 3–4
Abenabi Gathering
Beaver Pond–Chilson Beach
Franklin, MA
(508) 528-7629

June 3–4
Hawks Flight Intertribal Powwow
Perris, CA
(909) 923-3553, Chuck Reddich

June 3–4
Annual Maryland Indian Heritage
Society Powwow
Brandywine, MD
(301) 372-1932

June 3–4
Native American Powwow
Starrett at Springs Creek
Starrett City, NY
(718) 642-2725

June 7–11
Smoky Mountain National American
Indian Powwow
Sevier County Fairgrounds
Sevierville, TN
(800) 826-2401
(615) 453-5900

June 9–11
Red Earth Native American Cultural
Festival
Myriad Convention Center & Plaza
Oklahoma City, OK
(405) 427-5228

June 9–11
NAES College Powwow
Mather Park
Chicago, IL
(312) 761-5000

June 9–11
Lower Sioux Annual Powwow
Lower Sioux Reservation
Morton, MN
(507) 697-6185

June 9–11
Treaty Day Commemoration
Ceremonial Grounds
White Swan, WA
(509) 865-5121 ext. 328

June 9–11
Annual Will Rogers Indian Club
Powwow
Webster County Fairgrounds
Marshfield, MO
(417) 468-3003, Ed Webb
(417) 256-4698, Mary Roark

June 10
St. Clair's Feast Day
Santa Clara Pueblo, NM
(505) 753-7326 ext 206, 255

June 10
DQ University Graduation Powwow
Davis, CA
(916) 758-0470

June 10
Gathering of Native Americans
Arts & Crafts Show
Civic Plaza
Albuquerque, NM
(505) 768-3487, 3466, Linda

June 10–11
Davis Lake Annual Powwow
Davis Lake Camp
Suffolk, VI
(804) 539-1191

June 10–11
Powwow in the Park
McArthur Park
Little Rock, AR
(800) 228-0936

June 10–11
Honoring Our Veterans Annual
Powwow
Bay Mills College
Brimley, MI
(906) 248-3208

2nd weekend June
Big Wind Crowheart Powwow
Crowheart, WY
(307) 856-1117

2nd weekend June
Sac& Fox All Indian Pro Rodeo
(5½ mi. south on Hwy 377)
Stroud, OK
(405) 273-0579

2nd weekend June
First Peoples Powwow
Camp Rotary, MI
(313) 756-1350

2nd weekend June
Annual American Indian Film
& Video Competition
Oklahoma City, OK
(918) 747-8276, Gloria Pasternak

2nd weekend June
Cannon Ball Annual Flag Day
Celebration
Cannon Ball, ND
(701) 854-3618

2nd weekend June
Annual Cheyenne Homecoming
Powwow
Lame Deer, MT
(406) 477-6284, LeRoy Pine

2nd weekend June
Return to Pimitoui Powwow
Wm. H. Sommer Park
Peoria, IL
(309) 685-7843

2nd weekend June
Annual White Earth Powwow
White Earth, MN
(218) 983-3285

2nd weekend June
Annual Indian Fair
Museum of Man
Balboa Park
San Diego, CA
(619) 239-2001, Carla Edwards

2nd weekend June
Lenni Lenape Nanticoke Powwow
Salem Fairgrounds
Salem, NJ
(609) 455-6910

2nd weekend June
Southern Cascade Annual Powwow
Intermountain Fairgrounds
McArthur, CA
(916) 243-1741, Bev LeBeau
(916) 335-5090, Rex Harrison

2nd weekend June
Klamath Salmon Festival
Klamath, CA
(707) 482-5585

2nd week June
Barrie, Powwow
Barrie Fairground
Barrie, ONT CANADA
(705) 721-7689

2nd week June
Wollomononuppoag Indian
Council Powwow
Attleboro, MA
(508) 822-5061

2nd weekend June
Powwow
Manitou, ONT CANADA
(807) 482-2940

Mid-June thru mid-August
Red Cloud Indian Art Show
Heritage Center
Pine Ridge, SD
(605) 867-5491, Brother Simon

June 11–12
Traditional Powwow
Comstock Riverside Park
Grand Rapids, MI
(517) 487-5409

June 15–17
NAIA Powwow
Halle Stadium
Memphis, TN
(901) 789-9338 or 725-6869

June 15–17
Mowa Choctaw Indian Powwow
Choctaw Reservation
Mt. Vernon, AL
(205) 829-5500

June 15–17
Mowa Choctaw Tribal Powwow
Tribal Grounds
Mt. Vernon, AL
(205) 829-5500

June 15–18
Rebirth of the Traditional Spiritual
Gathering
North Carolina Indian Cultural
Center
Pembroke, NC
(910) 521-4178

June 16–18
Annual Children Are Sacred
Benefit Powwow
Cincinnati, OH
(513) 745-0908, Art Wasson

June 16–18
Woodland Powwow
The Deer Creek Music Center
Noblesville, IN
(317) 841-8900

June 16–18
Whitesand Powwow
Armstrong, ONT CANADA
(807) 583-2177

June 17
Auburn Native American Day
Eskhart City Park
Auburn, IN
(219) 925-1522

June 17
Virginia Indian Heritage Festival
Jamestown Settlement
Williamsburg, VA
(804) 229-1607

June 17
Trail of Tears Art Show
Cherokee Historical Society
Tahlequah, OK
(918) 456-6007, Myrna Moss

June 17–18
Annual Powwow
Sariia, ONT CANADA
(519) 336-8410

June 17–18
Wepawaug River Village Powwow
Eisenhower Park
Milford, CT
(203) 878-8898

June 17–18
Annual Gathering of All Nations
Old Athletic Field–Orleans Street
Stillwater, MN
(612) 439-2185

June 17–19
Iowa Tribal Powwow
Perkins, OK
(405) 547-2402

3rd weekend June
Annual Silver Star Powwow &
Indian Market
Kaiser Convention Arena
Oakland, CA
(415) 554-0525

3rd weekend June
Red Mountain Powwow
Ft. McDermitt, NV
(702) 532-8800

3rd weekend June
Chipeta Park Annual Powwow
Chipeta Park
Nederland, CO
(303) 258-7321

3rd weekend June
Annual Sam Yazzie Jr. Memorial
Powwow
Lakachukai, AZ
(602) 787-2301

3rd weekend June
Annual All My Relations Powwow
& Feast
Swinomish Gym
LaConner, WA
(206) 466-2355

3rd weekend June
Delta Park Powwow & Encampment
Delta Park
Portland, OR

3rd weekend June
Homecoming of the Three Fires
Comstock Riverside Park
Grand Rapids, MI
(616) 774-8331

3rd weekend June
TIHA Powwow
Llano City Park
Llano, TX
(817) 498-2873

3rd weekend June
Red Bottom Celebration
Fraser, MT
(406) 477-6284

3rd weekend June
Custer Battlefield Re-enactment
Hardin, MT

3rd weekend June
AICA Annual Powwow
Van Hoy Campground
Union Grove, NC
(704) 464-5579

3rd weekend June
Annual Traditional Gathering
Powwow Grounds
Mole Lake, WI
(715) 478-3957

3rd weekend June
Annual Wapusun Powwow
Lake Wapusun Campgrounds
Wooster, OH
(216) 628-5796, Curt Baltzzer

3rd weekend June
Porcupine Powwow
Porcupine, ND
(701) 854-7231
(701) 554-3430, Clay Dogskin

3rd weekend June
Chief Joseph & Warriors Memorial
Powwow
Lapwai, ID
(208) 843-2253, 7141

3rd weekend June
Ring Thunder Traditional Powwow
St. Francis Indian School
Rosebud, SD
(605) 747-2381 ext. 120, 2298

3rd weekend June
Wakeby Lake Annual Powwow
Glen Farms
Portsmouth, RI
(401) 683-5167

3rd weekend June
Eastern Delaware Nations Powwow
Forksville Fairgrounds
Forksville, PA
(717) 924-9082

3rd weekend June
Yavpai Prescott All Indian Powwow
Pagant Bingo Area
Prescott, AZ
(602) 445-8790

3rd weekend June
Carthage Powwow
Municipal Park Stadium
Carthage, MO
(417) 358-4974

3rd weekend June
Creek Nation Festival & Rodeo
Okmulgee, OK
(918) 756-8700

3rd weekend June
Powwow
Rosseau River, MAN CANADA
(204) 427-2139

3rd weekend June
Big Foot Memorial Riders
Honoring Wacipi
Soldiers Creek, SD
(605) 747-2336, Dorothy Jones

3rd weekend June
Annual Stewart Indian School
Powwow & Reunion
Stewart Indian School Museum
Carson City, NV
(702) 882-1802

3rd weekend June
Annual Yosemite
Indian Days Big Time
Yosemite Valley, CA
(209) 372-0294, Jay Johnson 8-5

3rd weekend June
Summer Powwow
Wildwood Acres
Harford City, IN
(317) 348-1223

3rd weekend June
Worchester Indian Cultural Art
Lodge Powwow
(Pratt Junction off Rte 12)
Sterling, MA
(508) 754-3300

3rd weekend June
Pequot & Narragansett Joint Powwow
Crandall Farm
Westerley, RI
(401) 346-1100

3rd weekend June
Indian Hills Powwow
Indian Hills Campground
Tehachapi, CA
(805) 822-4623 or 822-1118

3rd weekend June
CT River Powwow Society Strawberry
Moon Powwow
Ferry Hill Park
Rte. 160
Rocky Hill, CT
(203) 684-5407

3rd weekend June
Annual Lansing Indian Center
Powwow
Lake Lansing Park North
Lansing, MI
(517) 487-5409

3rd weekend June
Annual Sokaogon Traditional
Powwow
Crandon, WI
(715) 478-5190

3rd weekend June
Sahewamish Powwow
Mason County Fairgrounds
Shelton, WA
(206) 426-9871

Father's Day weekend
Community Powwow
Arapahoe, WY
(307) 856-6117

Father's Day weekend
All Indian Rodeo
Birch Creek, MT
(406) 338-7522

June 18
Annual All Native Day
Capilano Reserve, BC CANADA
(604) 253-1020

June 18–21
Opasquiak Annual Powwow
Pas Reserve, MAN CANADA

June 22–26
Eskasoni Annual Powwow
Cape Breton
Nova Scotia CANADA
(902) 379-2800

June 23
Anishinaabe Way Annual Powwow
Hayward, WI
(715) 634-3041, 5841

June 23
American Indian World Peace Day
Custer Battlefield
Hardin, MT
(406) 638-2621

June 23–25
Plains Powwow
The Deer Creek Music Center
Noblesville, IN
(317) 841-8900

June 23–25
Siksika Nation Fair
Gleichan, AB CANADA
(403) 734-3833, Harlon or
Faron McMaster

June 23–25
Kapown Days
Grovard, AB CANADA
(403) 751-3921

June 23–25
Mentor Annual Festival
Wild River Ranch
Mentor, AL
(404) 215-0604

June 24–July 30
Annual Festival of Native
American Arts
Cococino Center for the Arts
Flagstaff, AZ
(602) 779-6921

June 23–25
Annual Heber City Powwow
Wasatch Fairgrounds
Heber City, UT
(801) 645-4918

June 23–25
Chin–Qua–Pin
El Paso County Fairgrounds
Calhan, CO
(719) 392-1116 or 475-8896,
Kristeen Craig or Eugene Redhawk

June 23–25
Flagstaff All Indian Days Powwow
Aspen & Laroux
Flagstaff, AZ
(602) 774-1330

June 23–25
Annual Great Lakes Powwow
Hannahville, MI
(906) 466-2342

June 24
Red Thunder Powwow
Zoar State Forest
Aylett, VA
(804) 769-4447

June 24–25
Chicago AIC Annual Midwest
Regional Princess Powwow
Lake County Fairgrounds
Grayslake, IL
(312) 275-5871

June 24–25
Annual Woodland Gathering
Minnetrista Cultural Center
Muncie, IN
(317) 282-4848

June 24–25
Plains Indians Powwow
Buffalo Bill Historical Center
Cody, WY
(307) 587-4771, Faith Bad Bear

June 25
American Indian Music Festival
Estuary Park
Oakland, CA
(510) 452-1235
(510) 452-1243, FAX

4th weekend June
Indian Days Celebration
Rosebud, SD
(605) 474-2381, Rose Cordier,
or Alberta Widshot

4th weekend June
Annual Powwow
Saddle Lake, AB CANADA
(403) 726-3829, Celina McGilvery

4th weekend June
Badlands Celebration
Brockton, MT
(406) 768-5151

4th weekend June
Annual "Keeping the Traditions"
Powwow
Miami Valley Council for
Native Americans
Xenia, OH
(513) 275-8599, James Cain

4th weekend June
Stommish Water Festival
Lummi Stommish Grounds
(15 miles northwest via I-5 exit 260
to WA 540)
Ferndale, WA

4th weekend June
Graduation Powwow
Oglala Lakota College
Kyle, SD
(605) 455-2321

4th weekend June
TOPIC Powwow
South Shore Science Center
Norwell, MA
(617) 337-4308

4th weekend June
St. Francis Indian Day Celebration
St. Francis Indian School
Rosebud, SD
(605) 747-2298

4th weekend June
Coquille Indian Tribe Powwow
Brandon, OR
(503) 888-4274, Sharon Parrish
(503) 267-4587

4th weekend June
Heart Lake First Nation Treaty Days
Heart Lake Indian Reserve
Lac La Biche, AB CANADA
(403) 623-2130 or 623-2146

4th weekend June
Santee Annual Wacipi
Santee, NE
(402) 857-3509, Charles LaPlante

Last weekend June
Annual Potowatomi Powwow
Shawnee, OK
(800) 880-9880
(405) 275-3121

Last weekend June
Eastern Shoshone Powwow
Fort Washakie, WY
(307) 332-9106

Last weekend June
San Joaquin Indian Council Powwow
Three Rivers Lodge
Manteca, CA
(209) 858-2421

June 29–July 1
Stoney Nation Canada Day
Celebration & Rodeo
Morley, AB CANADA
(403) 881-2200

June 30–July 1
Calico Dancers Annual Good Time
Powwow
Moreau Recreation Park
South Glen Falls, NY
(518) 793-3471

June 30–July 2
Poundmakers Powwow
St. Albert, AB CANADA
(403) 458-1884

Mid–June thru mid–August
Red Cloud Indian Art Show
Heritage Center
Pine Ridge, SD
(605) 867-5491, Brother Simon

1st week of July
4th of July Powwow & Open Rodeo
Nespelem, WA
(509) 634-4711

July 1
Teslin Band Canada Day Celebration
Teslin, BC CANADA
(403) 390-2530

July 1
Heat Moon Festival & Potluck
Nipmuck Reservation
Webster, MA
(508) 943-4569

July 1–2
Native American Indian Powwow
Indian Plaza
Rte 2 Mohawk Trail
Charlemont, MA
(413) 339-4096
(603) 882-6607, Little Bear
Vendor Info

July 1–2
Arts & Crafts Fair
Indian Pueblo Cultural Center
Albuquerque, NM
(505) 843-7270

July 2–4
Annual Oneida Powwow
Norbert Hill Road
Oneida, WI
(414) 869-2083

July 4th weekend
Early Summertime Greasy Grass/No
Water Districts Powwow, Amateur
Rodeo & Celebration
Lodge Grass, MT
(406) 638-2601

July 4th weekend
File Hills First Nations Powwow
Star Blanket Powwow Grounds
Balcarres, SASK CANADA
(306) 334-2206

July 4th weekend
Tonkawa Powwow
Tonkawa, OK
(405) 628-2561

July 4th weekend
Annual Pawnee Indian Veterans
Homecoming & Powwow
Football Field
Pawnee, OK
(918) 762-2108

July 4th weekend
July 4th Powwow
Ceremonial Grounds
Cherokee, NC
(800) 438-1601

July 4th weekend
Annual Northern Cheyenne Powwow
Lame Deer, MT
(406) 477-6284, 6285, Barbar Sprang
8252, Tony Prairiebear

July 4th weekend
Annual 4th of July Celebration
Arlee, MT
(406) 745-4572, Pat Pierre

July 4th weekend
Annual Northern Ute Powwow
& Rodeo
Fort Duchesne, UT
(801) 722-5141 ext. 156,
Venita Taveapont
2249, Ron Wopsocks

July 4th weekend
July 4th Celebration
Tonta Apache Reservation
Payson, AZ
(602) 474-5000

July 4th weekend
Leech Lake Powwow
Veterans Memorial Grounds
Cass Lake, MN
(218) 335-6211

July 4th weekend
Mount Tum Tum Native American
Encampment
Territorial Park
Amboy, WA
(206) 247-5258, Barbara Waggener

July 4th weekend
Iron Lighting Powwow
Eagle Butte, SD
(605) 964-2542

July 4th weekend
Chief Taholah Days
Quinault Reservation
Taholah, WA
(206) 276-8211

July 4th weekend
Annual Chumash Intertribal Powwow
Santa Ynez, CA
(805) 686-1416

July 4th weekend
Annual 4th of July Powwow
Three Rivers Indian Lodge
Manteca, CA
(209) 858-2421

July 4th weekend
Wakpamni Lake Powwow
Batesland, SD
(605) 867-5821

July 4th weekend
Annual Manitoulin Island Traditional
Powwow
Manitoulin, ONT CANADA
(705) 377-5362

July 4th weekend
July 4th Celebration Powwow
& Rodeo
Window Rock, AZ
(602) 871-6645, 6702, 6478

July 4th weekend
4th of July Celebration in
Hoopa Valley
Hoopa, CA
(916) 625-4211 or 625-4239

July 4th weekend
Annual Powwow
Fort Kipp, MT
(406) 786-5370

July 4th weekend
July 4th Celebration
Hopi Reservation
Oraibi, AZ
(602) 734-2441

July 4th weekend
Indian Days Encampment & Powwow
White Swan Pavilion
White Swan, WA
(509) 865-5121

July 4th weekend
Shoshone-Paiute Annual Powwow
Owyhee, NV
(702) 757-3161

July 4th weekend
Bear Soldier Powwow
MacLaughlin, SD
(701) 854-7231 ext. 200

July 4th weekend
Annual Sisseton–Wahpeton Wacipi
Agency Village
(7 mi. south on Hwy 700)
Sisseton, SD
(605) 698-3911

July 4th weekend
Annual Red Cliff Traditional Powwow
Red Cliff, WI
(715) 779-3701

July 4th weekend
Powwow
Fort Alex, MAN CANADA
(204) 367-4504

July 4th weekend
Goodfish Lake Treaty Celebration
Goodfish Lake, AB CANADA
(403) 636-3622, 2077

July 4th weekend
Annual Chippewa Powwow
Shunk Road Reservation
Sault Ste. Marie, MI
(906) 635-4960

July 4th weekend
Kiowa Gourd Clan Celebration
City Park
Carnegie, OK
(405) 726-2996, Glenn Hamilton

July 4th weekend
Annual Veterans' Regional Memorial
Gathering
Chiloquin High School Football Field
Chiloquin, OR
(503) 783-3057, Quentin Bettles
(503) 783-2865, Pricilla Bettles

July 4th weekend
Quapaw Tribal Powwow
Beaver Springs Park
Quapaw, OK
(918) 542-1853

July 4th weekend
Mashpee Wampanoag Powwow
Heritage Park ret 130
Mashpee, MA
(508) 477-0208

July 4th weekend
AIICO Powwow
Garrett County Fairgrounds
McHenry, MD
(301) 963-7284

July 4th weekend
Annual 4th of July Celebration
Mescalaro Apache Reservation, NM
(505) 671-4495

July 3–8
Kapown Adventure Days
Hilliard Provincial Park
AB CANADA
(403) 751-3921

July 4
Nambe Waterfall Ceremonial
Nambe Pueblo
(north of Santa Fe, NM)
(505) 455-2036

July 7–8
Passaquoddy Tribe Annual
Indian Days
Petter Dana Point
Princeton, ME
(207) 796-2301 ext. 15,
Eva Sockabasin

July 7–9
American Indian Exposition & Sale
Ventura County Fairgrounds
Ag Building
Ventura, CA
(209) 221-4355

July 7–9
Prairie Island Mdewakanton
Dakota Wacipi
Prairie Island, MN
(800) 554-5473, Posie Johnson

July 7–9
Annual Black Hills & Northern Plains
Powwow & Art Expo
Rushmore Plaza Civic Center
Rapid City, SD
(605) 341-0925
(605) 342-6249, FAX

July 7–9
Kansas City Indian Club Powwow
Wyandottee County Fairgrounds
Kansas City, KS
(816) 421-7608

July 7–9
Wahpeton Dakota Nation
Annual Powwow
Wahpeton, SASK CANADA
(306) 764-6649

July 7–9
Aspen Celebration for the
American Indian
Aspen, CO
(303) 925-6400

July 8–9
Wukwemdong Sashoodenoug
Powwow
Kettle & Stony
Point, ONT CANADA
(519) 786-6680

July 8–9
Narragansett & Pequot Nations
Powwow
Crandall Farm
Westerly, RI
(401) 364-1100

July 8–9
Gateway to the Nations
Floyd Bennert Field
Brooklyn, NY
(718) 832-4884

July 8–9
Powwow
Tekawitha Island
Kahnawake, QUE CANADA
(514) 632-8667, Barbara Big Bear

2nd week July
National Powwow 9
Iroquois County Fairgrounds
(State Highway 49 north of
Crescent City, IL)
(708) 969-7131, Byron Loehman

2nd week July
Sac & Fox Nation 31st Annual
Powwow
(5.5 miles south of
Stroud, OK)
(918) 968-3526, Ron Harrie Sr.

2nd weekend July
Alexis Annual Powwow
Glenevis, AB CANADA
(403) 967-2225, Ellis Kootenay

2nd weekend July
North American Indian Days
Browning, MT
(406) 338-7521

2nd weekend July
American Indian Art Festival
Mission Plaza
San Luis Obispo, CA
(408) 623-2379, Sonny or
Elaine Reyna

2nd weekend July
Annual Mission International
Powwow
Mission, BC CANADA
(604) 826-1281, JoAnne Hanuse

2nd weekend July
Little Hoop Traditional Powwow
Mission, SD
(605) 747-2342

2nd weekend July
Hays Powwow
Hays, MT
(406) 358-2205

2nd weekend July
Afraid of His Horse Ceremonial
Pine Ridge, SD
(605) 867-5670

2nd weekend July
Arikara Celebration & Powwow
White Shield, ND
(701) 627-4781

2nd weekend July
Bear River Powwow
Lac Du Flambeau, WI
(715) 588-3286

2nd weekend July
Apache Tears Spirit Powwow
Crescent Community Club, Hwy 97
Crescent, OR
(503) 433-2461, Linda Wilcox
(503) 433-2677

2nd weekend July
Taos Powwow
Taos Pueblo Buffalo Field
Taos, NM
(800) 732-TAOS
(505) 758-1028

2nd weekend July
Yellowquill Powwow
Yellowquill Reserve, SASK CANADA
(306) 332-2281

2nd weekend July
Whitefish Bay First Nation Powwow
Whitefish Bay, ONT CANADA
(807) 226-5411

2nd weekend July
Yukon First Nations Cultural Festival
Brook's Brook
Yukon, CANADA
(403) 667-7631, Yvonne

2nd weekend July
4th Annual Cedar Grove Powwow
Bidwell Park
Chico, CA
(916) 894-5068, Jenifer Rivera
(916) 345-7738, Peter Ratner

2nd weekend July
Algonquin Indian School Powwow
Roger Williams Park
Providence, RI
(401) 781-2626 or 941-2582

2nd weekend July
Dove Crest Johnny Cake Festival
Rhode Island
(401) 539-7795

2nd weekend July
Annual Indian League of Americas
Powwow
Rte 55
Barrysville, NY
(718) 836-6255, Jim Kavanaugh
(914) 858-8309, Patricia Rice

July 9
Annual Celebration of the Feast Day
of the Blessed Katerai Tekawitha
Heart Catholic Church
Miami, OK
(918) 674-2587

July 9
Five Civilized Tribes Competitive
Arts Show
Muskogee, OK
(918) 683-1701
Lynn Thornley

July 9–16
International Brotherhood Days
Porcupine, SD
(703) 764-1953, Mike Bugelski
(703) 250-4161, evenings

July 9–16
Lone Feather Council Powwow
Penrose Equestrian Center
Colorado Springs, CO
(719) 475-8896

July 13
Hiawagha Powwow
Ironwood, MI
(906) 932-1122

July 14
Annual Feast
Cochiti Pueblo, NM
(505) 465-2244

July 14–16
Saskatchewan Handcraft Festival
Alex Dillabough Centre &
Battleford Arena
Battleford, SASK CANADA
(306) 653-3616

July 14–16
Honor the Earth Powwow &
Homecoming Celebration
Lac Courte
Oreilles Ojibwe Reservation
(11 miles east of Hayward, WI)
(715) 634-8924, Stony Larson

July 14–16
Enoch Powwow
Enoch, AB CANADA
(403) 470-4471, Beatrice Morin

July 14–16
Temagami First Nation Traditional
Powwow
Lake Temagami, ONT CANADA
(705) 237-8980

July 14–16
Annual Powwow
Chase, BC CANADA
(604) 679-3203

July 14–21
Festival of the Midnight Sun
Yellow Knife, NWT CANADA
(403) 873-4262

July 14–23
Cheyenne Frontier Days
Frontier Park
Cheyenne, WY
(800) 227-6336

July 15
Annual Big Time Festival
Kule Loklo Village
Pt. Reyes, CA
(415) 663-1092

July 15–16
Massachucetts Center of Native
American Awareness Annual
Towwa KeeswushPowwow
Marshfield Fairgrounds
Marshfield, MA
(617) 884-4227

July 15–16
Annual Monacan Indian Powwow
Sedalia Center
Big Island, VA
(804) 929-6911, George White Wolf
(804) 384-3972, Roy Johns

July 15–16
Keepers of the Western Door
Veterans Memorial Park
Salamanca, NY
(716) 945-4971

3rd weekend July
Comanche Homecoming
Sultan Park
Walters, OK
(405) 492-4988

3rd weekend July
Quileute Days
La Push, WA
(206) 374-6163, Scott Churchill

3rd week July
Cold Lake First Nation Treaty Days
Cold Lake, AB CANADA
(403) 594-7183

3rd weekend July
Antelope Powwow
Mission, SD
(605) 856-2703

3rd weekend July
Standing Arrow Powwow
Elmo, MT
(406) 849-5541, Clarenda Burke

3rd weekend July
Iron Ring Celebration
Poplar, MT

3rd weekend July
All Indian Stampede & Pioneer Days
Fallon, NV
(702) 423-2544, 3634

3rd weekend July
Flandreau Santee Sioux Wacipi
Flandreau, SD
(605) 997-3891

3rd weekend July
Ethete Powwow
Ethete, WY
(307) 332-2056

3rd weekend July
Charlotte Native American Festival
College ST
Charlotte, NC
(704) 527-7187

3rd week July
Council Oak Powwow
Town Hall Rte. 138
Dighton, MA
(508) 669-5008

3rd weekend July
Little Beaver Powwow
Jicarilla Apache Tribe
Dulce, NM
(505) 759-3242

3rd weekend July
Annual Corn Creek Traditional
Powwow
Rosebud, SD
(605) 462-6281 or 344-2206

3rd weekend July
Poundmaker Band Powwow
Paynton, SASK CANADA
(306) 398-4971, Brian Tootoosis

3rd weekend July
Peguis Annual Powwow
Peguis, MAN CANADA
(204) 645-2359

3rd weekend July
Mandaree Celebration & Powwow
Mandaree, ND
(701) 759-3311

3rd weekend July
Kainai Days
Standoff, AB CANADA
(403) 737-3753, 3998

3rd weekend July
Blood Tribe Native Arts Festival
Kainai Sports Arena
Standoff, AB CANADA
(403) 737-3753
(403) 737-2336, FAX

3rd weekend July
Annual Squilax Powwow
Squilax, BC CANADA
(604) 679-3203

3rd weekend July
Mississauga Powwow
Mississauga, ONT CANADA
(705) 627-3468
(705) 356-2568, Linda

3rd weekend July
Milk's Camp Traditional Powwow
St. Charles Bonesteel, SD
(605) 835-8495

3rd weekend July
Kickapoo Tribe of Kansas Powwow
(7 miles west of Horton, KS)
(913) 486-2131, Norene Negonsott

3rd weekend July
Carry the Kettle Powwow
Carry the Kettle Reserve
Sinaulta, SASK CANADA
(306) 727-2135, Jeff Eashappie

3rd weekend July
Annual Aspen/Snowmass
Celebration
Snowmass Rodeo Grounds
Snowmass Village, CO
(303) 920-2873

3rd weekend July
Annual Eight Northern Indian
Pueblos Artists & Craftsmen Show
San Juan Pueblo, NM
(505) 852-4265 ext. 112, Leon Tafoya

3rd weekend July
Bay City Powwow
Bay City, MI
(517) 772-5700, April

3rd week July
Weengushk Celebration
Walpole Island, ONT CANADA
(519) 627-1476

July 16–17
Wilkeson 2nd Annual Powwow
Wilkeson, WA
(206) 897-8892, Peter and
Diane DeCory

July 17–21
Birdtail Cultural Week
Spiritual Grounds
Beulah, MAN CANADA
(204) 568-4540

July 19–21
Annual World Eskimo Indian
Olympics
Big Dipper Arena
Fairbanks, AK
(907) 452-6646
(907) 456-2422, FAX

July 20–23
Annual Intertribal Indian Village
& Powwow
Salinas Municipal Stadium
Salinas, CA

July 21–23
Paul Band Powwow
Duffield, AB CANADA
(403) 892-2691
(403) 892-3760

July 21–23
Annual Keweenaw Bay Traditional
Powwow
Ojibwa Campground
Baraga, MI
(906) 353-6623, Chiz or Gerry

July 21–23
Rainbow Dancer Powwow
Springfield, IL
(217) 525-2698, Paul Carlson

July 21–23
Cheyenne Homecoming Powwow
Clinton, OK
(405) 323-2222

July 21–23
Kihekah Steh
(Hwy 20 West)
Skiatook, OK
(918) 446-0564

July 21–23
Bitterrot Valley Good Nations
Powwow
Daly Mansion Grounds
Hamilton, MT
(406) 961-4705
(406) 642-3769

July 21–30
Annual Great Northern Arts Festival
Inuvik, NWT CANADA
(403) 979-3536, Charlene Alexander

July 22
Cherokee of Hoke County
International Festival
Arabia Road
Rockfish, NC
(919) 875-0222

July 22–23
Annual Honoring Our Heritage
Powwow
Clio Lereman Park
Clio, MI
(313) 239-6621

July 22–23
Buffalo Days Powwow & Tipi Village
Head Smashed In Buffalo Jump
Fort MacLeod, AB CANADA
(403) 553-2731, Louisa Crowshoe

2nd to last weekend July
Back to Batouche Days
Batoche Historical Park
(1 hr. northeast of
Saskatoon, SASK CANADA)
(306) 343-8285, Claude Petit

4th weekend July
Wallowa Band Nez Perce
Descendants Friendship Feast
& Powwow
Wallowa, OR
(503) 886-2422

4th weekend July
Annual Homecoming Celebration
Veterans Park
Winnebago, NE
(402) 878-2272, 2772

4th weekend July
Sarcee Four Nations Celebration
Bragg Creek, AB CANADA
(403) 281-9722, 4455

4th weekend July
Chief Joseph Days
Joseph, OR
(503) 432-1015

4th weekend July
Annual White Mountain Native
American Art Festival &
Indian Market
Blue Ridge School
Pinetop, AZ
(602) 367-4290

4th weekend July
Milk River Powwow
Fort Belknap, MT
(406) 535-2621

4th weekend July
Annual Eastern Navajo Fair
Crowpoint, NM
(505) 786-5244

4th weekend July
Onion Lake Powwow
Onion Lake Reserve
(30 mi. north of Lloydminster)
SASK–AB CANADA
(396) 344-2107, Denise Waskewitch

4th weekend July
Fort Totten Annual Wacipi
Fort Totten, ND
(701) 766-4221, Elmer White or
Georgia DuBoys

4th weekend July
Annual West Moberly Powwow
Moberly Lake, BC CANADA
(604) 788-3663

4th weekend July
Little Eagle Monument Celebration
Little Eagle, SD
(701) 854-7564

4th weekend July
District Four Veterans Honoring
Wacipi
Rosebud, SD
(605) 747-2381

4th weekend July
Grand River Powwow
Six Nations Reserve
Brandfort, ONT CANADA
(519) 445-4391, Evelyn

4th weekend July
TsuuT'ina Nation Annual Powwow
& Rodeo
Bragg Creek, AB CANADA
(403) 281-4455 or 238-2677

4th weekend July
Alkali Lake Powwow
Williams Lake, BC CANADA
(604) 440-5611

4th weekend July
Sweetgrass Indian Celebration
Powwow
North Battleford, SASK CANADA
(306) 937-7475, (306) 937-2990,
(306) 937-9002

4th weekend July
Honoring Our Heritage Powwow
Genessee County Fairgrounds
Mt. Morris, MI
(313) 239-6621

4th weekend July
Annual Rising–Falling Water Festival
& Powwow
Showplace Exhibition Grounds
Richmond, VA
(804) 769-1018
(804) 443-4221

4th weekend July
Sturgeon Lake Powwow
Sturgeon Lake, SASK CANADA
(306) 764-1872, Terry

4th weekend July
Village Indian Trade Days
Knife River Indian Villages
National Historic Site
Stanton, ND
(701) 745-3309
(701) 745-3708, FAX, Fred
Armstrong

4th weekend July
Native American Indian Powwow
Indian Plaza
Rt 2 Mohawk Trail
Charlemont, MA
(413) 339-4096
(603) 882-6607, Little Bear
Vendor Info

July 24
Annual Native American Fair
& Powwow
Hassanamisco Reservation
80 Brigham Hill Rd.
Grafton, MA
(508) 393-2080

July 28–30
American Indian Exposition & Sale
Alameda Fairgrounds
Hall of Commerce
Pleastanton, CA
(209) 221-4355

July 28–30
Ochapowace Indian Celebration
Powwow
Grounds
Broadview, SASK CANADA
(306) 696-2425

July 28–30
Kawacatoose Powwow
Quinton, SASK CANADA
(306) 835-2466

July 28–30
Muskeg Lake Veterans Traditional
Powwow
Muskeg Lake, SASK CANADA
(306) 466-4914

July 28–30
T'suu Tina Rodeo & Powwow
Bragg Creek, AB CANADA
(403) 281-4455

July 28–30
Grand Celebration Powwow
Grand Casino
Hinckly, MN
(612) 384-7771

July 28–30
Suquamish Nation Youth Powwow
Capilano Park
100 Mathias Rd.
North Vancouver, BC CANADA
(604) 986-2120, Gloria Nahanee

July 28–30
Squamish Nation Powwow
100 Mathias Rd.
Capilano Reserve
North Vancouver, BC CANADA

July 28–30
First Nations Powwow
Tri County Fairgrounds
Bishop, CA
(619) 872-4927

July 28–30
Piegan Nation Annual Celebration
Brockett, AB CANADA
(403) 965-3940

July 29–30
Annual Powwow
Middlesex Fairground
Westford, MA
(617) 884-4227

July 29–30
Kekionga Gather of the People
Lawton Park
Ft. Wayne, IN
(219) 420-6043

July 29–30
Traditional Intertribal Powwow &
Living History Encampment
Alpine Hills
St. Rte 39
Dover, OH
(216) 364-1298, Beverly Angel

July 29–30
Thunderbird Dancers Powwow
Queens County Farm Museum
73-50 Little Neck Parkway
Floral Park Queens, NY
(212) 598-0100
(718) 347-3276

Last weekend July
Navajo Artists Exhibition
Museum of Northern Arizona
Flagstaff, AZ
(602) 774-5211

Fifth weekend July
Fort Randall Powwow
Lake Andes, SD
(605) 384-3641

Fifth weekend July
Wikwemikong Powwow
Manitoulin Island, ONT CANADA
(705) 859-3122

Fifth weekend July
Long Plain First Nation Powwow
Long Plain, MAN CANADA
(204) 252-2731

Fifth weekend July
Wososo Wakpala District Celebration
Between He Dog &
Upper Cutmeat, SD
(605) 747-2263
Lorraine Walking Bull

Fifth weekend July
Indian Hill Powwow
Oklahoma City, OK
(405) 391-9580

Fifth weekend July
Annual Lake of The Eagles
Traditional Powwow
Eagle River, ONT CANADA
(807) 755-5526

Fifth weekend July
Annual Little Elk's Retreat
Church on the Hill
Mt. Pleasant, MI
(517) 772-5700

Fifth weekend July
MCNAA Native American Powwow
Walpole, MA
(617) 884-4227

Fifth weekend July
Dove Crest Powwow
Rhode Island
(401) 539-7795

Last weekend July
Annual Seafair Indian Days
Daybreak Star, Discovery Park
Seattle, WA
(206) 285-4425

Last weekend July
Fort Missoula First Nations Powwow
& Celebration
Missoula, MT
(406) 721-9071

First long weekend after Batouche
Crescent Lake (Tokyo) Homecoming
Days
Yorktown, SASK CANADA
(306) 782-0494

Full moon Fri–Sat–Sun August
Omaha Powwow
Macy, NE
(402) 837-5391

August (date TBA)
Sahtu Dene Games
Fort Franklin, NWT CANADA
(403) 598-2231

August 1–6
Treaty & York Boat Days
Norway House, MAN CANADA
(204) 359-6704, 4355
Anthony Apetagon

August 3–5
Innu Nikamu Festival
Maliotenem, NWT CANADA
(418) 927-2985

August 4–5
Annual Bell Powwow
Bell Powwow Grounds
(southeast of Stilwell, OK)
(918) 696-5693
(800) 484-9133 ext. 5292

August 4–6
United Indians of Delaware Valley
Annual Powwow
Playhouse in the Park
Fairmont Park, PA
(215) 574-9020

August 4–6
Kaw Nation Powwow
Kaw Lake
Kaw City, OK
(405) 269-2552

August 4–6
Oak Lake Sioux Powwow
Pipestone, MAN CANADA
(204) 854-2959

August 4–6
Kalispel Salish Annual Fair
USK, WA
(509) 445-1178 or 445-1112

August 4–6
Honoring Sobriety Powwow
Mash Ka Wisen Treatment Center
Sawyer, MN
(218) 879-6731

August 4–7
American Indian Traditional
Preservation Committee Annual
American Indian Arts & Crafts Fair
and Competition Powwow
Rogue River Community College
Grants Pass, OR
(503) 474-6394
(503) 479-8770

1st weekend August
Rocky Boy Powwow
Rocky Boy Agency
Havre, MT
(406) 395-4291, 4707

1st weekend August
Indian Days Fair & Powwow
North Fork Recreation Center
Sierra Mono, CA
(209) 877-2115

1st weekend August
Annual Powwow
Santa Ysabel Reservation
Julian, CA

1st weekend August
Festival
Pojoaque Pueblo, NM
(505) 455-2278

1st weekend August
First Peoples Festival
Royal British Columbia Museum
Victoria, BC CANADA
(604) 387-3701

1st weekend August
YA-KA-AMA Acorn Festival
6215 Eastside Rd.
Forrestville, CA
(707) 887-1541

1st weekend August
United Lumbee Nations
High Eagle Warrior Society Powwow
Round Mountain Community Center
Round Mountain, CA
(916) 336-6701

1st weekend August
Menominee Contest Powwow
Woodland Bowl
Keshena, WI
(715) 624-5318, Carrie Wau Kau
(715) 799-4581, Julia Pyawasay

1st weekend August
Annual North Peace Stampede
Laccardinal Park (6 miles from
Grimshaw, AB CANADA)
(403) 338-2184

1st weekend August
American Indian Federation Powwow
Stepping Stone Ranch
West Greenwich, RI
(401) 231-9280

1st weekend August
Beaver Lake First Powwow
& Fish Derby
Beaver Lake (8 km southeast of
Lac LaBiche, AB CANADA)
(403) 623-4549, Cliff or Gary

1st weekend August
Mesquakie Powwow
Tama, IA
(515) 484-4578

1st weekend August
Eno-Occaneechi Powwow
Membane, NC
(919) 563-3091

1st weekend August
Passamaquoddy Annual Powwow
Pleasant Point Reservation
Perry, ME
(207) 853-2551

1st weekend August
Lheit-Lheit Powwow
Prince George, BC CANADA
(604) 963-8451
(604) 963-8324, FAX

1st weekend August
Hawk Haven Powow
Meeker, OK
(405) 279-2174

1st weekend August
Annual Powwow
Sunchild First Nation
Rocky Mountain House
AB CANADA
(403) 989-3740

1st weekend August
Powwow
Big Grassy, ONT CANADA
(807) 488-5552

1st weekend August
Kahkewistahaw Powwow
Broadview, SASK CANADA
(306) 697-2831 or 696-3291

1st weekend August
Parmalee Traditional Powwow
Parmalee, SD
(605) 747-2136, 2381

1st weekend August
Massacre Canyon Powwow
Trenton, NE
(308) 285-3322

1st weekend August
Oglala Nation Powwow & Rodeo
Pine Ridge, SD
(605) 867-5821

1st weekend August
Annual Kitsap Indian Center Powwow
Erlands Point Road
Bremerton, WA
(206) 692-7460

1st weekend August
Standing Rock Wacipi
Fort Yates, SD
(701) 854-7451, 3431

1st weekend August
Kiowa All Indian Rodeo
Fairgrounds
Andora, OK
(405) 654-2300

1st weekend August
Oklahoma Indian Nation Powwow
Cheyenne Powwow Grounds
Concho, OK
(405) 262-0345

August 4–5
Annual Bell Powwow
Southeast of Stillwell
Stillwell, OK
(918) 696-5693

August 5
Annual Virginia Native American
Cultural Center Powwow
Poor Farm Park
Ashland, VA
(804) 648-6222

August 5–6
Honor the Earth Powwow
Tri County Fairgrounds
Northhampton, MA
(413) 253-7788

August 5–6
Standing Buffalo Powwow
(6 mi. west of Ft. Qu'Appelle
Standing Buffalo Reserve)
SASK CANADA
(306) 332-4685, Bryon Goodwill

August 5–6
O Dawa Homecoming
Ottawa Indian Stadium
Harbor Springs, MI
(616) 348-3410

August 5–6
Wagon Trails Annual Powwow
4051 St. Rt. 46 S.
Jefferson, OH
(216) 527-5765, Don Lane

August 5–6
Houston Indian Market
& Southwest Showcase
Houston, TX
(806) 355-1610, Randy Wilkerson

August 6–13
Elders & Youth Annual Powwow
Pipestone National Monument
Pipestone, MN
(612) 724-3129

August 7–12
Annual Indian Exposition
Caddo County Fairgrounds
Anadarko, OK
(405) 247-6651

August 8–10
Prince Albert Indian & Metis
Friendship Centre Powwow
Prince Albert, SASK CANADA
(306) 764-3431, Brenda Sayese

August 8–13
Annual Intertribal Indian
Ceremonial
Red Rock State Park
Gallup, NM
(800) 233-4528, Larry Linford

August 10–13
Shoshone-Bannock Festival & Rodeo
Ft. Hall, ID
(208) 238-3700

August 11
St. Clair's Feast Day
Santa Clara Pueblo, NM
(505) 753-7326 ext. 242

August 11–13
Lower Brule Fair & Powwow
Lower Brule, SD
(605) 473-5561

August 11–13
Annual IICOT Powwow of
Champions
Tulsa State Fairgrounds
Tulsa, OK
(918) 836-1523

August 11–13
Ermineskin Powwow Celebration
Hobbema, AB CANADA
(403) 585-3741, Audrey Ward

August 11–13
Nesika Illahee Powwow
402 Park Way Government Hill
Siletz, OR
(800) 922-1399, Karen Bell

August 11–20
International Native Arts Festival
Calgary, AB CANADA
(403) 233-0022
(403) 233-7681, FAX

2nd weekend August
Saquache Powwow
Saquache, CO
(719) 655-2696, Ruth Horn

2nd weekend August
Annual LacVieux Desert Powwow
Old Village Rd.
Waters Meet, MI
(906) 358-4106

2nd weekend August
Annual Native American Festival
Mile High Middle School
Athletic Field
Prescott, AZ
(602) 445-1270, Ann Hale

2nd weekend August
Mohican Contest Powwow
Stockbridge–Munsee Reservation
"Many Tribes Park"
Bowler, WI
(715) 793-4111, 793-4270

2nd weekend August
John Smith Indian Band Powwow
Birch Hill, SASK CANADA
(306) 764-1282

2nd weekend August
Paumanauke Powwow
Tanner Park
Copiage, NY
(516) 661-7558

2nd weekend August
Bullhead Powwow
Bullhead, SD
(701) 854-7231

2nd weekend August
Omak Stampede
Omak, WA
(800) 933-6625

2nd weekend August
Little Shell Powwow
Newtown, ND
(701) 627-4781

2nd weekend August
Native American Craft Days
Bridgeport, CA
(619) 934-3342

2nd weekend August
Heart Butte Indian Days
Heart Butte, MT
(406) 338-7276

2nd weekend August
Sac & Fox Annual Powwow
Tama, IA
(515) 484-4678, 484-5358

2nd weekend August
Piapot Indian Celebrations Powwow
Piapot Reserve, SASK CANADA
(306) 781-4848

2nd weekend August
Powwow
Grassy Narrows, ONT CANADA
(807) 488-5552

2nd weekend August
Annual Assembly
Metis Nation of Alberta
St. Albert, AB CANADA
(403) 451-2870 or 455-2200

2nd weekend August
Annual Southern California Indian
Center Powwow
Orange County Fairground
Costa Mesa, CA
(714) 530-0225

2nd weekend August
Annual Crow Creek Powwow
Stephan, SD
(605) 245-2304, 2434

2nd weekend August
Powwow
North West Bay, ONT CANADA
(807) 486-3407

2nd weekend August
Annual Driftpile Powwow
Driftpile, AB CANADA
(403) 355-3615

2nd weekend August
Swan Lake Traditional Powwow
Swan Lake, SASK CANADA
(204) 836-2848

2nd weekend August
Honoring All Veterans Powwow
Lebanon, IN
(317) 482-3315

2nd weekend August
Kikino 5th Annual Silver Birch
Rodeo
Kikino Metis Settlement
AB CANADA
(403) 623-2635
(403) 623-7080, FAX

2nd weekend August
Clear Creek All Indian Powwow
Ed Woodington Farm
Nevada, MO
(417) 944-2745

2nd weekend August
Annual West Texas Homecoming
Powwow
Amarillo Civic Center
Amarillo, TX
(806) 273-6504, Dwain McGehee

2nd weekend August
Grass Mountain Traditional Wacipi
Grass Mountain, SD
(605) 747-2154, Ike Schimidt

2nd weekend August
Roaming Buffalo Singers Annual
Powwow
Buffalo Village Store
Union St. (off Rte. 116)
Plainfield, MA
(508) 226-5712

2nd Saturday August
Hoopa Sovereignty Day Celebration
Hoopa, CA
(916) 625-4211

2nd Sunday August
320th Narragansett Indian Powwow
Narrangansett Church Old Mill Rd.
Charleston, RI
(401) 364-1100
(401) 364-9832, George Hopkins

2nd Sunday August
Roasting Ears of Corn Feast
Lenni Lenape Historical Society
Allentown, PA
(215) 797-2121

August 11–13
Annual Macon Festival
Coliseum
Macon, GA
(404) 215-0604

August 11–13
Annual Bad River Powwow
New Odanah Powwow Grounds
Odanah, WI
(715) 682-7102

August 11–13
Muskoday Traditional Powwow
Muskoday, SASK CANADA
(306) 764-1282
(306) 763-1623, Randy Bear

August 11–13
Zuni Arts Cultural Expo
Tribal Grounds
Zuni Pueblo, NM
(505) 782-2869

August 11–13
Annual Red Lake Nation Powwow
Red Lake, MN
(218) 679-3341

August 12
Annual Fiesta
Zia Pueblo, NM
(505) 867-3304

August 12–13
"Who Will Mourn for Logan"
Powwow Festival
Brooke Hills Park Rt 27
Wellsburg, WV
(304) 737-1207

August 12–13
Grand Portage Rendezvous
Grand Portage, MN
(218) 475-2277

August 12–13
Annual Traditional Powwow
Trinity Farm
Pataskala, OH
(614) 228-0460

August 12–13
Annual Mountain Springs Powwow
Mountain Springs Camping Resort
Sharletsville, PA
(215) 488-6859

August 12–13
Shishquwaning Annual Traditional
Powwow
Shishquwaning, ONT CANADA
(705) 283-3292

August 12–13
Deseronto Traditional Powwow
Deseronto, ONT CANADA
(613) 396-3424

August 12–13
Annual Leonard J. Pamp Memorial
Traditional Powwow
10½ mile Rd.
Burlington, MI
(616) 729-9434

August 14–20
"Three Fires Confederacy" Gathering
of the Anishabe
Ojibways of Garden River
Sault Ste. Marie, ONT CANADA
(705) 946-6300

August 15
Annual Cataldo Mission Pilgrimage
Old Mission
Cataldo, ID
Mass, Feast, Powwow
(208) 274-5871, Father Connally
(208) 682-3814, Mission Office

August 16–21
Annual Crow Fair Celebration,
Powwow & All Indian Rodeo
Crow Agency, MT
(406) 638-2601

August 17–20
Meeker Powwow
Meeker, CO
(303) 878-3403

August 18–19
Long Lake Cree Nation Powwow
Long Lake, AB CANADA
(403) 826-3333

August 18–20
Denioo Days
Fort Resolution, NWT CANADA
(403) 394-4556, Tausia Lal

August 18–20
Mille Lacs Annual Powwow
Powwow Grounds
Mille Lacs, MN
(612) 532-4181 ext. 810

August 18–20
Chief Looking Glass Powwow
Kamiah, ID
(208) 935-2502

August 18–20
Beardy's & Okemasis Powwow
Beardy's & Okemasis Reserve
Duck Lake, SASK CANADA
(306) 467-4523

3rd weekend August
Annual Kamloopa Powwow
Kamloops, BC CANADA
(604) 828-9700, 9819
(604) 372-8833, FAX

3rd weekend August
Twin Buttes Celebration & Powwow
Twin Buttes, ND
(701) 627-4781

3rd weekend August
Wazi Paha Oyate Festival
Kyle Fair & Powwow
Kyle, SD
(605) 455-2321

3rd weekend August
Grand Ronde Powwow
Grand Ronde, OR
(503) 879-2035, Dakota Whitecloud

3rd weekend August
Quinnetuqut
Haddam Meadows State Park
Haddam, CT
(203) 282-1404

3rd weekend August
White River Powwow
White River, SD
(605) 259-3670

3rd weekend August
Wakpala Powwow
Wakpala, SD
(701) 854-7231

3rd weekend August
AICI Annual Traditional Powwow
Boone County Fairgrounds
Lebanon, IN
(317) 482-3315, Nancy Malaterra
(317) 573-6319

3rd weekend August
Sandy Bay Annual Powwow
Sandy Bay Reserve, MAN CANADA
(204) 843-2603, Wilifred Spence

3rd weekend August
83rd Annual Chief Seattle Days
Suquamish, WA
(206) 598-3311

3rd weekend August
Klamath Treaty Days Celebration
Chiloquin, OR
(503) 783-2005, Marc McNair
(503) 783-2219, Roberta Tupper

3rd weekend August
Big River Annual Powwow
Debden, SASK CANADA
(306) 724-4700
(306) 724-2161, FAX

3rd weekend August
Sagamok Powwow
Sagamok, ONT CANADA
(705) 865-2942, Robert

3rd weekend August
Annual O-Sa-Wan Powwow
The Wulf Family Farm
(4 mi north of Rte 20 on Hwy 23)
Marengo, IL
(815) 568-7997

3rd weekend August
Annual NiMiWin Intertribal Powwow
Spirit Mountain Ski Resort
Duluth, MN
(218) 726-0130

3rd weekend August
Abenaki Nation & State Parks
Powwow
Salisbury State Park
Salisbury, MA
(508) 698-0766

3rd weekend August
Native American Indian Powwow
Indian Plaza, Rt 2 Mohawk Trail
Charlemont, MA
(413) 339-4096
(603) 882-6607, Little Bear
(vendor info)

3rd weekend August
Santa Fe Indian Market
Santa Fe Plaza & De Vargas Mall
Santa Fe, NM
(505) 983-5220

3rd weekend August
Annual Community Powwow
Central Park Horse Arena
Rio Linda, CA
(916) 441-0918

August 19
American Indian Hobbyest Powwow
Flying W Ranch
Kelletsville, PA
(412) 331-6129, Tom Mance

August 19–20
Celebrating Our Traditions Powwow
(north of Traverse City)
Peshawbestown, MI
(616) 271-3538 ext. 228

August 19–20
Mohegan Wigwam Powwow
Ft. Shantok Park (off Rte 32)
Uncasville, CT
(203) 848-9252

August 19–21
Annual Baltimore Indian Center
Powwow
5th Regiment Armory
113 South Broadway
Baltimore, MD
(410) 675-3535

August 23–26
Annual Competition Songhees
Powwow
(off Admirals Road)
Victoria, BC CANADA
(604) 388-3475, FAX
(604) 388-4517, Lillian Sam

August 24–27
Frog Lake First Nations Powwow
Frog Lake, AB CANADA
(403) 943-3737, work
(403) 943-2207, home
Angeline Bedand

August 24–27
Annual Ponca Powwow
Ponca City, OK
(405) 762-8104

August 25–27
Big Sky Powwow
Lewis & Clark Fairgrounds
Helena, MT
(800) 654-9085

August 25–27
Annual St. Croix Wild Rice Festival
St. Croix Tribal Center
Hertel, WI
(715) 349-2195

August 25–27
Abegweit Powwow
Panmure Provincial Park
Prince Edward Island, CANADA
(902) 892-5314

August 25–27
White Bear Annual Powwow
White Bear Reserve
(9 mi. north on Hwy 9)
SASK, CANADA
(306) 577-2406, Irene Lone Thunder

August 25–27
CT River Powwow
Farmington Polo Club
Farmington, CT
(203) 684-6984

August 25–27
Oil Discovery Celebration
American Legion Park
Poplar, MT
(416) 448-2546

August 25–27
Annual Rosebud Fair & All
Indian Rodeo
Rosebud, SD
(605) 747-2381

August 25–27
Yorkton Friendship Centre Powwow
Yorkton, SASK CANADA
(306) 782-2882

August 25–27
Chief Anaham Annual First Nations
Days Family Sports & Music
Celebration
Dave Means Park
Williams Lake, BC CANADA
(604) 394-4212

August 25–Sep 3
The Wandering Spirit Art Show
Canim Lake Band
100 Mile House, BC CANADA
(604) 397-2227
(604) 397-2769, FAX

August 25–September 4
Canim Lake Band Summer Art Show
100 Mile House, BC CANADA
(604) 397-2227
(604) 397-2769, FAX, Alex Archie

August 26
American Indian Festival
Market Square
Alexandria, VA
(703) 820-3397
(703) 883-4686

August 26
Native American Festival
Swiss Heritage Village
Berne, IN
(219) 589-8007

August 26
Annual Muskegon Traditional
Powwow
Hackley Park
Muskegon, MI
(616) 759-7016

August 26–27
Three Fires Homecoming Powwow
& Traditional Gathering
Hagersville, ONT CANADA
(905) 763-1133
(519) 445-4548

August 26–27
Annual Powwow
Windsor, ONT CANADA
(519) 948-8365

August 26–27
Annual Intertribal Powwow
Sonoma County Fairgrounds
Santa Rosa, CA
(707) 539-5352

4th weekend August
Annual Makah Days
Neah Bay, WA
(206) 645-2201

4th weekend August
Spokane Falls Northwest Indian
Encampment & Powwow
Riverfront Park
Spokane, WA
(509) 634-4711, Eddie Palmenteer

4th weekend August
Council of Three Rivers Powwow
Indian Center
200 Charles St.
Pittsburgh, PA
(412) 782-4457

4th weekend August
Annual Anishinabeg MomWeh
Powwow
Tri-Township School
Rapid River, MI
(906) 786-0556

4th weekend August
Red Scaffold Powwow
Red Scaffold, SD
(605) 964-4594

4th weekend August
Silver Buckle Rodeo & Sports Days
Ahtahkakoop Band Reserve
Shell Lake, AB CANADA
(306) 468-2326, Chuck or
Darrell Saskamoose

4th weekend August
Powwow
Wabigoon, ONT CANADA
(807) 938-6504

4th weekend August
Cherry Creek Powwow
Cherry Creek, SD
(605) 964-2542

4th weekend August
Native American Heritage Days
Ft. Laramie Treaty Days
Ft. Laramie National Historic
Site, WY
(307) 837-2221, Gary Candelaria
(307) 261-7511, Rod Sanders

4th weekend August
Appalachian State University
Annual Powwow
Varsity Gym
Boone, NC
(704) 256-2724, Darin Grant
(704) 265-3104, Shawn Watkins

4th weekend August
Seminole Intertribal Powwow
Seminole Municipal Park
Seminole, OK
(405) 257-6573

4th weekend August
Delaware Indian Heritage Festival
& Powwow
Tuscarawas County Fairground
Dover, OH
(216) 343-1047

4th weekend August
Nansemond Indian Tribal Festival
Lonestart Lodge
Chuckaluck, VA
(804) 483-4236

4th weekend August
Lake Quinsigamond Powwow
Lake Park Lake Ave.
Worchester, MA
(508) 832-8173

4th weekend August
MCNAA Apsqe Powwow
Johnson Middle School Field
Robbins Rd. (off Rte 27)
Walpole, MA
(617) 884-4227

4th weekend August
Annual South Charleston Powwow
Oakesfield Stadium
South Charleston, WV
(501) 253-7364

September (TBA)
Annual Snolqualmie Tribal
Gathering & Powwow
Snoqualmie Middle School
North Bend, WA
(206) 333-6551

September (TBA)
Annual World Championship Stick
Game Tournament
Powwow Grounds
Arlee, MT
(406) 745-2951
(406) 726-3115

September 1–3
Dancing For The Big Rock
Burns Park
N. Little Rock, AR
(800) 228-0936

September 2
Annual Nansemond Indian Tribal
Festival
Lone Star Lodge
Chuckatuck, VA
(804) 485-9809, William Langston
(804) 483-4236, Sandy McCready

September 2–3
Mornuinntown Powwow
Highgate Rd.
Morauian Reserve, ONT CANADA
(519) 692-3936

September 2–3
Morariantown Delaware Powwow
Thamesville, ONT CANADA
(519) 692-3836

September 2–3
Annual Northern Cherokee Powwow
Blue Grass Festival Park
Clinton, MO
(816) 694-3656

September 2-3
Iroquois Indian Festival
Iroquois Indian Museum
Howes Cave, NY
(518) 296-8949

September 2-4
Annual First Light Powwow
Powwow Grounds
Athens, ME
(207) 654-3981

1st weekend September
Annual California All Indian Market
Mission
San Juan Bautista, CA
(408) 623-2379, Sonny or
Elaine Reyna

1st weekend September
Michinemackinoug Powwow
Marquette Museum
St. Ignace, MI
(906) 643-8173, Shirley Brown

1st weekend September
Annual Indian Summer
Festival of the Arts
Sechelt, BC CANADA
(604) 885-4673

Labor Day weekend
Labor Day Weekend Celebration
Powwow Grounds
Black River Falls, WI
(608) 254-4404

Labor Day weekend
Midwest's Ultimate Powwow
(next to Mequakie Bingo-Casino,
5 mi. west of Toma, IA)
(800) 728-4263

Labor Day weekend
Numaga Indian Days Celebration
Reno Sparks Indian Colony
Reno, NV
(702) 324-4600, Dan Thayer

Labor Day weekend
White Mountain Apache Tribal
Fair & Rodeo
White River, AZ
(602) 383-4621

Labor Day weekend
Annual Cheyenne River Sioux Fair
& Rodeo
Eagle Butte, SD
(605) 964-4426

Labor Day weekend
Cherokee National Holiday &
Powwow
Tahlequah, OK
(918) 456-0671

Labor Day weekend
Cheyenne & Arapaho Powwow
Colony Park
Colony, OK
(405) 323-3542, 4877

Labor Day weekend
Wee-Gitchie-Ne-Me-E Dim Powwow
Leech Lake Reservation
Cass Lake, MN
(218) 335-8289

Labor Day weekend
Puyallup Tribe's Annual Powwow
& Salmon Bake
2002 E. 28th (Exit 135 off I-5)
Tacoma, WA

Labor Day weekend
Indian Nations of Kansas Powwow
Lake Shawnee
Topeka, KS
(913) 272-5489, Mike Ballard
(913) 478-4804

Labor Day weekend
Eufaula Powwow
Eastside Park
Eufaula, OK
(918) 689-5066

Labor Day weekend
Spokane Tribal Fair & Powwow
Wellpinit, WA
(509) 258-4060

Labor Day weekend
Awokpamani Omaha Traditional
Powwow
Poplar, MT
(406) 768-5155

Labor Day weekend
Kla How Ya Days
Tulalip Tribal Grounds
Marysville, WA
(206) 653-4585

Labor Day weekend
Pyramid Lake Rodeo & Elders Day
Nixon, NV
(702) 574-0140

Labor Day weekend
Stockton California Indian Days
Edison High School
(209) 952-6931

Labor Day weekend
Camp Pollock Powwow
Sacramento, CA
(916) 363-2836, Jeph Downing

Labor Day weekend
Labor Day Powwow
Ethete, WY
(307) 856-6117

Labor Day weekend
Turtle Mountain Ni-Mi-Win
Celebration
Dunseith, ND
(701) 477-6451 ext. 126

Labor Day weekend
Shoshone Indian Fair
Fort Washakie, WY
(307) 323-9423

Labor Day weekend
Annual White Buffalo Council
Powwow
Tallbull Memorial Park
(in Daniels Park
South of Denver, CO)
(303) 936-2688, John Emhula

Labor Day weekend
Shinnecock Powwow
Shinnecock Reservation
Southhampton, NY
(516) 283-6143

Labor Day weekend
Nakota Labor Day Classic Powwow
Morley, AB CANADA
(403) 881-3949

Labor Day weekend
Choctaw Nation Labor Day Festival
Tribal Grounds
Tushkahoma, OK
(405) 924-8280, Nancy Belvin

Labor Day weekend
KEE-BOON-MEIN-KAA Powwow
St. Patricks Park
South Bend, IN
(616) 782-6323

Labor Day weekend
Labor Day weekend Powwow
Caddo Tribal Grounds
(5 mi. east of Binger, OK)
(405) 656-2344

Labor Day weekend
Ottawa Powwow & Celebration
Adowe Park
Miami, OK
(918) 540-1536

Labor Day weekend
Bull Creek Traditional Powwow
(17½ miles east of Winner
on Hwy 44 by Dixon, SD)
(506) 747-2381

Labor Day weekend
Tecumseh Lodge Annual Powwow
Tipton 4-H Grounds
Tipton, IN
(317) 773-4233
(317) 675-4353, Barbara Scott
or John Ellis

Labor Day weekend
Omaha Urban Indian Powwow
NP Dodge Park
Omaha, NE
(402) 451-8026, Mike

Labor Day weekend
Pacific Coast Indian Club Annual
Powwow
Barona Indian Reservation
Lakeside, CA
(619) 484-4784, Sammie Dominquez
(619) 443-6910, Boxie Phoenix

Labor Day weekend
Mountain Eagle Indian Fest
Hunter Mountain
Hunter, NY
(315) 363-1315

Labor Day weekend
Annual Arkansas Festival
Eureka, AR
(501) 253-7364

Labor Day weekend
Annual Seneca Intertribal Powwow
Kenneth Young Gallery
Lawtons, NY
(716) 337-3946

Labor Day weekend
Indian Arts & Crafts Market
Santo Domingo Pueblo, NM
(505) 465-2812

Labor Day weekend
Annual AIM Powwow
Fort Snelling, MN
(612) 724-3129

Labor Day weekend
Labor Day Powwow
C B Smith Park
Ft. Lauderdale, FL
(305) 476-7672

Labor Day weekend
Annual Powwow
Camp Calumet
Lake Ossipee, NH
(203) 643-5116, Quiet Bear
(603) 647-5374, Chuck or Cassandra

Labor Day weekend
FICA Labor Day Weekend Powwow
Pembroke Pines, FL
(305) 476-7672, Joe Braun

Labor Day weekend
LIHA Powwow
Sanborton, NH
(603) 783-9922

Labor Day weekend
Lebanon Powwow
Riverpark
Lebanon, OR
(503) 258-6193, White Raven

Labor Day weekend
Native American Indian Powwow
Indian Plaza
Rte 2 Mohawk Trail
Charlemont, MA
(413) 339-4096
(603) 882-6607, Little Bear
Vendor Info

Labor Day
Annual Labor Day Traditional
Powwow
Helmet Haus
Grove City, OH
(614) 433-6120

Labor Day
Protect the Earth Powwow
HTE Powwow Grounds
Lac Courte, WI
(715) 766-2725

September 5
Five Civilized Tribes Masters
Art Show
Muskogee, OK
(918) 683-1701, Lynn Thornley

September 6–10
Annual Navajo Nation Fair
Window Rock, AZ
(602) 871-6478

September 8–9
Annual Wacipi For Lakota Oyate
6946 Princeton
Glendale Rd. (Rt. 747)
Cincinnati, OH
(513) 745-0908, Art Wasson
(513) 844-1059, Lorie Lightfield

September 8–10
Annual World Championship Stick
Game Tournament
Powwow Grounds
Arlee, MT
(406) 745-2951 or 726-3115

September 8–10
Six Nations Fall Fair & Powwow
Ohsweken, ONT CANADA
(519) 445-2956, Glenda Porter

September 8–10
Indian Summer Powwow
Henry Maier Festival Park
Milwaukee, WI
(414) 774-7119

September 8–22
Annual Lawrence Indian Arts Show
Haskell Indian Junior College
Lawrence, KS
(913) 864-4245, Maria Martin

September 9
Annual WVNAC/NASC Intertribal
Powwow
West Virginia University Montainlair
Morgantown, WV
(304) 363-8151, Sharon Huskin
(304) 449-1790, Linds Karus

September 9
Annual Bristow Powwow
Bristow, OK

September 9–10
Hawk Flight Powwow
Perris, CA
(714) 492-5416

Weekend after Labor Day
Trail of Tears Intertribal Powwow
Recreation Complex
Hopkinsville, KY
(502) 886-8033, Beverly Baker

2nd weekend September
Indian Heritage Festival & Powwow
Martinsville, VA
(703) 666-8600, Mabel Peters

2nd weekend September
Annual Raccoon Mountain
Indian Festival
Chattanooga, TN
(706) 735-6275, Chipa Wolf

2nd weekend September
Coharie Powwow
Clinton, NC
(919) 564-6909

2nd weekend September
Annual Championship Powwow
Traders Village
2606 Mayfield Road
Grand Prairie, TX
(214) 647-2331, Doug Beich

2nd weekend September
United Tribes International
Championship Powwow
United Tribes Technical College
Bismark, ND
(701) 255-3285 ext. 360

2nd weekend September
United Tribes Indian Art Exposition
Bismark Civic Center
601 E. Sweet Ave.
Bismark, ND
(701) 255-3285 ext. 360

2nd weekend September
Annual Frontier Day & Powwow
Longs Landing
Council Bluffs, IA
(712) 325-1770

2nd weekend September
Annual Southern Ute Tribal
Fair & Powwow
Sky Ute Downs
Ignacio, CO
(800) 772-1236, Alden Naranip

2nd weekend September
Annual Indian Summer Festival
7th & Alma
San Jose, CA
(408) 971-9622

2nd weekend September
Seminole Nation Days Powwow
Miccosukee Mission
Wewoka, OK
(405) 257-6287

2nd weekend September
Annual Moberly Powwow
Rothwell Park
Moberly, MO
(816) 263-3009

2nd weekend September
Powwow
White Dog, ONT CANADA
(807) 927-2068

2nd weekend September
Annual Sycuan Powwow
El Cajon, CA
(619) 445-0109

2nd weekend September
Shakopee Mdewakanton Powwow
Mystic Lake Casino
Prior Lake, MN
(612) 445-8900

2nd weekend September
Annual California Indian Council
Foundation Powwow
Borchard Park
Newberry, CA
(310) 457-5496

2nd weekend September
Lenni Lenape Festival
Round Valley Youth Center
Lebanon, NJ
(215) 797-2121

2nd weekend September
Annual Nanticoke Indian Powwow
Millsboro, DE
(302) 945-3400

2nd weekend September
Maidu-Miwok Big Time Powwow
Auburn, CA
(916) 885-2752 or 885-3701

2nd weekend September
Indian Ceremonials Harvest Dances
& Feast
Starved Rock, IL
(815) 667-4976

2nd weekend September
Grand Valley American Indian
Lodge Powwow
Riverside Park
Grand Rapids, MI
(616) 791-4014, Ike Peters

2nd weekend September
Nipmuc Council of
Chaubunagungamaugg
Annual Powwow
Greenbriar Park
Oxford, MA
(508) 943-4569

2nd weekend September
Annual Iroquois Arts Festival
Duchess County Fairgrounds
Rhinebeck, NY
(914) 758-6526, Tina

2nd weekend September
Annual Kit-Han-Ne Powwow
Country Paradise Park
West Kittanning, PA
(412) 548-8823

2nd weekend September
Native American Apprecitation Day
Cumberland County Fairgrounds
Cumberland, ME
(207) 339-9520

2nd weekend September
Chief Red Blanket Memorial Powwow
Plug Pond
Haverhill, MA
(617) 884-4227

2nd weekend September
AISSI Annual Festival & Powwow
Brandywine, MD
(301) 372-1932

2nd weekend September
Moon of the Ripe Corn Powwow
Bluffton, OH
(419) 648-2388

September 9–10
Seneca Indian Fall Festival
The Saylor Bldg.
Irvine, NY
(716) 532-5777

September 9–10
Annual Kiser Lake Powwow
Kiser Lake Gun Club
St. Paris, OH
(513) 663-4345

September 9–10
Hawks Flight Intertribal Powwow
Perris, CA
(909) 923-3553, Chuck Reddich

September 9–16
Pine Nut Festival
Walker River Paiute Reservation
Schurz, NV
(702) 773-2306

September 10
Annual Trade Feast
Miwok Park
Novato, CA
(415) 897-4064

September 13–16
Pendleton Roundup
Pendleton, OR
(800) 524-2984

September 14–16
Guilford Native American Association
Cultural Festival & Powwow
Castle McCulloch
Jamestown, NC
(919) 273-8686

September 14–16
Annual Children's Powwow
Hannahville Reservation
Wilson, MI
(800) 682-6040

September 14–17
Schemitzun
Hartford Civic Center
Hartford, CT
(203) 536-2681

September 15
Gojiiya Feast Day
Jicarilla Apache Reservation
Dulce, NM
(505) 759-3242

September 15–16
Oklahoma Indian Art Market
Town Square
Okmulgee, OK
(918) 756-2324

September 15–16
Cabin Creek Powwow
Village Park
Langley, OK
(918) 782-3449

3rd weekend September
Choctaw Powwow
Arrowhead State Park
Canadian, OK
(405) 924-8280

3rd weekend September
American Indian Cultural Festival
Pismo Beach, CA
(408) 623-2379, Sonny or
Elaine Reyna

3rd weekend September
Annual Salmon Homecoming
Celebration
The Seattle Aquarium
Seattle, WA
(206) 386-4300

3rd weekend September
Indian Summer Festival
Bartlesville, OK
(918) 336-2787

3rd weekend September
GLICA Maple Syrup Festival
Tyngsborough State Forest
Tyngsborough, MA
(508) 453-7182, Frank Greenhalgh

3rd weekend September
Ogden Powwow
Fort Buenaventura State Park
Ogden, UT
(801) 621-4414 or 392-1638

3rd weekend September
Annual Honoring of the Youth
Powwow
Custom House Plaza
Monterey, CA
(408) 375-0095, Donna or White Bear

3rd weekend September
Flin Flon Native Heritage Festival
& Powwow
Flin Flon, MAN CANADA
(204) 687-3900, Leslie or Helen

3rd weekend September
Annual Ameridan Indian Days
Fort Zumwalt Park
O'Fallon, MO
(314) 272-1964

3rd weekend September
Annual Choctaw Intertribal
Association Pittsburg County
Powwow
Fairgrounds
(west of McAlester, OK)
(918) 423-2667, Dena Cantrell

3rd weekend September
Elbow River Intertribal Day Powwow
Max Bell Arena
Calgary, AB CANADA
(403) 264-1155, Wayne Courchene

3rd weekend after Labor Day
Council Tree Powwow & Native
American Art Show
Delta, CO
(800) 436-3041, Wilma Erven

3rd Saturday September
TIHA Powwow
Llano City Park
Llano, TX
(817) 498-2873

September 15–17
Great Mohican Indian Powwow
& Rendezvous
Londonville, OH
(419) 994-4008, Allen Combs
(419) 994-4097, Doug Shannon

September 15–17
GLICA & Bedford VA Hospital
Powwow
200 Springs Rd.
Bedford, MA
(508) 453-7182

September 15–17
Treaty Four Powwow
Fort Qu'Appelle Rexentre
Fort Qu'Appelle, SASK CANADA
(306) 332-8236
(306) 332-1874, Judy Pinay

September 16
Annual Santa Rosa Junior College
Powwow
Medicino Lawn Area
Santa Rosa, CA
(707) 528-6170

September 16
Keepers of the Dream Powwow
Lake County Fairgrounds
Crown Point, IN
(219) 663-4889

September 16
Festival of San Jose De Los Lagunas
& Arts Crafts Fair
Old Laguna Pueblo, NM
(505) 552-6654

September 16–17
Indian Summer Powwow
Brian Timmis Park
Hamilton, ONT CANADA
(519) 751-8082
Anna Marie Madahbee

September 16–17
Kentuckian Powwow
Powwow Grounds
Louisville, KY
(502) 637-2529

September 16–17
KNASG Annual Powwow
Louisville Zoo
Louisville, KY
(502) 634-8374

September 16–17
Ramapough Four Winds Powwow
Thomas Bull Memorial Park
Goshen, NY
(201) 529-1171

September 16–17
Annual NACC Powwow
Dome Arena
Rochester, NY
(716) 346-3939

September 16–17
Brighten The Vision Powwow
The Dome Center
Henrietta, NY
(716) 482-1100

September 22–24
Indian Summer Festival & Powwow
Victor, NY
(716) 924-5848

September 22–24
Dancing Rabbit Creek
Commemoration
Tribal Grounds
Mt. Vernon, AL

September 22–24
Winfield Annual Powwow
Winfield, TX
(615) 569-4960

September 22–24
Eastern Plains Festival
Leavenworth County Fairgrounds
Tonganoxie, KS
(913) 863-2312

September 22–24
New Jersey American Indian Center's
Fall Powwow
Warren Road, NJ
(908) 525-0066

September 23
California Indian Day Celebration
Auberry, CA
(209) 855-8523

September 23
Sapulpa Indian Days Powwow
Creek County Fairgrounds
Sapulpa, OK
(918) 224-9322

September 23
Northern Plains Powwow
Elmer Center
Sioux Falls, SD
(800) 658-4797

September 23–24
Wawaskinga Annual Competition
Powwow
Whitefish River First Nation
Birch Island, ONT CANADA
(705) 285-0210, Kiki McGregor
(705) 285-0177, Leon or
Patty Lightening

September 23–24
Curve Lake Annual Powwow
Curve Lake, ONT CANADA
(705) 675-8045

September 23–24
Millers Fall Harvest
Millers Tree Farm
Idaville, IN
(219) 278-7021

September 23–24
Lake Reba Powwow
Richmond, KY
(614) 377-2565

September 23–24
University of Massachusetts
Intertribal Powwow
Campus Center Pond
Amherst, MA
(413) 545-4932

September 23–24
Grandma's Annual Powwow
Frank Liske Park
Harrisburg, NC
(704) 282-1030

4th weekend September
National Indian Days
Pavillion
White Swan, WA
(508) 865-2800

4th weekend September
Kituwah
The American Indian National Arts
Exposition & Powwow
Asheville Civic Center
Asheville, NC
(704) 252-3880, Gail Gomez

4th weekend September
Fall Festival & Intertribal Contest
Powwow
Sioux City American Indian Center
Sioux City Convention Center
Sioux City, IA
(712) 255-8957

4th weekend September
Chicahominy Festival
Tribal Center
Providence, VA
(804) 829-2261

4th weekend September
Annual Middle Tennessee Powwow
Wilson County Fairgrounds
Lebanon, TN
(615) 444-4899, Don Yahola

4th weekend September
California Indian Days
Placer County Fairgrounds
Roseville, CA
(916) 920-0285, Loranda Sanchez

4th weekend September
Annual Northern Plains Tribal
Arts Show
Sioux Falls, SD
(800) 658-4797

4th weekend September
Annual Michigan Celebration
Field House
University of Michigan–Dearborn
Detroit, MI
(313) 593-5390

4th weekend September
Traditional Gathering
Monmouth Battlefield Park
Cliffwood Beach, NJ
(908) 390-1642

4th weekend September
Native Heritage Celebration
Porterville Fairgrounds
Porterville, CA
(209) 784-4509

4th weekend September
Annual California Indian Days
Celebration
Balboa Park
San Diego, CA
(619) 281-5964

4th weekend September
The Mounds Traditional Powwow
Starin Park
Whitewater, WI
(414) 473-7748

4th weekend September
Turning Leaves Festival
Old Indian Festival Area
Thornton, IN
(317) 436-2202

4th weekend September
Annual Council of Three Rivers
Powwow
Dorceyville, PA
(412) 782-4457

4th weekend September
Annual Western Michigan State
University Powwow
Wings Stadium
Kalamazoo, MI
(616) 375-5376, Phil Francisco
(616) 387-3390, David Knapp

4th weekend September
Eagle Wing Press
Black Rock State Park
Watertown, CT
(203) 729-0035

4th weekend September
Baxoje Fall Powwow
White Cloud, KS
(913) 595-3367

September 24
Great Swamp Massacre Powwow
Tribal Grounds
Kingston, RI
(401) 364-1100

September 24–25
Council of 3 Rivers
Singing Wind Sight–Dorceyville
Pittsburgh, PA
(412) 782-4457

September 29–October 1
Day of the Wolf Intertribal Powwow
Bullitt County Fairgrounds
(25 mi. south of Louisville, KY)
(502) 955-7965, Ida Creighton

September 29–October 1
American Indian Exposition & Sale
San Mateo Expo Center
Oak Hall
San Mateo, CA
(209) 221-4355

September 30
Annual Powwow
West Valley College
Sarasota, CA
(408) 370-6954, Celia Paz Cavanaugh
(408) 741-2025, Campus Center

September 30–October 1
Annual Native Cultural Festival
Vanier College Sports Complex
Montreal, QUE CANADA
(514) 937-5338, Jennifer La Billois

September 30–October 1
Indian Trail Powwow
Indian Trail, NC
(704) 331-4818

September 30–October 1
Annual American Indian Music
Festival & Powwow
Crissy Field
San Francisco, CA

October (date TBA)
Native American Powwow
Hagerstown, MD
(410) 675-3535, Barry Richardson

October (date TBA)
"Lady of the Drum" Memorial
Mini Powwow
Skagit Valley College
Mt. Vernon, WA
(206) 428-1261, Brenda Baker

Month of October
Annual Cherokee Heritage Art Show
Museum of the Cherokee Indian
Cherokee, NC
(704) 497-3481

October 1
Narragansett Nation Annual
Fall Festival
Indian Long House Rte. 2
Charlestown, RI
(401) 364-1100

1st weekend October
Coastal Bend Council Intertribal
Powwow
Memorial Coliseum
Corpus Cristi, TX
(512) 883-9980

1st weekend October
Wind, Rain & Fire Powwow
Rising Sun Campground
Monterey, IN
(219) 542-4780

1st weekend October
Shiprock Navajo Fair
Shiprock, NM
(505) 368-5108

1st weekend October
Two Rivers Native Film & Video
Festival
Holiday Inn Metrodome
Minneapolis, MN
(612) 292-3221, Juanita Espinosa

1st weekend October
Homecoming Powwow
American Indianist Society
Camp Marshall (off Rte 31)
Spencer, MA
(508) 852-6271

1st weekend October
Canadian Thanksgiving Powwow
Mt. Currie, BC CANADA
(604) 894-6867

1st weekend October
Okiciyapo Festival
Lawrenceville, GA
(404) 921-4840, Paul Eddy

448 / Appendix

1st weekend October
Chickasaw Nation Annual Festival
& Rodeo
Pennington Creek Park
Tishomingo, OK
(405) 371-2175

1st weekend October
Annual Mesa College Powwow
San Diego, CA
(619) 627-2706, Pierre Romero

1st weekend October
Cherokees of Georgia Gathering
& Powwow
Tribal Grounds
St. George, GA
(904) 275-2953

1st weekend October
Day of the Wolf Annual Intertribal
Powwow
Bullit County Fairgrounds,
(next to I-65, 25 miles south of
Louisville, KY, exit 112)
(502) 955-7965, Ida Creighton

1st weekend October
Wolf Moon Powwow
New location TBA
Lucerne Valley, CA
(619) 248-7818, after 8 p.m.

1st weekend October
Dighton Intertribal Council Powwow
Dighton, MA
(508) 669-5008

1st weekend October
Annual Native Cultural Festival
Westmont High School
Montreal, QUE CANADA
(514) 937-5338, Dolores Andre or
Pierre Thibeault

1st weekend October
Annual Powwow
Roundup Club Arena
Nowata, OK
(918) 273-2301

1st weekend October
Indian Summer Powwow
Camden, AR
(501) 231-4205

1st weekend October
Runnin Water Powwow
Lock & Dam Park
Rome, GA
(706) 232-1714, Frank Blair
after 5 p.m.
(404) 295-4382, Tommy or
Bonnie Cox

1st weekend October
Annual Fall Festival
Fairmont Park
Philadelphia, PA
(215) 574-9020, Yvonne Bernardino

1st weekend October
Annual Western Michigan University
Powwow
Kalamazoo, MI
(616) 349-5387

1st Saturday October
Monacan Indian Tribal Bazaar
St Paul's Episcopal Church
Amherst, VA
(804) 946-2531

1st Saturday October
Annual West Valley College Powwow
Learning Services Lawn Area
14000 Fruitvale Ave.
Saratoga, CA
(408) 867-2200 ext. 3642, Diana

1st Saturday October
Mason School Powwow
2812 N. Madison
Tacoma, WA
(206) 596-1139

October 6–7
Cumberland Native American
Powwow
Memorial Indoor Arena
Fayetteville, NC
(910) 483-8442

October 6–7
Fayetteville Powwow
Memorial Arena
Fayetteville, NC
(910) 483-8442

October 6–9
Sovereignty Celebration
Humanities Center
Red Lake, MN
(218) 679-3341

October 7–8
Hutash Harvest Festival
San Marcos Campground
Santa Barbara, CA
(805) 965-4688

October 7
Annual Intertribal Powwows
United Indians of Virginia
Chicahominy Reservation
Providence Forge, VA
(804) 865-6814, Raymond Adams

October 7
Salem Area Fall Powwow
Polk County Fairgrounds
Rickreal, OR
(12 mi. west of Salem)
(503) 623-8971, Cookie Spencer

October 7
Providence Intertribal Social
Trinity United Methodist Church
375 Broad St.
Providence, RI
(401) 621-2312

October 7
Harvest Moon Festival & Potluck
Nipmuck Reservation
Webster, MA
(508) 852-6271

2nd weekend October
Annual Native American Powwow
Pee Dee Trade School
Allensville Rd.
McCoil, SC
(803) 523-5269 or 523-6790

2nd weekend October
Kiowa Black Leggings Ceremonial
Indian City USA
Anadarko, OK
(405) 247-3987

2nd weekend October
Spirit of the People Powwow
Myriad Convention Center
Oklahoma City, OK
(800) 375-3737

2nd weekend October
Annual Intertribal Arts Experience
Hara Arena
Dayton, OH
(513) 376-4358, Marcy Elter or
Jan Abel

2nd weekend October
First Nations Cultural Festival
Big Four Building
Calgary Stampede Grounds
Calgary, AB CANADA
(403) 273-9855

2nd weekend October
Bay Area Indian Alliance Powwow
Kaiser Convention Arena
Oakland, CA
(510) 452-1235

2nd weekend October
Harvest Festival
Greater Lowell Indian Cultural
Association
Tyngsborough State Forest
Tyngsborough, MA
(508) 453-7182

2nd weekend October
Annual Intertribal Powwow
Thomas Square
Honolulu, HI
(808) 734-5171, evening
(808) 841-7357, day

2nd weekend October
American Indian Gathering
College Dome Community College
of Beaver County
Monaca, PA
(412) 775-8561, Alex Gladis

2nd weekend October
Annual Juried Arts Festival
Rancocas Reservation
Rancocas, NJ
(609) 261-4747

2nd weekend October
Rama's Annual Thanksgiving
Powwow
Rama/Chippewayan First Nation
Reserve
Rama, ONT CANADA
(705) 325-3611, George St. Germaine

2nd weekend October
Native American Indian Powwow
Indian Plaza
Rte 2 Mohawk Trail
Charlemont, MA
(413) 339-4096
(603) 882-6607, Little Bear
Vendor Info

2nd weekend October
Annual Chumash Intertribal Powwow
Santa Ynez, CA
(805) 686-1416 or 934-5233

2nd weekend October
A Time of Thanksgiving
Lenni Lenape Historical Society
Allentown, PA
(215) 797-2121

October 7–8
Nikaneet Annual Powwow
Maple Creek Arena
Maple Creek, SASK CANADA
(306) 662-7513, Glen Oake

October 8
3rd Annual Indigenous People's Day
Powwow & Indian Market
Martin Luther King Park
Berkeley, CA
(510) 452-1235

October 8–10
Paucatuck Eastern Pequot Harvest
Moon Powwow
CT River Powwow Association
Highland Orchards Resort Park
(Junction of I-95 & Rte 49)
CT (location TBA)
(203) 684-6984, Geoff or Elaine

October 8–16
Native American Student Art Show
The Heard Museum
Phoenix, AZ
(602) 252-8840

October 13–14
Annual Native American Heritage
Festival & Powwow
Roanoke, VA
(703) 342-5714, days
(703) 362-1833, evenings, Britt Rossie

October 13–14
Waccamaw–Sioan Powwow
Buckhead Bolton, NC
(919) 655-8778

October 13–15
NAIA Fall Powwow & Festival
Dupont–Tyler Middle School
(8 mi. east of Nashville, TN)
(615) 726-0806, Georgia Magpie

October 13–15
American Indian Exposition & Sale
Monterey Fairgrounds
Salinas Room
Monterey, CA
(209) 221-4355

October 13–15
Four Nations Powwow
Lewiston, ID
(208) 843-2003

October 13–16
Tahlequah Indian Territory Festival
Tahlequah, OK
(918) 456-3742

October 14–15
Annual Indian Gathering
Community College of Beaver
County
Mongca, PA
(412) 775-8561, Alex Gladis
(412) 774-9098, Georgem Tew

October 14–15
Indian Art Show & Sale
Arrowhead Trading Post
Catoosa, OK
(918) 266-3663

October 14–15
Reservation Wide Championship
War Dancing
Community Center
St. Ignatius, MT
(406) 883-3313, home
(406) 745-3523, work, Pat Pierre

October 14–15
Battle of Big Cabin Creek Powwow
Langley, OK

October 14–15
Hawks Flight Intertribal Powwow
Perris, CA
(909) 923-3553, Chuck Reddich

October 14–16
Annual Hagerstown Powwow
Hagerstown Junior College
Hagerstown, MD
(410) 788-0254

October 15
Five Civilized Tribes Masters Show
Five Civilized Tribes Museum
Muskogee, OK
(918) 683-1701

October 15–16
Fort Mojave Days
Needles, CA
(602) 326-4591, Iris Jackson

October 15–16
Fire Hawk & Blue Sky
Annual Powwow
Wolf Den One Jct. 44 & 101
Pomfret, CT
(203) 429-2668

October 15–16
Annual Apigsigtag Ta Powwow
University of New Hampshire
Durham, NH
(603) 862-2050

3rd weekend October
Fall Festival & Powwow
Native American Indian Association
of Tennessee
Hermitage Landing
Nashville, TN
(615) 726-0806

3rd weekend October
Apache Days
Globe, AZ
(602) 425-4495

3rd weekend October
Mesa Powwow
Mesa Southwest Museum
Mesa, AZ
(602) 644-2230

October 20–21
Annual South Texas Powwow
Palmer Pavillion
McAllen, TX (Way South)
(210) 686-6696, Robert Soto

October 20–21
Annual All-Native Festival
Edmonton, AB CANADA
(403) 479-1980

October 20–21
Meherrin Indian Tribe Powwow
Winton, NC
(919) 348-2166

October 20–22
Las Vegas Indian Days
Community College–Pecos
& Cheyenne
North Las Vegas, NV
(702) 642-6674, Ms. Squaw

October 20–22
American Indian Art Festival
& Market
Dallas, TX
(214) 891-9640

October 21
Thunderbird American Indian
Dancers Powwow
McBurney YMCA
215 W. 23rd St.
New York, NY
(201) 587-9633, Louis Mofsie

October 21
Annual Los Medanos College
Pittsburg, CA
(510) 706-2303, Zoe Watkins

October 21
NASA Powwow
University of Arkansas
Fayetteville, AR

October 21
Akdar Shrine Fall Powwow
Akdar Shrine
21st St.
Tulsa, OK

October 21–22
Best of the Best Powwow & Native
American Arts Festival
Rockland Community College
Field House
Suffern, NY
(914) 357-8424, Howard Glinsky
(704) 497-3370, General Grant

October 21–22
6th Annual AITA Powwow
Tribal Center
Toledo, OH
(419) 249-2601

October 26
American Indian Heritage Powwow
Univerity of Illinois
Chicago, IL
(312) 996-4515

4th weekend October
Comanche War Dance & Powwow
Cache, OK

October 27–29
Amigos Social Powwow
Amigos Complex
Tucson, AZ
(602) 622-4900

October 27–29
Mid Columbia River Powwow
Celilo, OR
(503) 298-1559

October 27–29
National Indian Days Powwow
Irataba Hall Manatoba Park
Parker, AZ
(602) 669-9211 or 669-2357

Nov. 1 thru Dec. 31
Stewart Museum Indian Arts & Crafts
Exhibition and Sale
Carson City, NV
(702) 882-1808

Nov. 3–5
American Indian Exposition & Sale
The Terrace
Austin, TX
(209) 221-4355

Nov. 4
Pepewarr Powwow
Armory
Elm St.
Middleboro, MA
(617) 884-4227

Nov. 4
American Indian Heritage Festival
Tony Burger Center
3200 Jones Road
Austin, TX
(512) 414-3849

1st weekend Nov.
Manitoba First Nations Powwow
Winnapeg Arena
Winnapeg, MAN CANADA
(204) 857-4381

1st weekend Nov.
Pima Maricopa Art Festival
Sacaton, AZ
(602) 963-4323

1st weekend Nov.
Carmel American Indian Festival
Carmel, CA
(408) 623-2379, Sonny or
Elaine Reyna

1st weekend Nov.
Annual Okinapi Traditional Powwow
Enoch Recreation Centre
AB CANADA
(403) 455-3242, Francis Bad Eagle

1st weekend Nov.
Annual AIA Orland Powwow
Fairgrounds (on West Hwy 50)
Orlando, FL
(407) 862-9676, Melissa McRoe

1st Saturday Nov.
Mason School Powwow
2812 N. Madison
Tacoma, WA
(206) 596-1139

1st weekend Nov.
Annual Veterans Powwow
Reckard Armory
University of Maryland–College Park
College Park, MD
(301) 540-0966, Linda Tsonetokoy
(301) 762-1572, Delia Reeves

1st weekend Nov.
Annual Eastern Michigan Powwow
Bowen Field House
Ypsilanti, MI
(313) 487-2377

1st weekend Nov.
Oglewanagi Powwow
Chapparell's Bingo Hall
Akron, OH
(216) 225-3416, Donna Seward

Nov. 8–12
Annual American Indian
Film Festival
San Francisco, CA
(415) 554-0525, Michael Smith

Nov. 10
Veterans Powwow
LCO Ojibwe Reservation
Hayward, WI
(715) 799-5166 or 799-5100
Luke Beauprey

Nov. 10
Pawnee Veterans Day Dance
Round House
Pawnee, OK
(918) 762-3962

Nov. 10
Veterans Gathering
Round House
Pawnee, OK
(918) 762-3624

Nov. 10–11
American Indian Exposition & Sale
Airport Convention Center
San Antonio, TX
(209) 221-4355

Nov. 10–12
Red Nations Powwow
Loos Stadium Field House
Dallas, TX
(214) 263-4039

Nov. 10–12
North Bay Clan Fall Powwow
Lower Creek Muscogee Tribe
3733 Co. Rd. 2321
Lynn Haven, FL
(904) 763-6717, Chief Woods
(904) 265-3345

Veterans Day
Veterans Day Powwow
Owyhee, NV
(702) 757-3161

Veterans Day
Veterans Day Powwow
Chemawa Indian School
Salem, OR
(503) 399-5721

Veterans Day
Veterans Day Powwow
Blue Earth Indian Nation
Council Bluffs, IA
(712) 325-1770

Nov. 11
National Museum of the American
Indian Powwow
City College, Manhattan Borough
Community College
Manhattan, NY
(212) 598-0100 ext. 29

Nov. 11
Restoration Celebration
Siletz, OR
(503) 444-2532, Karen Bell

Nov. 11
Veterans Powwow
DQ University
Davis, CA
(916) 758-0470

Nov. 11–12
Rimrock Rendezvous
"A Celebration of Contemporary &
Traditional Native American Arts"
Mt. Shasta Mall
Redding, CA
(916) 873-4834

Nov. 11–12
Annual Indoor Native Arts &
Crafts Show
Centennial Gym
Bloomsburg, PA
(717) 389-4574, Madeline Foshay

Nov. 11–13
Great American Indian Expo
Richmond State Fairgrounds
Richmond, VA
(410) 788-0254
(804) 764-0956, Jan Sullivan

Veterans Day weekend
Veterans Day Celebration
Toppenish Community Center
Toppenish, WA
(509) 865-5121

Veterans Day weekend
Veterans Day Powwow
Yuma Praying Grounds
Yuma, AZ

Veterans Day weekend
Veterans Day Powwow
Nespelem Community Center
Nespelem, WA
(509) 634-4711

Veterans Day weekend
Veterans Memorial Powwow
Hopi Civic Center
Oraibi, AZ
(602) 734-2441 ext. 215

Veterans Day weekend
NLAKA'PAMUX Nation's
Traditional Veterans Remembrance
Powwow
Kumsheen School
Lytton, BC CANADA
(604) 455-2467

Veterans Day weekend
Veterans Day Rodeo & Fair
San Carlos Apache Reservation
San Carlos, AZ
(602) 475-2361

Veterans Day weekend
Veterans Powwow
Panee Memorial Agriplex
Hobbema, AB CANADA
(403) 585-3739

Nov. 17–18
NMAI Expo & Powwow
Javits Center
New York, NY
(212) 825-6920

2nd weekend Nov.
Oglewanagi Powwow
866 Wilbeth Rd.
Akron, OH
(216) 225-3416, Donna Seward

Midmonth Nov.
Great Plains Indian Art Show & Sale
Sioux Falls, SD
(605) 336-4007

3rd weekend Nov.
Native Arts & Crafts Show and Sale
Aboriginal Artisan Art & Craft Society
Big Four Building, Stampede Park
Calgary, AB CANADA
(403) 486-0069, Martha
(403) 444-4225, Val

3rd weekend Nov.
Twin Eagles Powwow
Hilltop Campground (Hwy 80)
Haughton, LA
(903) 687-3449

Nov. 18
Mashpee Wampanoag Winter Social
& Potluck
United Church Village Community
Center
Mashpee, MA
(508) 477-0208

Nov. 18
National Native American Heritage
Day Powwow
Concord, MA
(617) 884-4227

Nov. 18
All Nations Indian Youth Powwow
YWCA West Tulsa
Tulsa, OK
(918) 762-3962

Nov. 18–20
Annual Fredricksburg Powwow
Fredricksburg Fairgrounds
Fredricksburg, VA
(410) 788-0689

Nov. 21–27
Annual National Native American
Cultural Arts Festival
Baltimore American Indian Center
Festival Hall
Baltimore, MD
(410) 675-3535

Nov. 24–25
Thanksgiving Powwow
Inland Native American Association
San Bernardino, CA
(714) 889-2444

Nov. 24–26
American Indian Traditional
Preservation Committee Annual
American Indian Arts & Crafts Fair
National Guard Armory
Merlin, OR
(503) 474-6394 or 479-8770

Nov. 24–26
Annual South Carolina Intertribal
Cultural Arts Festival & Powwow
Hory Fairgrounds
Loris, SC
(803) 776-9582, Ron Reams

Nov. 25
Thunderbird American Indian
Dancers Powwow & Auction
McBurney YMCA
215 W. 23rd St.
New York, NY
(201) 587-9633, Louis Mofsie

Nov. 25–27
Native American Month Social
Powwow & Indian Market
Amigos Complex
36 St. & 4th Ave.
South Tucson, AZ
(602) 622-4900

1st Saturday after Thanksgiving
Yip Nie Iswa Festival
Catawba Nation
Rock Hill, SC
(803) 324-5214
(803) 366-9150, FAX

Thanksgiving weekend
Annual Powwow
Fort Duchesne, UT
(801) 722-5141

4th weekend Nov.
American Indian Market
Phoenix Civic Plaza
Phoenix, AZ
(602) 252-1594

4th weekend Nov.
LIHA Powwow
Tchfkunchte Campground
Folsom, LA

4th weekend Nov.
Native Arts & Crafts Show and Sale
Aboriginal Artisan Art & Craft Society
Convention Centre
Edmonton, AB CANADA
(403) 486-0069, Martha
(403) 444-4225, Val

Month of Dec.
Scandinavian/Indian Christmas
Jacobsen House
Norman, OK
(405) 879-5935

Dec. (date TBA)
Winter Traditional Powwow
Toys for Tots Giveaway
Indian Heritage School
1330 N. 90th
Seattle, WA
(206) 298-7895

Dec. (date TBA)
Quinapiac Dancers Winter Dance
Eagen Center
Mathews St.
Milford, CT
(203) 263-3610

Dec. (date TBA)
Mashpee Wampanoag Winter Social
& Potluck
United Church Village Community
Center
Mashpee, MA
(508) 477-0208

Dec. (date TBA)
"Heritage Through My Hands"
Indian Art Show
Head Smashed In Buffalo Jump
Fort MacLeod, AB CANADA
(403) 553-2731, Louisa Crowshoe

Dec. 1–3
American Indian Exposition & Sale
Santa Clara County Fairgrounds
Fiesta Hall
San Jose, CA
(209) 221-4355

1st weekend Dec.
All Indian Rodeo
PIRA Rodeo Grounds
Colorado River Reservation
Parker, AZ
(602) 669-2357

1st weekend Dec.
Annual Powwow
University of St. Thomas
St. Paul, MN
(612) 962-5950

1st Saturday Dec.
Mason School Powwow
2812 N. Madison
Tacoma, WA
(206) 596-1139

Dec. 2–3
Heritage Through My Hands Native
Craft Show/Celebration
Head Smashed In Buffalo Jump
(near Ft. McLeaod, AB CANADA)

2nd weekend Dec.
Annual Chicago American Indian
Center Powwow
Navy Pier
Chicago, IL
(312) 275-5871, Diane Maney

Dec. 9–10
American Indian Exposition & Sale
Marin Center Exhibit Hall
San Rafael, CA
(209) 221-4355

Dec. 11
Christmas Powwow
DQ University
Davis, CA
(916) 758-0470

Dec. 11
Nickommo Festival
United Church of Christ
Webster, MA
(508) 943-4569

Dec. 16
Thunderbird American Indian
Dancers Powwow
McBurney YMCA
215 W. 23rd St.
New York, NY
(201) 587-9633, Louis Mofsie

Dec. 26–Jan. 1
Miccosukee Art Festival
Miccosukee Reservation
(25 miles west of
Miami, FL)
(305) 223-8380 ext. 346
Debbie Tiger

This calendar does not include all events. Many come and go each year. All will be worth a full day's journey to visit. Call to verify dates.

Check local Indian centers, clubs, and Native American programs at your nearest college or university. Quite often they will sponsor an event in conjunction with Indian awareness week or an anniversary, or sometimes they will have a monthly event.

Information for this events calendar derives from a powwow calendar compiled by Liz Campbell, published by the Book Publishing Co., Summertown, Tennessee. For a copy of her calendar, send $7.95 plus $1.50 postage to Powwow Calendar, P.O. Box 490, Chimacum, WA 98325.

Index

460 / Index

Index / 465

Totem, 189
Trail of Tears, 59, 61, 62, 68
Treaty of 1868, 11
Treaty of Fort Laramie, 51
Treaty of Medicine Lodge, 65, 109
Treaty of New Echota, 59
Treaty-making era, 23
Tree of Life, 4
Tribes. See individual listings
Trust patents, 25
Tsalagi, 58. See Cherokee
Tulalip tribe, 222
Tumwater tribe, 194
Tunica tribe, 230
Turquoise jewelry, 325-328
Turtle Island, 1, 365
Turtle Mountain Ojibwa, 52
Tuscarora tribe, 172. See Iroquois
   Confederacy
Tygh tribe, 359

Ugakhpa, 87. See Quapaw
Umatilla tribe, 199
U.S. Constitution, 168
U.S. government Indian termination
   policy, 354
Umpqua tribe, 191-194, 196; agriculture, 192; government, 194; history, 192-195
Utah, State of, 134-137
Ute tribe, 116-118, 134-137; history, 135-137; language, 135; Northern, 134-137; Southern, 117, 136

Valentine's Day Treaty, 79
Victorio, 284. See White Mountain
   Apache
Virginia, State of, 173-174
Viejas Kumeyaay, 359

Wailaki tribe, 359
Walker River Paiute, 132
Wallawalla tribe, 198
Wampanoag tribe, 165-166
Wapato tribe, 194
Wappo tribe, 343
Warm Springs tribe, 195-197
Wasco tribe, 198-199
Washakie, 13. See Shoshone
Washington, State of, 200-223

Washita massacre, 43
Washoe tribe, 132-133
Wichita tribe, 94
Wikiup, 191
Winipig, 47. See Winnebago
Winnebago tribe, 47, 185
Winnemucca tribe, 129
Wintun tribe, 360-361
Wisconsin, State of, 174-185
Wiyot tribe, 361-362
Wooden Cup, 2
Wounded Knee massacre, 97
Wovoka, 125
Wyandotte tribe, 95
Wyandot, 95. See Wyandotte
Wyoming, State of, 105-112

Yahi tribe, 362
Yakama tribe, 222-223
Yamhill tribe, 194
Yankton Sioux, 102-103
Yanktonai tribe, 37
Yaqui tribe, 275-276
Yavapai tribe, 286-287
Yavapai-Apache tribe, 286
Yellowstone National Park, 21
Yokuts tribe, 358-359
Ysleta pueblo, 332-333
Yuchi tribe, 95
Yuki Indians, The, 362
Yuki tribe, 362
Yuma. See Quechan
Yurok tribe, 345, 362-363

Zía pueblo, 328
Zuñi pueblo, 328, 332

Titles from John Muir Publications

Rick Steves' Books

Asia Through the Back Door, $17.95
Europe 101: History and Art for the Traveler, $17.95
Mona Winks: Self-Guided Tours of Europe's Top Museums, $18.95
Rick Steves' Baltics & Russia, $9.95
Rick Steves' Europe, $18.95
Rick Steves' France, Belgium & the Netherlands, $15.95
Rick Steves' Germany, Austria & Switzerland, $14.95
Rick Steves' Great Britain & Ireland, $15.95
Rick Steves' Italy, $13.95
Rick Steves' Scandinavia, $13.95
Rick Steves' Spain & Portugal, $13.95
Rick Steves' Europe Through the Back Door, $19.95
Rick Steves' French Phrase Book, $5.95
Rick Steves' German Phrase Book, $5.95
Rick Steves' Italian Phrase Book, $5.95
Rick Steves' Spanish & Portuguese Phrase Book, $7.95
Rick Steves' French/German/Italian Phrase Book, $7.95

City·Smart™ Guidebooks

City·Smart Guidebook: Cleveland, $14.95
City·Smart Guidebook: Denver, $14.95
City·Smart Guidebook: Kansas City, $12.95
City·Smart Guidebook: Minneapolis/St. Paul, $14.95
City·Smart Guidebook: Nashville, $14.95
City·Smart Guidebook: Portland, $14.95
City·Smart Guidebook: Tampa/St. Petersburg, $14.95

Unique Travel Series

All are $10.95 paperback, except as noted.
Unique Arizona
Unique California
Unique Colorado
Unique Florida
Unique Georgia ($11.95)
Unique New England
Unique New Mexico
Unique Oregon ($9.95)
Unique Texas
Unique Washington

Travel+Smart™ Trip Planners

American Southwest Travel+Smart Trip Planner, $14.95
Colorado Travel+Smart Trip Planner, $14.95
Eastern Canada Travel+Smart Trip Planner, $15.95
Florida Gulf Coast Travel+Smart Trip Planner, $14.95
Hawaii Travel+Smart Trip Planner, $14.95
Kentucky/Tennessee Travel+Smart Trip Planner, $14.95
Michigan Travel+Smart Trip Planner, $14.95
Minnesota/Wisconsin Travel+Smart Trip Planner, $14.95
New England Travel+Smart Trip Planner, $14.95
Northern California Travel+Smart Trip Planner, $15.95
Pacific Northwest Travel+Smart Trip Planner, $14.95

A Natural Destination Series

Belize: A Natural Destination, $16.95
Costa Rica: A Natural Destination, $18.95
Guatemala: A Natural Destination, $16.95

Other Terrific Travel Titles

The 100 Best Small Art Towns in America, $15.95
The Big Book of Adventure Travel, $17.95
The Birder's Guide to Bed and Breakfasts: U.S. and Canada, $17.95
Indian America, $18.95
The People's Guide to Mexico, $19.95
Ranch Vacations, $22.95
Understanding Europeans, $14.95
Watch It Made in the U.S.A., $16.95
The World Awaits, $16.95

Automotive Titles

The Greaseless Guide to Car Care, $19.95
How to Keep Your Subaru Alive, $21.95
How to Keep Your Toyota Pick-Up Alive, $21.95
How to Keep Your VW Alive, $25.00